The Future of Industrial Relations

The Future of Industrial Relations

Global Change and Challenges

JOHN R. NILAND

RUSSELL D. LANSBURY

CHRISSIE VEREVIS

SAGE Publications

International Educational and Professional Publisher

Thousand Oaks   London   New Delhi

Grateful acknowledgment is given to the *International Journal of Human Resource Management,* in which chapters 12, 13, 14, and 15 previously appeared, and to the *Comparative Labor Law Journal,* in which chapters 2, 3, 5, and 6 previously appeared.

For information address:

SAGE Publications, Inc.
2455 Teller Road
Thousand Oaks, California 91320

SAGE Publications Ltd.
6 Bonhill Street
London EC2A 4PU
United Kingdom

SAGE Publications India Pvt. Ltd.
M-32 Market
Greater Kailash I
New Delhi 110 048 India

Printed in the United States of America

Library of Congress Cataloging-in-Publication Data

The future of industrial relations : global change and challenges /
    edited by John R. Niland, Russell D. Lansbury, and Chrissie Verevis.
        p.   cm.
    Papers selected from the Ninth World Congress of the International
Industrial Relations Association, held in Sydney, Australia, from 30
Aug. to 3 Sept. 1992.
    Includes bibliographical references and index.
    ISBN 0-8039-5547-2
    1. Industrial relations.   2. Comparative industrial relations.
3. Labor policy.   4. Trade-unions.   5. Labor market.   I. Niland,
John R.   II. Lansbury, Russell D.   III. Verevis, Chrissie.
IV. International Industrial Relations Association. World Congress
(9th : 1992 : Sydney, N.S.W.)
HD6971.F87   1994
331—dc20   93-48901

94   95   96   97   10   9   8   7   6   5   4   3   2   1

Sage Production Editor: Rebecca Holland

Contents

PART V: Industrial Relations and Political Transformation

PART VI: Labor Market Policies and Practices

PART I

Introduction

in *Industrialism and Industrial Man* (1960) still has relevance to contemporary developments. In that work, the authors concluded that there was a central logic to industrialization that could be seen in every society, although different societies took separate paths on their way to industrialization. These variations related primarily to the approaches taken by the elites who organized the industrialization process. The central problem of industrial relations became not "capital versus labour" but "the structuring of the labour force . . . how it gets recruited, developed and maintained" (Kerr, 1973, pp. 280-281).

Support for this thesis was provided by Simitis (1986), who viewed the juridification of labor relations as the inevitable consequence of industrialization. Over time, the state would act to transform society from one based on status and individual contractual arrangements to one that was subject to comprehensive regulation. The state would thereby change its role from "contemplative" to "activist."

The argument presented by Bellace could appear to be in conflict with the widely held view that the late 1980s and early 1990s have been characterized more by deregulation and a withdrawal by the state from an interventionist role. However, Bellace claims that deregulation, in many cases, actually involved a process of reformulation of the "web of rules" so that the state could achieve its market objectives more effectively.

The state now acts not only through the enactment of legislation but also through a portfolio of regulatory mechanisms, which include administrative measures and ministerial decisions. Examples can be drawn from both underdeveloped countries and newly industrializing countries to demonstrate over time the expanding role of the state in industrial relations. In Korea, for example, the national government has been the prime architect of nation building as well as the prime mover of economic development (see Zappala & Lansbury, 1991).

One of the most interesting examples of the expanding role of the state has been at the supranational level in the European Community. The passing of the Single European Act in 1986 acted as a catalyst for policies of economic and social integration. The Charter of Fundamental Social Rights, of 1989, identified 12 basic principles, 2 of which are directly related to industrial relations: freedom of association and collective bargaining, as well as information, consultation, and participation rights.

There is also the prospect, during the 1990s, that an EC directive on European-level works councils will be approved (see Gold & Hall, 1992). However, there is still a long way to go before full harmonization of European industrial relations is achieved. Hence, it may be premature to proclaim the full encompassing role of the state in European industrial relations.

Some commentators, such as Clarke (1993), argue that when surveying the European scene today, it is difficult to see much of a convergence in industrial relations. Furthermore, while there are a number of similar influences at work in Europe (and other parts of the world), these are leading to some diverse outcomes. Streeck (1988), for example, has noted the growing variety in the use of technology and the structure of work organization, whose trend has been described as an "explosion," with different strands of development moving away from each other in different directions, as opposed to "implosive convergence" toward one central "best practice."

Trade Unions and the Future

The importance of the role of the state is also taken up in the second theme, on trade unions and the future. Davis (1992) notes that throughout the world unions are often closely related to the state, and "pluralist" unions (which are the norm in Western industrialized nations) tend to be the exception rather than the rule. Indeed, the term *union* can often be misleading since it describes such a diverse range of institutions often operating under very different circumstances. Indeed, even within Western industrialized market economies, the roles and functions of unions vary considerably and have been undergoing significant change.

The sharp decline in union density, which has been experienced in many developed market economies during the past decade in particular, has caused the union movement to reconsider its role and even its future viability. Ben-Israel and Fisher (1992) warn that unions in many countries are engaged in a struggle for survival, and that their future will be determined by their ability to influence the policies adopted by employers and governments, as well as their success in convincing workers to join and remain in their ranks. Other commentators, such as Wever (1992), question whether unions are likely to survive in the United States, where they are struggling to adapt to new management strategies and structures and to organize members in nontraditional areas.

Visser (1992) shows that unions in different countries have demonstrated a wide range of responses to changing circumstances. Membership density has remained strong in some European countries, particularly those in the Nordic region, compared with North America. Visser argues that smaller countries with a well-established welfare state and a tradition of social partnership (such as Sweden and Norway) have maintained their level of unionization more successfully than larger countries with a more adversarial system of industrial relations (such as the United States).

Australia presents a somewhat curious case, having experienced a sharp decline in union density during a period of Labour government and strong cooperative between the union movement and the state through the Accord (see Lansbury & Davis, 1992). An analysis of the decline in union density in Australia by Peetz (1990) may have broader application. His analysis suggests that at least half of the decline in unionization was due to structural change in the mix of industries, sectors, and occupations. Peetz also discerned a decline in public support for unions in Australia during a period when their collective behavior could be characterized as the most moderate and responsible for several decades. One of the possible reasons for this is that workers perceived that their unions had been too cooperative with employers and government, allowing real wages to fall while the profit shares to capital rose.

By contrast, in Britain, where the Thatcher government conducted a strong campaign against the union during the 1980s, many unions had recovered ground which they had lost during the decade (see Sussex, 1989).

Davis (1992) considers strategic alternatives facing unions in the 1990s as they strive to recruit and retain members. He argues that unions must seek influence in decision making at both government and industry levels. At the same time they must beware of diverting their attention away from the workplace and becoming too remote from their membership.

Hammarström (1992) pursues a similar argument, but emphasizes the need for high levels of union competence and strong organization in order to bargain with employers over issues such as job design, career planning, and training. To be relevant, argues Hammarström, unions need not only to pursue better wages and conditions, but also to support members in gaining stimulating and challenging jobs in a safe and healthy environment. Clearly there is much to be learned from unions that have managed to adapt to economic and structural changes. However, even in countries, such as Sweden, which have been traditional union strongholds, new strategies are required to maintain and develop their roles in the future.

Human Resource Management and Industrial Relations

The emergence of human resource management (HRM) as a new concept in the area of labor-management relations can be traced back more than 20 years. In the *Harvard Business Review* of July/August 1965, Miles contrasted human resources with human relations, and argued that management should focus attention on all organization members as "reservoirs of untapped resources." As Purcell (1992) indicates, however, HRM has become a contentious issue in recent times, with some commentators raising concerns that the word *resource* implies that labor is simply a commodity to be utilized and disposed of according to the exclusive needs of the firm.

In Legge's view, the increasing use of the term *HRM* is no more or less than a reflection of the rise of the "new right": "our new enterprise culture demands a different language, one that asserts management's right to manipulate, and ability to generate and develop resources" (Legge, 1991, p. 40). Against this, however, can be set a more positive view that HRM is concerned with "a coherent, positive and optimistic philosophy about management . . . built around the possibility of achieving personal growth in an integrated, human organisation" (Guest, 1990, p. 17). The fact that the theme of HRM had not previously been discussed at the World Congress of the IIRA reflects the ambivalence, if not hostility, with which HRM has been viewed by many industrial relations scholars.

For those who followed the system's approach to industrial relations pioneered by Dunlop (1958), and others who pursued a more radical approach to the subject (e.g., Hyman, 1987), HRM has been regarded as embodying a pluralist philosophy that was "both a product of and a cause of significant concentration of power in the hands of management" (Purcell, 1992).

Yet the debate surrounding HRM has forced a reevaluation of the scope and nature of industrial relations as a field of study, generating a broader perspective and incorporating insights from a wider range of social sciences (see Lansbury & Westcott, 1992). Although some commentators may argue that industrial relations originated as a broadly based, interdisciplinary field (e.g., Laffer, 1974), it has tended to become more focused on bargaining between unions and management. Purcell argues that HRM has "forced open the boundaries to the study of industrial relations in the firm both vertically (the strategic, functional and workplace levels) and horizontally (technology, manufacturing systems, financial controls . . . and even marketing)."

One of the key issues explored by several of the papers in this collection is whether the rise of HRM and the decline of unionization means the end of collective forms of representation and bargaining within organizations. The experiences of Europe seem to differ from those of North America in this regard. In a number of European countries collective bargaining coexists alongside new forms of management, to create what Storey (1992) calls "dualism" and Regini (1992) class "pragmatic eclecticism." Unions and collective bargaining are retained partly as a result of the legal framework, partly due to high levels of unionization, and partly as a feature of the social democratic version of HRM at a macro level, which is represented by the European Community's social charter.

A number of researchers also refer to the movement away from adversarial relationships toward integrative bargaining, partnership, and cooperation. Regini, however, argues that countries in which the state seeks to impose collective consultation (e.g., France and Spain) have tended to be less successful than those that have used a more voluntaristic approach (e.g., Italy). However, cases where industrial relations approaches (such as collective representation) have been combined with HRM have depended on employers cooperating with union representatives, and unions adopting a less adversarial approach. This is akin to what Kochan and Dyer (1992) call "mutual commitment," a new form of shared ideology that has characterized many successful examples of labor-management cooperation in the United States.

Another issue of interest examined in some of the papers is why some of the success stories of HRM have not been diffused more widely. Kochan and Dyer refer to the growing "greenfield site" phenomena, which use innovative HRM practices but often become "experimental islands in a sea of traditional practices." In the United Kingdom, Newell (1991) found that, from the employees' perspective, greenfield sites often failed to live up to their initial promise. Newell suggested that it may simply be a matter of time before greenfield sites become "brownfields" or revert to standard, traditional forms of employee involvement. This implies that some aspects of HRM may simply be a passing fad.

Purcell concludes, from these and other examples, that for the positive aspects of HRM to flourish and become more widely diffused, it may be necessary for the state to play a more interventionist role. The example of the Accord between the trade union movement and the Labour government in Australia, which has fostered award restructuring at the national level as well as micro-level reforms through enterprise-based bargaining, demonstrates how HRM and industrial relations reforms may be combined (see Davis & Lansbury, 1993; Mathews, 1992).

In a similar vein, Kochan and Dyer contrast the situation in the United States, where there has been virtually no action on the part of national policymakers to create the required environment or substantive policies to encourage greater employee involvement and participation, with countries such as Germany, where unions, management, and the state have collaborated to ensure effective forms of representation and participation to achieve long-term strategic change.

Industrial Relations and Political Transformation

In Eastern Europe, Africa, Latin America, and other parts of the world, the past decade has been characterized by significant change, if not transformation, of the political and economic environment. The relationship between political transformation and industrial relations, however, is by no means simple or straightforward. Galin (1992) argues that the main question to be answered is "whether the relationship between political transformation and industrial relations lives up to expectations, or by some quirk of irony, ends up producing the opposite effect?" In other words, does reality fit the myth? The myth which Galin examines is that governments, in most nondemocratic regimes, are the dominant actor, while the trade unions are at best tolerated, closely controlled, and often repressed.

According to this myth, it follows that political transformation will induce a complete overhaul of industrial relations, whereby trade unions will emerge as strong and vigorous legal partners in collective bargaining. However, as a number of scholars reveal, trade unions can experience an abrupt setback in their status once the transition toward democracy begins.

In many African countries during the colonial period, trade unions enjoyed privileged positions and forged alliances with nationalist governments. After independence, however, many of these countries established one-party systems or were brought under military rule. In some cases, unions were co-opted into the state apparatus, although sometimes they campaigned successfully and persuaded the ruling powers to accept union rights to implement particular economic and political policies. The emergence of a significant although divided union movement in South Africa, in recent years, demonstrates the diversity of outcomes for industrial relations arising from political change. It remains to be seen, however, what will be the role of trade unions under majority rule in South Africa.

Some of the most interesting recent developments have been in Eastern Europe, where the dismantling of communist regimes has led to diverse outcomes for trade unions and industrial relations. In Poland, the new industrial relations environment that resulted from the establishment of the democratic government in 1989 has witnessed the emergence of two centers of trade unionism (see Florek, 1992).

The former communist-aligned trade unions have survived in the form of the All Poland Trade Union Alliance, but are no longer under one-party control. Solidarity, the union-based organization that played a decisive role in bringing an end to communist rule in Poland, has subsequently split into several factions and has found it difficult to compete successfully for members against other trade unions. Unionization has also declined from 95% to 45%. Similar trends are apparent in other Eastern European countries, where internal divisions have weakened the new "free unions," since the end of the communist era. In Hungary, acute conflict between the seven trade union confederations led to intervention by the newly elected government, which passed two trade union acts in 1991 (see Héthy, 1992).

An interesting case is provided by Hong Kong, where unions were not active under the colonial government and did not apply pressure for improved labor legislation or redistribution of wealth and resources to the workers until the 1980s. The process of decolonization and the transfer of sovereignty to China in 1997 have widened divisions within the union government. The Hong Kong Federation of Trade Unions has supported moderation in the democratization process, in line with China's position. By contrast, the more outspoken independent unions have favored a more democratic political framework. Most unions have called for the inclusion of labor rights such as collective bargaining in the Basic Law, which will determine the structure of Hong Kong's future legislature, even though their overall influence is marginal. It remains to be seen what roles the unions will play in the post-1997 era (see Levin & Chiu, 1992).

Galin concludes that with the transition to democracy, unions often face both external and internal problems. While unions may be granted new formal rights by a democratic government, it may be difficult to exercise these rights as a result of both external pressures, from employers or the state, and internal problems. In the case of Solidarity in Poland, for example, the union faced external competition as well as internal power struggles, thereby losing the support of its membership. Thus, unions may find the transition to democracy much more difficult than they anticipated.

Labor Market Policies and Practices

The powerful influence of the international economy on national economies is highlighted by Pang Eng Fong (1992) in his examination of the macro/micro interface in labor market policy and practice. All of the papers in this section deal with industrialized countries, although Pang also draws some interesting comparisons with developing countries. The rise of internationalized product markets has not only diminished the traditional powers of unions but also reduced the effectiveness of national macro-economic policies to influence the labor market. While governments have an important role in creating the appropriate environment for investment and economic development, they may find themselves in conflict with the global interests of multinational enterprises that play significant roles in their economies.

Pang suggests three ways of considering the general theme under discussion. First, one may examine how key macro-economic variables affect and are affected by labor market policies and institutions. Common external shocks in the past two decades were greeted with very divergent macro-economic responses. Dell'Aringa and Lodovici (1992) illustrate this by showing how the "Swedish model" changed significantly in the 1980s as it became apparent that the long-held solidaristic wage and active labor market policies were no longer sufficient to ensure fast growth and an acceptable trade-off between employment and inflation. From their survey of OECD countries, Walsh and Brown (1992) conclude that centralized or coordinated bargaining structures rest too heavily on wage restraint as a strategy. The real challenge is to develop strategies to promote productivity and bargaining.

Second, one may analyze how national economic changes and labor market policy and institutions affect wage developments at the industry and enterprise levels. Gregory and Daly (1992) argue that the centralized wage determination system in Australia has led to narrower earnings distribution than in the United States, but has achieved a higher degree of equity. However, other commentators argue that the outcome of the centralized system may also have weakened labor flexibility and contributed to poorer macro-economic performance by Australia. Zeytinoglu (1992) examines how economic and social conditions have led to the rise of nonstandard forms of work, which have been to the disadvantage of women. This situation is unlikely to change, she argues, unless there are changes in macro social institutions to bring about a more equal sharing of responsibilities between men and women, and a greater social value attached to nonstandard forms of employment.

Third, one may analyze how a firm's policies on labor are influenced or shaped by external conditions. Belanger and Breton (1992) argue that, in responding to international competitiveness, employers may pursue either a strategy that emphasizes stronger managerial controls or one that seeks to foster creativity and participation among their workers. Eyraud (1992) also emphasizes the importance of "rapport" between the firm and the market conditions. However, such contrasts can be overstated, and a degree of convergence between Japanese and U.S. practices is occurring as a result of competitive pressures, which may lead to the development of a new model of the firm.

Pang provides a useful final observation in relation to the changing nature of the world economy and implications for the labor market policies. In the faster growing Asian countries, especially the "tiger economies" of East Asia, rapid growth and the relative absence of institutional rigidities have helped to smooth the adjustment process. As these economies mature, and the work force begins to demand a higher quality of life, many of the welfare and related "social wage" issues that have concerned the older industrialized societies may become major concerns. Hence, the key issues of industrial relations and human resource management may become increasingly universal.

Conclusion

This volume provides a useful guide to current debates in the area of international and comparative industrial relations. The five themes do not encompass all issues of concern to workers, unions, employers, and governments throughout the world, but they do highlight some major issues. The papers demonstrate the value of an interdisciplinary approach to these issues, as well as the importance of adopting both international and comparative perspectives. Gladstone remarked in a previous IIRA congress volume: "history has demonstrated that there is resiliency in labour relations systems which seem to have a great capacity to adjust to new challenges and therein find the seeds for their own renewal and survival" (Gladstone, 1989, p. 6).

It remains to be seen whether long-established systems of industrial relations are currently undergoing such a radical transformation that new forms of relationships between the parties will be formed that have little in common with the past. This will provide a challenge for future research.

References

Bamber, G. J., & Lansbury, R. D. (Eds.). (1993). *International and comparative industrial relations: A study of industrialised market economics.* London: Routledge; Sydney: Allen & Unwin.

Belanger, J., & Breton, G. (1992). Economic restructuring and the regulation of labour in Canada. *Proceedings of the Ninth World Congress of the International Industrial Relations Research Association.* Sydney: IIRA.

Bellace, J. (1992). The role of the state in industrial relations. *Proceedings of the Ninth World Congress of the International Industrial Relations Research Association.* Sydney: IIRA.

Ben-Israel, G., & Fisher, H. (1992). Trade unions in the future: Organisational strategies in a changing environment. *Proceedings of the Ninth World Congress of the International Industrial Relations Research Association.* Sydney: IIRA.

Clarke, R. O. (1993). Conclusion: Towards a synthesis of international and comparative experience of nine countries. In G. J. Bamber & R. D. Lansbury (Eds.), *International and comparative industrial relations: A study of industrialised market economics* (pp. 245-274). London: Routledge; Sydney: Allen & Unwin.

Davis, E. M. (1992). Trade unionism in the future. *Proceedings of the Ninth World Congress of the International Industrial Relations Research Association.* Sydney: IIRA.

Davis, E. M., & Lansbury, R. D. (1993). Industrial relations in Australia. In G. J. Bamber & R. D. Lansbury (Eds.), *International and comparative industrial relations: A study of industrialised market economics* (pp. 100-125). London: Routledge; Sydney: Allen & Unwin.

Dell' Aringa, C., & Lodovici, M. S. (1992). Industrial relations and labour policies in European countries. *Proceedings of the Ninth World Congress of the International Industrial Relations Research Association.* Sydney: IIRA.

Dunlop, J. T. (1958). *Industrial relations systems.* New York: Holt, Rinehart & Winston.

Eyraud, F. (1992). The relationship between the enterprise and the market in the assessment of skills: A comparative perspective. *Proceedings of the Ninth World Congress of the International Industrial Relations Research Association.* Sydney: IIRA.

Ferner, A., & Hyman, R. (Eds.). (1992). *Industrial relations in the new Europe.* Oxford: Basil Blackwell.

Florek, L. (1992). The impact of industrial relations on political transformation in Poland. *Proceedings of the Ninth World Congress of the International Industrial Relations Research Association.* Sydney: IIRA.

Galin, A. (1992). Myth and reality: Trade unions in industrial relations in the transition to democracy. *Proceedings of the Ninth World Congress of the International Industrial Relations Research Association.* Sydney: IIRA.

Gladstone, A. (1989). Introduction. In A. Gladstone, R. Lansbury, J. Steiber, T. Treu, & M. Weiss. *Current issues in labour relations* (pp. 1-10). Berlin: de Gruyter.

Gold, M., & Hall, M. (1992). Report on European-level information and consultation in multinational companies: An evaluation of practice. Dublin: European Foundation for the Improvement in Living and Working Conditions.

Gregory, R., & Daly, A. (1992). Who gets what? Institutions, human capital and black boxes as determinants of relative wages in Australia. *Proceedings of the Ninth World Congress of the International Industrial Relations Research Association.* Sydney: IIRA.

Guest, D. (1990). Human resource management and the American dream. *Journal of Management Studies, 27*(4), 377-387.

Hammarström, O. (1992). Local and global: Trade unions in the future. *Proceedings of the Ninth World Congress of the International Industrial Relations Research Association.* Sydney: IIRA.

Héthy, L. (1992). Political changes and the transformation of industrial relations in Hungary. *Proceedings of the Ninth World Congress of the International Industrial Relations Research Association.* Sydney: IIRA.

Hyman, R. (1987). Strategy or structure? Capital, labour and control. *Work, Employment and Society, 1*(1), 25-33.

Kerr, C. (1973). *The future of industrial societies: Convergence or continuing diversity?* Cambridge, MA: Harvard University Press.

Kerr, C., Dunlop, J. T., Harbison, F., & Myers, C. (1960). *Industrialism and industrial man: The problems of labor and management in economic growth.* Cambridge, MA: Harvard University Press.

Kochan, T. A. (1993). Foreword. In G. J. Bamber & R. D. Lansbury (Eds.), *International and comparative industrial relations: A study of industralised market economics* (pp. v, vi). London: Routledge; Sydney: Allen & Unwin.

Kochan, T. A., & Dyer, L. (1992). Managing transformational change: The role of human resource professionals. *Proceedings of the Ninth World Congress of the International Industrial Relations Research Association.* Sydney: IIRA.

Laffer, K. (1974). Is industrial relations an academic discipline? *Journal of Industrial Relations, 16*(1), 62-73.

Lansbury, R. D., & Davis, E. M. (1992). Employee participation: Some Australian cases. *International Labour Review, 131,* 231-248.

Lansbury, R. D., & Westcott, M. (1992). Restructuring Australian industrial relations: Dawn or twilight of a golden age? *Journal of Industrial Relations, 34*(3), 396-419.

Legge, K. (1991). Human resource management: A critical analysis. In J. Storey (Ed.), *New perspectives on human resource management* (pp. 19-40). London: Routledge.

Levin, D., & Chiu, S. (1992). Decolonisation without independence: Political change and trade unionism in Hong Kong. *Proceedings of the Ninth World Congress of the International Industrial Relations Research Association.* Sydney: IIRA.

Mathews, J. (1992). The industrial relations of skills formation. *Proceedings of the Ninth World Congress of the International Industrial Relations Research Association.* Sydney: IIRA.

Miles, R. (1965, July-August). Human relations or human resources? *Harvard Business Review,* 148-163.

Newell, H. (1991). *Field of dreams.* Doctoral thesis, University of Oxford.

Pang, E. F. (1992). The macro/micro interface in labour market policy and practice. *Proceedings of the Ninth World Congress of the International Industrial Relations Research Association.* Sydney: IIRA.

Peetz, D. (1990). Declining union density. *Journal of Industrial Relations, 32*(2), 197-223.

Purcell, J. (1992). Human resources management: Implications for teaching, theory, research and practice in industrial relations. *Proceedings of the Ninth World Congress of the International Industrial Relations Research Association.* Sydney: IIRA.

Regini, M. (1992). Human resource management and industrial relations in European companies. *Proceedings of the Ninth World Congress of the International Industrial Relations Research Association.* Sydney: IIRA.

Simitis, S. (1986). The jurdification of labor relations. *Comparative Labor Law Journal, 7*(2), 93-142.

Storey, J. (1992). The take-up of human resource management by mainstream companies: Key lessons from research. *Proceedings of the Ninth World Congress of the International Industrial Relations Research Association.* Sydney: IIRA.

Streeck, W. (1988). Change in industrial relations: Strategy and structure. *Proceedings of an International Symposium on New Systems in Industrial Relations.* Tokyo: Japan Institute of Labour.

Sussex, E. (1989). *Workers and trade unions in a period of structural change* (Working Paper No. 25). Geneva: ILO, International Employment Policies.

Visser, J. (1992). Union organisation: Why countries differ. *Proceedings of the Ninth World Congress of the International Industrial Relations Research Association.* Sydney: IIRA.

Walsh, J., & Brown, W. A. (192). Corporate pay policies and the internationalisation of market. *Proceedings of the Ninth World Congress of the International Industrial Relations Research Association.* Sydney: IIRA.

Wever, K. (1992). On the future of trade unionism in the United States. *Proceedings of the Ninth World Congress of the International Industrial Relations Research Association.* Sydney: IIRA.

Zappala, J., & Lansbury, R. D. (1991). Recent industrial relations trends in Korea. *Labour and Industry, 4*(2), 235-257.

Zeytinoglu, I. U. (1992). Part-time and other non-standard forms of employment: Why are they considered appropriate for women? *Proceedings of the Ninth World Congress of the International Industrial Relations Research Association.* Sydney: IIRA.

PART II

The Changing Role of the
State in Industrial Relations

2 \ The Role of the State in Industrial Relations

JANICE R. BELLACE

The question of the role of the state in industrial relations is one that for much of the past century has been cast in ideological terms. That is, authors have tended to present as a matter of theory what the role of the state in capitalist or Communist society should be, with references to the situation in actual countries used mainly for the purpose of further probing the ideal model.

In the past few years, the actual examples of Communist governments have declined so greatly in number and significance that it no longer seems relevant to include an extended discussion of the role of the state in a Communist society in this report. As testament to this observation is the fact that with only one exception, none of the papers written on this theme considered the role of the state in a Communist society.

Analytical Frameworks

The perspective from which one should analyze the role of the state in industrial relations is little discussed in industrial relations literature. Obviously the state has a role in industrial relations, and this role reflects the government's ideological and political orientation. Much of a descriptive nature has been written in this vein. For much of this century, industrial relations scholars have focused on the differences in the role of the state in Communist as opposed to capitalist societies. Yet, in the last decade of the twentieth century, this focus seems outdated. Today, we look at market

19

economies and ask why governments with a similar political orientation, facing similar economic constraints, pursue markedly different industrial relations policies. This is a question infrequently asked and rarely answered by scholars. To consider this question, the relevant industrial relations literature was reviewed. Two classic books, both more than 30 years old, continue to provide a useful analytical framework for discussing the state and industrial relations.

John Dunlop (1958), in perhaps the most influential work of the past 50 years, *Industrial Relations Systems,* laid down a general framework for conceptualizing an industrial relations system. The model Dunlop set forth was composed of actors (labor, management, and the state), each with its own ideology and power, interacting to produce outcomes, which Dunlop labeled "rules," within a context of technological, market, and power constraints. Dunlop's work sparked an enormous amount of discussion among industrial relations scholars, and even today, it provides a framework for analysis that cannot be ignored.

Dunlop's work spurred a vast amount of research. Because the field of industrial relations has traditionally focused on the union-management relationship, it is not surprising that much of the research on the actors in the national industrial relations systems has concentrated on the union as actor. The employer has been less studied. In many countries, government, in the sense of an actor with an ideology, has been almost ignored.

Many scholars have criticized Dunlop's *Industrial Relations Systems,* asserting that the model is static. Providing a dynamic dimension to the Dunlopian model are Kochan, Katz, and McKersie (1986) in their major work, *The Transformation of American Industrial Relations.* The proposition that actors in the industrial relations system can exercise strategic choice in industrial relations was raised as a theoretical issue by Kochan, Katz, and McKersie. They focused on the actors at enterprise level, and more specifically on the strategic choices open to management.

The question that the topic of this chapter raises is whether the state, as an actor in the industrial relations system, can exercise strategic choice, and if so, when and how does it do so.

John Dunlop's *Industrial Relations Systems* has endured as a persuasive model for analyzing industrial relations. First published in 1958, it is often deemed the most influential book in the field of industrial relations since the Second World War. It is still a work with which scholars must contend. In contrast, a work co-authored by Dunlop with Kerr, Harbison, and Myers shortly thereafter is now not so often cited. Nonetheless, this work, *Industrialism and Industrial Man* (Kerr, Dunlop, Harbison, & Myers, 1973), has made an indelible imprint on anyone discussing the topic of industrialization. The argument that there is a universal logic of industrialization, and the view that the process of industrialization can be usefully divided into chronological stages for purposes of analysis, are broadly accepted.

Some have criticized *Industrialism and Industrial Man* for a perceived disingenuity of a political nature: the substitution of industrialism for capitalism, with the apolitical notion of industrial society defusing the negatives features deemed inherent in capitalist society. In Marx's writings, capitalism was the historical epoch that preceded socialism. Moreover, the configuration of capitalism featured in Marx's writings was inseparably linked with an industrial society. Standard Marxist thinking adhered to the tenet that capitalism contained the seeds of its own destruction, an event that would occur when impoverished workers revolted. In *Industrialism and Industrial Man,* industrialization is an analytical concept that is severed from Marxist historical notions. Industrialization can occur and industrial society can exist under a capitalist or a socialist system, with the critical difference the identity of the industrializing elite.

In light of the events in Central and Eastern Europe in the past 5 years, the continuing validity of the analytical framework set forth in *Industrialism and Industrial Man* cannot be doubted. Thirty years after the book's publication, the authors appear eerily prescient. If a revised edition were to be written now, little would change, but subsequent events would provide the material for copious annotation. Perhaps the authors of *Industrialism and Industrial Man* were able to articulate theses with global validity because their research approach was consciously and avowedly comparative. They expressed a desire to relate the experiences of various industrial and industrializing nations into a common intellectual framework.

The State's Role at
Stages of Industrialization

In responding to the question, when does the state intervene in industrial relations, most scholars have followed the framework laid down in *Industrialism and Industrial Man.*

EARLY STAGES OF INDUSTRIALIZATION

Nearly all scholars agree that in the early stages of an industrial revolution, the state is hostile to workers and the emerging labor movement. The reasons for this hostility vary, and seem to relate to the period in which the industrial revolution began.

Prior to World War I, industrialization created a working class and thus disrupted the settled social order of pre-industrial society, based mainly on property. In capitalist countries, the state, which was closely aligned with the upper and growing middle classes, acted to defend the interests of those classes. A review of state pronouncements (for instance, legal decisions, statements of legislators) does not reveal any specific economic strategy nor even any specific concern with economic growth. Neither does there appear any articulated belief on the part of legislators and judges that the lot of workers, over time, would be improved by the doctrines to which they adhered. Rather, the state typically acted to protect the property interests of employers. To do this, new doctrines were developed. Property rights became linked to notions of freedom of contract. Workers joining together in an association became an unlawful combination, a conspiracy. In some countries, the association's behavior contravened a new legal notion tied to the free market: antitrust. In most countries, the reaction of the state to unions in the early stages of industrialization was outright hostility, and the state's role was one of legally sanctioned suppressor.

After World War II, the reaction of the state in newly industrializing countries apparently changed, but this may be more form than substance. In many such countries, the state itself was newly formed, often following an independence movement. During the drive for independence, the political parties that would subsequently govern were often aligned with nascent unions. Once independence was attained, these same persons faced the problem of creating an independent economy, a process that necessarily coincided with industrialization. At this point strong, independent unions became a liability to the state's economic plan. As a consequence, the state's posture toward labor became hostile to labor, but the expression of that hostility varied considerably from the nineteenth-century pattern. This difference may have occurred for two reasons.

First, the leaders of those countries industrializing after World War II were familiar with the experience of both Communist and Fascist states. In both, the state's posture toward workers and unions was operationally similar. Unions were viewed as an instrument of the state and, as such, were brought under the control of the party and the state. Although called "unions," unions in such countries served to organize and control the workers and were necessarily incapable of performing the role accorded unions under a system of free collective bargaining. The lesson to be learned was that unions could exist, and collective agreements could be signed, without the state's losing control of labor relations.

Second, the typical post-1950 industrializing nation was a member of certain international organizations, such as the International Labor Organization, that demanded formal allegiance to certain principles as a condition of membership. Hence, these states were motivated not to outlaw unions and ban collective bargaining. Nonetheless, history had demonstrated that a nation could have the appearance of a strong labor movement without, in reality, having independent unions. In many newly industrializing countries, the state proceeded on the basis that certain policies had to be followed for economic growth, and that groups in society, including workers, could not be allowed to interfere with the implementation of these policies. In such a system, the state took the position that the welfare of workers was the responsibility of the state, not of independent unions. Unions, then, became adjuncts of the state, rather than organizations freely chosen by workers to represent them with an independent voice. Although the exact details of implementation have varied by country, the pattern is remarkably similar. Citing the state's economic plan, the state would act to suppress strong labor unions that might challenge the party in power, and to curb collective bargaining so that it existed in form only.

MIDDLE PHASES OF INDUSTRIALIZATION

Once a nation has industrialized, the changed social order must somehow be accommodated. In the industrial relations sphere, normally there is some movement away from antagonistic employer-union relations limited solely to a few terms and conditions of employment. Although this shift can be gradual, it appears that in many countries there is a "paradigm break," that is, a period in which the parties consciously changed the system that was generally viewed as inadequate or unworkable in light of the new social realities. In many countries, some major disruption precipitated the change. The immediate event has often been a period of extremely militant labor unrest, including general strikes, shutdown of parts of the economy, and so on. On closer inspection, this unusual labor unrest can usually be traced to some other event, such as the devastation of war, or an extremely deep recession.

Using Professor Adams' (1992) categorization, this marks the state's change of posture to one of tolerance. Generally, there is recognition that the working class (which by now has significant purchasing power) is an important and valuable part of society, and that unions have a useful role to play in economic life. Beyond that, the pattern varies.

Two variants on this theme deserve mention. The first occurs when the paradigm break occurs in a country that has just lost a war, and the industrializing elite has been discredited but, for the most part, is still in place. In such cases, powers outside the country may have a significant role in imposing aspects of the new arrangement. What is normally a purely national process becomes greatly complicated, as the antagonistic national actors must also respond to a foreign influence. The second is only now occurring in Central and Eastern Europe. Here, the industrializing elite has, in a sense, collapsed, without its successor yet in place. There is a definite paradigm break. Yet the movement toward a new arrangement is tentative, because even the identity of the actors, let alone their programs and preferences, is still in flux.

LATE STAGES OF INDUSTRIAL SOCIETY

The role of the state in the late stages of industrialism varies greatly, as a survey of the advanced market economies reveals. In all, the state tolerates unions, although in some the level of toleration is quite low. In all, the state seeks to protect myriad individual rights, through either legislation or administrative regulation. In some, however, the state can be said to encourage employee representation by erecting structures that require labor participation inside the firm. In others, very substantial managerial control of labor prevails, with workers compelled to seek individual redress through legal means outside the workplace.

The issue of participation is an updated version of the property rights struggle of an earlier era. In the early stages of industrialization, legal doctrines favor those who have property. In the late stages, legal doctrines favor those who own shares in the company. The notion that nonshareholders should be accorded a say, with shareholders, concerning the company's direction represents a societal shift. In several Western European countries, this occurred in the 1970s. Laws were either enacted or significantly revised to grant workers information and consultation rights, often through bodies at the workplace or company level. In a few countries, the notion that workers should have a determinative say on some matters, without relying on strike power, has been accepted.

This concern with non-adversarial employee participation modes may also presage postindustrial society, where most rank-and-file workers will make nothing, but will be engaged in services. Some have already dubbed this new era "the information age." In a society where knowledge is power, a continued expansion of information and consultation rights seems predictable.

The Means of State Intervention

The authors of *Industrialism and Industrial Man* concluded that there is a central logic to industrialization that can be seen in every society, although different societies take separate paths on the way to industrialization. The authors noted that these variations relate primarily to the approaches taken by the elites who organize the industrialization process. The authors pinpointed the central problem of industrial relations around the world as "not capital versus labour" but "the structuring of the labour force—how it gets recruited, developed, and maintained" (Kerr et al., 1973, pp. 280-281).

JURIDIFICATION OF LABOR RELATIONS

Supporting this view, and its adherence to convergence theory, is Professor Spiros Simitis in his work, *Juridification of Labor Relations* (Simitis, 1984, 1986; Zacher, 1984). Simitis views juridification as the inevitable consequence of industrialization in all democratic societies; it is not a peculiar feature of certain cultures or national characters. The term *juridification* refers to the activity by which the state steers labor relations in certain prescribed directions. Over time, the state acts to transform a society based on status and individual contractual arrangements to a society subject to comprehensive regulation. The state is no longer "contemplative" but "activist."

In terms of industrial relations, the state acts to counter an inevitable aspect of industrialization: the relegation of labor to treatment as an article or commodity. The employment relationship of pre-industrial society, based on personal status, disappears in the early stages of industrialization and is replaced by contractual arrangements. Initially, the state is reactive. The state first acts to countermand the harshness of certain of these contractual arrangements, on the grounds that labor is not a commodity. The state justifies the legitimacy of this interference with contractual arrangements by pointing to the extreme or exceptional results of the arrangements, or by arguing that the parties affected cannot be considered fully capable of bargaining. As a result, the juridification of labor relations typically begins with restrictions on child or female labor. Often, the next intervention limits the maximum number of working hours. Legislation mandating certain minimum safety standards in factories and mines, and methods of payment for workers, are also typical of the early stages of industrialization.

Such legal regulation marks an unequivocal break with the orientation of law in the pre-industrial society (be it a civil or common-law society). The legislature comes to accept that it is necessary, legitimate, and in fact desirable to intervene in the employment relation to achieve economic and social objectives.

In most democratic industrial societies, the state during the reactive phase justifies its interference with individual contractual arrangements by targeting what it deems "abuses" of the free market system. In the next stage, however, the state is no longer bound by this concept. Rather, it acts to modify the natural but politically undesirable outcomes of an unfettered free market. This change in scope of state intervention often occurs during the middle stage of industrialization. For example, unemployment becomes a problem the state must combat. Typically, various measures are devised as a cushion for unemployed workers and their families. Initially, some form of unemployment compensation fund is devised. Then, the state may establish labor exchanges to assist unemployed workers in finding new jobs. Next, the state begins to promote occupational training, an activity that often motivates the state to develop job-creation schemes.

In the late stages of industrialization, the web of regulation becomes comprehensive. Labor market problems of lesser dimension receive attention. For example, standards are promulgated for individual dismissal to prevent unfair dismissals. The problem of atypical workers is considered. Now, the state's activist role is well understood. Groups not yet advantaged by the state's intervention lobby for protection. An interesting example of this is the enactment of antidiscrimination legislation in many countries during the past 30 years. Groups who feel disadvantaged in the labor market petition the state to act so that they have equal access to the labor market.

The reach of juridification now extends beyond labor relations to the population as a whole. The impact of industrialization is recognized as extending beyond the employment relation. For instance, in the past 25 years, legislation mandating occupational safety and health standards has tended to precede environmental protection legislation by only a few years. Hence, even though labor law (in the broad meaning of the term) may provide the paradigm for the juridification of labor relations, this phenomenon cannot be fully appreciated without resorting to many other areas of the law, such as social security, unemployment compensation law, employee retirement and benefits law, tax provisions, and so on. The web of regulation may be so complex that adjustments must be made. In some contexts, this has been called "deregulation." This process, however, should not be seen as the state's removing itself from intervention in setting labor market policy. Rather, as examples from the past decade illustrate, deregulation has merely meant a process of reformulation of the web of rules so that the state could better achieve its labor market objectives.

The process of juridification encompasses more than legislation. The state acts through a portfolio of regulatory mechanisms, including administrative measures and ministerial decisions. In many countries, judges do more than interpret law; they often, for all practical purposes, make law. As Simitis has observed, when the political authorities are unprepared to settle social conflicts, a condition of legislative escapism prevails and judicial activism replaces legislative inactivity (Simitis, 1986, p. 104). This reluctance of the authorities to act can occur on any issue, but is particularly likely to occur with respect to industrial conflict.

was one of industrial relations: to maintain a hardworking, disciplined, committed labor force without permitting workers to increase their share of the profits of their labor. Because disruption of industrial production would have played havoc with the state's strategy of being a reliable exporter, industrial peace became an end in itself.

For nearly 30 years all forms of industrial conflict were suppressed, on the grounds that it was a threat to rapid economic growth that could not be tolerated. In the 1960s the state acted indirectly to achieve this, as the vast labor surplus of the period permitted employers to end labor unrest easily by dismissing militant workers. Unions did exist, but their bargaining power was quite weak due to market conditions, and the state had accorded them no independent bargaining role. In the 1970s, as the labor market tightened, unions could have achieved gains at the bargaining table if the state had allowed free collective bargaining to occur. Beginning in 1971, however, the government, by a special presidential decree, effectively banned collective bargaining in the normal sense of the term, outlawed strikes, and made all disputes subject to automatic government determination. Bowing to international standards, Korea did not ban unions per se, but during this period of authoritarian corporatist repression, unions were permitted to exist only if they performed virtually none of the normal functions of a union.

In light of Korea's growing prosperity and the very high level of education of its populace, the question became when, not if, students and workers would act to change the system, for it was difficult to see how such repression could continue with less than martial law in force. A series of large-scale antigovernment demonstrations led to democratic political reforms in June 1987. Tensions that had built up led to a wave of militant labor disputes and a sharp upswing in union organizing. In 1989 the government resumed an interventionist policy, albeit considerably diluted from its earlier form. Korea is at the point of a paradigm break. The system of industrial relations that emerges will likely be in place for decades. Professor Park sees the choices as liberal pluralism or liberal corporatism. Because Korean unions have little experience in using free collective bargaining to achieve their aims and in advancing their political agenda, and because Korean society has been conditioned to accord the state the role of primary actor in the regulation of society, Park predicts that Korea will opt for liberal corporatism.

Central and Eastern Europe

The countries of Central and Eastern Europe present a situation that theorists had previously not considered: economies moving from state socialism to capitalism for the most part during the middle stages of industrialization. That wrenching changes will occur is accepted, but the dimensions of these changes remain unknown. Professor Swiatkowski (1992) explores this transition in industrial relations in the countries of Central and Eastern Europe, with particular reference to Poland.

Although the political environment is changing rapidly, institutions from the prior regime remain. Whether these are viable institutions that will survive the transition period is not yet known. In most countries, unions at the national industry level were essentially political bodies that served as the transmission belt of state economic policy. What the actual function of workers' committees at workplace level was, is less well understood. It is likely that these workplace level organizations will continue to exist. The question is whether they will serve as a consultative body, such as a works council, or whether they will act as a local union body engaging in bargaining. It may be that workers' organizations at workplace level will be quicker to make the change from a political to a bargaining mode. Certainly, it will occur more quickly in countries where unions and workers have some tradition of being in active opposition to the government, as in Poland.

What may be more difficult to change rapidly is the orientation of the government. Although legislators may have rejected the policies of state socialism, the privation concomitant with an immediate and total embrace of free market economics will be difficult for any freely elected government to bear for any significant amount of time. Not only is there no recent tradition of a passive state actor, but the experience of other countries indicates that liberal corporatism may be a feasible policy.

In the sphere of industrial relations, the speed of the change almost requires state direction in recognizing unions and collective bargaining, even though there is strong distrust of state intervention in industrial relations. The old system has been discarded, but a new system has not yet evolved. Yet the state must respond to the disappearance of the old system. To enact legislation on unions and collective bargaining, the legislators must act in reference to some form of unionism and must envision some form of collective bargaining. For instance, no statute can be drafted without considering the answers to some of the following questions: Will bargaining occur at industry level or at plant level; will collective agreements be legally enforceable; what topics can be included in a collective agreement; when will resorting to industrial action be permitted; will more than one union be permitted to represent one group of workers; and how will the identity of the workers' representative be determined?

One unique feature of the dilemma in Central and Eastern Europe is the amorphous nature of the employer constituency. In all other countries, the state acts with an identifiable employer community. Traditionally, the theoretical debate has focused on the question of whether the state inevitably champions the interests of employers at the expense of the workers. How the state will act vis-à-vis the interests of employers, when there is not yet an entrepreneurial class in the society, is a new question. Further complicating the picture is the possibility that some of the most important private-sector employers may be foreign concerns who bring precious capital into the country, but who also possess their own notions of the appropriate degree of state intervention.

ADVANCED MARKET ECONOMIES

The remaining papers written for this theme relate primarily to advanced market economies, with particular reference to Japan, North America, and Europe. These indicate that the state can make very different strategic choices.

Japan

Professor Sugeno (1992), in his discussion of Japan, depicts a country, which, since the end of World War II, has consciously followed an approach he concedes bears a significant resemblance to liberal corporatism. In promoting high economic growth, the state undoubtedly had a strong guiding role in socioeconomic developments, but it would be overstatement to say it controlled the other actors in the system. Moreover, in aiming for an export-driven recovery, the Japanese government, unlike Korea, did not hold back workers' wages to an extreme extent. The Japanese government's attention to the link between desired human resource management policies and legislation, especially labor legislation, is unusual. Equally atypical is the state's reaction to a period of militant labor unrest. Rather than suppressing free collective bargaining in the 1950s, the state used the whole range of measures at its disposal to rein in what were deemed to be extremist elements (the "Red Purge") and to encourage the ascendancy of moderate union leaders. In this stage, the state also contributed to the stabilization of labor relations by establishing procedures for labor dispute adjustment and adjudication.

The emphasis the Japanese government has placed on employment security has no parallel in the policies of other countries at a similar stage of development. For instance, Sugeno notes that the government's initiation of the productivity movement in the mid-1950s could have led to substantial conflict if productivity improvements had led to layoffs. Instead, the government-backed Japan Productivity Center agreed on the following principles with the national labor organization SODOMEI: (a) Since the productivity movement is designed to enhance employment security, displaced workers will not be made redundant but will be relocated by the employer; (b) labor-management consultation must be promoted in order to determine the concrete measures to be taken to increase productivity; and (c) the benefits of increased productivity must be distributed fairly among management, workers, and customers.

Professor Sugeno observes that Japanese industrial relations underwent a transformation during the industrial restructuring after the 1973 oil crisis. The government strongly encouraged unions and employers in the major industries to engage in joint consultation, so that the parties could come to their own agreements on specific measures to be taken to achieve large-scale employment adjustment without resorting to redundancies. Sugeno identifies two other developments, which together accomplished the transformation of Japanese industrial relations. First, three major public enterprises were privatized. This caused a reorganization of Japan's most militant unions. Second, the existing four major union confederations, with different ideological orientations, were consolidated into RENGO, the All Japan Trade Union Federation. RENGO supports collective bargaining in a free market system, but strongly emphasizes extensive consultation and participation in national politics. Both developments were initiated by the government.

In the past decade, the state's strong support of consultation has been demonstrated by the state's establishment of trilateral councils. Much of what is written about Japanese industrial relations focuses on their enterprise-centered basis. Sugeno, however, draws attention to the trilateral councils that function to absorb demands and opinions of labor and management, and to foster consensus on the direction and content of labor policies. He highlights the fact that through these councils, the government has been actively involving unions and employers in its labor policies. He views this as one of the important subsystems supplementing the enterprise-centered industrial relations of Japan.

Australia, Canada, and the United States

These three countries have in common the traditions of the same mother country, Britain. The craft-based structure and the adversarial bargaining approaches of British unions were the basis for the formation of unions in the New World. British common-law doctrines of property, contract, and tort structured the thinking of jurists in the New World when labor disputes came before them. Despite this, the approaches the legislature took in regulating labor relations have varied greatly among the three.

Braham Dabscheck (1992) details the basis for Australia's industrial tribunals, which regulate relationships between employers and employees, including wage disputes. The establishment of these tribunals at the turn of the century marked Australia's deliberate rejection of laissez-faire econom-

escape from or destroy bargaining. Although the legislative framework officially designed to aid in the expansion of bargaining remained in place, employers found ways to make use of it to thwart the establishment of bargaining (Lawler, 1990).

In Britain, the Thatcher government has been less subtle in attempting to throttle the unions and, in so doing, the process of collective bargaining. During the 1980s several acts were passed designed to make unions less effective (see Towers, 1989, for details). Government withdrew its long-term policy of officially encouraging all government employees to join unions and participate in bargaining. It also ended a policy in which government departments required that their contracts with suppliers have a clause stating that "the contractor shall recognise the freedom of his workpeople to be members of trade unions" (Hepple & Fredman, 1986). It used to be government policy to engage in bargaining, in part to be a model for relations in the private sector. The Thatcher government explicitly ended that policy.

The second interpretation also receives some support. Whatever their actual policy, most contemporary governments officially permit the existence of unions and of collective bargaining. There are almost no nations in the contemporary world that have general policies forbidding all employees to belong to unions and to engage in collective bargaining. There are, however, several countries that do not permit unions and collective bargaining to some employees. The Thatcher government in England disbanded one union of government employees and forbade them to engage in bargaining (Hepple & Fredman, p. 192). Public sector workers are not permitted to bargain collectively in Germany and in Japan. In recent years Canadian federal and provincial governments have increasingly resorted to back-to-work legislation to end strikes of government workers, and have often overridden collective bargaining in order to impose conditions of employment (Sack & Lee, 1989).

This general overview suggests that the theory, which holds that government policy moves in a unilateral direction away from suppression toward encouragement, is not entirely satisfactory. Some developments over the past two centuries support the proposition, but others do not. Neither industrialism nor modernism rigidly dictates policy. Governments instead have a choice. Desiring to be seen as "modern," few contemporary governments have an overall policy of outlawing all unions and all collective bargaining. Nevertheless, in recent years some governments have moved away from general encouragement toward suppression, and many others forbid some employees to engage in collective bargaining. Given that governments have a choice, one may ask what factors are associated with any given choice. In other words, under what circumstances do governments choose suppression, toleration, or encouragement?

Determinants of Government Policy

Repression. Both Rimlinger and Jacobs noted that in all of the countries that they addressed, unions and collective bargaining were repressed early in the course of economic development. With the advent of the industrial revolution, medieval institutions began to crumble, and the philosophy of liberalism began to gain ground. In this milieu, according to Windmuller, governments "perceived their primary responsibility to be the protection of the freedom of the market place and the sanctity of the individual contract of employment [and] as long as they considered trade unions to be a major threat to both, the purpose of intervention by the public authorities was the suppression, or at the very least the tight containment, of unions" (1987, p. 121). In short the new rash of legislation was motivated by liberal philosophy.

Clearly economic liberalism was an important factor in the development of U.S. policy. In the United States unions and collective bargaining were found to be criminal conspiracies in constraint of trade, by a court in 1806, and for the next quarter-century the "doctrine of conspiracy" was invoked many times. According to Chamberlain and Kuhn, "until 1834 convictions could be readily counted on" (1965, p. 15). It was not until another court case, settled in 1842, that unions and collective bargaining were permitted under certain circumstances.

Liberal philosophy also played a large role in the introduction of the Combination Acts in Britain. The formal rationale was that employee (as well as employer) combination amounted to a conspiracy in constraint of trade and was as a result contrary to the public interest. While this reason was no doubt of considerable importance in a country in which the political elite had strongly embraced liberal capitalist principles, nevertheless it was not the whole story. The French Revolution of 1789 caused considerable rumblings in Britain, and the power elite had good reason to fear that a similar attempt may be made in the United Kingdom. As Atiyah (1979) has noted, "After the outbreak of the Revolutionary Wars . . . [the authorities] saw any association of workmen as a possible source of subversive or revolutionary ideas" (p. 529). As a result the Combination Acts were designed in part to prevent the emergence of employee organizations that might act as a revolutionary catalyst.

A different rationale supported the Loi Le Chapelier of 1791, which forbade combinations in France. The motivation for this act was that there should be no associations intermediate between the individual and the state. Instead the state should be directly responsible to the citizenry. In short its philosophical basis was to enhance direct democracy. Its inspiration came not from economic theory, but rather from the philosophy of J. J. Rousseau.

In reality, however, it was used to suppress worker organizations (Jacobs, 1986, p. 198; Kendall, 1975, p. 13).

As noted above, government suppression of unions and collective bargaining occurred not only early in the nineteenth century but also much later. The German anti-Socialist laws effectively outlawed unions in 1878. As in France the rationale for these laws was more political than economic. Socialism was considered to be a threat to the dynastic elite ruling Germany, and the dual strategy of outlawing Socialist organizations and putting into effect many of the social programs called for by the Socialists was designed to defer the threat (Grebing, 1969, pp. 55-56).

Japan outlawed unions in 1900, ostensibly because their propensity to strike was a threat to the public peace. In fact the government was concerned because the union movement "centered in the industries related to armament and by the fact that it was led by socialists" (Okochi, 1958, p. 26). In short the rationale was more political than economic.

As noted above, when the USSR was established the Bolshevik government did not permit free unions and collective bargaining. To the extent that free unions agitating for the improvement of conditions of employment were a manifestation of class consciousness, such institutions were no longer needed in the Soviet Union, which had come to be a worker state. A new "productionist" role was more suitable for them. They would act as transmission belts between the leaders of the party and "the masses." In short, militant trade unions, aggressively forwarding the interests of their members, were considered to be obsolete and a contradiction in a society in which the state existed for the benefit of the working class and owned the means of production. Beyond the formal rhetoric, control of the unions was part of a more general strategy of the Communist party to control all aspects of society.

Like that of the Communists the Fascist repression of independent unions and free collective bargaining was based on the proposition that the state is responsible for the totality of economic and political relationships, and thus cannot permit competing power bases or decision-making sites that are likely to arrive at courses of action contrary to the overall policy framework of the state (Ramm, 1986).

Colonial powers, too, generally suppressed worker organizations in the nineteenth and early twentieth centuries (Kerr, Dunlop, Harbison, & Myers, 1962). While generally permitting unions and collective bargaining to exist, typically they have passed controls so tight that the institutions appear to be closer to the ones in the Soviet Union than to those in the West. Uncontrolled unions, it was feared, would likely divert funds to consumption rather than investment (Deyo, 1981). As noted above, the extent of propaganda in many developing countries urges unions to engage in productionist activities—

training, setting up cooperatives, and the like—instead of trying to win their members higher wages by using the threat of a strike. As in the West, however, the motivation was not entirely economic. As Roberts and De Bellecombe (1966) have noted, "The opposition to strikes manifested in Africa is based much more on a fear that they will be used to create conditions that will lead to the overthrow of the present political leadership, than on any appreciation of the effect of stoppages arising from a failure of collective bargaining" (p. 217).

The objective of the anti-union legislation introduced by the Thatcher government in the 1980s was to provide business executives with greater flexibility so that they would be able to respond more effectively to labor market signals (Towers, 1989). Philosophically, the Reagan administration in the United States was very close to the Thatcher government with regard to its belief that "market forces" should be able to operate with a minimum of constraint (Wheeler, 1987).

Both Germany and Japan have outlawed bargaining for civil servants. In Germany the rationale is that because civil servants have a special position of public trust, collective bargaining is inappropriate (Ramm, 1975). This rationale was, at one time, held by many governments, including those in North America. In most countries, however, it has fallen by the wayside. Civil servants argued that as citizens they were entitled to rights equivalent to other citizens; they also argued that since the state bargained with many entities (e.g., suppliers of services and the like), there was no reason why it should not bargain with its own employees. In Japan the reasoning seems to be more pragmatic. Collective bargaining for government employees was legalized by the occupying powers after World War II, but when this policy led to strikes and an increase in radical rhetoric, the policy was reversed, and bargaining in the public sector was outlawed and has remained illegal ever since.

Another critical factor leading the state to repress labor organization is the political pressure exerted by business. In all countries business executives prefer to have full authority to make all decisions necessary for the functioning of the enterprise, including decisions over terms and conditions of employment. As a result business interests continually lobby governments to adopt policies that will enhance their control of employment relations. In countries where business interests are very strong (e.g., the United States), government policy tends to be repressive. In countries where business interests are considered to be more critical to the public welfare than are labor interests, policy tends to be repressive. During the 1980s this has been a major factor in policy shifts in Europe and the United States, where the threat of competition from Japan and the newly industrializing nations of Korea,

become the more important than all of the others. Thus, where unions have political influence (e.g., Scandinavia), they are likely to insist that governments fully support collective bargaining.

The analysis here suggests that a policy of government encouragement of collective bargaining may be expected where, in addition to the factors that are associated with a policy of tolerance: (a) A Social Democratic or Labour party controls the government; (b) collective bargaining is considered to have positive consequences for economic growth; (c) bargaining is regarded as an effective and necessary means of conflict control; and (d) organized labor has a great deal of political influence. In addition government is likely to follow a policy of encouraging unionization and policy consultation (but not free collective bargaining) where there is a serious political threat to the nation, and a pluralist democracy is in place. A government is likely to engage in suppression of unions where there is a political threat to the nation, and the government is controlled by a nondemocratic elite.

Consequences of Government Policy

Do government policies have their intended effect? If government decides that it wants to encourage unions and collective bargaining, does union membership increase and the practice of collective bargaining become more prevalent? Contrarily, if government chooses to suppress unions and collective bargaining, do employees refrain from union activity? In Table 3.1 below, periods in several countries in which government policy was unequivocally designed to encourage or discourage unions and collective bargaining/consultation are identified. Also noted are the development of union membership and the practice of collective bargaining/joint consultation during the identified periods.

Although it would be inappropriate to draw firm causal conclusions from the data above, nevertheless they certainly are consistent with the proposition that the extent of union membership and collective bargaining is to a large degree a function of government policy. Where governments adopt an unequivocal policy of encouragement, union membership and the practice of collective bargaining expand.

If the proposition is in fact true, one may infer from it that where union membership is low and the practice of collective bargaining is restricted, those conditions are probably the result, in part at least, of less than enthusiastic government support.

The data also suggest that a policy of discouragement may not have the intended results. Unions continued to exist and function in several countries during periods of suppression, although they certainly did not prosper. The

TABLE 3.1 Notable Periods of Government Encouragement and Discouragement

Where/When	Union Membership	Practice of Collective Bargaining/Consultation
Encouragement		
U.S. 1917–1920	grew	grew
U.S. 1932–1947	grew	grew
France 1936–1938	grew	grew
Germany 1915–1921	grew	grew
Japan 1945–1948	grew	grew
Sweden 1936–?	grew	grew
France 1980s	decreased	grew
France 1968–1973	grew	grew
U.K. 1940–1945	grew	grew
U.K. 1973–1979	grew	grew
France 1915–1920	grew	grew
Discouragement		
U.K. 1799–1824	erratic	sporadic
U.S. 1806–1842	erratic	sporadic
Japan 1901–1925	flat	little
Germany 1878–1890	submerged	little
Germany 1933–1945	none	none
France 1791–1860	nascent	little
France 1940–1945	submerged	little
U.S. 1980s	decreased	decreased
U.K. 1980s	decreased	probably decreased
Japan 1938-1945	none	none

SOURCES: Ayusawa (1966); Berghan & Karsten (1987); Hepple & Fredman (1986); Lorwin (1964); Okochi (1958); Rojot & Despax (1987); Taft (1964); Taylor & Witney (1975).

inability of governments to effectively destroy the propensity of workers to organize is indicated by events following the lifting of bans in some of the countries. In Germany the anti-Socialist strategy of Bismarck was a total failure. When the anti-Socialist laws lapsed, union membership grew rapidly. The same occurred in both Germany and France after World War II, when the Fascist laws against union membership were lifted. A similar development is now occurring in some of the Eastern European countries; Hungarian developments are notable (Lado, 1991).

One cannot conclude, however, that suppression is entirely ineffective. There was little or no collective bargaining in Germany and Japan during the Fascist eras. Recent developments in the United States and Britain also indicate the efficacy of government policy in thwarting union membership and the practice of collective bargaining.

That government policy is an art instead of a science is suggested by some of the unintended consequences that have resulted from policy initiatives. In recent years one of the most dramatic examples is that of France. In the early 1980s the Socialist government of Mitterand passed legislation explicitly designed to encourage the spread of collective bargaining. Indeed the purpose was to have collective agreements cover the entire work force (see e.g., Aldir, 1989; Bridgford, 1990). To accomplish that end, legislation was passed requiring employers to negotiate on an annual basis with employee representatives at the enterprise level over wages and hours of work. It was assumed that the legislation would have positive consequences both for unions, who were designated as the appropriate bargaining agents for the employees, and for the practice of bargaining. In fact bargaining spread as intended, but union membership collapsed. A thoroughly convincing explanation for this extraordinary development has still not been offered. Nevertheless, some of the factors involved have been identified. First, French unions are very ideological and their primary method is agitation rather than sober bargaining. Thus a government mandate to bargain was not an especially beneficial event for them, as it would have been for unions in, for example, the United States or the United Kingdom, where bargaining is indeed their primary function. Second, according to experts, French workers are tired of the ideological posturing of the unions and, since bargaining is now mandatory and will occur regardless of whether they support the unions, many have chosen to withdraw their support. Third, employers have been seizing the initiative to involve employees in workplace level decisions, and thus employees may consider the unions to be less necessary than in the past. Fourth, unemployment has been high in France during the 1980s, and union membership often falls during periods of unemployment. Thus the negative effects of unemployment may have swamped the potentially positive effects of government policy.

Some Conceptual Issues in the
Analysis of Collective Bargaining Policy

In the above discussion there are two quite different types of factors giving rise to government policy. One type has to do with the rationality of a given policy. A policy of encouragement, for example, may be seen as rational because the evidence suggests that such a policy increases democracy, enhances economic growth, effectively channels potentially disruptive conflict, and helps the state win the cooperation of organized labor in the pursuit of the general welfare. These types of rationales are of importance in legitimizing policy, and thereby obtaining obedience to the rules stemming from the policy (see, e.g., Hepple, 1986, p. 27). Much policy analysis in industrial relations is in essence an assessment of the evidence for or against such propositions. The intensive U.S. debate during the 1980s, on the economic consequences of unionization, is of this character (see, e.g., Freeman & Medoff, 1984).

Another factor identified above has to do with political reality rather than rationality. Regardless of the evidence either in favor or against the rationality of a given course, governments often feel compelled to adopt or continue with a policy because of the political forces acting on them. For example, despite considerable academic evidence that collective bargaining is beneficial to economic performance, the government of the United States has not adopted a policy of encouraging collective bargaining, in part due to its ideological make-up, and in part due to the strength of political forces opposed to that course of action. In the world war periods many European governments adopted a policy of encouraging unionization and consulting with labor and management on issues of national concern, not because they were convinced of the public welfare benefits of that course of action, but rather because they felt compelled to do so under the circumstances. In the First World War period, the 1917 Revolution in Russia produced considerable fear that similar worker-based revolutions might occur in the West unless worker concerns were addressed and worker representatives were integrated into political decision making.

Another observation is that it is useful to make a conceptual distinction between policy and law. *Policy* refers to government intentions and behavior, whereas *law* refers to statutes or judicial decisions. Sometimes law reflects policy, but sometimes it does not. Britain is a good example. The British industrial relations tradition is said to be "voluntarist" because government, instead of passing extensive regulatory legislation, has permitted unions and management to work out their own arrangements. In their recent updating of Kahn-Freund's *Labour and the Law,* Davies and Freedland (1983) continually emphasize this point, as have many other authors. But, despite the absense of extensive legislation, the policy of British governments in the twentieth century has not been neutral, as the policy of voluntarism is sometimes interpreted to imply. In fact British policy has been to encourage collective bargaining. It has done so by notifying all public servants that collective bargaining is the preferred means of establishing conditions of work; by requiring government suppliers to recognize the freedom of their workers to join unions and engage in collective bargaining; and by directly intervening in many disputes in order to pressure intransigent employers to recognize unions and negotiate with them. These "policies" went largely unnoticed by British labor experts fixated on the romance of "voluntarism"

Freeman, R., & Medoff, J. (1984). *What do unions do?* New York: Basic Books.

Grebing, H. (1969). *The history of the German labour movement.* London: Oswald Wolff.

Hepple, B. A., & Fredman, S. (1986). *Labour law and industrial relations in Great Britain.* Deventer, The Netherlands: Kluwer.

Hepple, B. (Ed.). (1986). *The making of labour law in Europe.* London: Mansell.

Héthy, L. (1991). Industrial relations in Eastern Europe: Recent developments and trends. In R. J. Adams (Ed.), *Comparative industrial relations, contemporary research and theory.* London: HarperCollins.

Jacobs, A. (1986). Collective self-regulation. In B. Hepple (Ed.), *The making of labour law in Europe.* London: Mansell.

Kendall, W. (1975). *The labour movement in Europe.* London: Allen Lane.

Kerr, C., Dunlop, J. T., Harbison, F. H., & Myers, C. A. (1962). *Industrialism and industrial man.* London: Heinemann.

Kochan, T. A., Katz, H. C., & McKersie, R. B. (1986). *The transformation of American industrial relations.* New York: Basic Books.

Lado, M. (1991, August). *Workplace relations in the changing of industrial relations and economic guidance in Hungary for the past 20 years.* Paper presented to an international colloquium on Workplace Industrial Relations and Industrial Conflict; Laval University, Quebec.

Lawler, J. J. (1990). *Unionization and deunionization.* Columbia: University of South Carolina Press.

Lorwin, V. (1964). *The French labour movement.* Cambridge, MA: Harvard University Press.

Ogle, G. E. (1990). *South Korea, dissent within the economic miracle.* London: Zed Books.

Okochi, K. (1958). *Labor in modern Japan.* Tokyo: The Science Council of Japan.

Panford, K. (1988, January). State-trade union relations: The dilemmas of single trade union systems in Ghana and Nigeria. *Labour and Society, 13*(1), 37-53.

Ramm, T. (1975). Labour relations in the public sector of the Federal Republic of Germany: The civil servant's role. In C. Rehmus (Ed.), *Public employment labor relations: An overview of eleven nations.* Ann Arbor: Institute of Labor and Industrial Relations, The University of Michigan/Wayne State University.

Ramm, T. (1986). Epilogue: The new ordering of labour law 1918-45. In B. Hepple (Ed.), *The making of labour law in Europe.* London: Mansell.

Rimlinger, G. (1977). Labor and the government: A comparative historical perspective. *Journal of Economic History, 37*, 210-225.

Roberts, B. C., & De Bellecombe, L. G. (1966). Development of collective bargaining in former British and French African countries. In A. Ross (Ed.), *Industrial relations and economic development.* London: Macmillan.

Rojot, J., & Despax, M. (1987). France. In R. Blanpain (Ed.), *International encyclopedia of labour law and industrial relations.* Deventer, The Netherlands: Kluwer.

Sack, J., & Lee, T. (1989). The role of the state in Canadian labour relations. *Relations Industrielles, 44*(1), 195-223.

Slomp, H. (1990). *Labor relations in Europe.* New York: Greenwood.

Taft, P. (1964). *Organized labor in American history.* New York: Harper & Row.

Taylor, B., & Witney, F. (1975). *Labor relations law* (2nd ed.). Englewood Cliffs, NJ: Prentice-Hall.

Towers, B. (1989, January). Running the gauntlet: British trade unions under Thatcher. *Industrial and Labour Relations Review*, 163-188.

Wheeler, H. (1987). Management-labour relations in the USA. In G. Bamber & R. D. Lansbury (Eds.), *International and comparative industrial relations.* London: Allen & Unwin.

Windmuller, J. (1987). Comparative study of methods and practices. In *Collective bargaining in industrialized market economies: A reappraisal*. Geneva: ILO.
Zeytinoglu, I. (1986, Fall). The impact of the ILO's freedom of association standards of African labor laws. *Comparative Labor Law Journal, 8*(1), 48-87.

Commonwealth of Australia. The Australian Constitution specifies the various powers assigned to the Commonwealth Parliament; powers not so assigned being the responsibility of the respective state parliaments. During the conventions consideration was given to whether the Commonwealth Parliament, and hence government, should be assigned an industrial relations power. The granting of such a power was opposed by the champions of states' rights. Against this, it was argued, there would be no machinery to deal with disputes that spread across state borders. As Higgins (1915, p. 13) maintained in the *Harvard Law Review,* "Just as bushfires run through artificial State lines, just as rabbits ignore them in pursuit of food, so do, frequently industrial disputes." At the 1898 Convention it was decided, by a vote of 22 to 19, to grant the Commonwealth Parliament a limited industrial relations power.[6] Section 51, paragraph XXXV of the Australian Constitution states that:

> The Parliament shall, subject to this Constitution, have the power to make laws for the peace, order and good government of the Commonwealth with respect to . . . Conciliation and Arbitration for the prevention and settlement of industrial disputes extending beyond the limits of any one state.

Section 51, paragraph XXXV, is an indirect power. The Australian (Commonwealth) government is undoubtedly the only national government in the world that does not enjoy a direct industrial relations power with respect to the private sector. The Constitution forces the Commonwealth government to delegate powers of conciliation and arbitration to industrial tribunals, who are charged with the responsibility of settling and preventing interstate industrial disputes. Subject to other powers in the Constitution, the Commonwealth government cannot directly legislate on industrial relations with respect to such issues as wages, hours of work, working conditions, and so on. If it is desirous of achieving certain industrial relations outcomes, it is forced, like other parties, to argue its case before the federal industrial tribunal.[7]

State governments are not precluded from becoming directly involved in industrial relations. On a number of occasions important developments with respect to conditions have been established at the state level by legislation. Such examples would include the introduction of the 40-hour week, annual and long-service leave, apprenticeship and training, and health and safety standards. Notwithstanding their direct industrial relations powers, state governments have legislated, or brought into being, industrial tribunals. At the risk of making a rash historical generalization, state tribunals have tended to follow the lead of the federal tribunal with respect to matters of national or major importance. Furthermore, state governments have enacted legislation requiring their respective tribunals to follow the major decisions of the federal tribunal.[8]

The federal tribunal has consistently maintained and guarded its independence from the government of the day. Members of the tribunal maintain that they base their decisions on the quality of the submissions presented before them, and their judgment concerning the best, or most appropriate, course of action that should be adopted at a particular point in time. Mr. Justice Foster perceived the independence of the federal tribunal so strongly that he referred to himself and his colleagues as the "economic dictators of Australia" (Perlman, 1954a, p. 32).

Other members of the tribunal, however, have sought to maintain the fiction that they hand down decisions that are immune from biases and value judgments. For example, in the 1952/1953 Standard Hours and Basic Wage case (*77 CAR 477*, at 506 and 509) it was claimed that:

> The Arbitration Court is neither a social nor an economic legislature . . . it is not the function of the Court to aim at such social and economic changes as may seem to be desirable to the members of the tribunal. . . . The Court is not . . . a social or an economic legislature and . . . theories and policies should play no part in its determinations.

The claim that industrial tribunals do not concern themselves with social or economic reforms, and that they are not influenced by theories and policies, has a very hollow ring. The various personnel of tribunals pride themselves on the fact that they hand down reasoned decisions. They hear evidence and argument, are referred to past decisions and principles, and after careful and due deliberation hand down a decision. It is difficult in the extreme to conceive how members of an industrial tribunal, in arriving at a reasoned decision, can exclude theories and policies from their deliberations. William Jethro Brown, president of the South Australian Industrial Court from 1916 to 1927, has pointed out that members of tribunals like to maintain that it is the "law," rather than themselves, that makes decisions. He argues that:

> Lest they should innovate prematurely or capriciously, they have affected as a profession of faith that they cannot innovate at all . . . and, in so far as they have innovated, they have sought to conceal the fact from themselves as well as the public. (Brown, 1906, p. 291)[9]

Industrial tribunals have been a prominent feature of Australian industrial relations for almost a century. Notwithstanding this, however, only a few scholars have penned theoretical tracts that have sought to analyze and

Activist arbitration has been developed as an alternative view of the role of industrial tribunals, in an attempt to overcome problems associated with judicial arbitration and Mark Perlman's concepts of administrative and autonomous arbitration. Activist arbitration perceives members of industrial tribunals as being autonomous and independent. The personnel of industrial tribunals have their own views concerning how industrial relations issues should be resolved.[17] Members of industrial tribunals, under this view, enunciate new principles and develop new schemes to confront the various and diverse problems associated with industrial relations regulation. As the personnel of the various tribunals have been wont to maintain, they have been prepared to be innovative and experimental in responding to the needs of a progressive age. It might be useful, in fact, to regard industrial tribunals as constituting a quasi-permanent Royal Commission, charged with the responsibility of drawing the attention of the parties, the government(s), and the general public on how to reform and improve industrial relations.

With activist arbitration, industrial tribunals, via their decisions, speeches, and public statements of members and informal methods, seek to gain the parties' acceptance of the various schemes that they (tribunals) develop to resolve industrial relations problems. It is as if they are seeking to convince the parties of the wisdom of following the tribunal's lead down an ideal path of industrial relations regulation.[18] It is the propensity of tribunals for developing principles, of searching for the means of discovering and implementing "a new province for law and order" that is the source of both the problems that they encounter and the controversies in which they become involved.

At first blush, activist arbitration, with its notions of tribunal independence and autonomy, may appear similar to judicial arbitration. Unlike judicial arbitration, however, activist arbitration does not perceive industrial tribunals as being able to dominate the parties. Activist arbitrators interact or bargain with the parties in seeking to achieve the implementation of their "ideal" solutions to the problems associated with industrial relations regulation. Activist arbitration is also different from Mark Perlman's administrative and autonomous arbitration, where tribunals, in different ways, fulfill the needs of the parties. With activist arbitration it is quite conceivable that the parties will object to solutions proposed by industrial tribunals. While activist arbitration rests on an assumption of tribunal independence, it recognizes that tribunals do not operate in a vacuum; that they are confronted by parties that seek to restrict, restrain, and influence their decision-making ability. Industrial tribunals are just like other parties who find themselves caught up in the continuing struggles that constitute the real world of Australian industrial relations.

Australia's system of industrial relations is distinguished from that of other nations by the existence of industrial tribunals that regulate relationships between employers and employees. In a series of articles published in the *Harvard Law Review,* Higgins claimed that industrial tribunals would usher in "a new province for law and order." Industrial relations would not be left to what the Webbs referred to as "the higgling of the market"; industrial tribunals would interpret the public interest in responding to problems associated with industrial relations regulation.

In seeking to divine solutions to the issues of the day, industrial tribunals have been propelled to the center stage of discussions concerning Australian industrial relations. A tradition has been created of industrial tribunals furnishing solutions to industrial relations problems. By being so central to decision-making processes, industrial tribunals have been exposed to criticism and attack by those who have been opposed to the solutions they have devised. This penchant for tribunals becoming involved in controversy, of "stirring up peace," to coin a phrase Edmund Barton, Australia's first Prime Minister from 1901 to 1903, and member of the High Court from 1903 to 1920, once used to describe Higgins (Rickard, 1984, p. 274), in turn, has added to the mystique or aura of industrial tribunals as institutions in fearless pursuit and guardians of the public interest.[19]

In December 1920 the *Harvard Law Review* published a third article by Higgins.[20] The article concluded with the following words (Higgins, 1920, p. 136):

> Where there are more wills than one, there must come collision of will—and disputes; and even if the directors of industry were to be elected there still would be need for regulation. Regulation has come to stay.

As Australia prepares for a new century, it is conceivable that the experiment with industrial tribunals will come to an end. There are straws in the wind that the forces of international competition will bring about the destruction of the "new province for law and order." Notwithstanding what the future may have in store for us, Higgins's prophecy concerning regulation provides the key to gaining an understanding of Australian industrial relations in the twentieth century.

Notes

1. Over the years there have been four changes to the name of the major federal industrial relations tribunal. From 1904 to 1956 it was called the Commonwealth Court of Conciliation and Arbitration; between 1956 and 1973, the Commonwealth Conciliation and Arbitration Commission; between 1973 and 1989, the Australian Conciliation and Arbitration Commission; and since 1989, the Australian Industrial Relations Commission.

2. See Macintyre and Mitchell (1989) and Rickard (1976) for an examination of this period.

3. For further information on progressivism see Mowry (1946, 1958), Greer (1949), Kolko (1963), Lasch (1966), Weibe (1967), Gould (1974), and Roe (1984).

4. For the record, Beatrice Webb described her meeting with Higgins in the following terms (Austin, 1965, p. 76): "In the evening Mr. Higgins, a leading Melbourne lawyer and politician, came to dine with us. He is a bald-headed small-eyed man, of medium height; with a cultivated mind and a pleasant manner. He is not nearly so agile and astute as Isaac; but he is more anxious to find out the truth and act accordingly. His fault is a curious coldness and perhaps a lack of decision; he hesitates between complete opportunism and rigid adherence to theoretic principles; a hesitation which is emphasised by a slight stammer. He was rather pessimistic about Victorian politics: convinced of the honesty of the Government, but deploring the lack of intellectual leadership and the drifting of the policy according to the crude ideas of the majority of members, or the irresponsible advice of the 'Age.' 'They take a good idea and they spoil it' is Mr. Higgins' attitude towards many of the representatives of his community."

5. See for example the introduction to the 1902 edition, the discussion of arbitration and the national minimum wage. Webb and Webb (1902, pp. xxi-lvi, 222-246, 766-784).

6. For an account of these debates, see Rickard (1984, pp. 96-98).

7. See McCallum, Pittard, and Smith (1990) for further discussion concerning the role of the Constitution, and its interpretation by the High Court, in governing the operation of the Australian system of industrial relations.

8. Both legislation, and the tribunals themselves, have, in the past two decades, sought to achieve greater cooperation and coordination between tribunals. For a more detailed examination of these developments, see the *Australian Journal of Labour Law* (May 1990), which is devoted to "Joint State/Federal Arrangements in the Settlement of Industrial Disputes."

9. For a recent example of this, see Isaac (1989).

10. Only a handful of studies have been conducted concerning the work of individual tribunal members. See d'Alpuget (1977), Dabscheck (1983), Rickard (1984), Larmour (1985), and Vernon (1986).

11. For earlier work in this tradition, see Campbell (1945) and Sharkey (1961).

12. Also see Kitay and McCarthy (1989).

13. Higgins, for example, was involved in some celebrated clashes with Prime Minister William Morris Hughes. For details, see Higgins (1920), Lee (1980), and Rickard (1984). At the time of this writing, the Industrial Relations Commission is involved in a very public clash with the Hawke Labour government and the Australian Council of Trade Unions, with respect to the Accord Mark VI and the implementation of enterprise bargaining.

14. For a critical examination of such views, see Dabscheck (1989, pp. 113-141).

15. For examples of this view, see Kelsall (1960) and Niland (1978).

16. Like his father, Selig Perlman, he was interested in examining the role of outsiders, or "intellectuals" in industrial relations. To his credit, Mark Perlman sought to understand industrial tribunals through "Australian eyes," rather than overseas models.

17. There can, of course, be disputes between members of a tribunal concerning the best course of action to be adopted. For examples of such clashes, see d'Alpuget (1977), Dabscheck (1983), and Kitay and McCarthy (1989).

18. See Dabscheck (1983) for further development of these views.

19. In saying this, it should be realized that there is no such thing as the public interest. There are many publics, all in pursuit of their own interest. The point is that industrial tribunals develop their own solutions to problems of the moment, which they seek to legitimate under the rubric of the public interest.

20. The *Harvard Law Review* also published two articles by William Jethro Brown. See Brown (1919, 1922).

References

Austin, A. G. (Ed.). (1965). *The Webbs' Australian diary 1898*. London: Pitman.

Australian Journal of Labour Law. (1990, May).

Brown, W. J. (1906). *The Austinian theory of law*. London: John Murray.

Brown, W. J. (1919, June). Effect of an increase in the living wage by a court of industrial arbitration upon vested rights and duties under preexisting awards. *Harvard Law Review*.

Brown, W. J. (1922, January). Law, industry, and post-war adjustments. *Harvard Law Review*.

Campbell, E. W. (1945). *History of the Australian labour movement: A Marxist interpretation*. Sydney: Current Book Distributors.

Dabscheck, B. (1983). *Arbitrator at work: Sir William Raymond Kelly and the regulation of Australian industrial relations*. Sydney: Allen & Unwin.

Dabscheck, B. (1989). *Australian industrial relations in the 1980s*. Melbourne: Oxford University Press.

d'Alpuget, B. (1977). *Mediator: A biography of Sir Richard Kirby*. Carlton: Melbourne University Press.

Encyclical Letter. (1960). Pope Leo XIII, *Rerum Novarum* [The Workers' Charter]. London: Catholic Truth Society.

Fisher, C. (1983). *Innovation and Australian industrial relations: Aspects of the arbitral experience 1945-1980*. Fyshwick: Croom Helm.

Gould, L. L. (Ed.). (1974). *The progressive era*. Syracuse, NY: Syracuse University Press.

Greer, T. H. (1949). *American social reform movements: Their pattern since 1865*. New York: Prentice-Hall.

Higgins, H. B. (1915, November). A new province for law and order—I. *Harvard Law Review*.

Higgins, H. B. (1919, January). A new province for law and order—II. *Harvard Law Review*.

Higgins, H. B. (1920, December). A new province for law and order—III. *Harvard Law Review*.

Isaac, J. E. (1989, September). The arbitration commission: Prime mover or facilitator. *The Journal of Industrial Relations*.

Kelsall, E. P. (1960, June). Psychological aspects of the failure of arbitration in Australia. *Australian Journal of Psychology*.

Kitay, G. B. (1984). *Federal conciliation and arbitration in Australia 1967-1981*. Doctoral thesis, Australian National University.

Kitay, J., & McCarthy, P. (1989, September). Justice Staples and the politics of Australian industrial arbitration. *The Journal of Industrial Relations*.

Kolko, G. (1963). *The triumph of conservatism: A reinterpretation of American history, 1900-1916*. New York: Free Press.

Larmour, C. (1985). *Labor judge: The life and times of Judge Alfred William Foster*. Sydney: Hale & Iremonger.

Lasch, C. (1966). *The new radicalism in America*. New York: Knopf.

Lee, M. (1980). *The industrial peace act 1920: A study of political interference in compulsory arbitration*. Master's thesis, Sydney University.

Macintyre, S. (1989). Neither capital nor labour: The politics of the establishment of arbitration. In S. Macintyre & R. Mitchell (Eds.), *Foundations of arbitration: The origins and effects of state compulsory arbitration 1890-1914*. Melbourne: Oxford University Press.

Macintyre, S., & Mitchell, R. (Eds.). (1989). *Foundations of arbitration: The origins and effects of state compulsory arbitration 1890-1914*. Melbourne: Oxford University Press.

McCallum, R. C., Pittard, M. J., & Smith, G. F. (1990). *Australian labour law: Cases and materials*. Sydney: Butterworths.

Mowry, G. E. (1946). *Theodore Roosevelt and the progressive movement*. New York: Hill and Wang.

tions about the degree of real union autonomy during that period. Nevertheless, when compared with other periods, the 1960s were a time when the constitutional and statutory rights of workers to organize, bargain, and engage in collective action were relatively respected. This did not necessarily imply, however, that the government's developmentalist policies were not applied. In fact, during this period, the government was very much interested in securing low-cost, disciplined labor. What characterized this period were the governmental means employed to achieve this goal: relying more on market forces rather than on institutional intervention. Cheap disciplined labor could be easily obtained through the market system because the labor market was characterized by an unlimited supply of labor.

When an economy is suffering from a labor surplus, the surplus generally weakens labor's position. Though labor may be organized, unions can hardly be strong, and the labor-management relationship can be characterized at best, as paternalistic or, at worst, as exploitative. Adam Smith, in 1776, correctly described the major features of labor-management relations when an unlimited supply of labor prevails in the early stage of industrialization:

> It is not, however, difficult to foresee which of the two parties must, upon all occasions, have the advantage in the dispute, and force the other into a compliance with their terms. . . . A landlord, a farmer, a master manufacturer or merchant, though they did not employ a single workman, could generally live a year or two upon the stocks which they have already acquired. Many workmen could not subsist a week, few could subsist a month, and scarcely any a year without employment. In the long run the workman may be as necessary to his master as his master is to him, but the necessity is not so immediate. (Smith, 1936)

In contrast to the era of Adam Smith, collective bargaining in Korea during the 1960s was formally institutionalized. Nevertheless, market forces in Korea during the 1960s worked against labor as they did in Smith's era. Since the Korean economy suffered from severe unemployment and underemployment during the 1960s, workers were more concerned with gaining any employment opportunity than with achieving favorable working conditions. These labor market conditions were largely the cause of the inequality between the bargaining positions of capital and labor. Consequently, the government was not required to intervene or suppress union activities in order to maintain its cheap labor policy.

In other words, labor repression through market mechanisms worked rather effectively in Korea during the 1960s. This period of market-driven repression, however, came to an end as the economy moved from a labor surplus to a limited labor supply in the early 1970s.

STAGE 2: AUTHORITARIAN CORPORATIVE REPRESSION
(1972 TO MID-1987)

From the early 1970s the Korean economy slowly moved into the period of a semi-limited or limited supply of labor. The unemployment rate dropped sharply from 8.2% in 1963, to 4.5% in 1970, and 4.0% in 1973. This significant decline in the unemployment rate suggests that the Korean economy had shifted to a different stage of development. There is a wide consensus that an Arthur Lewis-type economic turning point, that is, a movement from unlimited to limited labor supply, took place in Korea some time in the early or middle 1970s.[2] Accordingly, the market mechanism could no longer guarantee low-wage, disciplined labor, and the union sector could make substantial differences if free collective bargaining was allowed to occur.

Against this background, the Special Presidential Decree on National Security was introduced in December 1971, and the labor scene suddenly changed. The content of the decree and its associated regulations was as follows: (a) Unions were required to secure government approval prior to engaging in collective negotiation; (b) when disputes arose, government intervention would be automatic and subsequent government decisions would be both final and binding; and (c) strikes or lockouts were prohibited.

This decree lasted for a decade before ultimately being lifted in December 1981. In December 1980, however, the labor legislation, such as the Trade Union Act and the Labor Dispute Adjustment Act, was substantially amended to the extent that unions continued to be suppressed even after the decree was withdrawn.

Though the labor relations policy of the 1970s made negotiation difficult and completely banned workers' collective action, the government did not restrict union organizing. Korean unions had been successful in negotiating "union shop" clauses that required employees to join the union as a condition of employment. This success, and the government's benign neglect of organizing activities, contributed to the relatively high growth of union membership during the 1960s and 1970s. Nevertheless, the changes to the labor laws effected in December 1980 produced a sharp decline in union membership, which only rose again with subsequent legislative changes in 1987.

Unions were allowed to grow, but not allowed to act as an effective instrument to protect and improve workers' interests. Instead, they were a vehicle for easier corporate control over labor. A unique feature of the Korean industrial relations system emerged during this period, one labeled "unionism without free collective bargaining" (Bognanno, 1980).

In sum, the whole period from 1963 to 1987 could be characterized as state or authoritarian corporatism,[3] although the methods employed to repress

TABLE 5.1 Union Membership (in Thousands) and Penetration Rate (PR)

Year	Membership	PR(%)	Year	Membership	PR(%)
1963	224	20.3	1977	955	24.3
1964	272	23.3	1978	1,055	24.0
1965	302	22.4	1979	1,088	23.6
1966	327	22.7	1980	948	20.1
1967	378	22.2	1981	967	19.6
1968	413	21.1	1982	984	19.1
1969	445	21.3	1983	1,010	18.1
1970	473	20.0	1984	1,011	16.8
1971	497	19.7	1985	1,004	15.7
1972	515	20.4	1986	1,036	15.5
1973	548	20.4	1987	1,267	17.3
1974	656	22.1	1988	1,707	22.0
1975	750	23.0	1989	1,932	23.7
1976	846	23.3	1990	1,887	21.7

SOURCE: Korea Labor Institute, *Quarterly Labour Review*, 1990-1991.
NOTE: Penetration Rate = Membership/nonagricultural permanent employees

labor during this time varied. During the 1960s repression was achieved mainly through labor market forces, while during the 1970s it was implemented through direct government intervention.

From 1972 to 1987, however, Korean corporatism was basically paternalistic. Although labor was excluded from sharing political power, workers did share some economic benefits. The mechanism for the economic inclusion of labor, however, was mainly through rapid generation of new job opportunities, rather than through higher wages for those already employed. During the 1960s, rapid employment creation, especially for the unskilled migrant workers from rural areas, was a top priority in the government's policy. This task was successfully carried out through the rapid expansion of labor-intensive light industries, resulting in a decline of open unemployment from 8.2% in 1963, to 4.5% in 1970 (see Table 5.1).

Unemployment per se has not been a serious problem in Korea since the early 1970s. Since that time, the priority has shifted from dealing with unemployment to dealing with underemployment. One of the various causes of underemployment is skill mismatching. This became increasingly problematic during the 1970s and 1980s, primarily as a result of the rapid changes in industrial structure from light industries to heavy industries, and subsequently to high-tech industries. To minimize skill mismatching, the government strengthened vocational-technical education at the secondary level, expanded public vocational training institutes, and even legally mandated in-plant vocational training by most private enterprises.

In short, the government tried to include labor in economic development, mainly through the reduction of unemployment (job creation) during the 1960s, and through the reduction of underemployment (better skill matches) during the 1970s and the 1980s.

STAGE 3: IMMATURE PLURALISM (MID-1987 TO MID-1989)

A political turning point toward democratization took place in Korea in June 1987.[4] The government instituted democratic reforms, including the adoption of presidential elections by direct vote. This political reform was spurred by a series of antigovernment demonstrations initiated in May and July of 1987 by students and quickly followed and supported by many middle-class urban dwellers. Along with the political reform came a de facto relaxation of the government's long-standing suppression of labor union activities.

The political turning point of June 1987 created space for a wave of labor disputes and union organization. Until 1986 the average number of labor strikes in Korea had been approximately 200 a year. However, in 1987 the number shot up to about 3,700. Furthermore, not only did the number of labor disputes increase, but the militancy of the conflicts increased as well (see Table 5.2).

Several aspects of these recent labor developments are significant and deserve special mention. The first important transformation was that labor's demands were far-reaching, calling not only for wage increases but also for union autonomy, reform of labor laws, and participation in management. While the demonstrations initially began in the large industries, where workers were relatively better paid, they later spread to smaller companies. This implied that the problems were not simply bread-and-butter issues, but instead went to the heart of the authoritarian corporatist system, which had characterized Korea's industrial relations over the decades. In addition, white-collar workers in banks, insurance companies, and some public enterprises, who had traditionally been reluctant to join unions, also actively participated in these recent strikes. These changes suggest that a rationalization or modernization of industrial relations had become an issue for the total working population, not just a small segment of it.

The second major development in the recent labor movement was that union democracy became a dominant issue. In many cases, two unions claimed to represent one company's employees, with each accusing the other of being controlled by the company. Although this was an internal union problem, the dissension frequently brought about work stoppages. This confusion, in fact, was one of the direct consequences of authoritarian corporatism. As previously mentioned, during the 1970s and 1980s, the

TABLE 5.2 Number of Labor Strikes: 1963–1990

Year	Strikes		Year	Strikes	
1963	89		1977	96	
1964	126		1978	102	
1965	113		1979	105	
1966	104		1980	407	Park Assassination (10-26-79)
1967	105		1981	186	
1968	112		1982	88	
1969	70		1983	98	
1970	88		1984	113	
1971	101		1985	265	
1972	n.a.	Presidential Decree	1986	276	
1973	n.a.	on Nat'l. Security (12-6-71)	1987	3,749	Roh's Democracy
1974	58		1988	1,873	Declaration (6-29-87)
1975	133		1989	1,616	
1976	110		1990	322	

SOURCE: Korea Labour Institute, *Quarterly Labour Review*, 1990–1991.

government tightly controlled the labor movement and allowed only activities of licensed unions. Thus, workers frustrated by the licensed union activities turned to the dissident, unrecognized labor movement. Church-sponsored groups were the most active elements in the dissident labor movement in the 1970s. However, the early 1980s witnessed the development of a new source of antagonism. Groups of students expelled from universities for antigovernment activities initiated dissident labor activities. Though their membership was not large, they were very active, militant, and radical, both in their ideology and in their action. These groups called themselves democratic unions and demanded legitimacy by accusing the licensed unions of being company unions.

The third development was found in the pattern of labor disputes. The typical sequence had been illegal strikes first, followed by effective negotiation and bargaining between labor and management. This reversed the standard of most countries, where collective bargaining occurs first, followed by strikes only after the negotiations have come to an impasse. This unique characteristic of the Korean labor movement followed from the fact that collective bargaining practices had not been institutionalized in Korea. As already discussed, during the period of authoritarian control, labor disputes were frequently resolved by direct government intervention. Unfortunately, this government intervention deprived workers and management of the valuable opportunity of carrying out effective negotiations by themselves. Therefore, collective bargaining had no opportunity to take root in Korea.

During the 2-year period of immature pluralism, from June 1987 to June 1989, the government followed a laissez-faire policy toward labor. Consequently, for the first time in the history of the Korean labor movement, unions enjoyed complete freedom to organize, bargain, and strike. However, mainly due to the parties' lack of experience in free collective bargaining, negotiations at the workplace did not proceed smoothly. Collective bargaining was frequently considered to be a war that one party would win or lose, rather than a process requiring compromise in order to reach a fair agreement. Thus, both parties frequently employed an adversarial "take it or leave it" bargaining style, which caused negotiations to continue until one party surrendered. Two years of completely free labor relations came to an end in June 1989, when the government returned to a selective intervention policy.

STAGE 4: TRANSITION TOWARD MATURITY (MID-1989)

With increasing government intervention, Korea's industrial relations system has now entered into a new stage of development. From a theoretical perspective, three possible courses of development lie ahead: authoritarian corporatism, pluralism, and liberal corporatism.

Although the government and employers may wish to return to authoritarian corporatism, this avenue is not a plausible choice for the future of Korea for the following reasons. The postwar generation (those born after 1953) will occupy about 75% of the total labor force by the year 2000. By that year, approximately 20% of the labor force will be college graduates, and more than 55% of the labor force will be either high school graduates or college graduates (Korea Development Institute, 1986). This postwar generation, highly educated and exposed to western-style liberalism and individualism, will harbor much higher expectations and will not comply with the restrictions of an authoritarian corporatist system.

Furthermore, the Korean economy is expected to sustain its growth at an average annual rate of more than 7% until the year 2000. This means that Korea's per capita GNP will continue to increase from about $5,000 in 1990, to more than $10,000 by the year 2000, in 1990 prices (Korea Development Institute, 1986). In addition, the increasing pressure to open up the Korean economy will continue to intensify in the coming decade. As per capita income rises and internationalization of the Korean economy continues, the traditional values, culture, and human relations will change. It is highly unlikely that an authoritarian paternalistic industrial relations system can be maintained in such an environment.[5]

Another factor that precludes the readoption of such a system is that Korea will experience a growing need for a more liberal and participatory system of industrial relations from the demand side. The Korean economy is now

Kochan, T. A., Katz, H. C., & McKersie, R. B. (1986). *The transformation of American industrial relations*. New York: Basic Books.

Korea Development Institute. (1986). *Korea year 2000: Summary report*. Seoul: Author.

Lane, C. (1989). *Management and labour in Europe*. Aldershot, UK: Edward Elgar.

Park, S-I. (1988). Labour issues in Korea's future. *World Development, 16*(1).

Poole, M. (1986). *Industrial relations: Origins and patterns of national diversity*. London: Routledge & Kegan Paul.

Rodgers, R. A. (1990). An exclusionary labour regime under pressure: The changes in labour relations in the Republic of Korea since mid-1987. *UCLA Pacific Basin Law Journal, 8*(1).

Schmitter, P. C., & Lehmbruch, G. (1979). *Trends toward corporatist intermediation*. London: Sage.

Smith, A. (1936). *The wealth of nations*. New York: Modern Library.

Streeck, W. (1986). Industrial relations and industrial change: The restructuring of the world automobile industry in the 1970s and 1980s. *Economic Analysis and Workers' Management, 20*(4).

Williamson, P. J. (1989). *Corporatism in perspective*. London: Sage.

6 \ The Role of the State in Industrial Relations in Japan: The State's Guiding Role in Socioeconomic Development

KAZUO SUGENO

Post-World War II industrial relations in Japan have been characterized by dynamic developments and transformations, as reflected, for example, in the transition from confrontational to cooperative labor-management relations, the decline of labor disputes and strikes, the establishment of industrial autonomy and partnership, and changes in both external and internal labor markets. Such transitions have occurred against the backdrop of the drastic economic changes represented by the periods of economic ruin, economic recovery, economic growth, economic adjustment, and economic restructuring, which have arisen in that sequence. Indeed, Japanese industrial relations have changed their features along with these economic developments. In this sense, the developments in industrial relations represent a major aspect of socioeconomic development in the postwar history of Japan. This chapter describes the role that the state has played in the industrial relations aspect of the postwar development of the Japanese economy and society.

The term *state* will mainly refer to the government or, more precisely, the entire organization of policy making and implementation initiated by the bureaucrats of the relevant ministries, endorsed by the cabinet, and, if the decision involves legislative acts, the Diet. Yet this chapter will also discuss another important aspect of the state's function: the role of the management decisions in most cases. Another blow against the militant labor movement was the expulsion of Communist leaders from industries by the 1950 "Red Purge" movement, initiated by the Occupation Authority. Yet many vicious labor disputes still occurred during the recession after the end of the Korean War, and this type of labor-management confrontation continued through the 1960 Mitsui Miike Coal Mine dispute. This dispute, which involved economic dismissals of 1,300 coal miners, marked the climax of postwar militant unionism. The union and management confronted each other with a fierce 8-month strike and lockout, marked by many battles at the picket lines.

As described above, labor-management relations during the early postwar era were characterized by unions led by leftist leaders, the frequent use of industrial action, management's confrontational attitude in establishing management its prerogatives, the enterprises' direct resort to economic dismissals when adjusting the level of the work force, and the frequent occurrence and aggravated nature of labor disputes.

THE PROCESS OF TRANSFORMATION
OF INDUSTRIAL RELATIONS

In the 1960s and the early 1970s, a period of high economic growth, labor-management relations underwent gradual transformation. By the end of the 1950s, unions in the major corporations of the key industries came to be managed by more enterprise-conscious leaders. A typical pattern of the leadership change occurred when, in the process of a prolonged strike, a large number of dissatisfied members split away to form a second union, quickly gaining an overwhelming majority within the company's work force. Another pattern was the turnover of leadership within an existing union after the failure of a major labor offensive. In each of the two cases, the new union leaders advocated more cooperative labor relations and obtained paramount support from rank-and-file employees. The company also backed them from the beginning. The new union leaders took the basic position of seeking to enlarge the size of profits by cooperating with the company in increasing productivity. From such a perspective, the parties promoted joint consultation and other communication systems.

In the economy as a whole, however, the number of labor disputes with strikes steadily increased in the 1960s. This trend can be related to the increase in small-scale strikes of shorter duration in the context of the Spring Wage Offensives, which developed during this decade. The number of strikes continued to increase in the early 1970s, when the incidence and scale of strikes (the number of participants and workdays lost) reached their peak. According to the Labor Ministry's statistics, the high point was in 1974, when the number of disputes accompanied by strikes of half a day or longer was close to 10,000, and the number of participants was 3.6 million; the number of workdays lost that year was close to 10 million. This is attributable to the further development of Spring Offensives with the strategy of "general transportation strikes," the first oil crisis of 1973, and the ensuing inflation against which unions fought hard in the 1974 Spring Offensive. Another important factor was the aggravation of labor relations in the public enterprises, particularly in the National Railways. This caused not only the escalation of public employees' illegal strikes in the course of the Spring Offensives, but also the frequent disruption of National Railway services by the union's slowdown tactics in the early 1970s. The militancy of public employees culminated in an 8-day political strike in December 1975, to campaign for the recovery of the right to strike.

Japanese industrial relations underwent a transformation during industrial restructuring after the 1973 oil crisis. In order to meet the critical economic situation, unions and management in the major industries engaged in extensive joint consultation and agreed on employee attrition and relocation plans to implement large-scale employment adjustment without resorting to economic dismissals. They also worked out measures to further rationalize the production systems. In this way, they established the method of accommodating industries and enterprises to drastic environmental changes. Moreover, in the Spring Wage Offensives, unions scaled down their demands to avoid unemployment, and the parties formed the framework of negotiating substantial, but noninflationary, wage increases. The unions and management in major industries also established the practice of settling wage increases, bonuses, and reduction in working hours peacefully and autonomously. There has been no attempt to conduct general transportation strikes since the late 1970s, and even the public employee unions have reduced their militancy. Thus, the number of strikes dropped sharply to a minimal level in the late 1980s.[5]

There are two other major developments that contributed to the transformation of industrial relations. The first was the privatization of the three giant public enterprises (the National Railway, the Telephone and Telecommunication Public Corporation, and the Tobacco Monopoly Corporation) through legislation in 1984 and 1986. Particularly significant was the reshuffling of the national railroad organizations and employees by the break up of the National Railways into several regional railroad corporations. During this process, the National Railroad Labor Union, one of the most militant unions in the public sector, declined to the status of a minority union in each of the regional railway systems (cf. Suwa, 1987, p. 5).

The other major development was the consolidation of the four national labor organizations into RENGO, the All Japan Trade Union Federation, in

1989. Basically supportive of the free market system, RENGO seeks to promote worker welfare by more extensively communicating and negotiating with management at various levels and more actively participating in national politics.[6] The employers' associations welcomed such a labor-front unification and adopted a more flexible and receptive attitude toward labor's demands. RENGO and the Japan Employers' Federation are even in basic agreement on the necessity of improving the quality of working life and have been cooperating in substantial projects.

Compared to the early postwar relations, contemporary union-management relations, as formed through the above-described process, are clearly characterized by industrial peace and extensive communication. The former characteristic (industrial peace) is reflected by consensual negotiations with minimal incidence of strikes, and the latter by information and opinion sharing on a wide range of subjects through joint consultation procedures at enterprise and plant levels. The tension between unions and management seems to be largely diminished, and the power relationship may be looked upon as one of either equal standing or employer superiority.

THE STATE'S ROLE IN THE TRANSFORMATION
OF INDUSTRIAL RELATIONS

A further question to be addressed in this chapter is what kind of role the state has played in the above transformation of industrial relations. First, the state contributed to the maturation and stabilization of labor relations through its procedures for labor dispute adjustment and adjudication. The great majority of vicious labor disputes, which had occurred up until the 1960 Mitsui Miike Coal Mine dispute, were resolved through the Labor Commissions' vigorous conciliation efforts. In those unstable years, applications to the Commissions for conciliation and other adjustment procedures numbered more than 1,500 every year. Labor Commissions also played a central role in the mechanism of Spring negotiations. Especially conspicuous was the parties' reliance on the Commissions' adjustment procedures in the Spring Offensives. Most typically, until the mid-1970s, wage negotiations in the private railway industry and the National Railways—which were key bargaining points in the strategy of the Spring Offensives—were settled by the Commissions' conciliation, mediation, or arbitration efforts every year.

Thus, the number of applications for conciliation was at its peak in those years, the largest being 2,249 in 1974. As of 1977 the private railway unions stopped working with the National Railway unions and, since that year, the parties in the railroad industry have been agreeing on wage hikes independently, without seeking assistance from the Central Commission. Overall, the number of conciliation applications has dropped sharply in recent years, due to the parties' general inclination to settle their negotiations autonomously.[7] The same tendency exists with regard to the number of unfair labor practice cases brought before the Labor Commissions for their adjudication and adjustment efforts.

The second role played by the state is its more positive action for inducing change. In this respect one cannot ignore the impact of the "Red Purge" intervention during the period of postwar turmoil, and the recent reorganization of the National Railways, both of which had the effect of assisting or reinforcing the new trend of union movements in the respective periods. In addition, the government's initiation of the so-called productivity movement in the mid-1950s laid the groundwork for improved industrial relations. In 1955 the Japan Productivity Center was established by business circles, under the guidance of the Ministry of International Trade and Industry, in order to diffuse the productivity movement throughout the economy. In the prospectus of the Center, the goals of the movement were "to enlarge the commodity market, to increase employment opportunities, to elevate wage levels and to enhance the quality of life through decreasing the costs of production by effectively and scientifically utilizing materials, manpower and facilities, thereby promoting mutual interests of labor, management and general customers" (Ministry of Labor, 1955, p. 516). In order to overcome labor-management conflict arising from that movement, the Center agreed with SODOMEI, the national labor organization that participated in the productivity movement, as to three basic rules, which became the leading principles for industrial relations in the subsequent years:

1. The productivity movement will eventually enhance employment security. Redundancy of employees that can temporarily result from productivity increases shall be resolved not by layoffs but by relocation of workers;
2. labor-management consultation must be promoted in order to determine concrete measures to increase productivity;
3. the fruits of increased productivity must be distributed fairly among management, workers and the customers (Ministry of Labor, 1955, p. 516).

The third state role in the same direction was the setting up of forums for labor-management communication at the national and industrial levels. For example, in 1970, the Ministry of Labor instituted a top-level consultation mechanism called the "Industry and Labor Round-Table Conference." This is a forum in which the top leaders of government, labor, and management, as well as academic authorities, meet regularly to discuss basic labor policies after reviewing the general trend of the domestic and international economy. Subsequent to the 1974 Spring Wage Offensive, in which unions gained more than 30% wage increases with major strikes, the government utilized this forum to get union and management leaders to share a basic understanding of the circumstances of the national economy and to realize the necessity of shifting to more moderate and peaceful wage negotiations.[8] The Labor Ministry also set up various other tripartite councils to have the relevant parties deliberate on issues of labor policy, such as prevention of unemployment, standards for minimum wages and working time, safety and health, and other issues. These councils function to absorb demands and opinions of labor and management, and to foster a consensus on the direction and content of labor policies. Through these mechanisms the government has actively involved labor and employer organizations in its labor policies. This can be regarded as one of the important subsystems supplementing enterprise-centered industrial relations in Japan (Sugeno, 1989, p. 335).

Industrial Restructuring and the State's Role

An important feature of contemporary industrial relations in Japan is its capacity for adapting to structural changes in the industrial environment. The first notable adaptation was made in response to the two waves of oil shocks and entailed large-scale employment adjustment. Labor and management achieved this adjustment not by economic dismissals but by attrition and relocation, after engaging in extensive labor-management consultation.[9] The state's role in this process was to facilitate and support such autonomous efforts by subsidizing the costs for business suspension and employee retraining and relocation, under employment stabilization projects recently implemented in the 1974 Employment Insurance Law. From their institution, these projects were fully utilized by the shipbuilding, chemical, and other heavy industries in carrying out adjustment programs. Special legislation was further enacted, in 1977, to provide more extensive benefits and grants to workers and enterprises in these "structurally depressed industries."[10]

The next adaptation occurred in the process of industrial and regional restructuring precipitated by the sharp rise of the value of the yen in 1985 and 1987 (Inagami, 1987, p. 3; Kuwahara, 1987, p. 4). In this process, steel and other manufacturing industries further promoted restructuring and diversification of their businesses. Many plants were closed or scaled down, and redundant employees were transferred to other plants or newly created businesses. There was also a serious economic situation in the local towns and regions, which depended heavily on exporting industries gravely damaged by the soaring value of the yen. Facing such economic situations, the government assisted employee relocation and retraining in restructuring industries through various grant programs. It also made efforts for improving the employment situation in the depressed regions by extending the provision of unemployment benefits and by granting subsidies to enterprises that maintained or hired workers living within those regions.

The above-described industrial restructuring was promoted by the participation of industrial labor organizations in the relevant industries. In order to facilitate industries to overcome economic crises and prevent the growth of unemployment, these industrial unions promoted joint efforts with employers' industrial organizations to press the government to form and implement industrial and employment policies in accord with their mutual interests. As a result, coordination between the government and the industrial parties to overcome the difficulties of the relevant industries became a major feature of contemporary industrial relations in Japan. The greatest importance was always attached to the prevention of unemployment, to which end all kinds of ingenious efforts were exerted. In this sense, employment stability has become one of the most important principles of Japanese industrial relations.

The Ongoing Reform of the Employment System and the State's Role Therein

The fourth aspect of the state role in Japanese industrial relations is the transformation of employment systems now occurring under the guidance of the government.

FEATURES OF THE CONVENTIONAL EMPLOYMENT SYSTEM

The Japanese employment system has been characterized by long-term employment secured until workers reach mandatory retirement age.[11] Wages and employee status rise as the employee accumulates years of service. The employer promotes employees' career development by systematic job rotation and training. The advantage merit of such a system for workers has been its employment security, enabling them to live a stable economic life. The seniority principle has also given workers a sense of fair treatment, and the wage system has also reflected the increase of living costs over the workers' lifetimes. More fundamentally, the employers have regarded employees as valuable human resources to be protected and developed within the company.

Yet this sort of employment relationship has demanded employees' total devotion to their jobs, in exchange for the employer's assurance of stability over the employees' entire life. The employers also developed various personnel systems, such as the differentiation of wage increases, bonuses, and promotions by performance evaluations, to stimulate employees' hard work. The system has also been premised on the traditional division of roles between the sexes and has placed the male work force in the center. Thus, the employee-employer relationship has generated the notion of almost unlimited dedication by male employees. They were driven to severe competition with their peers and worked lengthy overtime hours, with only limited use of statutory annual leave. These male workers have been subject to the company's absolute transfer right and have been sent to locations where they frequently live apart from their families.[12] Thus, the system imposed on workers means a considerable sacrifice in respect of their family life. The system also made it difficult for women to harmonize working careers with child-care responsibilities. In addition, the employment system discouraged mobility of workers, by imposing various disadvantages on workers who shift employment from one company to another. In these respects, the system was quite rigid, recognizing only one career pattern, with entry shortly after graduation from schools, single-minded dedication until retirement, and little possibility for career breaks.

POLICIES AND FORCES INDUCING CHANGE

The Equal Employment Opportunities Law for Women

The above-described Japanese employment system has been placed under great pressure for change in recent years. For example, the enactment of the Equal Employment Opportunities Law, in 1985, regulated employers' discriminatory employment practices against women and provided measures to assist women in their working life. The momentum for the passage of the law was given by an international movement that had started in the 1975 United Nations Women's Year and peaked with the adoption of the UN Convention in 1980.[13] However, the law certainly also reflected the domestic social change, namely the large-scale entry of women into the labor market, which was caused, on the demand side, by a major expansion in the tertiary industries and the increased demand for part-time workers; and on the supply side, by the decreased burden of housework and the increased need for housewives to earn a supplementary income. Thus, the government sought to respond to a major social force as well as to fulfill an international responsibility.

Compared to its foreign counterparts, however, the law adopted a unique position, gradually reforming the male-centered employment system by encouraging employers' voluntary action, rather than mandating immediate integration of women into the Japanese work force.[14] Yet despite its weakness as an enforceable norm, the state's declaration of sexual equality has had considerable impact upon traditional personnel management, and has resulted particularly in increased employment opportunities for female college graduates. It has also had the effect of pressing larger companies to reorganize the traditional career path, based on sexual distinction, into seemingly sex-neutral classifications of management and clerical or operative tracks. More decisive, in this regard, than the law or any other governmental action, is the recent labor shortage and the projection of its long-term continuation, which have forced enterprises to adopt a major strategy of making full-scale use of women as part of their work force.

The Policy of Restructuring the Economy
and Enhancing the Quality of Working Life

The next movement for the reform of the Japanese employment system started with Japan's response to trade frictions. The Japanese government attempted to accommodate the international critics of aggressive Japanese industries. In 1985, just before the Tokyo summit, Japan adopted the basic economic policy of restructuring its economy from export-oriented to one based on domestic demand. For this purpose, whole-scale economic measures were designed, one of which was the drastic reduction of working hours. The government set up a goal of reducing per capita annual working hours from the present 2,100-hour level to an 1,800-hour level. As its first step, the government obtained a major revision of the Labor Standards Law in 1986. The revision reduced the 48-hour weekly maximum to a 40-hour maximum, to be enforced in stages by the early 1990s. Following this revision, the Ministry of Labor drew up exhaustive measures for attaining the 1,800-hour level by the early 1990s. The reduction in working hours has also become a major subject, along with wage increases, in the Spring negotiations since 1987, and the parties have attained significant progress in increasing weekly and other rest days.[15]

More important, the movement for reduction in working hours became part of a more fundamental movement for enhancing the quality of working life. Aware of the Japanese industries' strong position in the global market and the achievement of great national wealth, the Japanese workers came to realize that they were not enjoying the quality of life they deserved for their dedicated work. In contrast to this image of great national and corporate wealth is the life of typical "salaried men" working in the Tokyo metropolitan area, who commute 1 to 2 hours each day, engage in extensive overtime work, and have to pay off their large mortgages by monthly contributions. In addition, the extraordinary increase in land prices in recent years has deprived many urban workers of even the dream of owning a house (Kawakita, 1988, p. 5; Shimada, 1990a, p. 4). The lives of those working in local cities and towns are much better balanced, but those areas have also been adversely affected by the concentration of institutions and information in Tokyo.

From this "Tokyo problem" arose the general social feeling that there must be major reforms of political and economic systems in Japan so that national resources could be more fairly distributed to increase the comfort of people's lives. The movement for the reduction in working time came to be reinforced by such a general social feeling. The movement was even more significantly supported by a structural labor shortage in the Japanese economy.[16] Since young workers, who are so preciously sought after by industries, have a clear inclination to avoid workplaces with longer working hours, it has almost become an imperative for enterprises to increase weekly and annual holidays in order to attract workers and survive in the coming labor shortage period.

Policies Related to the Aging of the Population

The third stimulus for the reform of the employment system was the aging of the population, as a result of the declining fertility rate and increased longevity.[17] The fertility rate has been gradually declining in Japan in recent years, with the figure reaching a low of 1.57 in 1990. This gave rise to grave concern in the government and the ruling party concerning its adverse effect on the aging society.[18] Along with the tendency among women to go on to higher education and marry later, the difficulty of career women to reconcile child-care responsibilities with their jobs was considered to be a major factor for the trend toward having fewer children. Thus, the "1.57 shock" moved the political parties and the government to hurriedly take the concerted action of enacting a Child-Care Leave Law, in 1991. This law guarantees every parent caring for an infant of less than 1 year of age the right to take child-care leave from his or her employer until the infant becomes 1 year old. The law will not only facilitate women's efforts to pursue careers but also promote a general atmosphere in the workplace of respect for an employee's family life.

The increase in longevity is also having a major impact on the Japanese employment system.[19] A consequence has been the increase of older members of the work force and prolongation of working careers. The age limit for long-term employment typically had been 55 years until the early 1970s, but most male workers continued employment in the same or a different firm until their early or late sixties. This was partly due to the economic needs of the workers connected with the immaturity of the pension systems.[20] Various surveys have shown, however, that from a cultural point of view, Japanese workers have demonstrated their desire to continue their working life as long as possible.[21] In this situation, the government, from the late 1970s, had been pressing firms to raise the age limit to 60 years, first by administrative guidance, and then by the Old Persons' Employment Stability Law of 1986 (A. Watanabe, 1986, p. 5). As a result, the 60-year age limit had been adopted in about 70% of firms as of 1991. In recent years, the government has also been promoting the policy of urging firms to secure employment of workers who have reached the retirement age limit, either in the original or a related firm, until they reach 65 years of age. It has done this in particular by revising the above law in 1990. This policy is necessitated, on the one hand, by the insufficiency of employment opportunities for old workers despite their desire to continue working. But it is also based on the government's recognition of society's need to achieve active participation of the senior work force, given the projections of a long-term labor shortage.

In any event, the employment system that the government is now advocating is the 65-year age limit system, which will require a significant modification of traditional wage and promotion systems and the structure of work organizations. The 65-year limit model is also premised on the more flexible distribution of working time throughout one's working career, with a reduction in working time for the younger work force, possibilities of career breaks for child or aged-parent care, and reeducation and the options of earlier or partial retirement (Inagami, 1991, p. 5).

THE EMERGING PROFILE OF THE
MODIFIED EMPLOYMENT SYSTEM

All the trends and forces described above are working together to change the Japanese employment system, which was established during the period of high economic growth and reinforced during the period of economic adjustment.[22] As was discussed above, the direction of modification will be toward a more merit-based, individualistic, flexible, and family-oriented system. The concrete features are likely to be diversified career tracks for promotion and transferability to be opted for by individual employees, more differentiated career advancement among the age groups, the further integration of various "non-regular" workers, increases in and positive use of mid-career workers, greater distinction between company and private life through increased leisure, possibilities of career breaks for care and reeducation purposes, increases in women managers and professionals, and a greater variety of working styles for workers in their late fifties and early sixties. The point here is that the model of the new employment system will be molded under the strong influence of state labor policies.

Conclusion: The Characteristics of the State's Role
in Industrial Relations in Japan

The "occupation policy," which first paved the way for modern industrial relations immediately after World War II, established a legal framework based on trade union rights and principles of labor contracts. Faced with economic difficulties for the nation and the people, the state also made great efforts to construct infrastructures for securing a minimum economic life. During the decade of turbulent labor relations after the war, the state greatly contributed to resolving disputes and achieving mature labor-management relations through its adjustment procedures. Then, the transformation of labor-management relations proceeded, with the state playing a major role in the initiation of the productivity increase movement, promotion of joint consultation, and setting up of forums for labor-management communication at the national level. At the time when the transition to cooperative relations had almost been completed, Japanese industries entered a period of adjustment due to international economic fluctuations. The state assisted the parties' joint efforts for adaptation through its active industrial and employment policies. The structural changes in the industrial environment continued further, to the extent of necessitating transformation of Japanese employment practices, which had been established during the period of economic growth. The state has been working together with industry and labor to search for a new employment system to enhance the quality of working life and adapt to an aging society with a labor shortage.

Summarized in this way, a distinctive feature of postwar industrial relations in Japan is its dynamism, characterized by drastic social changes and industrial transformations. Another feature is the state's leading role in socioeconomic developments. Indeed, one may find in the Japanese system a model of socioeconomic development guided by the state.

The theoretical question raised here is how to define the structure of industrial relations in which the state plays such an important role. First, this is definitely different from the liberalism or neo-liberalism, in which the state seeks to abstain from intervention in the commodity and labor market as much as possible. In Japan, the government, through its policies, is involved in almost every social and economic issue. But, on the other hand, has the state intervention in Japanese industrial relations been so strong and comprehensive as to make the free market system nominal? Has the labor market, employment system, or labor-management relations been so strictly controlled by the state as to render it a special regulatory regime? Except for authoritative and coercive intervention during the "occupation" period, and the setting up of labor standards and social security system, state intervention in industrial relations has been rather indirect. It has been characterized by inducing the parties' voluntary action through administrative guidance or "endeavor obligation," or the technique of achieving de facto consensus through government-sponsored consultation machinery. Moreover, despite the state's involvement in a wide range of issues in labor relations, the dual or multitier structure of industries and the labor market has basically been left intact. Management flexibility also has been maintained (Sugeno, 1991, p. 5). One could assume, therefore, that state regulation is premised on the free market system.

The next question then is whether the structure of Japanese industrial relations can be described as corporatism or neo-corporatism. The author is inclined to answer in the negative. Japanese industrial relations are essentially enterprise-based, and the centralization of power in labor and management organizations does not seem to be developed enough to create competitive parties with an equal footing vis-à-vis the state in the participatory machinery at the national level (van Wolferen, 1990, p. 81). What one could find in the postwar development of Japanese industrial relations is rather the reliance of labor and management on the state in coping with environmental changes. Yet there is certainly a significant resemblance to corporatism in the mechanisms of Japanese industrial relations, defined by some experts as "loose neo-corporatism."[23] Perhaps the greatest characteristic one can find in the state's role in Japanese industrial relations is the coordination between the government and social parties, and the parties' (particularly the labor side's) reliance on the government in the steering of the dynamic and transitional industrial relations.

Notes

1. The government reacted to the short-lived Meiji labor movement by enacting the Police and Peace Law in 1900. Article 17 of this law prohibited inducement of strikes and other organizational activities. Yet, influenced by the recognition of worker rights in the newly created ILO, the government adopted the policy of recognizing moderate labor unionism led by the Japan Federation of Labor, while continuing to suppress the leftist union movement connected with socialism or communism. The government thus eliminated the notorious Article 17 from the Peace and Police Law in 1926. It also made unsuccessful efforts for enacting a Trade Union Law by submitting bills to the Imperial Diet several times over a period of more than 10 years.

2. With regard to the number of union members, the prewar labor movement reached its peak in 1936, with 420,000 workers. The peak organization rate was 8%, as of 1931.

3. For a thorough analysis of the prewar union movement and labor relations in Japan, see Gordon (1985).

4. The monthly amount of a typical pension became 10,000 yen in 1965, 20,000 yen in 1970, and 50,000 yen in 1973.

5. In 1988 the number of disputes was only 498 and the number of participants and workdays lost were 74,000 and 173,000, respectively.

6. RENGO is the largest national labor organization in the history of the Japanese labor movement, with the affiliation of 78 industrial federations and about 8 million workers. It represents 67% of all organized workers. See Nitta (1988, 1990).

7. The number of applications declined to 736 in 1984, and 531 in 1988.

8. On the organization and function of the Industry and Labor Round-Table Conference, see Mori (1981, p. 299).

7 \ Trade Unionism in the Future

EDWARD DAVIS

The proportion of workers covered by unions has declined sharply in many industrialized market economies. In countries such as France and the United States unions may now cover less than 15% of the work force. The first section of this chapter explores the rapidly changing economic, political, and social context within which unions operate, and pays attention to reforms within industrial relations. The second section examines the impact of change on unions and in particular discusses the extent to which structural change has contributed to the fall in union density. The third section investigates the strategic alternatives facing unions as they strive to recruit and retain members. The fourth section draws conclusions on the nature of the crisis confronting unions and the task ahead.

Preface

Unions are their members. The future condition and character of unions will necessarily depend upon their ability to attract and retain members. This in turn will be influenced by broader economic, political, social, and industrial relations developments, although, as Undy and others have argued, unions are not simply "acted upon" (Undy, Ellis, McCarthy, & Halmos, 1981, p. 350). The choices that they make, the strategies that they develop, and the energy and resources that they commit in their pursuit will also be important.

In Schregle's commentary on the comparative study of industrial relations, he pointed to the potential for confusion arising from use of the same label to describe different institutions (Schregle, 1981). He gave examples of "courts" and "bargaining" and indicated that both could refer to very differ-ent institutional forms and behavior in different countries. This is certainly the case with trade unions. Within Western economies unions, for the most part, operate independently of government in pursuit of improved wages and conditions for their members. Throughout the Communist world, however, and through much of Africa, Asia, Latin America, and the Middle East, unions are often tied closely to the state, with top union officials regularly appointed by the state. Their overriding function is to maintain and improve production. Writing in the late 1980s, Ross Martin remarked that union movements of this sort outnumber all others (Martin, 1989, p. 145).

There are also many unions throughout the developing world that are struggling against economic and political repression. Amnesty International has reported on the plight of unionists who have been imprisoned or ill-treated for the peaceful exercise of their human rights, including basic union rights. It has listed the distressing cases of many union activists who have been killed or who have "disappeared." The situation is described as serious in Brazil, Colombia, El Salvador, Guatemala, and Sri Lanka (Amnesty International, 1990).

The term *union* therefore can often be misleading since it describes such different institutions operating in very different circumstances. Interlinked with this, there is a broad spectrum of opinion about what unions do and what they should do. The terrain is controversial and contested. In Martin's study he distinguishes five viewpoints, classifying them as *Pluralists* (union as industrial regulators), *Syndicalists* (unions as social emancipators), *Marxist-Leninists* (unions as party instruments), *Organicists* (unions as moral forces), and *Authoritarians* (unions as state instruments). The Pluralists are the odd man out. For them, the function of unions is to primarily improve the situ-ation of their members through collective bargaining. The main function for all other groups is education, either to raise workers' consciousness toward the overthrow of capitalism or to promote well-being within the society or state (Martin, 1989, pp. 95-99).

The comparative study of industrial relations is strewn with warnings about the interpretation of data. Different countries often adopt different approaches to data collection, which renders comparison hazardous. This has achieved notoriety in the study of time lost through industrial disputes. The raw evidence may suggest that one country is more strike-prone than another. Alternatively, it may just be more efficient at data collection (Shalev, 1978). This chapter is concerned with union membership as a proportion of the total work force. Bamber and Lansbury comment that comparative union mem-bership data are even less reliable than most other comparative data (Bamber & Lansbury, 1992, appendix). Estimates of union membership generally come from the unions themselves, and there is no standard approach adopted in computing results. In addition, unions may have reason to either under-estimate or exaggerate membership size. Further issues arise in defining the groups that will or will not be counted as making up the work force. For instance, the American Bureau of Labor Statistics (BLS) excludes the armed forces and groups such as employers, the self-employed, the retired, the un-employed, and those employed in agriculture, forestry, and fishing. Gideon Ben-Israel and Hanna Fisher, among others, reiterate the importance of due caution when handling data on membership and density (Ben-Israel & Fisher, 1992). Further issues of comparability and interpretation are discussed by Visser in the OECD's *Employment Outlook* (OECD, 1991, pp. 98-100, 121-128).

The steep decline in union density experienced in many developed market economies has generated much concern. It has acted as the catalyst for research and conferences inquiring into the causes and character of the condition. Without doubt there have been those who have celebrated the slide of union membership, the associated loss of union income and diminished influence. Indeed it has been the goal of some governments, such as Mrs. Thatcher's, to achieve this end. Nonetheless scholars within industrial rela-tions have often emphasized the contribution that unions make to economic, political, and industrial life. For instance, three Australian researchers have contended that unions are a significant vehicle for the achievement of social justice, an essential attribute of a free society and a vital balance to the power of major corporate employers (Shaw, Walton, & Walton, 1991, p. 102).

In the United States, Freeman and Medoff challenged the prevailing negative perception of unions and unionism, arguing that unionism raised social efficacy, was often linked to increased productivity, and promoted greater economic equality (Freeman & Medoff, 1984, pp. 246-251). More recently, writing in the *Harvard Business Review,* Hoerr has stressed that unions can assist companies in their bid to improve competitiveness (Hoerr, 1991). For instance, unions can play a valuable role in encouraging teamwork within the workplace and can assist in the resolution of grievances. Unions therefore can promote greater flexibility and greater productivity; "strong unions can make stronger companies" (Hoerr, 1991, p. 31). The author also acknowledged that unionized employees enjoyed greater protection at work than their nonunion counterparts.

Writing in the mid-1980s Jack Barbash asked, "Do we really want labor on the ropes?" (Barbash, 1985). He inquired into the repercussions of the decline of unionism for American democracy; he wondered whether the benign aspects of human resource management would continue in the ab-sence of unionism's countervailing power; and he pondered on the possibility of an eventual union backlash prompted by more favorable labor market conditions. He warned that government and employer attempts to undermine and destroy unions might appear to contain short-run benefits, but the strategy risked aggravating class conflict over the longer term.

Recognition of the potential contribution of unions to economic and political life is a feature of the chapters in this section. There is therefore shared concern over the sharp decline of union density in many countries, and great interest in the strategic choices facing unions as they strive to stem and reverse the loss of membership.

Changing Context

The economic, political, and social framework within which unions operate has undergone enormous change in the past dozen years. The OECD's *Employment Outlook* noted that the 1980s were "more than a simple chronological interval" (OECD, 1991, p. 59). The decade "corresponded to a full cycle of economic activity, characterized first by a deep recession and then by the longest period of continuous economic expansion in the postwar period" (OECD). The decade ended with many countries in severe recession.

Political change, particularly in Europe, has been momentous. Eastern Europe has seen the disintegration of the Soviet Union while Western Europe has moved toward closer economic integration. Sweden's peak union council, the LO, has remarked:

Europe, from the Atlantic coast to the Urals, from Troms to Palermo, is undergoing the greatest and most comprehensive change since the end of the Second World War. The political map is being redrawn. The change is twofold. On the one hand there is the creation of the internal market in Western Europe, on the other hand, there is the economic and political breakdown of the communist dictatorships and the dawning of democracy in Eastern Europe. (LO, 1990, p. 2)

The OECD and various scholars have drawn attention to the structural changes that have occurred. Within the OECD the overall proportion of employment represented by the services sector rose from 57% in 1980 to 62% in 1988 (OECD, 1991, p. 44). A significant proportion of this growth was linked to the contracting out of service activities from firms within the business sector. Accompanying structural change has been a major increase in nonstandard forms of employment. The proportion of the work force engaged in part-time work, self-employment, and casual employment has risen in many but not all countries. Edward Sussex, in a report for the International Labor Organization, presented a useful schematic representation of the process of structural change (see Table 7.1):

other key matters before the Australian Industrial Relations Commission. It appears paradoxical that union density in both countries declined during the tenure of generally sympathetic governments.

This paradox aside, the importance of government is underlined in the experience of African unions. Ben-Israel and Fisher contend that within Africa:

> [T]he impact of government has been extreme: several governmental restrictions coincided with a fall in membership rates. The trade unions played a major role during the anti-colonist struggle. Following independence, however, when their leaders took on senior positions in the ruling establishment, they became partners to the governments' fears of union-inspired political reforms. To prevent them, African governments have taken official and unofficial steps against the unions: legislation, administrative harassment, penetration of security agents into the unions and their undermining from inside. (Ben-Israel & Fisher, 1992)

In an overview of developments in African unionism, Henley concludes that states, in pursuit of economic reform, are unlikely to tolerate union demands. Rather, they will be tempted to impose further restrictions on union freedoms (Henley, 1989, p. 308).

Major change to the conduct of industrial relations has also stemmed from a shift in employer tactics in several countries. Commenting on the experience of unions in Canada, Mona-Josee Gagnon has perceived increasing employer efforts to win and mobilize the commitment of employees (Gagnon, 1992). More attention has been paid to profit-sharing schemes, and managers have been encouraged to adopt more participative styles in their dealings with subordinates. Consensus and harmony are proclaimed goals: "It is precisely this which is new and important: this insistence on convincing us." Gagnon remains skeptical, pointing to the traditional sources of antagonism in the workplace. Nonetheless, as she argues, there are significant implications for unions as employers strive to capture their workers' allegiance "if the enterprise is the first identity pole, if the work team is the second, what room is left for trade union identity?"

Wever tells a similar tale in the United States (Wever, 1992). Under the pressure of increased international competition, employers sought to cut production costs. For many this meant major changes to workplace design and/or moves to new sites. In both cases many employers sought to reduce or eliminate union influence. Unionism then became associated with plant closures and job insecurity. Some employers, though, adopted the "soft" approach, utilizing human resource strategies that stressed the virtues of close communication between managers and employees, consultation, and involvement in decision making. Their goal was the same, to stave off or curtail union influence.

Manik Kher remarks on similar experience in India, where employers have been less ready to cede to union claims and have responded increasingly with counterproposals (Kher, 1992). There has been a steady stream of major employers closing plants in unionized areas and relocating in more backward zones, where labor is cheaper and nonunion. As in North America, there are also many enterprises taking the soft approach. Sensitive human resource management styles, with benefits for employees in education, health, recreation, and housing, have been designed to challenge the allegiance of employees to unions.

At the last World Congress of the International Industrial Relations Association, the focus was "Labor Relations in a Changing Social, Economic and Technological Environment." Attention was devoted to increased labor market flexibility and new employment patterns, structural change, the characteristics of the new labor force, and the issues surrounding equity and equality of treatment at work. The congress noted the rapid pace of change and the crumbling of long-held assumptions. As put by one Rapporteur, the stereotypical image of the male, union-organized, manual, and full-time work force was under siege (Brown, 1989, p. 1). A large and growing proportion of the new labor force was female, nonunion, white-collar, and part-time. Neither the pace nor the breadth of change has slackened. Exploration of the character and fortunes of unions must take account of the backdrop of change.

Impact of Change on Unions

Alfred Pankert's paper reports on the adjustment problems of 11 national union confederations in industrialized market economies (Pankert, 1992). The general impression is that unions have been assaulted by change and that adjustment has been painful and difficult. Britain's Trades Union Congress (TUC) has commented on the "plethora of developments" with which it has had to contend and the fact that "change is spread in so many directions" (Pankert, 1992). The TUC went on to say that the rapid changes have required short-term, immediate responses, which have made more difficult the development and pursuit of longer term strategies.

The peak councils surveyed indicated also that unions have been slow to react to structural change and to the increasing heterogeneity of the work force. The past two decades saw in many countries the contraction of manufacturing and construction, traditional union strongholds, and the expansion of the large and amorphous services sector, yet the composition of union membership altered little. Women and young people comprise an increasing proportion of the work force, but unions have paid insufficient attention to their recruitment and retention. Similarly, there has been an increase in nonstandard work, yet unions have often neglected the needs and interests of this burgeoning group.

Faced with challenges of this nature, Ben-Israel and Fisher have warned that unions are engaged in a "struggle for survival" (Ben-Israel & Fisher, 1992). Their future, they said, will be determined by their ability to influence the approach of employers and governments, and their success in convincing workers to join and remain in their ranks. Surveying the situation in the United States, Wever has questioned whether unions are up to the task. The challenges are to organize members in unfamiliar areas, adapt to new management strategies and structures, and articulate the emerging values and interests of American workers. The evidence of the past two decades would seem to lead to gloomy prognosis.

Jelle Visser has spent much of the past 10 years assiduously gathering and analyzing data on union membership (Visser, 1989, 1990, 1992). His research has demonstrated that there are very different levels of union density in comparable countries and that many of the countries explored experienced a decline in density from the mid-1970s. General points made by Visser were that density tends to be higher in European countries than in North America, higher in smaller countries and lower in "adversarial" systems (1992). There are, of course, exceptions in each of these cases. Factors with a bearing on this are the role of the welfare state in Europe, which has encouraged greater density; the importance attached to achieving consensus in small countries; and government and employer support for unions in countries with a relatively harmonious approach to industrial relations.

Visser compiled the excellent chapter on trends in union membership for the OECD's *Employment Outlook* (OECD, 1991, pp. 97-134). Table 7.1 presents data on the experience of 24 countries.

As indicated, union density increased for most countries between 1970 and 1980. Among notable exceptions were the United States, Japan, and France. Between 1980 and 1988, however, only Finland, Iceland, and Norway recorded clear increases in density. In some of the other countries the falls in density were large: United States, 28.7%; New Zealand, 23.5%; France, 36.8%; Netherlands, 29.2%; and Spain, 27.3%. The fall in France, which by 1988 had lost half of its 1975 membership, prompted discussion of the feasibility of unionism without members and alternative channels for worker representation (OECD, 1991, p. 102).

The United States has long stood out among comparable countries in terms of low union density. The peak density (as a proportion of nonagricultural workers) was approximately 35% in the mid-1950s. Commentators on

American unionism have customarily referred to the range of problems facing unions. These include the large area for unions to cover, fierce employer opposition, a hostile judiciary, and a labor force fragmented by ethnic and racial divisions (Galenson & Smith, 1978, pp. 11-33). Since the mid-1950s there has been a steady and apparently relentless decline in union density. As might be imagined this has give rise to much discussion. Scholars have pointed to the impact of structural and technological change, and the shift of plants from highly organized sectors in the East and Midwest to Southern states such as Florida, Texas, and Oklahoma, where unions have failed to gain a firm footing (Barkin, 1965, pp. 217-219).

Much the same story has been told in the 1980s and early 1990s (Ferman, 1984; Strauss, Gallagher, & Fiorito, 1991). Scholars such as Barbash and Kassalow have pointed to the repercussions arising from the decline of the steel, auto, and textile industries, and the rise of employment in the private white-collar, technical, and professional spheres (Barbash, 1985; Kassalow, 1984). Attention has been drawn to the discouraging impact of sustained high employment and to the repercussions of new employer tactics to remove and keep out unionism. There is also recognition that American unions have failed to respond adequately to the changing composition of the work force. They have failed to convince significant proportions of women, blacks, and Hispanics that unions can provide them with an effective service.

The American Federation of Labor-Congress of Industrial Organizations (AFL-CIO) conducted its own research into the plight of its affiliates. *The Changing Situation of Workers and their Unions* covered the familiar terrain, but in particular emphasized both the adverse impact of employer opposition to unions and the absence of legal support for union organization and bargaining: "The norm is that unions now face employers who are bent on avoiding unionization at all costs and who are left largely free to do so by a law that has proven to be impotent and a Labor Board that is inert" (AFL-CIO, 1985, p. 10). The report also discussed public perceptions about unions. It found that a majority of nonunion workers think that unions do not respond to the needs and desires of their members and often coerce members into action that they do not support.

A sharp decline in union density has fuelled debate within the Australian peak council. Labor force survey data revealed that union density in 1988 was 41.6%, down from 51.1% in 1976 (Davis, 1990, pp. 100-103; Peetz, 1990, p. 198). This led to considerable soul-searching at the 1989 ACTU Congress. One senior official stated, "our movement is in deep crisis. We either improve our performance and reorganise or we perish" (Davis, 1990, p. 100). According to the then-president of the Australian Council of Trade Unions (ACTU), unions had "failed on the basic." They had not responded on the structural shift in jobs that had led to increased employment of women, white-collar, and part-time workers. They had failed to rationalize their often antiquated structures, and they remained prey to conflict within their own ranks. A further comment at the Congress was that:

> [O]ur priority in the future must be to get unions to cooperate in an effort to unionise the 60% of the work force that is unorganised, rather than to have unions preoccupied in fighting one another for a bigger share of the shrinking unionised market. (Davis, 1990)

The fall in density has been closely examined by Peetz (1990). His analysis suggested that at least half of the decline in the 1980s was a result of the accelerating influence of structural change in the mix of industries, sectors, and occupations. Changes in establishment and firm size were noted to be contributing factors. Factors accounting for the residual decline included the increasingly unfavorable legislative environment in some states (notably Queensland), a deterioration in attitudes toward unions, and, more speculatively, the impact of human resource management strategies designed to attract Australian workers away from unions (Peetz, p. 221).

The middle point is of particular interest. Peetz discerned a deterioration in attitudes toward unions during the decade that their collective behavior was marked by moderation and responsibility, and time lost through industrial disputes fell significantly (Davis & Lansbury, 1992). By the early 1900s there was concern that centralized wage fixing and the adherence of unions to the commitment to make no extra wage claims had diminished union relevance in the eyes of workers. This was one of the factors leading to unions' renewed interest in workplace bargaining (see below).

Manik Kher provides a different emphasis in her account of the decline of Indian union density (Kher, 1992). She stresses that the traditional link between unions and political parties has become weaker and that unions are in the process of "depoliticization." Their reduction in political influence has been accompanied by diminishing industrial strength, visible in the failure of unions to win a string of major disputes. She makes particular reference to a textile strike in Bombay in 1982. The strike fizzled out after a year, with the workers involved suffering from starvation, loss of employment, and indebtedness. The defeat demoralized unions across India and gave encouragement to employers seeking to diminish union influence in their plants.

Evidently, many industrialized market countries witnessed significant declines in union density in the 1980s, and it is clear that economic factors, in particular structural change, played a major part. Nonetheless, no neat explanations emerge to explain the variations in experience across different countries. In research completed by Visser he examined union density, from 1980 through 1988, in nine sectors in 14 countries, resulting in 126 separate cases (OECD, 1991, pp. 107-109). There were 21 cases of growth in union density, 30 cases of stability (plus or minus 5% over the period), and 75 cases of decline. The study indicated varied experience across sectors within the countries examined.

Further research on the British and German experience is instructive. The study by Undy et al. of various British unions found "ample evidence of the ability of unions to influence growth trends through their own actions" (Undy et al., 1981, p. 162). Important ingredients were the extent to which unions were perceived as "delivering the goods," the efforts made to recruit new members, and pursuit of the closed-shop and check-off arrangements. Sussex came to a similar conclusion. The ravages of the 1980s did not decimate the ranks of all unions. For instance, 40% of the unions affiliated with the British TUC increased their membership in 1987, and by the late 1980s the West German peak council, Deutscher Gewerkschaftsbund (DBG), had recovered the ground lost since 1981 (Sussex, 1989, p. 39).

Visser discussed several hypotheses formulated to explain the differences in density (OECD, 1991, pp. 118-119). First, Kassalow has argued that union density is determined by the extent of industry-wide and multiemployer bargaining. The greater these elements are, the higher the union density. Conversely, devolution and enterprise bargaining are associated with lower levels of density. Second, Kjellberg has proposed that strong union density requires union involvement, both at the state and sectoral level and at the workplace. In support of this he points to France as an example of where unions lack influence at either level, and density is very low; and Sweden, where the opposite is the case, and density is high. Other hypotheses nominated by Visser for testing are that inclusive unionism incurs less employer opposition and results in higher density, and that higher levels of density are often found where unions deliver broader benefits, such as social insurance services and unemployment pensions. The next section will throw some light on these matters as the response of unions to the challenges of the 1980s are examined.

Strategic Responses

The 11 peak councils surveyed by Pankert were found to have initiated steps to respond to the changing composition of the work force (Pankert, 1992). For instance, policies have been widely formulated on the importance of discovering the needs and aspirations of women, young workers, and part-time workers. Information on this has been made available to union officials and workplace representatives, and relevant training has been provided for them. Many peak councils have also concluded that too many unions remain too small. They lack the organizational resources required to provide an adequate service for members. Affiliates have therefore been urged to pursue amalgamations, mergers, and rationalization. Hurdles encountered have been the resistance of many officials and members, who fear loss of influence and identity in the aftermath of a merger, and the considerable time and effort required to achieve amalgamation.

Many peak councils have pointed to the desirability of greater union involvement in public and industrial decision making. Low union involvement in these spheres is linked to the "vicious circle of low skills, low quality jobs, low wages and low productivity." This has been the complaint of the British TUC. The past dozen years have seen the "unions left out of the equation in so many areas of industrial and public life." Such peak councils are confident that influence within senior levels of government and industry will assist in lifting workplace performance. The vicious circle will be replaced by a virtuous circle of high skills, high-quality jobs, high wages, and high productivity. This outcome, of course, will be of benefit to unions, because they will be better placed to recruit and retain members. The Australian case, in which unions have enjoyed very significant influence within government and within industry decision making, suggests that there may be more to it than this. Influence in high places was not sufficient to avert a sharp decline in density.

Pankert comments on increased union interest in enterprise competitiveness and proclaimed desire for more cooperative industrial relations. Union councils have apparently concluded that better relations will facilitate their involvement in issues such as training and retraining, to the benefit of members and enterprises (Pankert, 1992). Gagnon warns, however, that union pursuit of cooperation with employers should not be at the expense of their identity. Unions must remain at some distance from their employers. She contends that consensus "has become an obsession, almost a spectre" (Gagnon, 1992). The risk, she contends, is that emerging unionism will lack coordination and ideology. Its role as a vehicle of challenge will be defunct. If unions no longer play the role of articulating the interests of employees, as distinct from employers, then their legitimacy may be challenged by new separatist movements.

Wever discusses the experience of American unions (Wever, 1992). Their task is to apply pressure to employers to change management practices. Managers must be encouraged to communicate and consult more effectively with employees. This is seen as opening doors to higher levels of performance and higher wages. She notes that union efforts to achieve involvement at high levels in enterprise decision making have had mixed results. Collaboration in the auto industry has contained some benefits for unions; in the airlines industry there have been some dramatic failures.

The AFL-CIO spelled out its strategic response in 1985. In the *Changing Situation* report, it argued for the creation of new categories of membership to facilitate recruitment of employees outside organized bargaining units. Unions should also seek to provide a wider range of services to broaden their appeal to members and potential members. For instance, unions should offer assistance in job training and access to fringe benefits such as cheaper health care. Other goals nominated were increased use of the electronic media, raising public awareness and understanding of unions, and imposition of greater pressure on employers to diminish their avoidance of unionism in their plants. The late 1980s saw great efforts by American unions to raise their visibility, with the "Union Yes" campaign supported by prominent actors and sports personalities.

Contemplating opportunities for unions in an integrated Europe, Jobert and Rozenblatt argue that their effectiveness will be influenced by their ability to develop a broader and more political role (Jobert & Rozenblatt, 1992). They will need to coordinate their approach to enhance their powers of persuasion in European economic and industrial decision making. Similarly national unions will need to combine and coordinate their efforts in dealing with multinational enterprises. The challenge will be to gain the necessary information to enable unions to shape their response and develop counterproposals. Jobert and Rozenblatt note several examples of the establishment of joint information committees bringing together the European offices of enterprise and relevant unions. They also indicate the growth of European sectoral union bodies, which are beginning to play a more important role. Nonetheless, they warn that too many unions remain indifferent and unresponsive to the economic integration occurring around them.

Olle Hammarström argues that unions face three policy alternatives (Hammarström, 1992). The first is a back-to-basics strategy, which relies on unions retaining a narrow focus on wages, conditions, and job security. Dues are kept relatively low and unions are discouraged from developing cultural and other services. This is the no-frills approach. The second strategy is the 24-hour union, which has a broad focus and provides multiple services, for instance, discounts available to members for insurance, travel, and other items. The third alternative is for unions to focus on improving workplace organization, and in particular increasing opportunities for members to undertake training and skill development.

Hammarström emphasizes that this requires high levels of union competence and strong union organization at the workplace. He concludes that unions must work and bargain with managers over issues such as job design, career planning, and training. In sum, "to be relevant to members in the 1990s unions need to engage not only in issues of wages and conditions but also support members in getting stimulating and challenging jobs in a safe and healthy environment" (Hammarström, 1992).

In the early 1980s the ACTU forged an agreement with the Australian Labour party, then in opposition. The agreement, known as the Accord, covered an array of issues, such as the treatment of prices and nonwage incomes, taxation, industrial relations legislation, industry development, technological change, immigration, social security, occupational health and safety, education, health, and Australian government employment. It also supported the return of centralized wage fixation conducted by the Australian Industrial Relations Commission. In 1983 the ALP won federal government and moved to implement the Accord. In the mid-1980s the Accord underwent a metamorphosis. It became a process of decision making with a number of further agreements reached between the ALP and the ACTU. The original pact was renamed Accord Mark 1, and subsequent agreements Mark 2-6 (Davis & Lansbury, 1992).

The benefits of the Accord were debated at every ACTU congress circa 1983. ACTU leaders argued that the Accord delivered influence to unions at the level of national, economic, industry, and social policy making. This influence had been used to ensure expansionary economic policy, reflected in a surge in employment from 1983 to 1990, and improved social and other benefits such as healthcare and superannuation. There were few dissenting voices at these congresses, and formal union support for the Accord was overwhelming (Davis & Lansbury, 1992).

The difficult economic circumstances of the mid-1980s, with relatively high inflation and stubborn balance of payments' deficits, forced renewed attention to union strategy. At the 1987 congress, two policy documents were debated: *Future Strategies for the Trade Union Movement*, and *Australia Reconstructed* (ACTU, 1987; Department of Trade, 1987). The thrust of both documents was that unions must maintain a broad focus:

> The economic circumstances have demanded that unions in pursuit of more jobs, greater job security and the capacity to increase living standards are more closely involved in the processes of production and not simply in the distribution of the receipts of production. This changed emphasis has meant that unions must be interested and involved at company and industry level about training, investment, production methods and industry policy. (ACTU, 1987, p. 5)

The ACTU recognized that unions were handicapped in the service of their members. In 1987 there were 326 unions covering 3.2 million members, with more than 150 unions with fewer than 1,000 members each. ACTU policy therefore called for radical surgery, using amalgamations and rationalization to reduce the number of unions to approximately 20. These unions would generally be industry-based, although there would be some occupational and conglomerate unions. The rationale was that the newly forged unions would be larger, better resourced, and better equipped to deliver improved services. The large reduction in the number of unions would also diminish demarcation tensions. Unions would spend less time engaged in internecine conflict.

The way forward for unions was elaborated at the 1989 ACTU Congress, in *Can Unions Survive?* (BWIU, 1989, pp. 40-51). This exhorted unions to press on with amalgamation plans. It also encouraged unions to devote more time to recruitment, to target groups such as women and young workers, and to strengthen links between union offices and rank-and-file membership. Taking a leaf from the AFL-CIO, it argued in favor of union development of services such as access to cheaper credit and housing and insurance, travel, and retail discount arrangements (BWIU, 1989, p. 46).

The early 1990s have been remarkable on two counts. The Australian union movement is in the throes of major change, with 21 union amalgamations achieved in the past 2 years. A further 70 are in progress. The contours are being redrawn, with the goal of 20 large unions appearing more attainable (Davis, 1992). Second, union leadership has called for workplace bargaining to play a much more important part in wage determination. The Australian Industrial Relations Commission, under great pressure from the federal government, unions, and most employer organizations, agreed to facilitate more bargaining in its October 1991 *National Wage Case Decision*. Unions hope that the return to bargaining will restore their relevance in the eyes of members and assist recruitment. Unions have not abandoned their interest in the broad agenda drawn up a decade ago; they have determined to exercise influence within the workplace as well as at the national level.

Conclusions

The role, form, and functions of unions differ from country to country. This chapter has looked mainly at unions within Western industrialized market economies. Even within this group a range of experience has been evident. Some countries, such as France and the United States, have witnessed sharp declines in union density, to the point where the future of unions has been put in question. Other countries suffered steep declines in density, but unions have continued to cover a significant proportion of the work force. Yet others, such as the Nordic countries, have retained high levels of density, and unions have remained influential actors within these societies. The case remains strong that unions have a vital role to play in the representation of employees at work. In addition, as argued by Freeman and Medoff, unions

8 \ Trade Unions in the Future: Organizational Strategies in a Changing Environment

GIDEON BEN-ISRAEL

HANNA FISHER

Trade unions worldwide are suffering from a decline in membership rates. This phenomenon is common among unions having different structures, functions, organizational bases, and legal bases. In other words, the phenomenon does not derive from the character of the union, although the extent of its prevalence in a specific union may be connected to the latter's particular characteristics.

The aim of this chapter is to analyze the phenomenon and its causes, while referring to changing environmental conditions and their influence on the parties to the industrial relations system. We shall present several economic, structural, and ideological factors that are generally recognized in literature as influencing the union's capability to recruit members, as well as the workers' inclination to join trade unions. The economic and structural factors are expressions of apparently irreversible trends; therefore, the problems facing the unions are not expected to be temporary ones. We shall also examine the attitudes and behavior of other parties—governments and employers—toward the trade union. These entities as well are affected by economic factors and in turn influence the state of the trade unions. By means of restrictive legislation and nonrecognition, both government and employers are capable of creating conditions that may hinder or even prevent the

135

establishment of unions. It is therefore important to distinguish between individuals joining an existing union and the establishment of a new union or the organization of a new workplace. We shall distinguish between the union as such and the workers as individuals and examine the differential influence of changing conditions on them. At the individual level we shall examine the factors that influence the inclination to join, refrain from joining, or leave the union.

At the union level we shall examine the behavior of the union under such conditions, and which unions are better equipped to survive. We shall analyze the options of the different labor movements and unions to cope with the various challenges with which they are faced.

Decline in Membership Density in Trade Unions

In most countries of the world, trade union membership levels are declining. This trend is apparent from secular data collected in various countries.[1] Because of different criteria used, the figures do not permit international comparisons of membership rates, however the long-term measurements in the same country demonstrate the trends.

EXAMPLES INDICATING THE EXTENT OF THE PHENOMENON

Lawler (1986) shows that in the United States membership rates fell from a peak of 30% to 19%. Troy (1990) refers to the decline in membership density, mainly in the private sectors in the United States and European countries.

In the United Kingdom there was a decline of 9% during 1980-1986 (Disney, 1990; Freeman & Pelletier, 1990).

In Japan, membership rates fell from 35% in 1970 to 29% in 1983 (Shimada, 1983; SOHYO News, 1986). The decline was due mainly to the fact that no new members were recruited, despite the significant rise in the labor force.

During the 1960s, when African countries won their independence, membership rates rose. Today (Henley, 1989), the rate is declining and in most African countries it is below 20% of the labor force. A considerable number of organized workers are civil servants or employees of state companies; the representation of the private sector in the trade unions is much smaller.

At the 1990 Asian/African Regional Meeting of Experts on Organization of the ICFTU, concern was expressed regarding the increasing number of nonorganized workers and the declining trend of membership rates in many of the countries of the region (Report of ICFTU-APRO, 1990a).

ECONOMIC AND STRUCTURAL EXPLANATIONS

The literature examines different explanations and reasons for the membership decline phenomenon and attempts to determine the dominant factors that gave rise to it (e.g., Disney, 1990; Henley, 1989; McCallum, 1989; Shimada, 1983; Troy, 1990).

It is not our intention to give preference to any particular explanation or to present a comprehensive and unequivocal model for forecasting membership trends according to economic characteristics. Our underlying assumption is that the complex of factors involved in the fall in membership, irrespective of whether it has direct or indirect influence on the state of the unions in different countries, is of importance to the unions to help them examine the alternative strategies for coping with the problems they are facing.

ECONOMIC FACTORS

Many scholars have dealt with the influence of economic variables on membership trends and have attempted to determine the nature of these influences. The prominent subjects discussed are the business cycle, wage and inflation levels, production methods and technological changes, the character of the products and the labor markets, occupational structure, and the unemployment rates.

The general argument is that the unions find it harder to increase membership during times of economic crisis and recession, under conditions of competitive domestic and international product markets, and in a situation of both surplus labor and unemployment.

Disney (1990) examined the impact of macroeconomic factors, such as the business cycle, wage inflation, and unemployment, on union density in the United Kingdom. He claims that these are the prominent explanatory factors of membership trends, if the general trend is taken into account in addition to fluctuations in the business cycle. He found that in the long run the higher the level of real wages, the lower the membership level. Furthermore, he discerned no long-term influence of unemployment rates on membership.

Trade agreements and the opening of international markets, which lead to changes in the product market and to competition, have increased the importance to the firm of reducing production costs, including labor costs. One of the ways of dealing with the problem is to transfer labor-intensive industries to developing countries where cheap labor is available. This is carried out through creation of international companies and by investment in developing countries, where the consideration of attracting foreign investors exerts pressure against unionization. At the same time, governments are pressured to create free trade zones and legally prohibit the establishment of trade unions in them.

The structure of developing economies is gradually changing, due to the introduction of sophisticated technology and the passage from labor-intensive manufacture to know-how intensive industries (e.g., microelectronics and onto-electronics). In these industries the proportion of indirect labor (planning, computation, control, marketing) is high. There is also a trend of transfer to the public, commercial, and personal services sectors, while the number of those employed in the industry is not rising. These changes affect the production system on the one hand, and the occupational structure as well as the character of the labor force required, on the other.

Production processes are becoming less standardized and uniform. The familiar plant floors, populated by a large number of workers doing the same type of work, during the same working hours and taking the same breaks, enabling communication among the workers, are less common. When they do exist, they are likely to be transferred to locations where there are other means to hinder unionization. Accordingly, the labor force in demand tends to be one that is better educated, more motivated, less homogeneous, and not always concentrated in one place. As will be shown below, these characteristics are related to low membership rates.

These changes in job characteristics are accompanied by a growth of the proportion of part-time and temporary workers, subcontractors and self-employed. Furthermore, the number of people working flexible hours or outside the workplaces is increasing. They tend to be scattered and mobile and are not tied to a single employer. All these factors create difficulties in their unionization (Brown, 1986; Terry, 1986).

Economic factors, the product market, the technology, the labor market, and occupational structure affect industrial relations as well as the attitudes and actions of the parties involved.[2] The attitudes and strategies of governments, employers, and unions, and the actions deriving thereof, determine both the capacity of the latter to organize new workplaces, and the inclination of workers to join the union. The influence of these factors is discernible through the characteristics of the workers and will vary according to the categories to which they belong.

The Influence of Government: Legislation, Creation of Social Climate, and Intervention in the Economy

The state of the national economy, as well as the nature of international competition, tends to encourage governments to prefer the employers who

authorities in order to mediate and allocate interests and implement policy. In this definition Lehmbruch refers to a system similar to the social partnership in Austria. He claims that similar forms of the model exist also in Germany, the Netherlands, Scandinavia, and Switzerland. The definition is founded on the assumption that the workers, the governments, and the employers agree on general economic goals and hold the same ideology regarding industrial relations. The union is willing to accept wage restrictions in order to advance the agreed economic goals. In parallel, the workers' representatives have considerable influence on working conditions and human resources management in the workplace. Comparing the situation in various European countries, Lehmbruch claims that the model is most effective in Austria, more than in Germany, where the unions are less centralized. In the Netherlands the corporatist system is institutionalized, from the point of view of the entities that are partners to the negotiations and bargaining. On the other hand, in Sweden, institutionalization is less formal, but negotiations are more centralized and take economic data into account.

Such a type of corporatism posits a concentrated and centralized union that is not guided by traditional class orientation. The political involvement of the union, and hence its access to the centers of decision making through the political channel, is a factor that can assist in implementing such a system (see also Dunkley, 1984, an analysis of the Austrian system, compared with Germany and Scandinavia, and details of the prerequisites for the existence of such a system).

Lash (1985) submits the most general definition: Corporatism or neo-corporatism is an institutional system in which the organized interests of labor and capital operate in one framework with the government. Within this framework, the workers' organizations act as social control agents for the workers. They agree to restrain wage demands in exchange for representative monopoly and a guarantee of economic growth. This definition includes centralized bargaining practices, which were common in Europe mainly during the 1950s and part of the 1960s. Lash points to the failure of the model in European countries (Germany, France, the United Kingdom, Italy) and in the United States. He also claims that in Sweden, which is regarded as the best example of this model of relations, the trend is toward decentralization of negotiations.

Lash regards as the main problem of corporatism the imbalance between centralized negotiation leading to egalitarianism, and economic interests that pull toward autonomy and isolationism. He claims that the trend toward pragmatism in the labor market and in employment in Sweden has caused a tendency to decentralize negotiations. This trend finds expression in the isolationism of the strong unions who do not regard the egalitarian wage policy of the LO as suitable for their own interests.

The phenomenon also exists in other places where the union was often less centralized originally than in Sweden. Unions experiencing difficulties sometimes adopt the way of fragmentation and competitiveness. In such a situation, the stronger unions, who believe they can attain more by acting independently, will show a tendency to withdraw. There are some who argue that unions are undergoing fragmentation and are transforming into shop-floor-level unions (Brown, 1986; see also Ofek & Rosenstein, 1987, on the isolationist inclinations of the unions in the General Federation of Labor in Israel).

On a theoretical level, Panitch (1980) also claims that such a structure is inherently unstable, since the union carries within it the kernel of a continuous struggle; changes in leadership or opposition from the ranks in the form of wildcat strikes can draw the union outside the circle of cooperation. Panitch claims that such a process is to be expected mainly under conditions of full employment.

Shimada (1983) describes the flexibility of the Japanese union on wage issues in an effort to maintain stability of employment at the expense of wage increases. Although negotiations are conducted at the plant level, there is a leading union and a full information transfer system. Shimada (1983) defines this as functional corporatism: cooperation between organized workers, organized capital, and the government, to achieve a common goal, namely, stable prices and full employment (referring to Lehmbruch's 1980 definition). In Japan, wage agreements are adapted to macroeconomic conditions, despite decentralized negotiations. Centralization finds expression in communication and in goal participation. Corporatism is also manifest in the high degree of the union's involvement in everyday management, such as work rates, promotion and transfer of workers, on-the-job training, and participation in joint committees.

In Singapore (Blum & Pataranapich, 1987) the unions form part of a tripartite mechanism aimed at improving the standard of living through increase of output. The government plays the leading role in this mechanism, and the employers have a free hand in handling matters. The main function of the trade union is to ensure industrial peace, to cooperate with management and see that production increases. This model was further strengthened in 1982. Union leadership has been supportive of the government's goals and plans for modern technology, growth, and increase in productivity. Even following the economic recession and wage freeze in 1985, cooperation continued and unions agreed to wage cuts. Singapore attempted to change to the Japanese model by introducing structural changes and creating workplace unions in order to increase the workers' identification with the workplace. Implementation of the initiative is still in process. The attempt to apply the Singapore corporatist model in Hong Kong was only moderately successful, partly because of limited membership rates and failure to reach agreement on joint objectives.

INFLUENCING WORKERS BY INCREASING
THE BENEFITS OF UNION MEMBERSHIP

If we regard the decline in membership rates as evidence of the fact that the expected benefits of membership are lower compared with its costs, then one way to recruit members is to increase the benefits. Workers have nonmaterial needs that can be provided by the union. An intelligent union will examine the members' indirect economic and social needs, and by finding the suitable ways and means of fulfilling them, will increase its attractiveness.

During recent years the number of unions that look beyond the direct economic sphere and representation in wage negotiations has been increasing. Yet, generally, preoccupation with other topics is still in its infancy, with the exception of the General Federation of Labor in Israel, which will be referred to below. The expansion of union functions is mentioned, for example, by Shalev (1980). Freeman and Pelletier (1990) also point to innovations in union services in the United Kingdom, such as credit cards, cheap mortgages, and so on.

PROFESSIONALISM

The most important way by which the union can deal with the challenges of government, employers, and the workers is to become more efficient and to use means that correspond to those at the disposal of the other parties. As already mentioned, employers use advisers and information in every field and subject; and the expectations of workers have also grown with the rise in their educational level. To be effective, the union must become a partner whose power is equal to that of the employers. It must foresee the steps they will take and adopt suitable defensive measures. Like the employers, the unions must have recourse to data, information, research, and advice of experts. They must outline professional plans of action and not limit themselves to reacting to the activities of others. One of the chief tools with which the unions can reach the public is the professional use of the media.

More then ever before, trade unions are employing legal and organizational advisers able to help them improve their strategies and tactics (Lawler, 1986). However, unions, especially those in the developing countries of Africa that are experiencing severe difficulties, do not always have the resources necessary to deal with the problem; and the union officials are low paid, which does not permit recruitment of higher-level staff (Henley, 1989).

Several unions, and especially the international trade union confederation, ICFTU, have recognized the importance of training and research and have initiated plans to improve the capability of unions to analyze economic data and social trends and present the facts at the bargaining table. The plan calls for training of union activists and representatives in the spheres of economics, statistics, and analysis of business data. ICFTU also encourages research within the union framework in developing countries by assisting in the development of research departments in the unions in Africa, Asia, and Latin America (Report of ICFTU-APRO, 1990a, 1990b). The overall aim of the plan is to raise the status of the unions in society in order to enhance their influence in the joint frameworks of employers and governments. The plan is also directed toward improving their capacity to represent the workers and recruit members.

THE HISTADRUT (GENERAL FEDERATION OF LABOR) AS A MODEL

Until the end of 1989 (the latest date for which data are available), the Histadrut succeeded in maintaining its level of membership.

In one form or another, the Histadrut applies the directions described above. The Histadrut is a general organization with a broad and stable membership base. Membership in the Histadrut is personal and not dependent on an organized workplace.

The Histadrut has a centralized mechanism of collective bargaining at the general level, as well as decentralized ones that, to a large extent, balance isolationist trends. It is linked to Israel's Labour party and operates through parliamentary channels to influence economic and welfare policy. According to the Labour party's regulations, the Secretary-General of the Histadrut is one of the party's most senior members of Knesset (Parliament).

Together with the employers and the government, the Histadrut is a member of joint committees and accepts general economic and social goals. A certain type of functional corporatism is manifest in the agreements that the Histadrut signed, with the employers and the government, which were aimed at achieving these general objectives. The "package deals" of 1970 and 1985 are worth mentioning, as well as other agreements that included concessions on wage increases and cost-of-living indexing in order to promote employment and economic growth.

Within the framework of the Histadrut, which by the nature of its comprehensiveness encourages wage equality, the isolationist trends of the trade unions can also be observed. They believe that, as a separate trade union, they will be able to achieve better economic gains for their members. Since they operate with professional workers whose inclination to join is relatively low, they hope that this strategy will help them maintain membership levels. To date, the balancing mechanisms have stopped these trends.

As in African countries, the Histadrut was instrumental in the establishment of the State of Israel. However, it developed on different lines from the African unions. Part of its leadership did indeed transfer to the government, but the Histadrut maintained its independent position and power, and even some of the national functions it had fulfilled during the period before Israel was a state. Therefore, it fulfills many functions that trade unions generally do not take upon themselves. For example: Within the framework of mutual aid, the Histadrut maintains health services through a sick fund to which most of Israel's population belongs; the Histadrut is responsible for the pension insurance of a considerable part of its members; the Histadrut maintains child day-care centers and kindergartens to help women who work outside their homes; the Histadrut maintains retirement homes for the elderly; it maintains educational and cultural services, community services, and leisure facilities, as well as a broad range of economic and consumer institutions.

As regards professionalism, the Histadrut maintains an Institute for Economic and Social Research, the task of which is to provide the decision makers with accurate information. There are also institutions responsible for training and development of Histadrut employees.

Notes

1. An international comparison of membership rates poses difficulties because of the different methods used by the unions to measure membership rates. Different countries relate the percentage of members to different potentials (labor force, employed, employed in the branch). Membership figures are mainly based on figures supplied by the unions, and are far from reliable.

2. For an analysis of membership trends and their causes, we regard "Workers and Their Organizations" (Dunlop, 1958) as two distinct factors in the industrial relations system.

3. A more profound analysis of these subjects and their effects is beyond the scope of this study.

4. Kassalow, for example, claimed that the absence of a labor party in the United States would prevent the trade unions from attaining a European level.

References

Arya, P. P. (1989). Workers' identification with his union and its correlates. *Indian Journal of Industrial Relations, 25,* 70-81.

Bain, G. S., & Elias, P. (1985). Trade union membership in Great Britain: An individual level analysis. *British Journal of Industrial Relations, 23,* 71-92.

Blum, A. A., & Pataranapich, S. (1987). Productivity and the path to house unionism: Structural change in the Singapore labour movement. *British Journal of Industrial Relations, 25*, 389-400.

Brown, W. (1986). The changing role of trade unions in the management of labour. *British Journal of Industrial Relations, 24*, 161-167.

Clark, G. L. (1989). *Unions and communities under seige and the crises of organized labor.* New York: Cambridge University Press.

Crouch, C. (1979). *The politics of industrial relations.* London: Fontana.

Davy, J. A., & Shipper, F. (1987). Union membership decline: Do the goals of unions reflect the changing values of workers? *Labour Studies Journal, 12*, 20-27.

Disney, R. (1990). Explanations of the decline in trade union density in Britain: An appraisal. *British Journal of Industrial Relations, 28*, 165-177.

Dunkley, G. (1984). Can Australia learn from Austria about income policy? *Journal of Industrial Relations, 26.*

Dunlop, J. T. (1958). *Industrial relations systems.* New York: Holt, Reinhart & Winston.

Freeman, R., & Pelletier, J. (1990). The impact of industrial relations legislation on British union density. *British Journal of Industrial Relations, 28*, 141-164.

Fullager, C., & Barling, S. (1989). A longitudinal test of a model of the antecedents and consequences of union loyalty. *Journal of Applied Psychology, 74*, 213-227.

Gallagher, D. G., & Clark, P. F. (1989). Research on union commitment: Implications for labour. *Labour Studies Journal, 14*, 52-71.

Henley, J. S. (1989). African employment relationships and the future of trade unions. *British Journal of Industrial Relations, 27*, 295-309.

Hundley, G. (1988). Education and union membership. *British Journal of Industrial Relations, 26*, 195-200.

Lash, S. (1985). The end of neo-corporatism?: The breakdown of centralised bargaining in Sweden. *British Journal of Industrial Relations, 23*, 215-239.

Lawler, J. J. (1986). Union growth and decline: The impact of employer and union tactics. *Journal of Occupational Psychology, 59*, 217-230.

Lehmbruch, G. (1977). Liberal corporatism and party government. *Comparative Political Studies, 10*, 91-126.

Levy, A. (1990). Heterogeneity and union membership determination. *Journal of Labour Research, 11*, 41-57.

Martin, R. M. (1983). Pluralism and the new corporatism. *Political Studies, 31*, 86-102.

McCallum, N. (1989). Trade union economic growth and politics. *Journal of Industrial Relations, 31*, 272-384.

Ofek, A., & Rosenstein, A. (1987). The comprehensiveness of the Histadrut compared with the isolationist tendencies of the trade unions. *Economic Quarterly*, 131. (In Hebrew)

Panitch, L. (1980). Recent theorisation of corporatism: Reflections on a growth industry. *British Journal of Sociology, 31*, 159-187.

Proposed decisions of the 16th convention of the general federation of labor in Israel. (1990). (In Hebrew)

Report of ICFTU-APRO Experts Meeting on Organization. (1990a, March). Singapore: Author.

Report of ICFTU-APRO Experts Meeting on Research. (1990b, May-June). Singapore: Author.

Schmitter, P. C. (1977). Introduction. *Comparative Political Studies, 10*, 3-6.

Schmitter, P. C., & Lehmbruch, G. (1979). *Trends toward corporatist intermediation.* London & Beverly Hills, CA: Sage.

Shalev, M. (1980). Industrial relations theory and the comparative study of industrial relations and industrial conflict. *British Journal of Industrial Relations, 18*, 26-43.

Shimada, H. (1983). Wage determination and information sharing: An alternative approach to income policy. *Journal of Industrial Relations, 25*, 177-189.

SOHYO News. (1986). Why unionisation retarded? *Report of the SOHYO Committee*, 5-31.

Terry, M. (1986). How do we know if shop stewards are getting weaker? *British Journal of Industrial Relations, 24*, 169-179.

Troy, L. (1990). Is the union in the decline of private sector unionism? *Journal of Labour Research, 11*, 111-143.

9 \ Local and Global: Trade Unions in the Future

OLLE HAMMARSTRÖM

Trade unions are one of the well-established institutions of the Western world. A movement that grew up with industrialism in the beginning of the last century has now been operating for more than 100 years in most Western countries.

The union movement has had its ups and downs. To some extent it follows economic cycles and political developments. The development of large industries with favorable conditions for unions such as steel, construction, and mining has also determined the size of the trade union movement. The largest national union movement of the world, that of the United States, started 200 years ago, in 1792, when an organization for shoemakers was started in Philadelphia (Mielke, 1982). The numerical strength peaked in the late 1970s, with more than 20 million members. The relative strength peaked in the late 1960s, when 23% the labor force was affiliated with trade unions. Since then the U.S. labor movement has lost members and is now down to 16% union affiliation (OECD, 1990). With a long period of Republican presidents in office, the political influence of the U.S. labor movement is also at a historically low level. It is not uncommon to hear predictions in the United States saying that we are witnessing the passing of the trade union movement. These archaic organizations, which build on solidarity and collective action, have no role in a modern society with more sophisticated methods for pricing labor and solving disputes. In other countries the picture is different. The trade union movement in Sweden has never before had as many members as today. Membership increased at a slow rate right through the 1980s, and the level of affiliation in 1990 was 86%.

Trade unions are basically democratic organizations. In the short term the union leadership has substantial control over the organization. But in the long term it is the members' activity, or lack of activity, that decides what the union is—and what it is not. This also means that unions to a degree are a reflection of current trends in society. The union is the membership—and the membership is a part of society.

The same term *union* is used throughout the world, but there are substantial differences between unions and the role they play in different countries. Each union reflects the problems, needs, and aspirations of its members. Unions are products of their respective history and of their relations to employers, government, and the general public.

The most recent decades have offered changing conditions for unions and union work. The 1960s were characterized by rapid economic growth, growth of consumption, and large-scale production. It was a time when resources were assumed to be unlimited, and man in production was regarded as an adjunct to the developing machines. Tayloristic production methods in the extreme and dreams of the unmanned factory characterized the industrialized countries.

As a reaction, the 1970s became a decade of regulation. People realized that nature suffered from exploitation and that man threatened the existence of life on earth. The consumption of raw materials and energy caused drastic effects on the environment. People were consumed in the production process. Calls to save the environment and to democratize life on the job became paramount. Legal regulation was extensively used as a method to attack the problems in the workplace and society at large.

Following this the 1980s became a period of reaction against regulation. If the 1970s were a decade favoring unions, the 1980s became a decade for the employers. The individual and the market were hailed. Free competition and market orientation became the answer. This was a problem to the union movement, an organization with an ideology based on collective action and solidarity. Union membership declined in many countries, as did the political influence of unions.

In Great Britain, the cradle of the union movement, union affiliation is at 43% (Däubler & Lecher, 1991), down 12 percentage points from a peak of 55% in 1979 (Visser, 1989, p. 241) and the Labour party has been on the opposition benches for an unusually long time. In France, union affiliation has fallen drastically and is currently around 13%, compared to almost 50% after the Second World War (Visser, 1989, p. 70). Union membership has fallen in Germany and Italy too. The falling membership is partly explained by structural changes: declining numbers of employees in areas where unions traditionally have been strong; declining proportion of manual workers and increasing proportion of white-collar employees, a less unionized category. Behind the falling membership in the industrialized countries are generally significant falls in private sector membership partly balanced by an increase in public sector membership. Many union movements are in crises (Bibes & Mourieau, 1991; Edwards, Garonna, & Tödtling, 1986).

Current Problems

MEMBERSHIP

The highest rates of affiliation to trade unions are found in Sweden, 86%; Finland, 77%; and Denmark, 73% (OECD, 1990). Union affiliation in these countries is around twice as high as in the large industrialized countries such as Germany, Italy, and the United Kingdom. Why have the unions in some countries managed better than those in other countries? There is obviously not one single factor that explains the difference. It is rather a complex mix of interrelated reasons, such as historic background, union policy, management policy, government policy, and legislation.

One common characteristic for unions with high affiliation rates is the aspiration to extend union activities beyond the traditional role of looking after wages and working conditions. In the Nordic countries, industrial democracy became a major union concern in the 1970s. Unions demanded a say in what was produced and how work was organized. The unions were prepared not just to oppose employers regarding wages and conditions of work but also to cooperate with management in developing companies and organizing production. Developments during the 1980s demonstrate that it has been possible for unions to combine a traditional adversarial role with a role of cooperation while maintaining and even increasing the membership.

The high affiliation rates in the Nordic countries are also partly explained by the high affiliation rate among white-collar employees. It appears that in countries where white-collar employees are organized in separate unions, the affiliation rate is higher than in countries where blue- and white-collar employees are organized in the same unions. In theory it is easy to argue in favor of minimizing the number of unions per workplace and for uniting all employees into one union. Industry unions have clearly taken priority over craft unions in most countries. But experience shows that where white-collar employees are organized in separate unions, a much higher affiliation rate has been reached. It is easier to recruit clerical workers and managers to a

level. Skills orientation, however, demands a high level of local union competence and activity. The development of competence must start with an analysis of the company business idea, including products, markets, and choice of technology. This should preferably be done jointly by union and management. To engage in this type of joint analysis and to organize the subsequent on-the-job and off-the-job training requires a strong local union organization. In the Nordic countries local union delegates by tradition are elected, they have a mandate to bargain, and the ratio of elected delegates to members is in the range of 1:10-20. This contrasts to countries such as Germany, France, and Italy, where local delegates often are appointed officials, they have a weak bargaining mandate, and the ratio of delegates to members is in the range of 1:20-40 (Kjellberg, 1983, p. 82). A more advanced union strategy requires a strong union presence at workplace level.

Challenges in the 1990s

END OF TRADE UNIONISM?

The union movement in countries such as France and the United States is no doubt in trouble, with affiliation rates in the 10% to 15% range. At a time when regulation is highly suspect, and individualism and market orientation are à la mode, the classic union profile is less attractive. The situation in Sweden, Finland, and Denmark, however, illustrates that unions can still attract a large segment of the work force. Rather than trying to sell the old union message in new wrapping, unions need to adapt to the needs and aspirations of the work force tomorrow. Looking at the experience of the Swedish union movement during the 1980s, my conclusion is that unions need to concentrate on two levels, the local and the global.

THE LOCAL LEVEL: WORKPLACE UNIONISM

To be relevant to the members in the 1990s, unions need to not only address issues of wages and working conditions but also support the members in obtaining stimulating and challenging jobs in a safe and healthy environment. In order to do this unions must get involved in analyses of business strategies. From these analyses unions, together with management, need to draw conclusions regarding work organization, career planning, training, and education. This type of work cannot be performed by full-time outside union officials. It requires a daily presence on-site and an ongoing relationship with management. As has been demonstrated in the Nordic countries, it is possible to activate local union representatives in this work. But it requires a higher density of elected union representatives than is common in most countries. And it requires that representatives are locally elected and are given a strong bargaining mandate. From a union point of view it is preferable if workplace representation is union based only, rather than based on all employees regardless of union affiliation. A number of European countries have traditionally had systems for employee representation that is not based on unions or union membership but on employment. Examples are the German Betriebsrat, the Italian Commissione interna, the French Comité d'entreprise, and the Dutch ondernemingsraad (Kjellberg, 1983). These are sometimes in effect controlled by the unions, but in other cases they live their own life independent of or even in competition with the unions. The Anglo-Saxon countries have a strong tradition of shop stewards. Their role is traditionally reactive, and they have not in general developed a constructive dialogue with management on investments, training, and other issues of business development. In Australia, an interesting reform period is in the process. A program called "award restructuring" has been in process since 1988, including changes in pay structures, training, and work organization (Hammarström & Hammarström, 1991). Special union-management committees are set up to administer these changes. This example is important for any union that wishes to be relevant during the coming decade.

INTERNATIONAL UNION NETWORKS

International union cooperation exists on a number of levels. At the peak union level there are confederations of national union centers. The largest and most important is the International Confederation of Free Trade Unions (ICFTU). The ICFTU was established in 1949 and has affiliates in most market economy countries. In addition, there are two other confederations of national centers. The World Confederation of Labor (WCL), previously called the International Federation of Christian Trade Unions, has affiliated organizations with a common religious orientation. The World Federation of Trade Unions (WFTU) has had affiliates in the Eastern and Central European countries and some Communist-led unions in the West and elsewhere. On the next level there are trade secretariats, most of which are affiliated with one of the international confederations. The trade secretariats affiliate with the national unions in the same industry or sector of the labor market. There are some 15 trade secretariats that are affiliated with the ICFTU. Both the international confederations and the trade secretariats have regional subdivisions, divided by continents or other geographical areas.

International union cooperation also takes place in relation to other international organizations such as the ILO, the OECD, and the European Community.

From a national and international horizon the system of international union cooperation looks reasonably well organized, with unions with the same political orientation affiliated with the same international network. The system seems reasonably efficient in relation to lobbying activities directed toward national governments and international organizations of employers and governments. But the system is not effective from a local workplace point of view. The local union representatives, whether they are active in a national or multinational company, have a growing interest in direct contact with local union representatives in other countries. In multinational enterprises the typical need is to get regular information on operations and conditions in other parts of the enterprise. Another frequent need is liaison in connection with structural changes, such as buying and selling of plants, transfer of production, and other changes that have significant effects on employment and employment conditions. These needs are frequently characterized by severe time constraints. Contacts must be established within days, and telephone and fax are more relevant than mail.

To meet the demands the international trade secretariats have started to build up enterprises committees in some of the larger multinational enterprises. The International Metalworkers Federation (IMF) has been particularly active in this field and has established some 10 enterprises committees. The International Federation of Commercial and Technical Employees (FIET) is also active in this field. One of the shortcomings of these committees is that they are limited to the unions that are affiliated to the relevant trade secretariat. It often means that important and representative unions in one or more countries are not included in the networks. From the point of view of a local union delegate who wants to get information and liaise with union delegates from other parts of a company, it is the competence and representativeness on the local level that are of importance, not whether a union is affiliated to one or the other of the trade secretariats.

Local union cooperation within the framework of the international union organizations also faces other problems. When a trade secretariat organizes a meeting for affiliated unions in a multinational company, the pressure is strong to include all affiliated unions. That seems fair and just from a membership point of view. But it means that meetings tend to be very big and costly. It is not only costly in regard to travel and accommodations but also because of the need for translation. The demand for total representation and having all unions included is, of course, appealing from a democratic point of view; but from a local union point of view, it is much more useful to have a meeting with a small number of relevant delegates than a large meeting where issues cannot be properly penetrated.

This problem was illustrated in connection with the merger of the Swedish ASEA and the Swiss Brown Boveri Corporation into the huge ABB. At the time of the merger the companies had operations all over the world, but the main production and the strategic management were centered in three countries: Switzerland, Germany, and Sweden. These were also the three countries that were primarily affected by the direct effects of the merger in terms of changes in production. In Sweden there are four significant unions organizing the employees. One is not affiliated to any trade secretariat, two are affiliated to IMF, and one is affiliated to IMF and FIET. In Germany there are two major unions, one affiliated to IMF and one to FIET; the same situation exists in Switzerland.

When the merger was announced a number of union representatives contacted each other to exchange information and to find out the positions of other unions. Because of internal rivalry between the German unions it was not possible to organize a joint meeting with all relevant unions. Instead, separate meetings were organized by the IMF-affiliated unions and by the FIET-affiliated unions. At a later stage joint union meetings were organized with top management of ABB. The chief executive officer of the company agreed to meet an international union group, but emphasized that the company did not wish to enter into negotiations with the trade secretariat and preferred to keep union-management relations "in house," that is, to include the local representatives only.

The ABB case illustrates the limitation of the present system for international union cooperation. If collaboration is limited to members of specific trade secretariats, large segments of the employees concerned might be left out of such cooperation. And if all unions affiliated to one trade secretariat are brought into the inter-union cooperation, meetings tend to be too big and costly and, as a consequence, can be held only at infrequent intervals.

One solution to these problems is to limit the role of the trade secretariats to the initial phases of establishing contacts. Once contacts have been made, local unions' delegates should be left to organize union contacts. In many companies it is logical to establish two levels of union participation, one being an inner circle of the major unions in the key establishment of the company. These unions, which have regular contacts with the strategic management, can form an overall picture of management thinking and where the company is going. It means a small group of union representatives can both develop a good overall understanding of the company position and problems and build up competence and a respected relationship with top management. The rest of the unions can form an outer circle that receives information from the inner circle and is called to meetings at longer intervals. With this model it should be possible to build an effective union structure at reasonable cost and offer top management a relevant group for discussions that is representative but not too big.

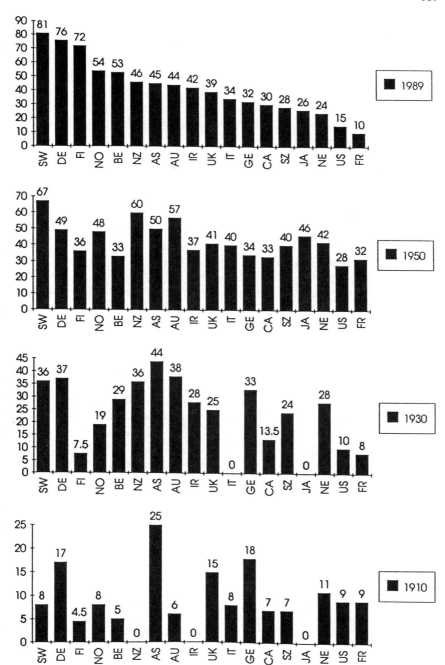

Figure 10.1. Union Organization Cross-Cultural Differences

unions and union organizing activities in cooperative industrial relations systems. However, for each of these generalizations there are awkward exceptions: the very low unionization rates in such European welfare states as France and the Netherlands; the Swiss and Dutch exceptions of weak unionism in the small-state group; the low degree of unionization in a cooperative system, such as Japan, or the large differences in unionization between such adversarial systems as the United States and the United Kingdom, or the divergence in unionization rates between the United States and Canada in recent decades.

In the OECD study a number of possible explanations, beyond the ones suggested above, were discussed; among these were factors relating to the industrial and occupational structure of the economy and the composition of the labor force, factors relating to the stability of the economy, factors relating to employer and government support for unions, legal and institutional aspects, and union organizing abilities. It was found that the structure of employment (for instance the proportion of employees working in agriculture, in manufacturing, or the proportion of female wage earners) contributed little to nothing to the explanation of the cross-national differences in aggregate unionization levels. Cyclical patterns in wages, prices, unemployment, and other economic indicators also failed to explain differences in levels (as opposed to short-time changes in such levels). It was hypothesized that the most promising avenue for explaining cross-national differences in unionization rates is to relate institutional (political and industrial relations) characteristics to strategic differences in employer, union, and worker behavior, that is, to the choices concerning union representation made by the three agents involved in the union membership decision (see Visser, 1991a, pp. 118-120).

In the present chapter I will probe this avenue a little further and develop and test an explanatory cross-national model of the determinants of unionization. Below I present the theoretical argument of the paper, summarized with a causal model. The empirical cross-national data which are used to test the model are presented in the section on data, followed by a presentation and discussion of the results in the final section.

THEORY

Restricting our comparison to democratic societies in which the decision to join or not join a trade union is a basic civil right, we assume that workers' decisions are central to the analysis of union membership. Obviously, these decisions do not occur in a social vacuum, but are influenced by the pressures of co-workers, union organizers, and employers. As is noted by Bain and Elsheikh (1976, p. 112) "the decision to join a union is rarely a completely voluntary act." Yet even in the rare case where unions and employers have agreed to a pre-entry closed shop and to union membership as a qualifying condition for employment, workers have a choice to refuse membership along with the job.

Although most economic studies of union growth treat unionization as if it were solely the outcome of workers' decisions (Fiorito & Greer, 1982; Hirsch & Addison, 1986; for a critique, Visser, 1990), it is more realistic to assume that the level of unionization is also the product of the activities of union organizers and of employers who accept or reject the presence of unions and union membership in the workplace. Rather than at individual workers, the activities of employers and union organizers are targeted at workplaces, establishments, or firms. It is also in the workplace, mainly, that the pressures of co-workers for or against the membership in each individual case are mostly felt, especially since the decline of company towns and the differentiation between work and life space in modern societies. It is in the workplace that the problem of finding people to punish free riders, and of safeguarding solidarity norms, are best solved (Elster, 1989; Hechter, 1987; Olson, 1965), but only if some union organization is present and this presence is recognized by employers. Typically, workers who are union members are part of networks of colleagues and friends in the workplace who are themselves union members, whereas nonmembers tend to know and contact mostly other nonmembers. Within a multivariate analysis of union membership in the Netherlands, this network variable was one of the strongest predictors of actual membership (van Rij, Kersten, Saris, & Visser, 1990).

The distinction between worker and workplace follows the "two hurdle model" proposed by Green (1988) and Disney (1990): There are nonmembers because there is no union available in the workplace that they might join, and there are nonmembers who fail to join a union despite the opportunity to do so. Only if there were always, for every worker and in each workplace, a union, could the decision to join a union be approached as a single-stage decision procedure. But as Disney correctly points out, this single-stage decision model is inappropriate when some individuals are in a position to choose (because there happens to be a union), and others are not (because there is no union). For the second group the choice would be to set up a union (or union local, or workplace organization), which is to solve and overcome the paradoxes of initiating collective action spelled out by Mancur Olson. The American sociologist C. Wright Mills, in his analysis of the extremely low degree and very unevenly distributed presence of collective organization among white-collar employees in his country, already noted that union availability in the work organization was the crucial variable, for "the question to organize or not to organize a union . . . is an entirely different proposition from joining or not joining a trade union" (Mills, 1951, p. 306).

We therefore make a distinction in our model between the determinants of workplace coverage (whether a union is available in the workplace for part or all of the work force) and the determinants of individual membership (why some people join and others don't if both have an equal choice, given the presence of a union). Disney asserts that the second stage of the decision process, in which workers weigh the costs and benefits of exercising their option to join (or leave) a union, is best analyzed in terms of macroeconomic or business cycle factors (Disney, 1990). While this may be true in a longitudinal study of unionization rates in one country, assuming that there are no significant shifts in union organization and workplace coverage, it is evident that in a cross-national comparative study we must place considerable weight on the first stage. My working hypothesis is that the (cross-time) rather invariant international differences in unionization rates can be explained by differences in workplace coverage. This variation in coverage results from international differences in employer and union behavior, that is, recognition and de-recognition strategies of employers, and representation and retention strategies of trade unions.

The plausibility of this approach is further strengthened by the fact that there appears to be no relation, over time or across nations, between social attitudes of workers concerning the desirability of unions or union membership (Nielsen, 1990). In cross-sectoral studies the expressed preferences of workers concerning union membership often contrast with actual membership. For instance, attitudinal surveys show a greater preference for unionism among women and youths (Bertl, Rudak, & Schneider, 1988, for Germany; Visser, Kersten, Van Rij, & Saris, 1991, for the Netherlands; Spilsbury, Hoskins, Ashton, & Maguire, 1987, for the United Kingdom; Kochan, 1988, and Moore, 1986, for the United States). Yet we find that fewer women than men take up actual membership, and that union density rates among young workers are lower than among workers in older age groups. Not surprisingly, personal characteristics and preferences of workers are less determining for actual union membership than the firm or market segment in which people are employed. This is the reason why, in multivariate (regression) analysis of the determinants of union membership, almost never is a significant relation with personal characteristics such as age, sex, marital status, and so on found once the researcher controls for workplace-related variables such as firm location (public or private sector), firm size, recognition, or union network.

The American historian Ruth Kornhauser has made the pertinent observation that over time union membership has become less self-selective. In the early days there were no unions to join for most workers; unions had to be founded before they could be joined. Under such conditions, she argued, "union membership will be selective rather than inclusive, and will result from the tendency of workers with similar characteristics to be drawn to unions." On the other hand, once unions have become established and accepted as legitimate representatives, they tend to incorporate most individuals in occupations and workplaces where they have been recognized and "there should be no association between union membership and attitudes prior to unionization, for union membership is no longer confined to individuals whose favorable orientation led them to unions" (Kornhauser, 1961, pp. 51-52). This, of course, describes the limit case of complete institutionalization when unions, once they gain a contract with the employer, can "blanket" all of the workers under the contract into membership, as is or has been the case in some workplaces in, for instance, New Zealand, Australia, the United States, and Great Britain.

In studies of the variation of unionization across workplaces, three variables in particular appear to be positively associated with union membership: (a) the *size* of the workplace, or rather the establishment or firms of which the workplace is part; (b) *employer recognition*; and (c) location in the *public or government* sector. These conditions are interrelated. Where employment is concentrated in larger units, the possibilities to initiate and maintain collective organization are larger. The costs incurred by employees, if they decide to join a union (employer retaliation, and so on), are probably lower because of the further social and emotional distance between employer and employees (Lockwood, 1958) and the greater likelihood of bureaucratic and impersonal forms of management control in large firms (Blau & Schoenherr, 1971). Moreover, many of the statutory provisions for worker representation (works council and health and safety legislation, for instance) are only available, or implemented, above a given minimum size of the work force (Visser, 1991b). For trade unions it is more efficient to organize a large plant than a small plant. Given the higher death rates of small firms, and a higher turnover rate of personnel, it will be less problematic to maintain collective organization in large firms. Although the relationship between unionization rates and firm size is empirically well established in a great number of countries (Bertl et al., 1988; Millward & Stevens, 1986; Visser, 1991a), it may not be linear. Bain and Elias (1985), for the United Kingdom, and Hirsch and Berger (1984) and Cornfield (1986), for the United States, have shown that in very large firms unionization levels may be lower. If employers want to keep unions out of the workplace, then the very large among them stand better chances to defeat unions, given fatter resources they can bring to bear in the competition over the allegiance of workers.

Whether employers do put up a fight to keep unions out depends on two main factors: the legal environment and the economic incentive for employers to follow an anti-union strategy. The more exclusive the bargaining contracts negotiated by unions are, and the larger the union mark-up on wages, the larger the incentive for employers to oppose unions (Blanchflower &

Freeman, 1990). *Bargaining coverage* and *centralization* are the two crucial variables related to the incentive of individual employers to choose a strategy of opposition to trade unions. Where coverage of union-negotiated contracts is extensive and unions negotiate inclusively, that is, for members as well as nonmembers, mark-up effects will either be absent or very small indeed. Statutory or voluntary extension of collectively bargained norms to non-organized employers, as is the case in a number of European countries, further reduces the incentive for individual employers to oppose unions. Rather than fighting unions on their own, employers will have an incentive to join an employers' associations since they have to bear most of the costs anyway. Centralization of collective bargaining in multiemployer units tends to reduce the wage differences between firms and help unions gaining a foothold in the small firm sector. Though we expect centralization and inclusive bargaining to increase unionization, mainly via the moderating influence on employer opposition, union organizers are faced with the difficulty that benefits cannot be privatized since nonmembers receive the same wages and benefits as members do. Centralization and inclusive bargaining are expected to help union organizers overcome the first hurdle, and to lower the set-up and maintenance costs of union organization in the workplace, while making it a harder task for union organizers to convince workers to take the second hurdle and actually join. Union organizers must therefore offer other, nonmaterial or ideological incentives (Pizzorno, 1966). Or they succeed in getting help from friends and lay claim on a selective benefit of some sort. One of the most effective benefits in this regard appears to be the union's involvement in unemployment insurance, job placement, and training (Pedersen, 1989; Visser, 1991a).

The legal environment is important insofar as it may or may not decrease the costs of union organizing by prohibiting certain types of employer retaliation, by allowing secondary picketing and solidarity strikes in favor of workers seeking to establish collective organization, and by guaranteeing statutory rights of workplace representation and collective bargaining. Government control by Socialist, Labour, or Left parties best explains the degree of legal support for union organization, both through the effect on legislation and on implementation of the law. Leftist government control is also related to the size of the public sector. Employer opposition to union organization is smaller in the public sector than in the private sector. The reasons mentioned by Clegg (1976, ch. 2) are: employment concentration, a wider use of bureaucratic and collective mechanisms of labor management, the absence of a clear employer role, and a wider coverage and fuller implementation of statutory norms. The greater stability of most public sector bureaus also contributes to the generally much higher unionization rates observed in this sector (see Table 10.1).

Finally, the variables that I have related to the strategic choices of employers and unions—coverage, centralization, Left government control, and workplace size—can themselves be related to three main cross-national differences: the *size of country*, the *industrial infrastructure*, and the degree of social, religious, ethnic, and linguistic *homogeneity* of the wage-earning population. The first two points are closely related (for an extensive elaboration on the argument, see Katzenstein, 1985; Stephens, 1979). Smaller countries tend to have more concentrated industries; the small size of the domestic market forced them to concentrate on export; heavier competition in world markets forced out the smaller firms. For the same reasons, smaller sized countries tend to have more specialized economies, especially if they industrialized comparatively late. These developments contribute to collective organization of employers and to a relatively high degree of centralization in employers' associations (Ingham, 1974; Sisson, 1987). Stephens observes that economic concentration and employer centralization have two main effects on unionization. One is mediated through the impact on bargaining structures, as is hypothesized above. The second effect is on what we may call the "target rate of unionization" aimed at by unions. Taking the example of the Swedish central employers' federation SAF, he argues that the development of strong centralized employers organizations and the effective use of the lockout instrument lowered the effectiveness of strikes (at the current level of unionization), and thus will raise the incentive for unions to organize all firms in the employers association (Stephens, 1979, 1990). Moreover, in concentrated and specialized economies we will find fewer unions, less inter-union competition, fewer craft or exclusive unions, and a more "rational" structure of mainly industrial unions. According to Stephens, the strength of craft unionism is inversely related to the level of union organization. It is hypothesized that such a union structure is related to a higher target rate ("open" versus "closed" unions) and is more efficient in the recruitment and retention of members, mainly because of a lower degree of task overlap and the use of modern administration techniques in larger and industrial unions (Streeck, 1981).

Finally, the social, religious, linguistic, and ethnic homogeneity is directly related to the degree of "class voting" and the strength of the political Left (Cameron, 1984; Korpi, 1983; Przeworski & Sprague, 1986). Societal homogeneity will also determine another aspect of trade union structure, that is, the degree of ideological and political unity (Sturmthal, 1953; Visser, 1990). My hypothesis is that divided unionism is associated with lower unionization rates, because under such conditions unions are less effective in convincing employers, governments, political friends, and others that "trade unions are a good thing." Hence, divided unions must live with lower levels of protection and benefits that can be offered to workers and members.

In other words, divided unions are more expensive from the point of view of workers, and must count on a higher degree of ideological identification and motivation. The argument of this section is summarized in the model portrayed in Figure 10.2.

THE DATA

Unionization Rates

The dependent variable is the total union membership, less retired and self-employed members, divided by the number of wage and salary earners and the unemployed (see Table 10.1). The sample consists of 18 advanced capitalist countries belonging to the OECD that have had democracies since the end of the Second World War (I have, however, excluded the two very small countries, Iceland and Luxembourg, in order to prevent a bias toward the theoretical argument of this study; separate regressions with both countries, however, do not show statistically significant results different from the ones shown in Table 10.3).

The results presented here refer to unionization levels in 1980. This year was chosen for reasons of comparability with the studies of Stephens (1990) and Wallerstein (1989). Separate regressions for 1970 and 1989 yielded highly similar results. It is recalled that between 1970 and 1980, or between 1980 and 1989, there was no dramatic change in the relative position of countries on the "unionization league," except a growing distance between the head and the tail. Although important in time series studies, it is of no consequence whether we calculate union density with or without the unemployed. The latter figure tends to be higher (except in Belgium, Denmark, Finland, and Sweden, where the unions are involved in the unemployment protection system), but it hardly affects the rank orders. Comparing the 3 years (1970, 1980, 1989) for which we have data on union density rates with and without the unemployed (Visser, 1991a, Table 1), the rank order correlation coefficient is .98.

Similar checks have been made regarding sectoral unionization data, since it would seem inappropriate to give too much weight to cross-national differences in unionization if sectoral density rates showed different rank orders between countries, as Clegg (1976, p. 13) believed to be the case. The correlations between the rankings of countries on the basis of the aggregate unionization rates presented in Table 10.1 and the rates for the private or public sector (Visser, 1991a, Table 4.6), or for manufacturing or commercial services (Visser, 1991a, Table 4.4), are all .80 or higher. Only the unionization rate in financial services shows a more divergent picture: an even larger variation between countries (c.v. = .67) and a different ranking, most notably of Japan.

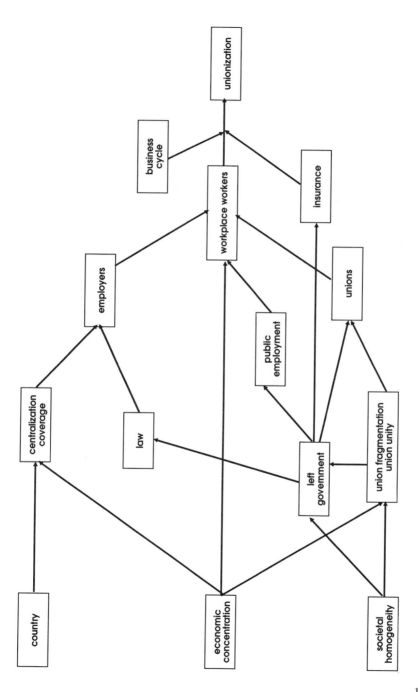

Figure 10.2. Determinants of Unionization (Causal Model With Arrows Between Variables)

175

Finally, I have also compared my measurement of the dependent variable with the data of others. In general, my union density figures for 1980 are much lower that those of Wallerstein (and Stephens) for 1978 or 1979, mainly because they use gross density figures (including pensioners and self-employed). However, the ranking of countries is not dramatically different: Between the data in Wallerstein's Table 1 (1989, p. 482; Stephens, 1990, Table 1) and the union density figures for 1980 presented in my Table 10.1, the rank order correlation coefficient is .95.

Size of the Labor Force

Like Wallerstein and Stephens I have used the natural log of the number of wage and salary earners plus the unemployed, as found in the OECD's *Labor Force Statistics*. Using the log of the potential membership rather than the absolute number implies that the percentage increment rather than the absolute increase in numbers matters for union density.

Economic Concentration

I have followed Stephens's operationalization and made use of his data. Based on a measure of the four-firm concentration ratio, that is, the percentage of employment, shipments, and production accounted for by the four largest firms in a narrowly defined industry, Pryor (1973) has computed a weighted average for 11 countries. Stephens (1979, Table 4.9) has added estimates for the other countries in the sample based on the size of the GDP.

Societal Homogeneity

Various measures have been used to measure diversity: the indices of ethnical and linguistic diversity developed by Taylor and Hudson (1972, pp. 271-274) which are also used by Stephens (1979, 1990); the index of religious diversity (Taylor & Hudson, 1972, pp. 275ff), as well as the combined indicator of heterogeneity based on ethical, linguistic, and religious diversity developed by Lane and Ersson (1987, p. 93). Unfortunately, this indicator is only available for the European countries in the sample.

Class Voting

Where political preferences are rooted in the social stratification of society, party preferences will differ across social strata. A simple procedure for gauging these differences is to dichotomize the social stratification continuum by placing workers in one group, and all others in a second group. The percentage point difference in support for Socialist or Left parties between the workers and the other occupational groups gives the well-known Alford-index for class voting. The data are taken from Korpi (1983, p. 35, Table 3.3).

Left Government

Control over the government by Socialist, Labour or Left parties is the best proxy for the political and legal support for unionization. Thus, rather than measuring in some way or another labor and industrial relation laws (see Freeman & Pelletier, 1989, for an interesting procedure) across time and nations, we use an index of cumulative Leftist participation from 1919 to the year of the union density figure in the analysis. This index gives each country between zero and three points for each year of Left party participation in the government depending on the Left's share of the parliamentary seats held by the government coalition, the party of the prime minister, and whether the government has a majority. With changes for Italy (I have included the PSI among the Left), I have used the figures of Wallerstein (1989, Table 3).

Public Employment

Public employment has been calculated on the basis of OECD *National Accounts Statistics,* and is given as a percentage of the dependent labor force. I have also calculated, on the basis of the OECD *Labor Force Statistics,* the percentage of wage and salary earners employed in industry (manufacturing, mining, utilities, and construction), the percentage working in agriculture, and the percentage of female employees. None of the latter variables made any significant contribution in explaining the cross-national differences in unionization rates.

Bargaining Coverage

Bargaining coverage, or the extent of collective bargaining, is defined as the proportion of employees under collective bargaining (and/or statutory) arrangements (Clegg, 1976). I have used the data listed under "scope of collective bargaining" in Cameron (1984, p. 165, Table 7.6), with some updates from the ILO (1987) overview of collective bargaining in industrialized market economies.

Centralization

Although our theoretical model calls for a measure of organizational centralization of employers' associations, comparative data are hard to come by. Instead, we have used, as have almost all others in the field (Blyth, 1979; Calmfors & Driffill, 1988; Cameron, 1984; Crouch, 1988; Dell'Aringa & Lodovici, 1989; Katzenstein, 1985; Schmitter, 1981; Tarantelli, 1986), an indicator of organizational centralization of trade unions on the assumption that both will be highly similar. The indicator of union centralization takes into account the level at which pay is mainly and usually determined (economy-wide, industry-level, company-level, plant or workplace), the involvement of confederal union officials, the centralization of strike funds, and the staff and financial resources of the confederations (Visser, 1990, pp. 175-177). This indicator has been extended beyond the 10 European countries studies by Visser to Belgium and Ireland on the bases of the DUES database (Ebbinghaus, Visser, & Pfenning, forthcoming). The centralization indicator closely follows the earlier one by Headey (1970), and I have extended the indicator to the non-European countries in the sample on the basis of his data.

Trade Union Fragmentation

Trade union fragmentation is a measure of the number of unions within each main confederation and the degree of potential political, ideological, or organization conflict between them. Thus, the highest score is given to a union system with few unions whose domains are clearly demarcated (as in the case of industrial unions) and who share the same political creed. This indicator of "intra-confederal unity" (Visser, 1990, p. 152) has been extended to the countries not included there on the basis of the number of unions, union type, and the degree of political factionalism within unions or confederations.

Trade Union Unity

This variable expresses the broad ideological, political, and organizational unity within union movements and is measured on the basis of the number of main union confederations and the degree of conflict between them, taking into account also the competition of minor or emergent confederations or autonomous unions. This measure of "inter-confederal unity" (Visser, 1990) has also been extended to all countries in the sample.

Table 10.2 presents a summary of the measurement of the explanatory variables.

RESULTS

The results of the analysis are shown in Table 10.3. In general, I repeat the inconclusive outcome of Stephens (1990): It is impossible to tell on strictly

TABLE 10.2 Determinants of Union Density, 1980

Equation	(1) (N = 18)	(2) (N = 18)	(3) (N = 18)	(4) (N = 18)
Constant	137.09*	174.88*	96.62*	98.95*
Size	−8.40**	−7.93**	−4.06**	−4.40**
Ethn. Divers		−1.33***		−.50
Left			.35*	.34*
(adj)R^2	.38	.41***	.73*	.72*

Equation	(5) (N = 18)	(6) (N = 18)	(7) (N = 18)	(8) (N = 18)
Constant	2.86	1.48	8.05	8.64
Concentration	28.40**	38.56*	18.39*	20.92*
Ethn. Divers		−30.25**		−11.60***
Left			.36**	.33*
(adj)R^2	.33	.45***	.73*	.74*

Equation	(9) (N = 18)	(10) (N = 18)	(11) (N = 18)	(12) (N = 18)	(13) (N = 18)
Constant	30.25*	3.90	15.74**	15.39**	6.59
Left	.43*		.28**	.30*	.29*
Class Vote		.54*			
Coverage		37.88*	39.59**	39.59**	56.16*
Fragmentation				−14.65***	
Centralization					−2.83***
(adj)R^2	.67**	.70*	.74*	.77*	.78*

NOTE: Level of significance: *.01; **.05; ***.1.

empirical grounds, whether "size of the potential membership" contributes more to the explanation of unionization levels than "economic concentration." Because of multi-collinearity, they cannot be entered in the same equation, as an inspection of the correlation matrix in Table 10.3 will tell. The correlation between the two variables is −.89. Each of the best explanations (equations 3 and 4, as well as 7 and 8) includes the variable "Left government," while the addition of "ethnic diversity" adds little to the explanation and even yields an inferior outcome when added to "size" and "Left government." The use of alternative diversity measures (linguistic, religious, or overall diversity) also yielded inferior results, mainly because of multi-collinearity problems. The use of the variable "class vote" instead of "Left" government produced highly similar though slightly inferior results. Generally, these outcomes are very similar to Wallerstein (who considered only size) and Stephens (who considered both size and concentration),

TABLE 10.3 Correlation Matrix: Dependent and Independent Variables

	Density	Size	Concentration	Ethnic Diversity	Overall Diversity	Class Vote	Left Government	Public Employment	Coverage	Centralization	Fragmentation	Unity
Density		-0.60	0.61	-0.30	-0.60	0.76	0.75	0.46	0.81	0.52	0.41	0.52
Size			-0.89	0.13	0.23	-0.43	-0.49	-0.15	-0.68	-0.49	-0.42	-0.37
Concentration				0.09	-0.09	0.41	0.43	0.10	0.53	0.35	0.27	0.38
Ethnic Diversity					0.75	-0.38	-0.34	-0.21	-0.51	-0.56	-0.24	-0.15
Overall Diversity						-0.52	-0.55	-0.74	-0.70	-0.38	0.17	-0.33
Class Vote							0.82	0.48	0.63	0.47	0.36	0.51
Left Government								0.75	0.73	0.62	0.55	0.45
Public Employment									0.46	0.30	0.11	0.33
Coverage										0.81	0.65	0.50
Centralization											0.75	0.29
Fragmentation												0.12
Unity												

though they used a sample of 20 nations (including Iceland and Israel) and a different measure of the dependent variable.

However, from equations 9 to 13 it can be seen that, in contrast to the positions taken by both Wallerstein and Stephens, we do not need either variable, "size of the potential membership" or "economic concentration," to explain cross-national differences in unionization. A model that uses the "nearer" variables is always more appealing on theoretical grounds. Participation of Left parties in the government in combination with bargaining coverage and either of the variables "union fragmentation" or "centralization" yields the best results. This is very close to the prediction of our theoretical model in paragraph 2. Only the variable "trade union unity," when added to equation 10 or 11, failed to add to the explained variance; multicollinearity problems (between coverage and unity) and, in general, the impossibility to enter more than three variables in a regression with only 18 cases prevent us from pursuing the issue further.

My overall conclusion in this short chapter is that size, economic concentration and, to a lesser extent, societal homogeneity are important to explain industrial relations outcomes, among them the level of unionization prevailing in a country in a given period of time. However, I have tried to argue on theoretical grounds and have presented empirical evidence that this influence is indirect, mediated through institutional and organizational characteristics of the national industrial relations system, as well as through political influences. This is preliminary evidence because we have deleted time and sequences from our model, and the model is intended as a reasonable first approximation. The next step should be to focus on the "when" question. When did the political, legal, institutional, or organizational changes take place, and how well do these changes relate to the movement of unionization rates? That analysis would have to include the second hurdle of the union membership process as well.

References

Bain, G. S., & Elias, P. (1985). Trade union membership in Britain: An individual-level analysis. *British Journal of Industrial Relations, 23*(1), 71-92.

Bain, G. S., & Elsheikh, F. (1976). *Union growth and the business cycle.* Oxford: Basil Blackwell.

Bertl, W., Rudak, R., & Schneider, R. (1988). *Arbeitnehmerbewusztsein im zeichen des technischen un sozialen wandels* [Worker consciousness in the age of technical and social change]. Dusseldorf: DGB/Hans Böckler Stiftung.

Blanchflower, D. G., & Freeman, R. B. (1990). *Going different ways: Unionism in the U.S. and other advanced OECD countries* (Discussion Paper No. 5). London: London School of Economics, Centre for Economic Performance.

Blau, P. M., & Schoenherr, R. A. (1971). *The structure of organizations.* New York: Basic Books.

Blyth, C. (1979). The interaction between collective bargaining and government policies in selected member countries. In OECD, *Collective bargaining and government policies.* Paris: Organization of Economic Cooperation and Development.

Bruno, M., & Sachs, J. (1985). *The economics of worldwide stagflation.* Oxford: Blackwell.

Calmfors, L., & Driffill, J. (1988). Bargaining structure, corporatism and macroeconomic performance. In *European policy: A European forum* (No. 6).

Cameron, D. (1984). Social democracy, corporatism, and labor quiescence: The representation of economic interests in capitalist society. In J. H. Goldthorpe (Ed.), *Order and conflict in contemporary capitalism* (pp. 143-178). Oxford: Clarendon.

Clegg, H. A. (1976). *Trade unionism under collective bargaining: A theory based on comparisons of six countries.* Oxford: Basil Blackwell.

Cornfield, D. B. (1986). Declining union membership in the post world war II era: The united furniture workers of America, 1939-1982. *American Journal of Sociology, 91*(5), 1112-1153.

Crouch, C. J. (1988, October). Trade unions in the exposed sector: Their influence on neocorporatist behaviour. In AA.VV., *Markets, institutions and co-operation: Labour relations and economic performance*, Aiel-lea Conference, Venice.

Dell'Aringa, C., & Lodovici, M. (1989). *Industrial relations and economic performance* (mimeo). 8th World Congress of the International Industrial Relations Association, Brussels.

Disney, R. (1990). Explanations of the Decline in trade union density in Britain: An appraisal. *British Journal of Industrial Relations, 28*(2), 165-177.

Ebbinghaus, B. O., Visser, J., & Pfenning, W. (forthcoming). *Trade union systems in Western Europe. A data-handbook* (Vol. 1). Frankfurt & New York: Campus.

Elster, J. (1989). *The cement of society.* Cambridge: Cambridge University Press.

Fiorito, J., & Greer, C. R. (1982). Determinants of U.S. growth: Past and future needs. *Industrial Relations, 20,* 1-32.

Freeman, R. B. (1990). On the divergence in unionism among developed countries. In R. Brunetta & C. Dell'Aringa (Eds.), *Labour relations and economic performance* (pp. 304-324). London: Macmillan.

Freeman, R. B., & Pelletier, J. (1989). The impact of industrial relations legislation on British union density. *British Journal of Industrial Relations, 28*(2), 141-164.

Green, F. (1988). *The distribution of union membership in Britain: An individual-based analysis* (mimeo). Leicester: University of Leicester.

Headey, B. W. (1970). Trade unions and national wage policies. *Journal of Politics, 32*(2), 407-438.

Hechter, M. (1987). *The principles of group solidarity.* Berkeley: University of California Press.

Hibbs, D. A., Jr. (1976). Industrial conflict in advanced industrial societies. *American Political Science Review, 70*(3), 1033-1058.

Hicks, A. (1988). Capitalism, social democracic corporatism, and economic growth. *Journal of Politics, 50*(2), 677-704.

Hirsch, B. T., & Addison, J. T. (1986). *The economic analysis of unions: New approaches and evidence.* London: Allen & Unwin.

Hirsch, B. T., & Berger, M. C. (1984). Union membership determination and industry characteristics. *Southern Economic Journal, 50*(1), 665-669.

ILO. (1987). *Collective bargaining in industrialized market economies: A reappraisal.* Geneva: Author.

Ingham, G. K. (1974). *Strikes and industrial conflict. Britain and Scandinavia.* London & Basingstoke: MacMillan.

Katzenstein, P. (1985). *Small states in world markets. Industrial policy in Europe.* Ithaca, NY: Cornell University Press.

Kjellberg, A. (1983). *Fackling organisering i tolv lander* [Trade union organization in twelve countries]. Lund: Archiv.

Kochan, T. A. (1988). The future of worker representation: An American perspective. *Labour and Society, 13*(2), 183-201.

Kornhauser, R. (1961). Some determinants and consequences of union membership. *Social History, 2.*

Korpi, W. (1983). *The democratic class struggle.* London: Routledge & Kegan Paul.

Korpi, W., & Shalev, M. (1980). Strikes, power, and politics in western nations, 1900-1976. In M. Zeitlin (Ed.), *Political power and social theory* (Vol. 1, pp. 301-334).

Lane, J-E., & Ersson, S. O. (1987). *Politics and society in Western Europe.* London: Sage.

Lockwood, D. (1958). *The blackcoated worker. A study in class consciousness.* London: Allen & Unwin.

Mills, C. W. (1951). *White collar. The American middle class.* New York: Oxford University Press.

Millward, N., & Stevens, M. (1986). *British workplace industrial relations 1980-1984.* Aldershot: Gower.

Moore, T. S. (1986). Are women workers "hard to organise"? *Work and Occupation, 13.*

Nielsen, H. -J. (1990). *American individualism and American labor union decline: A comparative perspective.* Copenhagen: Institute for Policy Studies Froskningsrapport, No. 1.

Olson, M. (1965). *The logic of collective action. Public goods and the theory of groups.* Cambridge, MA: Harvard University Press.

Pedersen, P. J. (1989). Langsigtede internationale tendenser i den faglige organisering og den politiske venstreflo/j [Longitudinal international trends in trade union organization and the political left]. *O/konomie e Politik, 62*(2), 91-99.

Pizzorno, A. (1966). Introduzione allo studio della participazione politica [Introduction to the study of political participation]. *Quaderni di Sociologia, 15*(3-4).

Pryor, F. (1973). *Property and industrial organization in communist and capitalist countries.* Bloomington: Indiana University Press.

Przeworski, A., & Sprague, J. (1986). *Paper stones. A history of electoral socialism.* Chicago: University of Chicago Press.

Scharpf, F. W. (1987). *Sozialdemokratische krisenpolitik in Europa* [Crisis and choice in European social democracy]. Frankfurt a/M: Campus.

Schmid, M. G. (1982). Does corporatism matter? Economic crises, politics and rates of unemployment in capitalist democracies in the 1970s. In G. Lehmbruch & P. C. Schmitter (Eds.), *Patterns of corporatist policy-making* (pp. 237-258). Beverly Hills, CA: Sage.

Schmitter, P. C. (1981). Interest intermediation and regime governability in contemporary Western Europe and North America. In S. Berger (Ed.), *Organizing interests in Western Europe: Pluralism, corporatism and the transformation of politics* (pp. 285-330). Cambridge: Cambridge University Press.

Sisson, K. (1987). *The management of collective bargaining. An international comparison.* Oxford: Basil Blackwell.

Spilsbury, J., Hoskins, M., Ashton, D. J., & Maguire, M. J. (1987). A note on union membership of young adults. *British Journal of Industrial Relations, 25.*

Stephens, J. D. (1979). *The transition from capitalism to socialism.* London & Basingstoke: Macmillan.

Stephens, J. D. (1990, July 9-13). *Explaining crossnational differences in union strength in bargaining and welfare* (mimeo). XIIth World Congress of Sociology, Madrid.

Streeck, W. (1981). *Gewerkschaftliche organisationsprobleme in der sozialstaatlichen demokratie* [The problems of union organization in the democratic welfare state]. Königstein/Ts: Athenaum.

Sturmthal, A. (1953). *Unity and diversity in European labor.* Ithaca, NY: Cornell University Press.

Tarantelli, E. (1986). *Economia politica di lavoro.* Turin: UTET.

Taylor, C. L., & Hudson, M. C. (1972). *World handbook of political and social indicators.* New Haven, CT: Yale University Press.

Therborn, G. (1986). *Why are some peoples more unemployed than others?* London: Verso.

van Rij, C., Kersten, A., Saris, W., & Visser, J. (1990). *Trade union membership and age. Determinants of joining and leaving; a first approach to the use of event history* (Working Paper No. 1), University of Amsterdam, Department of Sociology.

Visser, J. (1985). Vakbondsmacht en vakbondsgroei in West-Europa [Union power and union growth in Western Europe]. *Tijdschrift voor Arbeidsvraagstukken, 1*(1), 18-38.

Visser, J. (1988). Trade unionism in Western Europe. Present situation and prospects. *Labour and Society, 13*(2), 125-182.

Visser. J. (1989). *European trade unions in figures. 1913-1985.* Deventer, The Netherlands, and Boston: Kluwer.

Visser, J. (1990). In search of inclusive unionism. *Bulletin of comparative labour relations, 18.* Deventer, The Netherlands, and Boston: Kluwer.

Visser, J. (1991a). Trends in union membership. In OECD, *Employment outlook 1991* (pp. 97-134). Paris: Organization of Economic Cooperation and Development.

Visser, J. (1991b, September 23-25). *Employee representation in West-European workplaces: Scale and scope, strategy and structure.* Paper presented at the 3rd European Region Conference of the IIRA, Bari-Naples.

Visser, J., Kersten, A., van Rij, C., & Saris, W. (1991). Waarom zijn weinig vrouwen lid van de vakbeweging? [Why do so few women join unions?] In C. Bouw et al. (Eds.), *Macht en onbehagen. Veranderingen in de verhoudingen tussen vrouwen en mannen* [Power and unease. Changes in the social relations between men and women] (pp. 167-182). Amsterdam: SUA.

Wallerstein, M. (1989). Union organization in advanced industrial democracies. *American Political Science Review, 83*(2), 481-502.

11 \ On the Future of Trade Unionism in the United States

KIRSTEN S. WEVER

American unions have in recent decades suffered almost unparalleled declines. While unions once represented about 35% of American workers, they currently organize less than 16%. Their inability to gain mild labor law reform legislation in 1978 (under Democratic President Jimmy Carter) reflected waning influence in Washington, D.C. Falling real wages in the United States reflect the unions' growing weakness in collective bargaining. Media coverage of organized labor continues to focus on recent long, bitter, and often violence-tinged strikes, or—what is perhaps even more damaging to labor's public image—on the Teamsters' and other unions' links to organized crime.

While the political, economic, and social clout of American trade unions has eroded, until very recently most policymakers in the private and public sectors have failed systematically to consider the potentially dangerous effects of this decline. Yet the economic implications are disturbing. The decline of American unions coincides with the decline of American firms' "competitiveness" (Cuomo, 1988). Meanwhile, those advanced industrial countries that fared relatively well economically in the 1980s are promoting the production and rendering of high-quality, high labor-value-added goods and services; relying on a work force with high skill levels; and employing relatively flexible methods of organizing work and production.[1] German

AUTHOR'S NOTE: Portions of the argument presented in this chapter were first developed in Kochan and Wever (1991) and in earlier drafts of Wever, Berg, and Kochan (1993).

employers, for example, are known for capitalizing on labor as a comparative advantage in international markets—rather than treating labor or "human capital" as just another cost to be minimized. Thus, they are able to ensure high and rising standards of living. Moreover, in Germany, Japan, and other major advanced industrial states, sectoral competitiveness is closely associated with significant participation by workers and their representatives in the organization of work (e.g., training, internal labor markets) and production (Brewster, 1992; Kochan & Osterman, 1990; MacDuffie & Kochan, 1991; Wever, 1993). In short, it is possible—indeed, it is common—for firms in advanced industrial countries to accommodate and integrate labor interests into their competitive strategies, allowing both parties to the employment relationship to place the advancement of human capital at the top of their negotiating agendas.

Throughout the 1980s public debate in the United States about the role of labor in society and economy was informed by a peculiarly American perspective emphasizing decentralized, market-driven, individual actors, rather than groups and institutions capable of compensating for the deficiencies of markets (Lipset, 1977). According to the most extreme version of this account, unions as protectors of the *distinct* interests of workers have outlived their functions (Reynolds, 1990). Currently an alternative view may be emerging in the public debate. Within the first few months of taking office President Bill Clinton's Secretaries of Labor (Robert Reich) and Commerce (Ron Brown) established a blue ribbon commission (known as the Reich Commission) that is to reconsider American labor laws and the nature of employment relations more broadly. Arguably for the first time since the 1930s the old, new, and emerging interests of the American work force—and their links to the interests of society at large—are being systematically considered.

The Reich Commission is explicitly concerned with the relationship between economic democracy and economic efficiency, between worker participation and the ability to compete in high-skill, high-wage, high labor-value-added markets. It has been charged with issuing a comprehensive report in May of 1994, suggesting what form(s) of collective employee representation are economically and politically appropriate in the contemporary setting, how American labor law should be restructured to encourage these, and what further public policy measures might be needed to support these changes. In its deliberations the Commission is considering, among other things, employer-specific employee representation bodies patterned on the European works council model, as well as public policies designed to encourage greater employer investments in the skills of their employees.

The openness of the Clinton administration to a more integrated approach to labor law, as a component of a broader political economic institutional framework, is signaled also by the statements and writings of other advisers. For instance, Professor Laura d'Andrea Tyson, the head of the Council of Economic Advisors, has written extensively and persuasively on the linkages between trade policy, industrial policy, and employment relations policy (see, e.g., Levine & Tyson, 1990).

The current historical moment offers a rare opportunity for reshaping American employment relations, and the possibility that the unions might be able to exert substantial influence on the shape of public policy.

This chapter considers the causes of the decline of American labor over the past several decades; the challenges facing the unions as they attempt to revitalize their movement; existing experimentation with new forms of labor-management relations that represent early efforts to meet these challenges; and the likelihood that these experiments will translate into significant changes in the nature of employment relations in the coming years. The conclusion contains a few suggestions about the future of trade unionism in the United States, and of worker representation more generally, taking into account the broader institutional structures in which the employment relationship is embedded, and the possibilities opened up by emerging national political trends.

Background

The decline of American trade unionism over the past several decades stems from a confluence of closely interrelated factors, including structural economic changes, demographic shifts, growing employer willingness and ability to counter or avoid unions, the erosion of labor laws and their enforcement, and changing popular views about worker representation. The early seventies saw the beginning of the end of postwar American supremacy in international markets. Increased price competition placed pressures on unionized employers to lower costs. Traditional collective bargaining contracts, which rigidify internal labor markets, became less acceptable because they limit flexible resource allocation. Many employers located new production (and thus employment) in low-wage (typically nonunion) settings in the United States and abroad. Still unionized employers paying higher wages found it hard to compete against nonunion firms, prompting widespread adoption of union avoidance and investment relocation strategies. Trapped by tradition and labor law into channeling all their interests through collective bargaining and grievance procedures, trade unions were unable to affect these strategic investment decisions. No longer able to take wages out of competition, the unions were also unable to ease the competitive pressures underlying these decisions.

These investment shifts explain part of the loss of union membership, but another portion of that loss can be attributed to workers' own immediate interests and personal decisions under the changed circumstances. For several reasons, workers had fewer reasons to join unions, and in some cases saw reasons not to. Union jobs were increasingly associated with plant closings and job insecurity. The system of exclusive representation made it hard to carry membership across jobs. This is especially problematic among white-collar workers, who are more loyal to their careers than to their employers, and more likely to shift employers than blue-collar workers. Many companies developed sophisticated human resource policies, offering workers the kinds of benefits historically associated with unions, but without forcing workers to pay union dues and without the tension and rancor popularly associated with union-management relations in the United States. The increasingly conservative political environment of the 1980s in which these developments unfolded only served to reinforce the union movement's downward spiral.

New Strategies?

The decline of the American unions appears if anything to be overdetermined. The multicausal nature of this slide suggests that any attempt to reverse it must at the very least (a) target union organizing resources so they take into account demographic and sectoral shifts in employment; (b) counter and adapt to new employer investment and governance strategies and organizational forms; and (c) speak to the diverse and changing needs, expectations, and values of the work force (Kochan & Wever, 1991). Moreover, a successful strategy for the revitalization of American organized labor also requires changes in the political economic institutions within which employment relations are embedded. The current political climate raises the possibility of such institutional transformation, and thus establishes propitious conditions for a concerted new union strategy for articulating and representing workers' interests.

A high-performance economy hinges on a well-trained work force. Workers themselves have an interest in broad skills, which can be transferred relatively easily across firms, and thus enhance their bargaining leverage on the external labor market. Yet for a variety of reasons, American companies tend to emphasize narrow skills and to invest relatively less than their counterparts in other advanced industrial countries in their human resources (Wever & Berg, 1993). For instance, fearing that training investments will accrue to competitors if their newly trained employees take jobs at other firms, many American employers minimize training, and target training investments at company-specific skills that cannot easily be "poached." Research has found that while about one-third of American employers have adopted some aspects of a high-performance competitive strategy, focusing on the value added by human resources, most of this experimentation has been piecemeal, adopting some innovative human resource practices while rejecting others (Osterman, 1993). (This accounts for the simultaneous co-existence of strikingly different types of labor-management relations throughout the U.S. economy.)

In this regard the interests of the society and economy at large are more closely allied with those of workers than those of individual firms. Broad skills are best suited to the flexible production methods that are associated with high productivity and quality (Kochan & Osterman, 1990). They support a higher standard of living than can be achieved as the net aggregate result of the narrower skills profiles offered by individual firms acting purely in self-interest.

A successful American trade union revitalization strategy must articulate American workers' interests in employers' adoption of high-performance competitive strategies, and in the broad and ongoing training and further training components of such strategies. More specifically, three goals must be simultaneously pursued if labor is to address the structural causes of union decline. First, the unions must come to terms with the changing sectoral distribution and character of jobs themselves. Most jobs, and almost all new jobs in the United States, are in the service sectors. The new service jobs being created are highly diverse, requiring many different kinds of organizing strategies. Both highly skilled professional and technical service workers and employees in low-paying, low-skilled service jobs will be increasingly concerned with their skills. The U.S. education and training systems lag far behind those of our major competitors. Meanwhile, our standard of living is becoming more closely tied to broad, flexible skills. Training, retraining, and ongoing or further training will become more and more important to workers throughout the economy, as skills increasingly determine people's ability to get and keep stable employment, and to move across firms (Batt & Osterman, 1993; Lynch, 1990).

As noted above, American unions have typically focused more on the immediate job satisfaction of would-be members than on their potential (or actual) medium- or long-term sociopolitical interests. What is now called for is an approach that makes clear the links between skills, the quality of jobs, and thus the quality of working and home lives; the relationship between the work life and the home life; and potential job mobility. Not only must these interconnections be made clear, but the possibilities for enhancing skills, and thus easing work/home life tensions; advancing economically and occupationally, and so on; must be better organized.

A second aspect of a union revitalization strategy must speak to the fact that firms today are structuring themselves differently, and making decisions differently than when the traditional industrial relations system was taking root (Kern & Sabel, 1991; Kochan, Katz, & McKersie, 1986). Traditional Taylorist management practices concentrate decision making in the management hierarchy, above the level of the workplace or shop floor. Employees were traditionally told what to do, and "participation" occurred solely through collective bargaining conducted by the union at 2- to 3-year intervals. In the past strategic decisions concerning the kinds of investment firms would make, and where, did not affect workers as directly as they do today. "New" technologies were substantially similar to "old" ones, and were not accompanied by major changes in skills composition and in the organization of work and production. Investment abroad or in nonunion facilities was more often a supplement to, rather than a substitute for, investment at home. Jobs were not on the line as frequently, and when they were, it was not as hard for workers to move to other firms.

But today the devolution of decision-making power, and the increasingly important nature of strategic management decisions, require that worker interests be directly represented in these forums, rather than surfacing only periodically, in meetings with personnel departments during collective bargaining negotiations. What is needed is a model more closely resembling industrial relations systems that grant worker representatives rights to information about and influence over strategic management decisions through co-determination, and over decisions concerning the organization of work and (to a lesser extent) production through legislatively mandated, employer-specific representative bodies.[2]

Third, to recapture a significant proportion of American workers, the unions must understand the ways in which American workers' views of work, worker representation, and the workplace have changed. The United States is notorious for lacking a broad Socialist vision (or people able to articulate and broadcast that vision) of the sort that unites working-class interests in labor movements throughout Europe. Yet the strong and principled commitment of American workers to their sociopolitical as well as economic struggles is amply demonstrated throughout U.S. labor history. There is no reason to believe that American workers will not continue to heed appeals to principle (rather than pure economic gain). But they, like other workers, need their leaders to define those principles in ways that unite and move them.

Experiments and Innovations

Are American trade unions up to the tasks of organizing in unfamiliar arenas, adapting to unfamiliar management strategies and structures, and articulating and giving expression to the changing values and the emerging interests of American working people? We now turn to a brief survey of the evidence so far available.

ORGANIZING

For some time a number of American unions have been intensively involved in efforts to develop new organizing strategies, create new organizing resources and coordinating centers, attract workers in industries outside their traditional manufacturing strongholds, and organize workers in new categories of membership. Indeed, some unions have scored steady membership gains in recent years, and the American Federation of Labor and Congress of Industrial Organizations (the AFL-CIO, the unions' federation) has made some headway in organizing new "associate members," even as the overall percentage of organized workers has continued to drop.

However successful individual unions' efforts may be, the aggregate picture remains unsettling. Unions' organizing efforts are still concentrated in manufacturing, though it is in the service sectors that most new jobs are being created and most currently unorganized jobs exist. The financial cost of organizing the number of people who would have to be organized each year, just to maintain current union representation levels, dramatically exceeds the present economic resources of the unions.[3] In any case, most unions are not systematically addressing workers' needs for more secure and better structured internal labor markets, or more information about external labor markets.

ADAPTING TO NEW MANAGEMENT
STRUCTURES AND STRATEGIES

In the late 1970s and early 1980s managements and unions in the auto, steel, aerospace, telecommunications, rubber, airline, and many other industries began to experiment with various forms of labor participation in management decision making, both at strategic top management levels and at the point of production, on the shop floor or at the workplace (Kochan et al., 1986). Among the most innovative experiments are the joint training funds established originally in the auto industry in the early 1980s, and later in other sectors as well (Wever, Berg, & Kochan, 1993). These projects pool management and labor resources to enable the parties to establish training programs to help employees adapt to changing technological and work organizational requirements, and/or to transfer from one area of production to another. Thus, they both imply a strategic human capital investment on the part of the employer and entail labor participation in the organization of work at the point of production.[4]

But unfortunately most unions lack a clear central strategy regarding skills development, leaving local leaders without consistent standards or policies to apply in the concrete development of training projects. This strategic weakness can be seen in the well-known case of the Saturn Division of General Motors (GM) and the autoworkers union (the UAW). The union and company have been involved since the early 1980s in the joint design of the car and the plant, as well as the structuring of labor-management relations and corporate governance at the division. Saturn, perhaps more than any other case, involves labor in important decisions at the strategic and work-place levels of the labor-management relationship, and contains a significant and ongoing training component. While Saturn, after many delays, is now in production and appears to be a high-quality car, to date we have no systematic evidence concerning productivity or the scope and effects of labor participation. More to the point, there is no indication that the principles organizing work and production and structuring skills and the internal labor markets at Saturn will be introduced at other GM plants. Indeed, GM is considering expanding Saturn's operations on the basis of a more traditional model of labor-management relations. In any case, because Saturn is a "greenfield" site, it is not clear whether its essential innovations could be reproduced in older, more traditional plants. Finally, central union officials also remain divided about the political wisdom of pursuing a Saturn-style strategy throughout the auto industry (see Rubinstein, Bennett, & Kochan, 1993).

Other less striking innovations can be found throughout the auto industry and in dozens of other industrial sectors. There are doubtless even more cases of failed attempts at restructuring the labor-management relationship in the name of productivity and quality. Experiments with labor-management part-nerships in the airline industry, after its deregulation in the late 1970s, emerged and receded, sometimes in spectacularly hostile conflicts, on a regular basis. The apparently far-reaching partnership at Eastern Airlines, for instance, dissolved into a long strike and finally the company's ruin. Data are hard to collect on the many cases of labor participation in management that simply never got much past the planning phase.

To the extent that these departures from traditional, nonparticipative forms of labor-management relations are successful, they are nonetheless uni-formly isolated from organizational or institutional structures that could support, strengthen, or shape them over time. National union strategy generally does not consciously shape and support variations among local strategies—whether in regard to training or other aspects of the employment relationship. For that matter, on the employer's side corporate policy rarely plays any central coordinating role. Absent central employer or industry associations, and absent even a whole-hearted AFL-CIO endorsement of the concept of labor participation, it is hardly surprising that questions about labor's role in such matters, or about the importance of skills development as part of the labor-management relationship, have tended to find little resonance in public discourse.

Top-level labor-management discussions in the Collective Bargaining Forum, involving union presidents and top business executives, have considered and are continuing to talk about alternative industrial relations systems, including European-style works councils (Collective Bargaining Forum, 1991). The Forum is also actively considering a possible American system of national apprenticeship training. While such high-level talks undoubtedly enhance the mutual understandings of the individuals involved, it is unclear just what effect these discussions have on any concrete accomplishments in the world of work. The Forum too is an isolated institution, unrelated to and unendorsed by business peak associations (like the Chamber of Commerce or the National Association of Manufacturers [NAM]), by the AFL-CIO, or by other organizations that might more directly shape innovations in employment relations.[5]

Various state-level experiments with new forms of worker representation may hold out more promise than the experiments alluded to above. Principally, this is because such projects tend to tie changes in worker representation and employee-employer relations directly to preexisting institutions and organizations. Thus, for instance, the State of Wisconsin is in the process of developing training and further training projects in which labor, business, and local community groups are jointly involved in deciding what skills are needed, who should receive these and how they are to be conveyed (Rogers & Streeck, 1990). The State of Oregon is developing a comprehensive apprenticeship training program. The State of California, also innovating in the area of training, is considering the establishment, by legislative mandate, of a workplace-specific institution similar to the works council, to provide a minimal level of representation to all workers (unionized or not) around health and safety-related issues.

All of these programs entail some labor involvement in strategic decision making and workplace organization. What is promising about these innovations is that they appear to support the promotion of skills and worker representation by connecting them explicitly with other institutions structuring employment relations, such as junior colleges providing the classroom portion of vocational training, private industry councils (PICs) defining training needs, preexisting union apprenticeship and other kinds of training programs, and organizations to standardize various skill levels and types. But these experiments are all still in early stages, and cannot yet be fully evaluated.

ARTICULATING AND PROMOTING DIVERSE
WORKER VALUES AND INTERESTS

Can unions keep up with the changing needs and values of the contemporary labor force? Certainly the AFL-CIO, and specifically its Committee on the Evolution of Work (the CEW),[6] has come to accept the limitations of the "exclusive" model of representation. According to this model no worker at a given workplace[7] can be represented unless a majority of the workers at the workplace elect a single union to represent them. A worker cannot take union membership with him or her to another job (unless the new workplace happens to be organized by the same union he or she belonged to at the old workplace). Experimentation throughout the country with "associate membership" programs—not involving collective bargaining—offers workers various services for payment of less than full union dues. The Federation is also experimenting with new ways of organizing full members. However, none of these efforts is explicitly or centrally concerned with the career interests and long-term labor market needs of the workers the unions are trying to attract.

Finally, there are no national labor leaders articulating this or any other alternative vision or strategy that clearly distinguishes itself from the traditional approach, tied to New Deal political conditions, postwar economic conditions, and Taylorist organizational principles. The CEW, moribund since late 1989, has been revived as the possibility of labor law change was introduced with the Democratic party's accession to the White House. However, the unions have focused their lobbying efforts on a highly traditional labor law reform agenda, rather than trying to shape the public debate, and the Reich Commission's findings about the changing nature of workers' needs and interests (and in particular, the national skills deficit). Its main political goal, as the Reich Commission begins its work, is the passage of legislation that would safeguard workers' right to keep their jobs in the event of a strike. Unfortunately, this reinforces the public image of unions as being more concerned with battling employers than contributing to the economic health of the economy as a whole.

INSTITUTIONAL CONSTRAINTS

New organizing strategies, joint training funds, high-level labor-management talks—all these innovations are isolated from or incompatible with the institutions that structure employment relations both in and outside the workplace. Most American workers, working in nonunion workplaces, are unaffected by the traditional industrial relations system. To the extent that workers are covered by collective bargaining, most still lack any systematic representation of their skills-related and (internal or external) labor market-related interests. Labor has no systematic voice in standardizing or regularizing internal labor markets for workers in low-skill, low-wage service or manufacturing jobs, or in centralizing, organizing, and conveying information about external labor markets and career development opportunities to workers in higher skilled professional and technical jobs.

Meanwhile, there remain other formidable institutional and ideological obstacles to be overcome. The major piece of legislation governing labor-management relations in the United States—the Wagner Act of 1935—can be read to render works councils (or similar enterprise-specific bodies) illegal because of the danger that they might be dominated by employers. Recent rulings of the National Labor Relations Board support this reading of the law, and have led some companies to shy away from initiating employee participation programs (see Schlossberg & Reinhart, 1992). Many of the topics connected with participative labor-management innovations are not subjects about which the parties are legally required to bargain, leaving each side vulnerable to the other's abrupt withdrawal from such joint arrangements. Union access to strategic decision-making forums, via representation on boards of directors, raises possible conflicts of interest, since board members have a primary fiduciary responsibility to stockholders. Some employers claim to fear prosecution for violations of antitrust legislation if they engage in multiemployer projects that involve cooperation, say, around training matters (Hilton, 1991). The U.S. institutional landscape can appear more like a minefield for those interested in pushing back the frontiers of worker representation.

Conclusions

The decentralization, fragmentation, and laissez-faire approach of the parties to industrial relations in the United States lead to an obscuring of the important role of central institutions (organized business, organized labor, industrial relations, labor market, and training mechanisms) in helping labor and management navigate changes in their environments (international markets, political developments, and technological changes) and adapt to those changes. The contrast to a very different political economy illustrates the point. German unions have placed training and skills enhancement at the top of their strategic agenda. Regional, industry-wide, collective-bargaining contracts in a number of industries now include provisions for employers to provide workers with training and ongoing training, and particularly ongoing employee training and development, in some instances regardless of whether the technology for which workers are being trained has been or is about to be implemented. These contracts are negotiated between the unions and the employer associations. That negotiation is itself founded on continuous dialogue, at the level of national policy making, about the nature and role of training and skills issues in the changing political economy. The national apprenticeship training system is structured and run jointly by the parties to these debates, and trains somewhere between 60% and 80% of a given cohort of school leaders. Central unions in the metal working, chemical, printing, service, and other industries, representing every type of employee imaginable, develop strategies for how enterprise-specific works councils can plan skills and internal labor market strategies to cope with new technologies. These often proactive or preemptive strategies are developed with the councils via regular meetings, work groups with employees, and union seminars and courses. In short, all the institutions of worker representation, skills development, and employment relations, from collective bargaining and the apprenticeship system to the works councils and workplace agreements, play overlapping functions in the broad network of relationships that underlie the German skills base (Apitzsch, Klebe, & Schumann, 1988; Bahnmueller, Bispinck, & Schmidt, 1991; Bispinck, 1990; Mueller-Jentsch, 1992).

By and large, the practices of most American employers do not reflect the link—so prominent in Germany—between employee representation and high-performance work systems. With regard to training, in the United States the role of both the government and the unions is relatively limited. Thus, much training that occurs outside the firm is more or less independent of and irrelevant to the needs of companies adopting new technologies and/or modern and flexible methods of production. Employer-provided training tends to be highly firm-specific. In both cases, training fails to support employees' job mobility and employers' ability to capitalize on a broad conceptual knowledge base of the sort that best supports modern and flexible methods of production (MacDuffie & Kochan, 1991; Osterman, 1993). The competitive challenges facing the American political economy clearly suggest—and policymakers in Washington have begun to consider—a stronger role for employee representation and the public sector, which could benefit all parties by maximizing the breadth and relevance of skills transmitted in joint or tripartite training programs. The extension of such programs, and the creation of a nationally mandated, enterprise-specific works council-like organ, would certainly represent significant steps in this direction. Tax incentives for training investments, which would be governed by joint labor-management councils, could help induce firms to make human resource investments that would be good for the economy as a whole, but which they might not themselves undertake unless competitors were doing so as well (Wever & Berg, 1993). Some combination of these and other possibilities being considered by the Reich Commission will undoubtedly emerge in the form of public policy initiatives. As a result, the American institutional landscape may well change significantly over the coming years.

What remains less clear is the role that traditional organized labor—"exclusive" American unions patterned on the political economy of previous decades—will play in the employment relations system of the future. The positions taken by leading representatives of business and labor suggest a common opposition to any new national-level mechanism for representing employees' interests in management decision-making processes. It is too early to tell what other institution-building initiatives will emerge from the Reich Commission's deliberations, or how business and labor will either respond or try to influence the process.[8] But it is possible to imagine a scenario in which neither side identifies particularly strongly with the Commission's proposals. The Commission has only minimal business representation, and on that account it may not be able to reflect the chief concerns of the business community. Labor Secretary Reich has stated publicly that he is not sure whether traditional American unions have a place in the cooperative workplace of the future, alienating many in the labor movement. Union support for the works council concept is weak, at best. If neither business nor labor strongly endorses the Commission's recommendations, it is not clear how effective any institutional changes that emerge are likely to be. Under these circumstances the weak position of organized labor would probably become even more entrenched.

Alternately, it is possible to imagine a scenario in which employers seize the initiative themselves. Institutional changes in this case would be prompted not by public concern about the need for worker representation in the name of democracy, but rather by a growing conviction on the part of American employers and managers that, as Kern and Sabel (1991) suggest, it is self-defeating to simultaneously fight the battle against labor in the domestic political market and against competitors on the international economic market. To achieve a high-skill competitive strategy, American firms will have to accept higher levels of employee involvement, and possibly (but not necessarily) worker representation, than they have traditionally done. But there is every reason to believe that they will reject traditional U.S. unionism in their search for new forms of labor-management relations. Particularly if, as is likely, American labor law is changed to encourage a wider range of experiments with new forms of employee representation, employer-initiated experiments in employment relations are more likely to further weaken the unions' position in the national political economy.

The unions cannot preserve the American system of employment relations in its current form simply by reiterating demands for the protection and strengthening of the traditional industrial relations system. It is a question of when and how, not whether, new forms of employment relations will arise to accommodate the needs of the unique American version of the post-Fordist political economy. The possibility for significant institutional change has emerged for the first time in half a century. The institutional landscape can be influenced by employers' and union's strategies for change. Unless the unions seize the moment, however, the role of independent collective worker representation in the United States is most likely to decline further in the coming decade.

Notes

1. This has been termed the "high-performance" work system model (Osterman, 1993).

2. The works councils and their equivalents in Germany, France, Italy, the Netherlands, Sweden, and other advanced industrial states also play central roles in overseeing the in-house portion of apprenticeship training programs.

3. Based on calculations by Chaison and Dhavale, 1990.

4. The communications workers union (CWA) is engaged in particularly impressive joint training innovations in several companies in the telecommunications industry (Batt, 1991; Wever, Batt, & Rubinstein, 1993.)

5. The conservative position of the Federation is signaled in the comments of the AFL-CIO president Lane Kirkland, in an interview conducted by the author in August 1989: "We don't need [co-determination] and works councils; we have the most powerful collective bargaining structure in the world; we practically set up the German system, and it works for them but it's not for us."

6. The Committee on the Evolution of Work was founded by AFL-CIO Secretary-Treasurer Thomas Donahue in 1981, to consider long-term strategic issues facing the labor movement. The Committee met regularly and issued two reports in the early 1980s. It reconvened in 1987 for 2 years, but at that time failed to reach agreement on strategic problems and solutions under consideration, which at that time included the works council idea. It disbanded in 1989 and was reestablished in response to Bill Clinton's election and the emergence of possibilities for more labor influence at the national legislative level than had been possible during the 1980s.

7. What is really meant here is a bargaining unit, determined by the National Labor Relations Board, necessarily excluding supervisors and managerial personnel, and in any event not always coinciding with a geographical workplace.

8. Based on discussions with representatives of NAM, the Collective Bargaining Forum, and the AFL-CIO in 1993.

References

Apitzsch, W., Klebe, T., & Schumann, M. (Eds.). (1988). *BertVG '90: Der konflikt um eine andere betriebsverfassung* [The conflict over a different works constitution]. Cologne: Bund Verlag.

Bahnmueller, R., Bispinck, R., & Schmidt, W. (1991, March). Weiterbildung durch tarifvertrag [Further training through collective bargaining contracts]. *W. S. I. Mitteilungen, 44*(3).

Batt, R. (1991, August). *Joint labor-management training programs* (Working Paper). Cambridge: MIT, Sloan School of Management.

Batt, R., & Osterman, P. (1993). *A national policy for workplace training: Lessons from state and local experiments.* Washington, DC: Economic Policy Institute.

Bispinck, R. (1990). *Rationalization, work policy and trade union collective agreement policy in the F.R.G.* (Working Paper). Düsseldorf: Wirtschafts- und Sozialwissenschaftszentrum des Deutschen Gewerkschaftsbundes.

Brewster, C. (1992, June). *European human resource management: Reflection of, or challenge to, the American concept?* Unpublished paper, Cranfield School of Management, United Kingdom.

Chaison, G. N., & Dhavale, D. G. (1990). A note on the severity of the decline in union organizing activity. *Industrial and Labor Relations Review, 43.*

Collective Bargaining Forum, The. (1991). *Labor-management commitment: A compact for change* (B.L.M.R. 141). Washington, DC: U.S. Department of Labor, Bureau of Labor-Management Cooperation Programs.

Cuomo Commission on Trade and Competitiveness. (1988). *The Cuomo commission report.* New York: Simon & Schuster.

Hilton, M. (1991, March). Shared training: Learning from Germany. *Monthly Labor Review,* pp. 33-37.

Kern, H., & Sabel, C. (1991, January). *Trade unions and decentralized production: A sketch of strategic problems in the West German labor movement* (Working Paper). Cambridge: MIT, Department of Political Science.

Kochan, T., Katz, H., & McKersie, K. (1986). *The transformation of American industrial relations.* New York: Basic Books.

Kochan, T., & Osterman, P. (1990, December). *Human resource development and utilization: Is there too little in the U.S.?* (Working Paper). Cambridge: MIT, Sloan School of Management, Industrial Relations Section.

Kochan, T., & Wever, K. (1991). American unions and the future of worker representation. In G. Strauss, D. Gallagher, & J. Fiorito (Eds.), *The state of the unions.* Madison, WI: Industrial Relations Research Association.

Levine, D., & Tyson, L. (1990). In A. S. Blinder (Ed.), *Paying for productivity.* Washington, DC: Brookings Institution.

Lipset, S. M. (1977). Why no socialism in the United States? In S. Bialer & S. Sluzar (Eds.), *Sources of contemporary radicalism* (pp. 31-149). Boulder, CO: Westview.

Lynch, L. (1990, February). *The private sector and skill formation in the United States: A survey* (Working Paper). Cambridge: MIT, Sloan School of Management.

MacDuffie, J. P., & Kochan, T. (1991, January). *Does the U.S. under-invest in human resources? Determinants of training in the world auto industry* (Working Paper). Philadelphia: University, The Wharton School.

Mueller-Jentsch, W. (1992, May). *Works councils in Germany.* Unpublished paper, Universitaet-Gesamthochschule Paderborn.

Osterman, P. (1993, January). *How common is workplace transformation and how can we explain who adopts it?* (Working Paper). Cambridge: MIT, Sloan School of Management, Industrial Relations Section.

Reynolds, M. O. (1990, Winter). The creative destruction of unionism. *Forum for Applied Research and Policy, 5*(4).

Rogers, J., & Streeck, W. (1990, August 27). *Vocational training: Reflections on the European experience and its relevance for the United States* and *What is to be done? Policy recommendations to the commission.* Testimony before the Governor's Commission for a Quality Workforce, Center on Wisconsin Strategy, University of Wisconsin-Madison.

Rubinstein, S., Bennett, M., & Kochan, T. (1993). The Saturn partnership: Co-management and the reinvention of the local union. In B. Kaufman & M. Kleiner (Eds.), *Employee repre-*

sentation: Alternatives and future directions. Madison, WI: Industrial Relations Research Association.

Schlossberg, S., & Reinhart, M. (1992, September). Electromation and the future of labor-management cooperation in the U.S. *Labor Law Journal,* 608-620.

Wever, K. (1993). Learning from works councils: Five unspectacular cases from Germany. *Industrial Relations.*

Wever, K., Batt, R., & Rubinstein, S. (1993, June). *Workers' participation in work organization in the United States* (Monograph commissioned by the International Labour Organization). Geneva: ILO.

Wever, K., & Berg, P. (1993). Human resource development in the United States and Germany. *International Contributions to Labour Studies.*

Wever, K., Berg, P., & Kochan, T. (1993, July). *Employee skills development in institutional context: Comparing the United States and Germany* (Monograph commissioned by the Economic Policy Institute). Washington, DC: Economic Policy Institute.

PART IV

Human Resources Management and Industrial Relations

12 \ Human Resources Management: Implications for Teaching, Theory, Research, and Practice in Industrial Relations

JOHN PURCELL

This is the first time, I believe, that our association has devoted a congress theme to human resource management. To some this may be welcomed as a timely response to the new agendas for industrial relations evident in most countries. To others it may be a matter of regret indicative of the creeping managerialism that endangers the traditional concern with employers and employees, their collective organizations, and the role of the state. Cynics like Guest see it as an attempt to "offer new hope for those who had begun to despair of the long-term potential of industrial relations and personnel management as important academic subjects" (1990, p. 377). It has not gone unnoticed in Britain that a number of academic stalwarts of the labor movement now find themselves holding professorships funded by major companies under the title "Human Resource Management." Is it industrial relations by another name, like so many textbooks where the second edition is simply retitled, or like the MBA elective in a major British university where numbers were falling until it was retitled "Human Resource Management" with little change of content? It is now among the most popular, leading to a much needed flow of funds to the beleaguered department of industrial relations.

There is a more serious objection to human resource management in that increasingly our teaching is located in business schools where the underlying value structure is managerial and unitarist: Do our students really accept the inevitability of a conflict of interest between management and labor, or is the pursuit of human resource management covertly, or in places overtly, anti-union? Behind this is a sense of unease at the clash of academic values on the nature of scholarship. Those of us approaching well-known management texts in strategy, marketing, and operational management for the first time as our subject area seems to explode beyond the institutional bounds, often are astounded at the normative and prescriptive tone of much of what we read, what Mintzberg in strategy has labeled the "design school" (1990, p. 171). Is the teaching of human resource management a litany of what ought to happen, based on anecdotes of best practice? Is human resource management about presenting "a coherent, positive and optimistic philosophy about management . . . built around the possibility of achieving personal growth in an integrated, humane organization" (Guest, 1992, p. 17)? Is the very attraction of human resource management that it is acceptable because it fits the values and beliefs of managers and professional employees? Where is the detailed research, the evidence, the analysis of the contingencies surrounding the firm, the exploration of the attitudes and behavior of subordinate employees? Or is human resource management concerned primarily with the management of managers, as the few texts in strategy that mention human resource management imply (Porter, 1985, pp. 405-407)? If human resource management is no more than a study of the behavior of managers in seeking to gain competitive advantage, then we really do have cause for concern.

Some of these concerns are touched upon in the invited papers for this theme. Here I want, without undue repetition and regurgitation of the burgeoning literature in human resource management (hereafter referred to as HRM), to look at the origins and meanings of HRM, assess the hidden or latent consequences from an industrial relations viewpoint, and consider the union "problem" in relation to HRM. I then consider the evidence for the diffusion of HRM practices and conclude with a discussion of the limits to HRM and the implications for research, practice, and teaching in industrial relations. I do so with the aim not of providing definitive answers but of stimulating debate.

Origins and Meanings

The earliest reference I know of is a paper by Miles, in the *Harvard Business Review* in 1965, contrasting human resources with human relations. Here human resources is seen to go beyond the role of the manager under human relations of adopting "participative leadership policies as the least cost method of obtaining cooperation and consent." In human resources there is a concern with people's values and abilities:

> [W]hich focus attention on all organization members as reservoirs of untapped resources. These resources include not only physical skills and energy, but also creative ability and the capacity for responsible, self-directed, self-controlled behavior. Given these assumptions about people, the manager's job cannot be viewed merely as one of giving direction and obtaining cooperation. Instead, his primary task becomes that of creating an environment in which the total resources of his department can be utilized. (Miles, 1965, p. 150)

This remains a reasonable, if not very specific, statement of some of the central tenets to most, but not all, definitions of HRM as a theory of management, not of the firm; as a new way of managing employees associated with decentralization and empowerment; as a concern with flexibility and a wider range of unspecific, and unspecified tasks; as a means of organizing production beyond Taylorism; and as a holistic approach. It is not hard to see how goals of integration, commitment, flexibility and adaptability, and quality come to be incorporated in models of HRM, nor how the achievement of HRM is seen to be closely associated with business strategy. (For a critical analysis of the growth of human resource management, see Legge, 1991, pp. 19-40.)

Many authors contrast models of HRM with previous practice, and most refer to Taylorism, Fordism, and scientific management. In all such contrasts, often in the form of lists, like the well-known one of Walton (1985), the danger is stereotyping the past and idealizing the future; but such lists at least have the advantage of drawing attention to the component characteristics of HRM. Storey (1992), in the paper for this congress, classifies these into sets of issues, which taken together, constitute meaningful version of HRM. These four aspects are: (a) a particular constellation of beliefs and assumptions; (b) a strategic thrust informing decisions about people management; (c) the central involvement of line mangers; and (d) reliance upon a set of "levers" to shape the employment relationship, which are different from those used under proceduralist and joint regulative regimes typical of classical industrial relations systems. Heller (1992) argues that HRM has at last persuaded industrial relations scholars to recognize the contribution of other social science disciplines developed in industrial sociology, organizational behavior, and organizational psychology. The reason is that the integrated and holistic nature of HRM makes it difficult if not impossible to isolate industrial relations from employment relations and work relations, to use Gospel's classification (1983, pp. 12-17). In this sense HRM has forced open the boundaries to the study and practice of industrial relations in the firm, both vertically (the strategic, functional and workplace levels) and horizontally (technology, manufacturing systems, financial controls, training and development, and even marketing if "internal marketing" catches on, as in "our employees are our internal customers").

Kochan and Dyer (1992), in the their paper, use the term *mutual commitment* to delineate this type of management from other traditional forms. This is well illustrated by the requirements they specify at the strategic level: business strategies built around sources of competitive advantage such as quality, innovation, flexibility, speed, and customer service; key decision makers guided by a set of values that view employees as valued stakeholders; mechanisms for giving voice to employee and human resource inputs in strategy formulation and organizational governance processes. This is then matched by complementary policies at the functional and workplace level. Prieto (1992), in his paper, uses a not dissimilar model of high technology services developed by Crozier, where innovation replaces rationalization, quality supersedes quantity, and human resources is placed in a privileged position.

Extracted and listed in this way the models of human resource management easily become fantasized and divorced from any recognizable reality. If there are a few firms that meet all the criteria for human resource management, then their very exception must lead us to question not why others do not follow suit, but why these few exist in the first place. It is instructive to find that the classic firms always chosen as exemplars of sophisticated human resource management, such as Hewlett-Packard and IBM, have found it necessary to abandon some elements of their HRM policies, such as job security, in the face of market downturn. Similarly, Kochan and Dyer refer to another company in the same industry, Digital, and the effect of corporate downsizing on two plants noted for their manufacturing excellence. It is not surprising that once an idealized version of HRM is deployed—a description of what the world ought to be like—that those who search for it, like the pot of gold at the end of the rainbow, find that rhetoric outstrips reality by a wide margin.

There is an another meaning to the term that plays on the word *resource,* where labor is to be utilized and disposed of according to the exclusive needs of the firm. This "hard" version of HRM (Storey, 1991) is developed by Legge as "tough love," where business strategy in relation to meeting the needs of the product market or financial constraint might require the removal of "dead wood whose performance is not up to standard, transferring employees to other parts of the business, tying rewards closely to individual performance" (1991, p. 32). She goes on to argue that the use of the label HRM:

> [I]s no more or less than a reflection of the rise of the "new right." . . . Our new enterprise culture demands a different language, one that asserts management's

the legitimation of managerial authority and in the imagery of the firm as a team with committed employees working with managers for the benefit of the firm. It may be that the context in which the firm finds itself limits management's freedom of action, leading to what Regini calls in his paper "pragmatic eclecticism" and Storey refers to as "dualism." What is important is not just that the focus is on management's ability to implement change, but how this power shift affects classic industrial relations forms of analysis. It will be recalled that Dunlop's seminal work on the industrial relations system referred to the creation of "an ideology or a commonly shared body of ideas and beliefs regarding the interaction and roles of the actors which helps to bind the system together" (1958, p. 383). This was closely associated with the pluralist presumption, often criticized by radicals, of a balance of power. These comfortable assumptions are no longer applicable. Where is the balance of power evident in this quote cited by Storey of a major motor manufacturer: "The unions were invited to the party but they didn't seem to want to come. So the party went ahead without them." Or this quote from a personnel director on the implementation of performance related pay, a standard part of HRM:

> There is going to be a lot more focus on the individual; the individual's worth and talents he or she has and the contribution they make to the business; involving them in that part of the business they work in. That really involves being far more open, involving people far more in what they do; moving down the track to change the way in which we reward people. *All this begins with cutting the power of the trade unions in the traditional collective bargaining sense off at the knees.* (Kessler & Purcell, 1992)

There is not much evidence here of the sort of binding, shared ideology that Dunlop was referring to. It might be argued that Kochan and Dyer's description of "mutual commitment" constitutes a new form of shared ideology. If so, it is one where management is the dominant actor, and where we are concerned with relationships inside the firm; whereas Dunlop, for good reason, was concerned far more with external, system-wide relationships.

This is reflected in the process of decentralization in the institutions and procedures of industrial relations that has taken place to a greater or lesser extent in most countries, certainly in Europe, North America, Australia, and New Zealand. The shift to single employer bargaining, and within that toward the operating subsidiary company or establishment level, is especially marked in Britain (Purcell, 1991). This means that the study of wage fixing, of trade unions, and of collective bargaining has to be undertaken within the firm at the strategic, functional, and workplace levels. However, just as external trade union officers have been rendered marginal to the process change, there is strong evidence that the agents of change in management are not the personnel/HRM professionals but line or operational managers. This empowerment of line managers, noted by Savoie in his description of the Ford training program, is a typical requisite of HRM. It means that the traditional sources of research data, trade union officers and personnel managers, are no longer sufficient. Even the shop steward or lay union representative in the plant is likely to be marginalized (Marchington & Parker, 1990).

Part of the reason for this is the growth of individualism and the shifting definition of the employee's role. Once a move is made away from standardized, routine tasks embodied in a job description to an emphasis on flexibility and multi-skilling, seen in its most elaborated form in TQM (Hill, 1991), emphasis is placed on individual and team performance and the means of enhancing it. Heller refers to "motivated competences" in his paper, while Mathews provides an analysis of the shift in training from task and craft (static descriptions of requisites) to competences and a more sophisticated modelling of skills formation.

Two things follow. First, given the emphasis on the individual and each person's performance, it is inevitable that this is associated with an enhanced role for middle managers. As Hill makes clear, if TQM is associated with empowering employees, it also means enhancing the influence and involvement of line managers (1991, p. 561). Second, the linked concepts of control and democracy in organizations, at least at the workplace, take on the attributes of a positive sum game much more in accord with Tannenbaum's model (1986), than has often been allowed for. This is a quite different focus from that normally used in the study of industrial democracy and worker participation. Here attention is restricted to the operation of secondary institutions, such as joint consultative committees, works councils, and collective bargaining. An institutional focus is no longer appropriate once indirect representational systems become less important than means of direct involvement, not just via Quality Circles but through a transformation of the nature of tasks to teamwork. This is the basis of Heller's paper on motivated competences, in which "competence (that is to say experience, knowledge and skill) plays a dual role, mediated by participation, thereby associated with a positive motivational climate."

There are, of course, significant limitations to the participative role of employees, given the emphasis on the management prerogative and the unilateral nature of managerial power explicit in HRM. It has been argued in Toyotaism that this is: "because . . . participation and responsibility accorded to workers is limited. It is highly circumscribed by its being orientated to the rationalization of production and not any fundamental altering of the character of work" (Wood, 1991, p. 573).

The most significant feature of individualism is, as Storey notes, that the key levers used to shape the employment relationship have changed away from aspects of joint regulation seen most clearly in the failure of productivity bargaining (Ahlstrand, 1990). Now the key levers are selection according to attributes, often involving social-psychological tests, performance pay, individual contracts, enhanced flows of information, teamwork, and an emphasis on organizational culture and climate. It is not that these key levers have been "captured," so to speak, from collective bargaining. For the most part they were never covered in the bargaining agenda, but are new devices invented by management as a means of selecting, motivating, and controlling, via commitment, the individual employee. It is for this reason that collective bargaining can exist, in Europe at least, alongside these new forms of management to create what Storey calls "dualism," and Regini "pragmatic eclecticism." Unions and collective bargaining are retained partly as a reflection of the legal status given in some countries, partly as a historical residue and, perhaps, as a necessary feature of the social democratic version of HRM emerging in Europe.

The nature of the bargaining relationship is changed, however. A number of authors refer to the need for, or necessity of, moving away from an adversarial relationship toward integrative bargaining, partnership, and cooperation. Evidence is given that this is taking place. Where, as in France and Spain, the state seeks to impose collective consultation, the outcome, as shown by Regini, may be less satisfactory than achieved through voluntary means, as in the United Kingdom and Italy. In part employers have been prepared to continue to give voice to union representatives, and in part unions themselves have recognized that HRM has changed the collective bargaining agenda, and that competitive pressure makes the cost of disputes significantly higher. But this dualism is illustrative, argues Storey, of a "failure to work-out a coherent policy which embraces 'human resource management' and industrial relations [which] is surely a sign of instability."

The advance of human resource management and the decline in the importance, if not the practice, of collective bargaining may well mean that we are in a period of transition. Will the decline in trade union membership, visible in all OECD countries in the 1980s, continue, not just because of sectoral shifts but through the take-up of the key features of HRM? And what, if anything, will replace unions as the means of giving voice to employees in strategy formulation and organizational governance? It is already clear that "greenfield sites" are either operated as nonunion sites, or the role of the union is tightly constrained. For example, in the Toyota plant in the United Kingdom (which will start production in 1993), the members of the Toyota Members Advisory Board (the sole mechanism allowing for employee representation) will be directly elected by the employees, even though the Amalgamated Engineering Union has been "granted" recognition. This is more akin to the German Works Council, but without the legal powers that are seen as essential to the German system, and without regional or industry-wide collective bargaining.

The Limits to Human Resource Management

This brief reference to works councils draws attention to the most significant weakness of the practice and analysis of HRM. The danger is that the firm, usually a large employer, sees itself, or we treat it as, an isolated island, disconnected from the rest of society. Preoccupation with internal management practices and policies leads to gross simplification and crude assumptions made on the ability of management to pursue certain policies as though they are free agents. In part this derives from an exaggerated strategic choice analysis, where technological and market determinism is rejected, rightly, in favor of an implicit assumption that management can choose to do what they wish—they have strategic choice—bounded only by the need to survive and compete in the turbulent product market. This leads to an emphasis on internal power relations, leadership, and what Peters and Waterman called the 7-S framework of structure, systems, style, staff, skills, strategy, and shared values (1982, p. 10), as though all firms have an equal choice to develop the management recipes.

Beaumont (1992) has noted how the stress on the need to integrate human resource management with technological developments is:

> [L]ittle more than the basic message of socio-technical systems . . . [and] the major emphasis on the importance of a competitive, unstable product market in stimulating the need for flexible work practices and a close individual employee-organization identification process is simply rediscovering the organic management systems theory of Burns and Stalker [1961]. (p. 32)

We could add to the list the classic studies of 25 to 30 years ago which placed management behavior in context, such the well-known work of Woodward (1965) and Blauner (1964) on technology, Sayles (1963) on work groups under technology, and beyond them, the whole contingency school arising from Trist and others (Trist, Higgin, Murray, & Pollock, 1963) and the socio-technical approach. The critical questions that largely remain unanswered can be taken straight from the guiding assumptions of industrial sociology at its high point in the early 1960s; under what circumstances will a given approach to the management of labor tend to emerge? We do not have to be exclusively deterministic to argue that certain technologies, certain skill requirements, and certain organizational environments will be associated with a propensity for the firm and its managers to behave in certain ways toward its employees. We can add many other variables from ownership to national or socio-cultural factors. We can allow for strategic choice, provided that we recognize, study, and take account of the constrained nature of that choice. It seems to me that the study of human resource management has yet to come of age, and like most adolescents, there is a reluctance to learn from an older generation. We often accuse managers of adopting "not-invented-here" blinkers, but oddly, we are in danger of doing the same. This has implications for research since much human resource analysis is based on interviews with managers, their plans and intentions; and little serious work seems to be done on the context in which these are developed and applied, or how they actually affect the behavior of subordinate employees. A great deal remains to be done at the micro level of the firm, especially at the workplace, in terms of technology, skill mix, employee attributes, and policies of selection, appraisal, reward, and teamwork in the organizational context. The need is to explore the variety of approaches within HRM in terms of the contingent variables. How different is HRM, and why, in a finance house than in a hotel or an airline, for example?

A more sophisticated, research-based analysis might help to explain why HRM is not more diffuse through national and international economies and societies. Kochan and Dyer draw attention in their paper to the greenfield site phenomenon, where innovative HRM practices are developed but they generally fail to spread to other units within the firm. "As such they become experimental islands in a sea of traditional practices." Even research inside such "innovative" greenfield sites can lead us to question how far HRM policies actually affect the working lives of the employees. Newell studied three such companies in the United Kingdom in the late 1980s, and, unusually, was able to conduct an attitude survey among the employees. Interestingly, many companies withdrew their cooperation from the research once she asked to interview their employees, or "members," as many prefer to call them, preferring, perhaps, the comfort of their own rhetoric to harder evidence of employee commitment. In the three plants that remained in the study, the questionnaire, which was designed to compare attitudes with a wider, national sample of employee attitudes, revealed that the employees were less confident of their managers' ability to manage and more critical of management than was the case nationally. This did not necessarily mean that management was worse, but that the employees' expectations had been heightened by the careful selection process and the hype about the need for self-motivated, multiskilled, flexible employees. The actual experience of daily work was not sufficiently different to persuade the employees that their high expectations were being met. In part, there was a contradiction, between the promise of career advancement and promotion, and the design of the flat organization, another feature of HRM, which rendered it impossible to promote people to intermediary positions since there were none (Newell, 1991). This led Newell to suggest that the key issue in greenfield sites is ask how long it takes them to become "brown," to revert to standard, traditional forms of employee management, implying that for some organizations HRM might be a passing fad.

Kochan and Dyer point to much the same sort of difficulty. They note that national attitude surveys suggest that "there has been a particularly sharp decline in measures of employee trust in management and in their companies generally" [in the United States]. This leads them to focus on the factors that inhibit the diffusion of HRM practices, both upward to the boardroom and, more important, across different institutions and institutional decision makers, as well as across various firms and industries. Similarly, both Regini and Storey note the limitations to the adoption of full-blown HRM policies in European firms. Prieto draws attention to the consequences on interfirm relations, especially the small subcontract firms where tougher contracts seem to drive out the possibility of HRM or even traditional, stable labor management. "A mobilization of the labour force within an enterprise may be accompanied by—or pave the way for—a coercive mobilization in enterprises dependent upon it." Is this segmentation of the labor market, the division between "core" and "periphery," an inevitable feature of HRM, both inside large firms and between these firms and their subcontractors, thereby limiting the diffusion of HRM? Is "tough love" a more common attribute in practice than the soft "mutual commitment" model, especially at a time of economic recession?

It is almost always argued that a key attribute of HRM is its close association with strategy, both informing strategic decisions and deriving from them. This may mean, however, no more than labor management is made subservient to the needs of the firm. Attempts to find a link between corporate strategy and HRM rarely arrive at conclusive evidence that strategic decisions are informed by the needs of employees (Purcell, 1990). It is more often the case in large, diversified corporations that HRM is seen as an operational responsibility while the supremacy of financial management at the center is often noted, as in Kochan and Dyer's paper. This difficulty in gaining diffusion of HRM within companies is often linked to a call for companies to change their internal operating procedures toward networking and synergistic interdependencies, and to opt for longer term planning horizons typical of Japanese firms, but it is highly questionable whether the capital market in the United States and the United Kingdom will allow this to happen. A wider question remains on the diffusion of HRM between firms. This leads us back to the question of institutions in the labor market external to the firm.

Conclusion: A Broader View
of Human Resource Management

The trend toward the decentralization of national labor market institutions in Western Europe has triggered a neo-corporatist debate on the value of coordinated bargaining (e.g., see Soskice, 1990). Three elements of this debate are relevant here. First, it is asserted that the degree of coordination achieved is associated with superior economic performance seen in the income-employment trade-off. Second, it is not the existence of formal, joint institutions for coordination that is important, but the degree to which employers coordinate, formally or informally, their response to collective bargaining and labor market matters, seen most clearly in Japan and Germany. Third, the ability of employers, the state, and trade unions to generate a high degree of employment security leads to, and is itself a reflection of, the willingness of workplace trade unions and other forms of worker representation to emphasize longer term goals. While, for example, British unions are seen to be preoccupied with short-run perspectives in wage-bargaining, German unions and works councils "have a structure of incentives, including employment security, effective representation and participation, continuing retraining in broad skills, which gives them a long-term perspective in plant bargaining" (Soskice, 1990, p. 59).

The implication is that highly developed inter-firm relations and a complex network of institutions in the labor market beyond the firm (and a finance market capable of going beyond short-termism) provides fertile ground for the adoption of HRM. The more usual model of the individual firm standing alone in a generally hostile market is less plausible for the achievement of long-term goals in HRM.

This draws our attention back to the traditional subject matter of industrial relations. Once we question why it appears to be difficult to achieve a diffusion of "best" HRM practices beyond a small number of isolated cases, we find, through comparative analysis, fruitful sources of explanation in the degree of inter-firm cooperative relations; the extent, type, and form of labor market regulation; and a different conception for the role of the state. Kochan and Dyer draw attention to the fact that "there has been virtually no action on the part of national policy makers [in the United States] to create the environment or the substantive policies needed to encourage or require either firms or unions to act more forcefully . . . " By contrast, in Germany there are long-established practices where unions and management collaborate to develop industry training standards closely linked to the state's educational system.

This is where the paper by Mathews (1992) adds significantly to the debate. He notes that the process of award restructuring in Australia as part of the national accord policies, and to reflect the changing needs of major employers, has led to agreements at national level to rethink the notion of skill, learning space, and the reward of competences. Here, rather than HRM meaning that management are free to do what they wish unencumbered by national agreements, as in the United Kingdom and the United States, a more sophisticated, industry-wide approach has been adopted. This in turn is associated with a more integrative style of bargaining at both industry and firm level.

It must also be the case, given the coverage of awards across industries, that the game theory problem of free riders is diminished. The key need is to find a way back to the notion of collective action for mutual benefit, rather than as adversarial sparring partners. This in turn inevitably triggers a debate on public goods, especially the issue of training and development, where Britain and America, to name but two countries, are widely seen to have failed. The problem with isolated HRM firms, where the burden of high training, development, and reward strategies must be borne, is that low-cost producers can gain significant advantage in the short run, as Kochan and Dyer assert was the case in the U.S. domestic airline industry.

It is no accident that the models for best practice for HRM most often used all come from the same industry—computers—with IBM, Hewlett-Packard, Digital, Wang, and Apple often cited. There appeared to be an industry standard, in part because of the rapid change in technology, the need for diagnostic skills in manufacturing, and a predominance of professionally trained employees in each firm. It helped that the industry achieved continuous growth for very long periods, so that employment security was assured. It may be that this industry exhibited exceptional characteristics, not found in, say, hotels, steelmaking, insurance, or education. It is here that the ability to raise standards generally, across the whole of the industry, and exclude free riders, may well be associated with an enhanced capacity to implement HRM policies. However, this is critically dependent on employers and their willingness to seek inter-firm cooperative solutions. Again, game theory leads us not to be surprised that many might say it is a good thing, but few are prepared to act for collective interests unless they can be sure that all will. This is where the state plays a crucial role. It is often noted that there are extensive inter-firm relations and mutual responsibilities in Japan, which connect into government via a host of networks. Coordination is more normative than legislative in nature and probably much more powerful for that.

Ironically, then, students of HRM often begin with the weakening of external labor market institutions and the liberalization of management in the firm as necessary preconditions for the adoption of HRM, with all of its emphasis on new ways of managing employees and releasing their talent. Yet it appears that the more HRM is seen to be the preserve of each individual firm acting in isolation, the least likely it is that HRM practices will grow and flourish in the wider economy. In arguing for a wider diffusion of HRM, one is left pondering the need for a currently unfashionable, interventionist role for the state, especially in the area of training and development, such as in the training levy in Australia, and the creation of different forms of institutions in the labor market outside the firm. This in turn is very likely to involve trade unions in different agendas seen in the push for training and a longer term perspective beyond wage fixing. The study of formal institutions and informal means of inter-firm and multiparty collaboration is likely to return as an important theme as part of HRM in the future, especially once a tradition of comparative study is established.

References

Ahlstrand, B. W. (1990). *The quest for productivity: A case study of Fawley after Flanders.* Cambridge: Cambridge University Press.

Beaumont, P. B. (1992). The US human resource management literature: A review. In G. Salamam (Ed.), *Human resource strategies* (pp. 20-37). London: Sage.

Blauner, R. (1964). *Alienation and freedom: The factory worker and his industry.* Chicago: Phoenix Books.

Burns, R., & Stalker, G. M. (1961). *The management of innovation.* London: Tavistock.

Dunlop, J. T. (1958). *Industrial relations systems.* Carbondale: Southern Illinois University Press.

Edwards, P. K., & Whitson, C. (1991). Workers are working harder: Effort and shop-floor relations in the 1980's. *British Journal of Industrial Relations, 29*(4), 593-601.

Gospel, H. F. (1983). Management structures and strategies: An introduction. In H. F. Gospel & C. R. Littler (Eds.), *Managerial strategies and industrial relations.* London: Heinemann.

Guest, D. E. (1990). Human resource management and the American dream. *Journal of Management Studies, 27*(4), 377-387.

Guest, D. E. (1992). Right enough to be dangerously wrong: An analysis of the in search of excellence phenomenon. In G. Salamam (Ed.), *Human resource strategies* (pp. 5-19). London: Sage.

Heller, F. (1992). The under-utilisation of human resources in industrial relations theory and practice. *Proceedings of the Ninth World Congress of the International Industrial Relations Association.* Sydney: IIRA.

Hill, S. (1991). Why quality circles failed but total quality management might succeed. *British Journal of Industrial Relations, 29*(4), 541-568.

Kessler, I., & Purcell, J. (1992). Performance related pay: Theory and practice. *Human Resource Management Journal.*

Kochan, T. A., & Dyer, L. (1992). Managing transformational change: The role of human resource professionals. *Proceedings of the Ninth World Congress of the International Industrial Relations Association.* Sydney: IIRA.

Krafcik, J. F. (1988, Fall). Triumph of the lean production system. *Sloan Management Review,* 41-52.

Legge, K. (1991). Human resource management: A critical analysis. In J. Storey (Ed.), *New perspectives on human resource management* (pp. 19-40). London: Routledge.

Marchington, M., & Parker, P. (1990). *Changing patterns of employee relations.* Hemel Hempstead: Harvester Wheatsheaf.

Mathews, J. (1992). The industrial relations of skills formation. *Proceedings of the Ninth World Congress of the International Industrial Relations Association*. Sydney: IIRA.

Miles, R. E. (1965, July-August). Human relations or human resources? *Harvard Business Review*, 148-163.

Mintzberg, H. (1990). The design school: Reconsidering the basic promises of strategic management. *Strategic Management Journal, 11*, 171-195.

Mueller, F., & Purcell, J. (1992). The Europeanization of manufacturing and the decentralization of bargaining: Multinational management strategies in the European automobile industry. *International Journal of Human Resource Management*.

Newell, H. (1991). *Field of dreams*. Doctoral thesis, University of Oxford.

Peters, T. J., & Waterman, R. H. (1982). *In search of excellence: Lessons from America's best run companies*. New York: Harper & Row.

Porter, M. (1985). *Competitive advantage: Creating and sustaining superior performance*. New York: Free Press.

Prieto, C. (1992). Personnel management of the labour force: Sociological analysis of the major approaches. *Proceedings of the Ninth World Congress of the International Industrial Relations Association*. Sydney: IIRA.

Purcell, J. (1990). The impact of corporate strategy on human resource management. In J. Storey (Ed.), *New perspectives on human resource management* (pp. 67-91). London: Routledge.

Purcell, J. (1991). The rediscovery of the management prerogative: The management of labour relations in the 1980s. *Oxford Review of Economic Policy, 7*(1), 33-43.

Regini, M. (1992). Human resources management and industrial relations in European companies. *Proceedings of the Ninth World Congress of the International Industrial Relations Association*. Sydney: IIRA.

Savoie, E. J. (1992). Revitalising the middle manager. *Proceedings of the Ninth World Congress of the International Industrial Relations Association*. Sydney: IIRA.

Sayles, L. S. (1963). *Behaviour of industrial work groups: Prediction and control*. New York: John Wiley.

Schuler, R. S., & Jackson, S. J. (1987). Linking competitive strategies with human resource management practices. *The Academy of Management Executive, 1*(3), 207-219.

Soskice, D. (1990). Wage determination: The changing role of institutions in advanced industrialized countries. *Oxford Review of Economic Policy, 6*(4), 36-61.

Storey, J. (1991). From personnel management to human resource management. In J. Storey (Ed.), *New perspectives on human resource management* (pp. 1-18). London: Routledge.

Storey, J. (1992). The take-up of human resources management by mainstream companies: Key lessons from research. *Proceedings of the Ninth World Congress of the International Industrial Relations Association*. Sydney: IIRA.

Tannenbaum, A. S. (1986). Controversies about control and democracy in organizations. In R. N. Stern & S. McCarthy (Eds.), *The organizational practice of democracy*. London: Wiley.

Trist, E. C., Higgin, G. W., Murray, H., & Pollock, A. B. (1963). *Organizational choice*. London: Tavistock.

Walton, R. (1985, March-April). From control to commitment in the workplace. *Harvard Business Review*, 77-84.

Wood, S. J. (1991). Japanization and/or Toyotaism? *Work, Employment and Society, 5*(4), 567-600.

Woodward, J. (1965). *Industrial organization: Theory and practice*. Oxford: Oxford University Press.

13 \ Managing Transformational Change: The Role of Human Resource Professionals

THOMAS A. KOCHAN

LEE DYER

Can the United States maintain its traditional position of economic leadership, and one of the world's highest standards of living, in the face of increasing global competition? Concerned observers cite the following negative news: lagging rates of productivity growth, noncompetitive product quality in key industries, structural inflexibilities, and declining real wage levels and flat family earnings (Carnavale, 1991). Further, they offer a plethora of proposed solutions, covering both broad public policies and more specific firm-level policies and practices.

The latter often call upon organizations to do a better job of developing and utilizing their human resources (Cyert & Mowery, 1986; Dertouzos, Solow, & Lester, 1989; Marshall, 1987; Walton, 1987). Newly industrializing economies, such as Mexico, Brazil, and some of the Asian countries, compete in world markets with wages that range from 10% to 30% of those paid in more advanced countries, such as Japan, Germany, and the United States. For companies in the more advanced countries to compete in world markets, without lowering wages and living standards, requires not only ever-increasing levels of productivity, but also finding other sources of competitive advantage, such as high product quality, product differentiation, innovation, and speed to market.

But competing on these grounds often requires major organizational transformations in human resource policies and practices. This is especially the case for U.S. firms that have grown up under the legacy of scientific management and industrial engineering principles, which emphasize the separation of decision making from doing, and narrow divisions of labor and functional specialization. It is also true for unionized firms that have long done business under the New Deal model of labor relations, which emphasizes job control unionism and the separation of managerial prerogatives from worker and union rights.

Human Resources and National Competitiveness

The past decade has witnessed an explosion of interest in human resource management, and the growth of a number of new academic journals, professional societies, and industry-university research and educational partnerships. All of these share the view that human resource issues should be and, given the increased awareness of their importance, would be elevated to new levels of influence within corporate decision making and national policy making. In the United States these expectations and arguments have been voiced before, in some cases way before (Douglas, 1919; Slichter, 1919). Nonetheless, even today we find that the human resource function within many American corporations remains weak and relatively low in influence, relative to other managerial functions such as finance, marketing, and manufacturing (Kochan & Osterman, 1991). Moreover, despite the outpouring of academic writing on "strategic human resource management," little progress has been made in developing systematic theory or empirical evidence on the conditions under which human resources are elevated to a position where the firm sees and treats these issues as a source of competitive advantage. Nor is there much research that actually tests the effects of different strategies on the competitive position of the firm.

Countless national competitiveness commissions, and at least three national commissions sponsored by current or former Secretaries of Labor, have documented the need for the country, as well as individual firms, to invest more in human resources and encourage the development of workplace innovations to fully utilize employee talents, once developed. But so far these clarion calls have often fallen on either deaf or hostile ears. Corporate managements, for reasons we will document below, have not proven particularly enthusiastic. Responses from labor leaders have been mixed. Many of the recommended practices have been pioneered in nonunion firms, and some union leaders see them as inherently anti-union in nature. Yet the economic pressures of the 1980s led to a certain amount of joint union-management experimentation, and these experiences have produced a cadre of local and, to a lesser extent, national union leaders who are advocates. As yet, however, no clear vision or strategy on these issues has been articulated by the labor movement. And finally, there has been virtually no action on the part of national policymakers to create either the environment or the substantive policies needed to encourage or require either firms or unions to act more forcefully in this regard.

Why does the rhetoric so far outstrip the reality? One (although certainly not the only) answer is that theorists and researchers have cast their models of human resource management and related policy issues too narrowly. Specifically, they have relied too heavily on top management and human resource managers within corporations to drive the necessary transformation. Too little consideration has been given to the organizational and institutional contexts in which firms formulate and implement their human resource strategies and policies. Moreover, the literature has tended to treat each firm as an independent actor, whereas, as we argue below, it is now clear that the practices of individual firms are influenced not only by their own business strategies, technologies, and structures, but also by the practices of other firms in their product and labor markets, as well as by the activities of their suppliers and customers, of labor unions, and of public policymakers (Dyer & Holder, 1988). Thus, we see the need to bring labor and government back into our theories and models of human resource management policy and practice. To do this we need to integrate recent works from human resource management with research from industrial relations, political economy, and internal labor markets. We now turn to this task.

Generic Principles of Mutual Commitment Firms

Many terms have been used to describe firms that seek to treat human resources as a source of competitive advantage and to do so in a manner that preserves high standards of living: "high commitment" (Walton, 1985), "excellent" (Peters & Waterman, 1982), "best practice" (Dertouzos et al., 1989), "transformed" (Kochan, Katz, & McKersie, 1986), and "high commitment" (Lawler, 1986). We will use the term "mutual commitment" (Walton, 1985). We prefer this term since, as will be evident below, we believe that achieving and sustaining this approach requires the strong support of multiple stakeholders in an organization and in the broader economy and society in which the organization is embedded. Table 13.1 summarizes a set of generic principles that characterize the "mutual commitment" approach. It is important to realize that these are broad principles, which are operationalized in quite different forms across countries and firms. Therefore, they do

TABLE 13.1 Principles Guiding Mutual Commitment Firms

Strategic Level	Functional (Human Resource Policy) Level	Workplace Level
Supportive Business Strategies	Staffing Based on Employment Stabilization	Selection Based on High Standards
Top Management Value Commitment	Investment in Training and Development	Broad Task Design and Teamwork
Effective Voice for HR in Strategy Making and Governance	Contingent Compensation that Reinforces Cooperation, Participation, and Contribution	Employee Involvement in Problem Solving
		Climate of Cooperation and Trust

not translate into a universal set of "best practices," but rather stand as broad guidelines to be implemented in ways that conform to particular cultural or organizational realities. Further, much work remains to be done to (a) test the validity of these principles, (b) describe and analyze the different practices used to meet these principles, and (c) assess the interrelationships among the principles, practices, and important societal, organizational, and individual outcomes in different settings.

Table 13.1 organizes the principles according to the three-tiered institutional framework presented in Kochan et al. (1986). At the highest level of the firm, first it is essential that business strategies not be built around low costs, and especially not around low wages, salaries, and benefit levels, but rather around such sources of competitive advantage as affordable quality, innovation, flexibility, speed, and customer service (Carnavale, 1991). Second, key decision makers must be guided by a set of values and traditions—often referred to as organizational culture—that views employees as valued stakeholders in the organization, not as mere cogs in the machine. Within any given business strategy and strategic context, top managers have significant discretion in human resource matters, and values and traditions often dictate how, and how wisely, this discretion is used. Finally, at the strategy and policy-making level it is necessary that there be one or more mechanisms for giving voice to employee and human resource interests in strategy formulation and organizational governance processes. One possibility is the use of planning mechanisms to assure that human resource issues receive just due in the formulation of business strategies (Dyer, 1983; Schuler & Jackson, 1987). In other contexts informal labor-management information sharing and consultation might be used. In still others it might be more formal forms of worker representation in corporate governance structures (e.g., labor leaders on the board of directors, works councils).

Moving down to the human resource policy level, we suggest three additional principles that are important for achieving comparative advantage from human resources. First, staffing policies must be designed and managed in such a way that they reinforce the principle of employment security, and thus promote the commitment, flexibility, and loyalty of employees. This does not imply guarantees of lifetime employment, but it does imply that the first instinct, in good times and bad, be to build and protect the firm's investment in human resources, rather than to indiscriminately add or cut people as knee-jerk responses to short-term fluctuations in business conditions (Dyer, Foltman, & Milkovich, 1985). Closely related is the matter of training and development. Clearly, firms that seek competitive advantage through human resources must make the necessary investments to ensure that their work force has the appropriate skills and training not only to meet short-term job requirements, but also to anticipate changing job requirements over time. That is, they—and their employees—must be prepared to adopt the concept of lifelong learning.

The third critical principle at the human resource policy level concerns compensation. Basic compensation levels must be adequate to attract and retain a committed, cooperative, and involved work force, and the compensation structure must be seen as internally equitable by employees at various levels in different functions. Over and above competitive basic compensation levels and structures would be variable, or contingent, compensations schemes (e.g., bonus plans) designed to reinforce desired forms of quality, flexibility, and the like, as well as to provide the firm a means of controlling labor costs in tough times without reverting to layoffs.

Finally, we move to the level of day-to-day interactions of employees with their environment, supervision, and jobs. Here we see several principles as critical. Clearly, in selection high standards must be set regarding the level of skill, training, and educational preparation required of new recruits. The ability to learn and the willingness to continue to learn over the course of one's career become extremely important personal attributes for employees in mutual commitment firms. Second, the education and skills preparation of employees must be fully utilized on the job. This requires job and career structures that eschew narrow, Tayloristic job assignments in favor of flexible work organization that features expanded jobs and the free-flowing movement of employees across tasks and functional boundaries.

A third principle operant at the workplace level deals with opportunities for employees and/or their representatives to engage in problem solving and decision making in matters that involve their jobs and the conditions surrounding their jobs, what Lawler (1988) refers to as job involvement. The fourth and final workplace principle relates to the quality of relationships between employees, their representatives, and managers. A high conflict/low trust relationship (Fox, 1974) is seen as incompatible with the task of building and maintaining mutual commitment. This does not mean that all conflicts between employees and employers wither away. Indeed, we continue to assume that conflicting interests are a natural part of the employment relationship, but that these conflicts cannot be so all-encompassing that they push out the potential for effective problem solving and negotiations. Instead, they must be resolved efficiently and in a fashion that maintains the parties' commitment and capacities for pursuing joint gains.

Obviously, the above set of principles constitutes a caricature of actual organizations. No organization is expected to meet all of these principles perfectly, or through the same set of practices. Nonetheless, in the broadest sense it is postulated that when these principles are properly operationalized, they will come together in the form of an integrated system that, other things equal, will produce globally competitive business results as well as globally competitive standards of living for employees.

The preceding principles were presented as if each firm has total discretion over the choice of its human resource strategies, and as if each firm's choice is independent of the strategies followed by other firms. But neither of these is accurate. External factors, particularly the role of the trade unions, the state (government policy), and in some countries, industry associations, all influence and/or constrain the range of choices open to decision makers. Moreover, individual firms are heavily influenced by the strategies followed by others in their product and labor markets, supplier and customer networks, and industries. Thus, a critical factor is the rate and depth at which the concepts underlying these principles are diffused across different institutions and institutional decision makers, as well as across various firms and industries.

Extent of Diffusion
of Mutual Commitment Principles

Unfortunately, no single database currently exists that allows us to estimate precisely how widespread the principles reviewed above are in U.S. organizations today. It is probably fair to say that very few organizations have yet embraced the full set of principles in a coherent fashion. But clearly, the past decade has been a time of great experimentation with various of these principles, to the point that it is probably fair to say that most large firms, and perhaps even a majority of relatively small firms, have experimented with one or more of them at one time or another.

Supportive Competitive Strategies

We believe that one of the most powerful determinants and reinforcing forces for a mutual commitment human resources strategy lies in the nature of competitive business strategies. Clearly, many U.S. firms recognize this as well. In some ways, however, large U.S. firms suffer from the legacies of their prior successes in taking advantage of the vast size of the U.S. markets. For this reason, they have experienced more difficulty adapting to export markets, and the flexible production and differentiated competitive strategies needed to support mutual commitment human resource strategies (Carnavale, 1991; Piore & Sabel, 1984).

In the clothing industry, for example, despite the obvious difficulty of competing with imports from low-wage countries, American manufacturers and unions have made only limited progress in abandoning their traditional individual piecework and related mass production strategies, in favor of practices that would give them advantages in time to market and quick response to changing customer preferences (National Clothing Industry Labor Management Committee, 1991). As a result imports are taking a greater share of the market, both at the low price points, where mass production continues to dominate, and at the high price points, where styling, fashion, and variability in tastes matter most.

In the U.S. airline industry, the low-cost strategies of Continental and Eastern Airlines served to limit the success of the high growth and service differentiation strategies of firms such as American and Delta Airlines, in the first decade following industry deregulation (Kochan & McKersie, 1991). Thus, while low-cost strategies are difficult to sustain over the long run, especially when faced with competition from abroad, a significant number of American firms continue to give priority to this strategy, and thereby slow the pace of innovations in human resource practices.

Managerial Values
and Organizational Culture

As noted earlier, we continue to see top executive and line management support as a necessary condition for introducing and sustaining the types of human resource strategies described in Table 13.1. Yet there is little in the history of American management, or in the behavior of American management in the 1980s, to suggest that management alone, left to its own devices, will produce the transformations in organizational practices needed to sustain and diffuse the delineated human resource principles. While some, perhaps even many, top executives share supportive values, they are buffeted

by equally strong countervailing pressures that call for quick action taken to
bolster the short-term interests of major shareholders.

Consider, for example, the following description of the dominant managerial strategies of the 1980s, offered by the top human resource executive
at General Electric, one of the firms often cited as symbolizing exemplary
management practices (Doyle, 1989):

> Economic power in the Eighties—the power to launch and sustain the dynamic
> processes of restructuring and globalization—has been concentrated especially
> in the hands of the larger companies, along with the financiers and raiders who
> alternatively support or attack them. If the Eighties was a new Age of the
> Entrepreneur—and small business did in fact account for most of the new job
> creation in the United States—it was Corporate America that accounted for
> most of the economic disruption and competitive improvement; it took out
> people, layers and costs while rearranging portfolios and switching industries.
> . . . Across the decade in the U.S. alone, there was over a trillion dollars of
> merger and acquisition and LBO activity. Ten million manufacturing jobs
> were eliminated or shifted to the growing service sector. Deals were cut and
> alliances forged around America and around the world.
>
> From where the shots were called was well-known. Restructuring and glo-
> balization did not emerge from employee suggestion boxes; they erupted from
> executive suites . . .
>
> So competitive rigor—imposed by companies in their employer roles and
> demonstrated by their restructuring and globalizing moves—was widely accepted
> because its rationale was widely understood. Given this climate—along with a
> political environment of relative deregulation—companies in the Eighties could
> focus more on portfolios than on people; fire more than hire; invest more in
> machines than in skills.
>
> The obvious reality of tough competitive facts inspired fear in employees and
> gave employers the power to act. Shuttered factories and fired neighbors is re-
> structuring without subtlety: People could see the damage and feel the pain.

This, then, is the perhaps the dominant political environment of corporate
decision making and governance that must be taken into account in building
theoretical and action models in the human resource management arena.

Human Resources
in Business Strategy Formulation

Clearly, very few if any inroads have been made into top-level business
strategy formulation by either informal or formal forms of employee representation; the European experience remains distinctively European (Kochan
et al., 1986). Some progress has been made in bringing human resource

adjustment is often a function of the relative power and pressures exerted by shareholders, or of takeover threats. In this view, support for human resource initiatives involves a contest not only among functional units within the firm (e.g., human resources and finance), but also among the interests of employees, shareholders, and other stakeholders.

Purcell (1989) has noted that the trend toward divisional or profit center ("M-Form") organizational structures also serves as a constraint on the elevation of human resources to levels of strategic importance. In these structures human resource decisions tend to be decentralized to the divisional level. This reduces the likely effects of overall corporate value systems and policies, and increases the probability that decision horizons will be short-term.

Two recent international studies reinforce the importance of developing models that extend beyond the boundaries of individual firms. Both Walton (1987) and Cole (1989) stress the importance of national and industry-level infrastructures for supporting the diffusion of innovations in human resource practices across national economies. And both cite the lack of such infrastructures as a reason why the United States lags in this respect.

Thus, a stronger model of change, which considers internal political and external institutional and policy variables, is required if we are to understand and effectively promote the diffusion of human resource innovations across the American economy. While we do not pretend to have a well-developed and tested model in hand at this point, we offer the following as key propositions for testing in the interest of developing such a model:

Proposition 1: The capacity of any individual firm to initiate and sustain human resource innovations is constrained by the extent to which these innovations are similarly adapted by other firms in its product and labor markets, and customer and supplier networks.

The nub of this proposition is that no firm can transform its human resource practices alone. Human resource innovations are likely to suffer from what is called a "market failures" problem (Levine & Tyson, 1990). That is, while all firms and the macro economy would be better off if all firms invested in human resource innovations, any particular firm will fail to capture the benefits of such investments if others fail to follow suit. This is most clearly seen in the area of investments in training. Leading firms, such as Motorola, IBM, Ford, and General Motors, that invest a great deal in training and development run the risk of losing these investments to turnover, because their employees can attract a wage premium from firms that prefer to skim the labor market. This, in turn, reduces their incentives to invest below the level that would prevail if all firms were developing their own internal labor markets.

The importance of suppliers and customers participating in human resource innovations can clearly be seen in the context of total quality management efforts. Final assemblers can realize the full payoff of such efforts only if their suppliers meet corresponding quality standards. Thus, it is not surprising that such companies, and particularly Japanese plants operating in the United States, have demanded that their suppliers develop parallel quality improvement programs in order to become or remain a preferred supplier. Obviously, the reverse logic applies to customers. In one study of auto suppliers, for example, Gillett (1992) found that the extent of innovations in internal management systems varied directly with the expectations of the firms' customers. Change was quickest in coming and most far-reaching among those supplying Japanese customers, who not only demanded them but also facilitated their implementation. It was slowest and least extensive among those supplying divisions of American firms that were themselves less committed to similar innovations.

While a number of leading firms are now demanding higher quality from their suppliers, or are being required to provide it to their customers, so far their reach has been rather limited and narrowly focused. The general weakness of industry associations in the United States, along with the reluctance of firms to intervene in the human resource and labor-management relations affairs of their suppliers and customers, suggests that this avenue of change will have perhaps an important but limited impact. This, however, is a promising avenue for empirical research. It will be interesting to see, for example, if the pressures on suppliers, and of customers, produces a sustained and broad commitment to total quality, and whether this will carry over into areas of human resource management that face less direct, market-driven, across-firm pressure.

Proposition 2: Top and line management commitment is a desirable, but unlikely and generally insufficient condition for transforming human resource practices.

Virtually every article written on human resource innovations contains the obligatory final paragraph asserting the necessity for top management support for successful implementation. Yet, as previously noted, these managers are under many competing pressures from inside and outside the firm, and there is no reason to believe that employee and human resource considerations will tend to prevail in their strategic decision making and day-to-day actions. While some chief executives, particularly the founders of such major companies as Polaroid, IBM, Digital Equipment, and Hewlett-Packard, are well known for values that have long supported human resource innovations, such is not the case in most U.S. firms, where less visionary CEOs have risen through the ranks of finance, marketing, manufacturing, or law, with little or no formal exposure to the human resource function or need to demonstrate human resource management skills.

U.S. firms tend to promote and transfer managers rapidly, which also limits the power of managerial values as a driver of human resource innovations. Such rapid movement provides little incentive or opportunity for managers to develop the personal trust and commitment necessary to support such innovations. Under such circumstances, managers are likely to view investments in human resources as short-term costs that will at best produce payoffs for their successors. A study of innovations at a number of Chrysler plants found that the average tenure of a plant manager was less than 2 years, and each time the manager turned over, the process of change was noticeably slowed (Lovell et al., 1991).

The vast majority of top American executives believe that unions are unnecessary and undesirable in their firms (but perhaps not in the broader society). This value is often translated into a high priority for union avoidance and/or containment. This, of course, limits the options for human resource professionals within such firms since they must be careful to try to achieve desired innovations without the active involvement of union officials or, if unorganized, to introduce innovations in ways that avoid creating the collective equivalent of a union.

In brief, the values of top executives and line managers are an important source of support that needs to be garnered. But reliance on a strategy of expecting these values to develop naturally is likely to continue to create islands of innovation that do not diffuse or that are not sustained. Thus, legal, structural, or personal bases of power that elevate the influence of employee and human resource policy interests will need to supplement and reinforce the values and commitment of top executives and line managers.

Proposition 3: Human resource innovations require a coalitional, multiple-stakeholder change model.

If human resource professionals are in a relatively weak position in managerial hierarchies, and their more powerful line managers and top executives are only sporadic allies in the innovation process, a broader base of support and power will be needed to sustain innovations. The lessons of the historical models cited above suggest that these broader stakeholders include government regulatory agencies, employee and/or labor union representatives, and industry and/or professional associations. Historically, most democratic societies have relied on the pressure of unions to discipline and motivate management to upgrade human resource standards and practices. Continued decline in labor union membership in the United States not only weakens this potential source of pressure, but also creates a cycle of mistrust and adversarial tensions that limits the capacity of union leaders to work cooperatively with management on innovative programs. Union leaders instead come to feel threatened and, in turn, define their primary challenge as a fight for survival and legitimacy. Thus, a cycle of low trust and high conflict gets perpetuated in a way that drives out opportunities for jointly sponsored innovative activities. Reversing this cycle would go a long way toward the diffusion of the mutual commitment principles noted above.

Similarly, to subvert the "market failures" effect noted above, government policymakers will also need to be enlisted as part of a coalition supporting human resource innovations. This, in turn, requires a significant shift in the behavior, and perhaps the mindset, of human resource management professionals, who generally endorse voluntary industry efforts over government policies that would require or mandate innovative practices. This commitment to voluntarism is rooted both in an ideological predisposition to protect the prerogatives and autonomy of individual firms and in a recognition of the enormous diversity of the American economy. Yet herein lies a paradox. As long as these values and considerations dominate the politics of human resource management professionals, the diffusion, sustainability, and impact of the very principles they espouse is likely to remain quite limited.

Proposition 4: Human resource professionals need to be open to learning from international sources. Transferring innovations across national borders and organizational boundaries offers the best opportunities for achieving broad, non-incremental change in human resource practices.

One important lesson brought home forcefully by Japanese direct investment in the United States is that American managers perhaps have more to learn about human resource management from foreign competitors than they have to offer. The U.S. auto industry is perhaps the most visible example of this. Since the mid-1980s the most productive and highest quality auto manufacturing plants in the United States have been those that are Japanese-owned and -managed (Krafcik, 1988). The New United Motors Manufacturing Inc. (NUMMI) facility jointly owned by General Motors and Toyota, but managed by the latter, has received the most attention because it achieved benchmark levels of productivity and quality with an American work force and union, and with less technological investment than exists in most American-owned and -managed plants in the United States. The dominant lesson from this case is that there is much value in a holistic approach to human resource management that is integrated with the dominant production system, and that emphasizes the mutual commitment principles previously noted (Shimada & MacDuffie, 1986).

Indeed, the human resource approaches introduced in NUMMI and other Japanese firms represent fundamental changes that cut across all three levels of the framework introduced in Table 13.1. In some instances U.S. auto companies are attempting to achieve similar systemic changes in their facilities and in new organizations, such as GM's Saturn Division. Thus, the visible presence and high level of performance, achieved with a fundamentally different human resource management system than existed in comparable American facilities, has been an extremely powerful spur to transforming practices across this industry.

The lessons offered to the United States by other countries are not limited to Japan. Recently, policymakers and academics (and an increasing number of union leaders) have become interested in the German apprenticeship and training system, as well as German-style works councils. Because, however, these institutions require greater government and joint labor-business-government interaction and consensus, they have received only limited attention and support to date from the general business community and human resource managers and professionals.

Proposition 5: Documenting the effects of human resource polices on economic outcomes of interest to managers and employees is critical to sustaining support for these innovations. Learning networks that involve all the diverse stakeholders with an interest in these innovations can then speed the transfer, acceptance, and use of this knowledge in other settings.

NUMMI came to serve as such an important spur to innovation in the automobile industry because word of its economic performance levels spread so quickly. More recently, MacDuffie and Krafcik (1989) have shown that the positive performance effects of the NUMMI approach generalize to other facilities as well. As a result, the virtues of this approach are becoming even more widely accepted throughout the world auto industry. Unfortunately, this is all too rare an example. Few human resource practices or interrelated systems of practices are evaluated in as systematic and convincing a fashion as has been the case in the auto industry.

This approach was possible because the industry's major stakeholders accepted standard performance benchmarks (hours per car for productivity, and number of defects per car and/or number of customer complaints per car for quality) and then cooperated with university researchers to collect, analyze, and publish the results of across-plant and across-firm comparisons (without revealing the identity of individual plants or firms). This type of learning network stands as a model of what is needed to accelerate the process of knowledge generation and innovation diffusion.

Summary and Conclusion

In summary, we believe that the type of change model that is necessary to support diffusion of human resource innovations starts with a clear model of the generic principles or requirements that must be met; casts its vision internationally to discover world-class benchmarks; engages a broad coalition of human resource and labor advocates, both within and outside the firm, in a network that works together to promote and diffuse innovations; and then provides the analytic data required to evaluate and disseminate the economic effects of the innovations. With the strength of this broad base of support and harder evidence for the effects of the innovations, informed government representatives can then contribute by providing the national or macro-level infrastructure and policies needed to go from micro-firm specific islands of innovation to changes of sufficient scope and magnitude to make a difference in national competitiveness and standards of living. If this is done, the field of human resource management will have achieved its own transformation from the traditional image of personnel administration to a truly strategic orientation and contribution. If events fail to move in these directions, on the other hand, the voices of human resource managers and professionals in many firms are destined to remained buried deep within the managerial hierarchy, pleading for, but only sporadically receiving, the support and commitment of their more powerful managerial brethren.

Implications for Research

Obviously, this view requires a substantial investment in high-quality research to identify promising human resource innovations, and to evaluate their effects on organizational and individual outcomes of interest to multiple stakeholders. Presupposed is a broadened perspective of the relevant stakeholders to include not only top managers (and maybe stockholders), but also various types of employees, labor leaders, and purveyors of public policies. Also presupposed is a multinational—or global—view, as well as a corresponding willingness to learn from the lessons of other countries. All this may represent a particularly radical departure for U.S. scholars.

Certainly, there is no assumption here that prevailing sentiments, extolling the virtues of various forms of human resource innovations, and the new-found influence of today's human resource managers, represent either reality or inevitability. To achieve global competitiveness and satisfactory standards of living will require broadened perspectives of human resource systems, the development of more realistic models of organizational change, and a mountain of convincing evidence. Absent these, in the long run the prevailing rhetoric cannot help but fall on deaf ears.

References

Alper, W. S., Pfau, B., & Sirota, D. (1985, September). The 1985 national survey of employee attitudes executive report. Sponsored by *Business Week* and Sirota and Alper Associates.

Baron, J. N., Dobbin, F. R., & Jennings, P. D. (1986). War and peace: The evolution of modern personnel administration in U.S. industry. *American Journal of Sociology, 92*, 350-384.

Buller, P. F. (1988, Autumn). Successful partnerships: HR and strategic planning at eight top firms. *Organizational Dynamics*, 27-43.

Burack, E. (1986, Summer). Corporate business and human resource planning practices: Strategic issues and concerns. *Organizational Dynamics*, 73-86.

Carnavale, A. P. (1991). *America and the new economy*. Washington, DC: The American Society for Training and Development.

Cole, R. E. (1989). *Strategies for learning*. Berkeley: University of California Press.

Conference Board, The. (1990). *Variable pay: New performance rewards* (Bulletin No. 246).

Craft, J. A. (1988). Human resource planning and strategy. In L. Dyer (Ed.), *Human resource management: Evolving roles and responsibilities* (pp. 47-87). Washington, DC: Bureau of National Affairs Books.

Cyert, R. M., & Mowery, D. C. (Eds). (1986). *Technology and employment*. Washington, DC: National Academy Press.

Dertouzos, M., Solow, R., & Lester, R. (1989). *Made in America: Regaining the competitive edge*. Cambridge: MIT Press.

Douglas, P. (1919, July). Plant administration of labor. *Journal of Political Economy, 27*, 544-560.

Doyle, F. P. (1989, September 23). *The global human resource challenge for the nineties*. Paper delivered to the World Management Congress, New York.

Drago, R. (1988). Quality circle survival: An explanatory analysis. *Industrial Relations*.

Dyer, L. (1983). Bringing human resources into the strategy formulation process. *Human Resource Management, 22*(3), 257-271.

Dyer, L., Foltman, F., & Milkovich, G. (1985). Contemporary employment stabilization practices. In T. A. Kochan & T. A. Barocci, *Human resource management and industrial relations* (pp. 196-201). Boston: Little, Brown.

Dyer, L., & Holder, G. (1988). A strategic perspective on human resource management. In L. Dyer (Ed.), *Human resource management: Evolving roles and responsibilities* (pp. 1-35). Washington, DC: Bureau of National Affairs Books.

Fisher, A. B. (1991, November 18). Morale crisis. *Fortune*, pp. 70-82.

Foulkes, F., & Whitman, A. (1985, July-August). Marketing strategies to maintain full employment. *Harvard Business Review*, 4-7.

Fox, A. (1974). *Beyond contract: Trust and authority relations in industry*. London: MacMillan.

Gillett, F. (1992). *Supplier-customer relationships: Case studies in the auto parts industry*. Master's thesis, MIT.

Gordon, J. (1990, March). Who killed corporate loyalty. *Training*, 25-32.

Hay Group, The. (1991). 1991-92 Hay employee attitudes study. Author.

Jacoby, S. (1985). *Employing bureaucracies*. New York: Columbia University Press.

Kanter, D., & Mirvis, P. (1989). *The cynical Americans: Living and working in an age of discontent and disillusion*. San Francisco: Jossey-Bass.

Kochan, T. A., & Cappelli, P. (1983). The transformation of the industrial relations and personnel function. In P. Osterman (Ed.), *Internal labor markets*. Cambridge: MIT Press.

Kochan, T. A., & Dyer, L. (1976) A model of organizational change in the context of union-management relations. *Journal of Applied Behavioral Science, 12*, 58-78.

Kochan, T. A., Katz, H. C., & McKersie, R. B. (1986). *The transformation of American industrial relations*. New York: Basic Books.

Kochan, T. A., & McKersie, R. B. (1991). Human resources, organizational governance, and public policy: Lessons from a decade of experimentation. In T. A. Kochan & M. Useem (Eds.), *Transforming organizations*. New York: Oxford University Press.

Kochan, T. A., & Osterman, P. (1991). *Human resource development and utilization: Is there too little in the U.S.?* Paper prepared for the Time Horizons Project of the Council on Competitiveness, MIT.

Kochan, T. A., Osterman, P., & MacDuffie, J. P. (1988, Fall). Employment security at DEC: Sustaining values amid environmental change. *Human Resource Management Journal.*

Krafcik, J. F. (1988). World class manufacturing: An international comparison of automobile assembly plant performance. *Sloan Management Review, 30,* 41-52.

Lawler, E. E., III. (1986). *High involvement management.* San Francisco: Jossey-Bass.

Lawler, E. E., III. (1988). Choosing an involvement strategy. *The Academy of Management Executive, 2*(3), 197-204.

Lawler, E. E., & Mohrman, S. A. (1985). Quality circles after the fad. *Harvard Business Week, 63,* 65-71.

Levine, D. I., & Tyson, L. D. (1990). Participation, productivity, and the firm's environment. In A. S. Blinder (Ed.), *Paying for productivity* (pp. 183-236). Washington, DC: Brookings Institution.

Lovell, M., McKassie, R. B., Kochan, T. A., MacDuffie, J. P., Hunter, L., & Goldberg, S. (1991). *Chrysler and the UAW: Modern operating agreements.* Report to the U.S. Department of Labor, Bureau of Labor Management Relations and Cooperative Programs, Washington, DC.

MacDuffie, J. P., & Kochan, T. A. (1991, August). *Determinants of training: A cross-national comparison in the auto industry.* Paper presented at the 1991 meeting of the Academy of Management.

MacDuffie, J. P., & Krafcik, J. F. (1989, August 16). *Flexible production systems and manufacturing performance: The role of human resources and technology.* Paper delivered at Annual Meeting of the Academy of Management, Washington, DC.

Marshall, R. (1987). *Unheard voices.* New York: Basic Books.

National Clothing Industry Labor Management Committee. (1991). *A strategy for innovation.* New York: Author.

Nkomo, S. (1986, August). The theory and practice of HR planning: The gap still remains. *Personnel Administrator,* 71-84.

O'Dell, C. (1987). *People, performance, and pay.* American Productivity Center.

Peters, T. J., & Waterman, R. H., Jr. (1982). *In search of excellence.* New York: Harper & Row.

Pettigrew, A., & Whipp, R. (1991). *Managing change for strategic success.* Oxford: Blackwell.

Piore, M., & Sabel, C. (1984). *The second industrial divide.* New York: Basic Books.

Purcell, J. (1989). The impact of corporate strategy on human resource management. In J. Storey (Ed.), *New perspectives on human resource management* (pp. 67-91). London: Routledge.

Schuler, R. S., & Jackson, S. E. (1987, August). Linking competitive strategies and human resource management practices. *Academy of Management Executive,* 207-219.

Shimada, H., & MacDuffie, J. P. (1986). *Industrial relations and "humanware": Japanese investments in automobile manufacturing in the United States* (Working Paper). Cambridge: MIT, Sloan School of Management.

Slichter, S. (1919, December). The management of labor. *Journal of Political Economy, 27,* 813-839.

Thomas, R. J. (1992). *What machines can't do: Organizational politics and technological change.* Berkeley: University of California Press.

Walton, R. E. (1980). Establishing and maintaining high commitment work systems. In Kimberly & Miles (Eds.), *The organizational life cycle.* San Francisco: Jossey-Bass.

Walton, R. E. (1985). Toward a strategy of eliciting employee commitment based on policies of mutuality. In R. E. Walton & P. R. Lawrence (Eds.), *HRM trends & challenges* (pp. 35-65). Boston: Harvard Business School Press.

Walton, R. E. (1987). *Innovating to compete.* San Francisco: Jossey-Bass.

14 \ The Industrial Relations of Skills Formation

JOHN MATHEWS

Models of the industrial relations process are generally neutral as to the content of the issues dealt with in negotiations. The influential framework introduced by Kochan, Katz and McKersie (1986), for example, with its trio of strategic, sectoral, and enterprise levels for negotiations, provides a valuable template for the analysis of industrial relations processes and institutions, but it stops short of specifying the dominant topics of negotiations at the differing levels. Similarly, the patterns of industrial relations processes developed by Purcell (1981) make useful distinctions between "adaptive cooperation," "antagonistic constitutionalism," and "cooperative constitutionalism," for example, but do not seek in any general way to tie these categories to specific enterprise or trans-enterprise issues or link them with their underlying production systems.

In this chapter I shall be concerned with investigating the consequences for industrial relations theory and practice, of the emergence of a new province of negotiations connected with workers' skill formation, and the application and deployment of skill in the production process. Such a province extends the traditional domain of industrial relations, which arguably has been concerned with the negotiation of wages and immediate conditions of employment, or with matters that can be subsumed under the heading of "labor costs." Costs and control were the twin issues dominating such negotiations through most of the postwar period.

The industrial relations of skill denotes a different kind of negotiated relationship between the parties. It is concerned with the collective aspects of the processes, standards, and mechanisms of skills formation in the enterprise, paying particular attention to due process and to the public interests involved in standardizing skills and competency-based job classifications across different enterprises, as well as with the interface between enterprise skills formation processes and the public education and training systems. The industrial relations of skill covers such matters as the development through negotiation of the competency standards built into job descriptions, of the performance criteria attached to them, of the assessment procedures required to determine whether workers have achieved a given level of competence, of the mechanisms that provide workers with a pathway to move from one classification to another, and subsequently, to pursue a career within the same firm or within the industry. These are matters that are appropriate to enterprise-level negotiation.

More generally, the industrial relations of skill denotes negotiations at industry and sector level over the public recognition of industry skill standards, and the portability of qualifications from one enterprise to another. There is thus a significant social or public dimension to the industrial relations of skill, arising from the concern of labor movements and governments to maintain wide social access to skills formation pathways as a means of combating the incipient polarization tendencies that unregulated enterprise-level skills formation might be expected, and is observed, to promote.[1]

The arguments to be pursued in this chapter are fourfold. First, we shall investigate the links between the emergence of skills formation as a "new province" of industrial relations, and the rise of new production systems, which seek competitive advantage not through cost minimization and repetitive standardized production, but through promotion of quality and maximization of value addition. It will be argued that skill occupies a quite different significance in the latter production system, bringing it to the center of industrial relations concerns. Second, the categories of skill formation will be introduced and discussed, and the relations between them exemplified with a model of the skills formation process. This model utilizes the notions of an abstract "learning space" and a "training space," and it can be used to discuss the major issues arising in the negotiation of skills issues; in particular it allows us to develop an agenda for the industrial relations of skill, through alignment of the learning and training spaces at the enterprise and sector levels. Finally, we shall draw some implications of this analysis for the public dimensions of the skills formation process, seeking to account for its bias toward enterprise negotiation, and toward the promotion of cooperative frameworks within which common interests can be identified and pursued.

Skills and the New Production Systems

It is by now relatively uncontroversial to claim that a new production system is emerging in OECD countries, based on high quality, quick response, and high value-added product strategies. It stands in contrast with the standardized low value-added production system, based on mass production, that has dominated the twentieth century until the most recent decade. The lineaments of the new production system have been described by a number of recent authors, such as the MIT Commission on Industrial Productivity and its text, *Made in America* (Dertouzos, Solow, & Lester, 1989); the International Motor Vehicle Program, also based at MIT, and its text, *The Machine that Changed the World* (Womack et al., 1990), which introduced the notion of the "lean production system" as a generalization of the Toyota organizational innovations; the German industrial sociologists Kern and Schumann (1984), with their notion of the "new production concepts"; and the U.S. scholars Piore and Sabel (1984), who introduced the notion of "flexible specialization" in their influential text, *The Second Industrial Divide.*[2]

For the purposes of this chapter, we may accept the arguments advanced by the MIT Commission on Industrial Productivity. The Commission's analysis was centered on the role of mass production in shaping the prevailing concepts of productivity and efficiency, and in determining the prevailing patterns of industrial relations. As the MIT Commission noted, "The great success of the American economy in the twentieth century was a system of mass production of standard products for a large domestic market" (Dertouzos et al., 1989, p. 47). Competitive advantage lay with simple, low value-added products that could be produced at low cost in large numbers for undifferentiated mass markets. This system was replicated, with varying national adjustments, in virtually all OECD countries during the postwar period. It called for narrow jobs and the pursuit of efficiency through division of labor; for detail work to be regulated by machine and by close, untrusting supervision; for skills to be appropriated by Organization and Methods engineering departments, and to be confined to narrow trades, protected by demarcation and the front-end training model of apprenticeship. Deskilling was pursued as a conscious strategy, in order to cheapen labor and hence production; technological innovation was pursued to further deskill and eliminate the labor factor in the production process.

The paradigm shift in manufacturing, captured in the phrase "new production concepts," owes its origins to market segmentation and innovation on the demand side, and to the development of new work organization systems, such as teamwork and programmable flexible manufacturing and assembly systems, on the supply side. In the realm of complex value-added goods and services, these organizational innovations have given firms adopting them a competitive edge over firms that are still wedded to large-scale mass production as their strategy.[3]

The elements of the new production system are likewise relatively uncontroversial. First, production (of goods or services) is demand-driven, rather than driven by the accumulation of stocks or by the demands of production. This represents a fundamental shift, which appears in a new focus on the customer and on quick response as a generalized strategy. Second, competitive strategy is based on product and process innovation rather than cost minimization and repetitive production. Such a strategy calls for flexibility of process and adaptation of employees to different tasks, achieved through teamwork and multiskilling, and complemented by technological innovations such as programmable flexible manufacturing systems and flexible service cells. Third, it calls for devolution of responsibility, autonomy, and authority, which is best expressed through self-managing teams, and in any case through broadened job descriptions and elimination of middle levels of supervision. This broadening of tasks is achieved through the integration of functions that were previously fragmented, and the building in of functions (such as quality assurance) that were previously functionally distinct. Flexibility demands new management techniques such as JIT and TQM. Finally, the system's dependence on worker commitment and adaptability needs to be reflected in more cooperative industrial relations and recognition of workers' contributions, for example, through skills- and performance-based pay.

In both manufacturing and services, the new production systems require a linkage between work and skill that was quite foreign to the formerly dominant mass production system. This has been documented most strikingly in industries where the previous approach has led firms to the brink of bankruptcy, and they have saved themselves only by adopting a radically different approach to skills formation, as in banking and metalworking.[4]

In the OECD countries and in various sectors, the former job classification systems that divided processes into narrow tasks, and linked jobs exclusively with machines, are being restructured to provide an explicit link with skill, a flexibility in use, and a notion of career path through the upward progression by workers as they acquire skills and experience. In advanced firms this process was accomplished in the late 1970s or 1980s, resulting in broad job definitions succeeding each other in a skills and payments progression. In later arrivals, such as Australia, the same process is being gone through, but at a sectoral level rather than at the level of individual enterprises; this is the process known in Australia as award restructuring (Curtain & Mathews, 1990).

Workers in the new production systems are expected by firms to make contributions to productivity enhancement through the understanding of the big picture, that is, how each operation is shaped by context, and how contingencies can be accommodated within the overall process. This requires a novel approach to skill. In place of the narrow functionally specific skills of the formerly dominant mass production system, what are needed are generic and adaptive skills, of the kind that are generally deemed to be knowledge.[5]

The major reports cited above are in agreement that the competitive advantage enjoyed by firms employing the new production systems, lies in their functional flexibility and adaptability conferred by multifunctional, polyvalent, multiskilled workers. It is this insertion of skill into the productive process, in contrast to the Taylorist approach that was concerned with taking skill out of it, that drives the new industrial relations of skill.

A Model of Skills Formation

The notion of skills formation is broader than the traditional notion of training (Ford, 1988; Mathews, 1989a). Skills formation has an active component to it; it acknowledges that the process of knowledge acquisition occurs over time and builds on experience, in contrast with the "empty vessel" notion that underlies training and retraining. The categories of skill formation are competence, performance criteria, and elements that can be built up in modular fashion, as a wall can be built up from bricks. To be utilized, these competences need to be assessed and evaluated against standards.

In this chapter a model of the skills formation process is developed that brings these categories into direct relationship with one another. This approach offers advantages over indirect modeling exercises, such as the extensions of neoclassical economics into human capital theory or multifactor productivity, all of which introduce needless confusion with their reliance on an undefined and (virtually) unmeasurable notion of capital.

The Learning Space

We start with a state space formulation of a learning space.[6] The axes, or state variables, are the competences relevant to any particular industrial agreement (or award, in the Australian terminology). The values of the state variables are the levels of competence attained, these levels corresponding to the levels spelled out in general in the industrial agreement. *Skill* in this model is a point in the space, corresponding to a certain level reached in each of the competences by a particular individual. *Skill enhancement* is a transformation of the space, moving the original skill point to a location that is further from the origin (corresponding to the acquisition of higher levels in certain competences).

If skills acquisition occurs in one dimension only, then this will be termed *upskilling*, or vertical skills acquisition. If it occurs in more than one dimension, it will be referred to as *multiskilling*. If competence is acquired in a dimension where there was no previous level of competence, this will be referred to as *cross-skilling. Deskilling* would be represented by a competence (i.e., a dimension of the skill space) being removed, through a change in organization or technology or both.

Example 1. Steel Industry: In the steel industry in Australia, award restructuring, to accommodate the new production systems, has created three skills streams: for production workers, maintenance staff, and electricians. Six general job classification levels have been created, each succeeding the other in terms of higher levels of skill and responsibility, thereby creating career paths for all categories of worker. Competences relevant to the steel industry, over and above basic literacy and numeracy, are computer awareness/programming, metallurgy, advanced numeracy (e.g., statistical quality control).

We can represent these competences as the three axes of a three-dimensional learning space, with each axis containing six divisions, corresponding to each level reached. (The space in this case is actually a lattice, with $3 \times 6 = 18$ points of intersection.) This is shown in Figure 14.1. A worker will already have a certain skill, chosen arbitrarily in Figure 14.1 as point A. This point represents a skill tally as follows: computer awareness (level 2); metallurgy (level 1); advanced numeracy (level 1). The worker then undergoes training and accumulates experience, so that he or she acquires, for the sake of argument, two further modules of computer awareness (to level 4); three further modules of metallurgy (to level 4); two further modules of SQC (to level 3). This process of skills acquisition, or skills enhancement, takes the worker to point B, corresponding to levels 4, 4, and 3 on each axis, respectively. Point B is further from the origin than point A, showing that the worker at point B has greater skill than at point B. (This quantum could be measured, depending on the metric chosen for the space.)

Of course, where there are more than three competences it is impossible to show the space graphically. However a single point in the space can still be visualized by setting up an array, with columns the competences, and rows the levels. For the case of the steel example, the array is shown in Figure 14.2. Point A is now represented by the triplet (a1, a2, a3). Point B is the

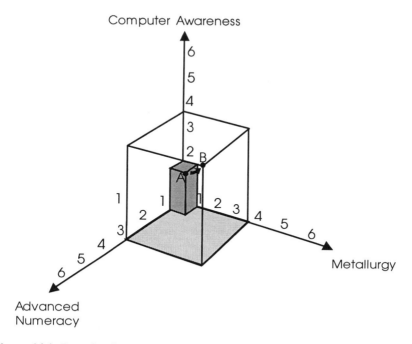

Figure 14.1. Learning Space: Steel Industry

triplet (b1, b2, b3) where b1 is two levels above a1, b2 is three levels above a2, and b3 is two levels above a3—corresponding to the process of skills acquisition given in the example. Representation in the array is not as neat as in a discrete space, but it has to be used to make sense of skills transformations involving more than three competences (which will normally be the case).

The learning space model clarifies several matters immediately. First, it illustrates the link between skills enhancement and wage premiums; it shows how a worker may progress from one level in the restructured job classification system to a higher one—by attaining the appropriate level (through training or experience) in each of the competences defined by the award. Thus the worker in our example, who is at point A, will be in Level 1 of the award, because he or she is at level 1 in two of the competences, namely, metallurgy and advanced numeracy. As an extra level is acquired in each of these competences, the worker can move to level 2 in the award, thus receiving a wage premium. At point B the worker has moved into level 3 of the award—and by acquiring one further increment in advanced numeracy, can move to level 4 in the award.

Levels	Computer Awareness	Metallurgy	Advanced Numeracy
6			
5			
4	b_1	b_2	
3			b_3
2	a_1		
1		a_2	a_3

Figure 14.2. Learning Array: Steel Industry

Second, it clarifies the notion of *assessment*, and in particular, *competency-based assessment*. Assessment is the process through which a worker may demonstrate that he or she has reached a certain level, or standard, of competence. It might be carried out by the employer through challenge tests, or by an educational institution through various assessment procedures, including exams, but also making allowance for experience. Assessment acquires an enhanced significance in the context of new production systems, because it will determine where a worker slots into an award classification, and hence will determine the worker's pay. In our example, the worker is assessed as starting at point A, and is assessed as ending at point B.

Third, it shows why assessment is in general carried out in terms of criteria of competence (criteria-referenced assessment), rather than in terms of one person or group being assessed as superior to another (norm-based assessment), which is the form familiar from educational settings.

The Training Space

In a similar way, we can construct a model of the activities of firms, and of the public education and training system, with regard to competency-based training, in terms of a training space. In this case the axes, or state variables, are the subjects taught, and the values along each axis are the modules, or units, through which the teaching proceeds. There is no time built into this model, as it is assumed that learners complete modules at their own pace.[7]

Points in this space represent entry points and exit points to and from training programs. The exit points should normally carry some kind of *certification*. The entry points should normally carry some form of *credit transfer*, offering students credit for modules and/or courses previously completed. The linking of courses together in a network of credit transfer between exit points and entry points is what we term *articulation*.

Example 2. Vehicle Industry Certificate: The restructuring of the vehicle industry award in Australia involves the development of an industry-wide training qualification, the Vehicle Industry Certificate. This proposed qualification will involve employees in undertaking study in "properly accredited training modules covering core, process and enterprise knowledge" (AIRC, 1989). For the sake of this example, let us name these subjects as:

- core subjects (automotive manufacturing)
- process subjects (assembly, basic maintenance)
- enterprise subjects (enterprise-specific procedures)

Each of these subjects will contain a certain number of modules, which can be displayed along each dimension of the teaching space, as shown in Figure 14.3. (In general there will be different numbers of modules per subject.) The origin represents a common entry point into this teaching space, where no credit is claimed for previous work. Point A (a1, a2, a3) represents an example of another entry point, in this case where credit is offered for previous courses completed or experience obtained on the job, at one automotive company or another. (Credit a1 is given in core subject, credit a2 for process subject, and so on.) Point B represents an exit point, where a qualification is obtained (in this case, the Vehicle Industry Certificate): It is awarded for completion of the specified modules b1, b2, b3 in each of the subjects. Point C represents a further exit point, involving a higher level qualification, that is, further modules completed. Point C might represent, for example, a Vehicle Industry Higher Certificate. The higher certificate would be well articulated with the lower Certificate if the modules in each course are comparable, so that credit for completing the lower certificate can be transferred across to the modules of the higher certificate.

As in the steel example, this vehicle industry case can be represented in array format, to cope with the problem that any more than three dimensions cannot be drawn graphically. The array corresponding to Figure 14.3 is given in Figure 14.4.

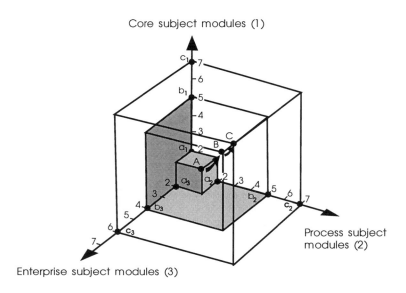

Core subject modules (1)

Process subject
modules (2)

Enterprise subject modules (3)

A (a_1, a_2, a_3) is entry point
B (b_1, b_2, b_3) is exit point corresponding to VIC
C (c_1, c_2, c_3) is exit point corresponding to VIHC, with B as entry point

Figure 14.3. Teaching Space: Vehicle Industry

The training space of the model thus provides us with a convenient means of exhibiting the notions of multiple entry and exit points for training (as opposed to the single entry and exit points, defined by juvenile apprenticeships, in the traditional skills system); of modular training offerings; and of articulation between one set of qualifications and another.

Among OECD countries, Sweden has advanced furthest in placing its public training system on a modular footing. The Swedish National Training Board (AMU) has developed a rationalized system of teaching along purely modular lines. For example, training in welding and sheet metal skills is offered through 32 separate modules, each lasting from 1 to 7 weeks. These are shown in Table 14.1. These modules can then be grouped to form broader qualifications, such as certificates and diplomas.[8]

The incentive for the education and training systems to move to this modular format for delivery of their courses is that it clearly matches up with the developments in skills acquisition associated with the industrial relations of skills formation. Subjects taught in modular format have the potential to

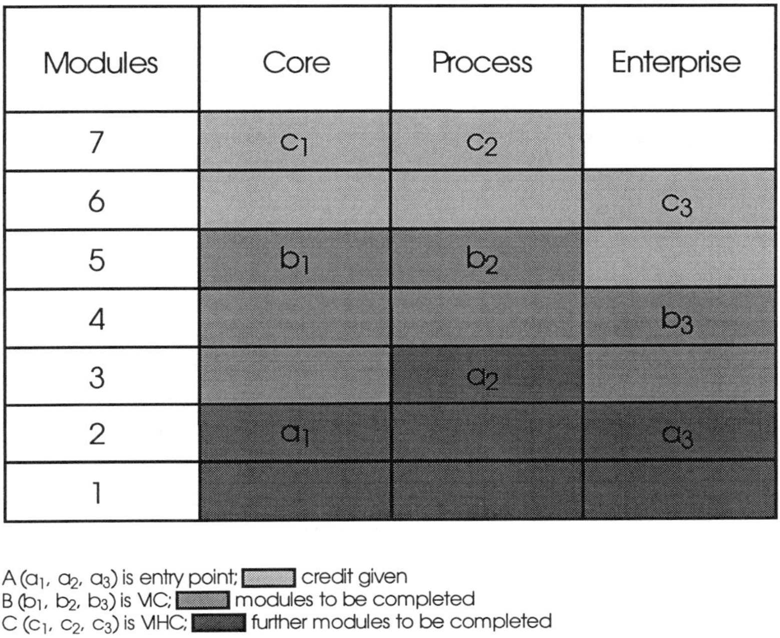

Modules	Core	Process	Enterprise
7	c_1	c_2	
6			c_3
5	b_1	b_2	
4			b_3
3		a_2	
2	a_1		a_3
1			

A (a_1, a_2, a_3) is entry point; ▭ credit given
B (b_1, b_2, b_3) is VIC; �◪ modules to be completed
C (c_1, c_2, c_3) is VHC; ▪ further modules to be completed

Figure 14.4. Teaching Array: Vehicle Industry

marry up with competences acquired on the job in modular progression. This brings us to the third element of the model.

Alignment of the Learning and Training Spaces

At the heart of the industrial relations of skills formation lies the challenge for firms, unions, and public authorities to align the qualifications, offered by the education and training systems, with the competences to be spelled out in restructured awards. In terms of our model, this corresponds to aligning the learning space and the training space so that they become one: Competences in the learning space will correspond with subjects in the training space, both being acquired and delivered in modular format.

Of course the education and training system can structure its course offerings like this only when the industrial relations system has determined the competence structure of the skills-based job classification systems. This

TABLE 14.1 Swedish AMU: Welding and Sheet Metal Modules

Module No.	List of Modules	No. of course weeks
32	Work test, TIG and metal arc welding	2
31	TIG welding of stainless steel pipes (small dimensions)	2
30	Metal arc welding of unalloyed and EHS steel pipes	2
29	Metal arc welding of pipelines. Downward welding	3
28	Welding tests. Oxy-acetylene, TIG and metal arc welding	1
27	Metal arc welding of thin-walled stainless steel pipes (2-3mm)	3
26	TIG and metal arc welding of stainless steel pipes	1
25	Metal arc welding of unalloyed steel pipes	3
24	TIG Welding of unalloyed steel pipes	1
23	TIG welding of stainless steel pipes	1
22	Oxy-acetylene welding of unalloyed and low alloyed pipes	3
21	Oxy-acetylene welding	6
20	Sheet metal work and assembling practice	7
19	Beading and folding	1
18	Circular bending	1
17	Edge pressing	2
16	Edge bending	1
15	Drilling and grinding	1
14	All-round sheet metal machining	2
13	Shearing	2
12	Basic numerical control technique	1
11	Metal arc welding procedure	2
10	Welding practice	3
9	Bending and straightening	1
8	Metal arc welding test	1
7	Metal arc welding in different positions	3
6	Oxy-acetylene and plastic cutting	1
5	MIG and MAG welding	3
4	TIG welding	3
3	Basic metal arc welding	6
2	Basic oxy-acetylene welding cutting and edging	4
1	Basic sheet metal work	4

makes clear where the initiative lies for skills formation in the context of the new production systems.

Example 3. Food Production Skills Formation: A U.K. Food Production course designed in Canada serves as a good example of these ideas in action. On completion, students are expected to be able to perform a range of jobs in the catering business. Each job is specified in terms of its constituent competences.[9]

Each competence has a performance standard attached to it, and a grading structure allowing for six levels of attainment in each competence. Hence

social science and management literature. But they have, quite often, been considered as a more or less obvious appendix of the more general change in the patterns of production. This chapter starts from the assumption that the two phenomena are only partly related. European employers' different policies of personnel management and industrial relations depend to some extent on the technological and organizational choices they make; but institutional factors play an even greater role, in a period in which previous models for action clearly appear inadequate and in which, as a consequence, uncertainty is growing (Streeck, 1987).

If this is so, to identify and explain the major differences in the policies of labor regulation prevailing in European companies is no less important than to stress the common trends. Although the challenges coming from international competition are to a large extent the same, and in spite of the effects produced by the single market, the variability of institutional factors at the national, sectoral, and company levels makes the perspective of a further convergence among the personnel and industrial relations policies of European companies rather unlikely. The cases discussed here serve to illustrate this hypothesis, showing both the trends that can be assumed as general and the differences that cannot be easily overlooked.

Common Trends in European Companies

In the early 1980s it was quite common to predict a major deregulation of the European industrial relations systems. The organizational, market, and political weakening of trade unions, after a decade in which they had enjoyed considerable power, seemed to prelude serious attempts by managers to restore their unilateral authority in the workplaces. The need for greater flexibility to compete in volatile markets was often interpreted as a need to break rules and institutions seen as unbearable constraints on the ability of firms to adjust rapidly. The generalized decline of tripartite concertation and of other attempts to regulate labor-management relations in a wider political context, and the shift of the center of gravity of these relations toward the workplaces, were considered major steps in the deregulation process, one which served precisely the need to restore unilateral authority and to get rid of unnecessary constraints. Finally, the rhetoric of a "free" (deregulated) market, so prominent among the American and British political elites, as well as the early attempts by American companies to develop personnel policies aimed at creating nonunion labor relations, convinced many observers that this was indeed the future for European industry as well.

To the extent that common trends emerged in European industry during the 1980s, however, these have largely pointed to the opposite direction.

Industrial adjustment to the changed economic situation has been mostly carried out not by attacking the unions, but by securing their support. The intensification of international competition, with regard to not only prices but also product quality, has implied for most companies a search for some cooperation by their work force. Human resource management and development have become more crucial, especially for firms adopting post-Fordist patterns of production, but this has generally not taken place to the detriment of industrial relations, as we will see in discussing the companies studied.

To be sure, firms can choose to rely exclusively on hierarchy and power, often accompanied by selective incentives, to achieve a greater degree of labor flexibility and adaptability to change. But, except for a few cases, this seems to have happened only where industrial relations were already very poor; and, even there, our cases show that managers did not force such institutional change as existing power relations would have made possible. Where, on the other hand, industrial relations were fairly developed, managers usually tried to take advantage of them, that is to turn them into a resource.

This search for a greater (than before) cooperation by their work force has led some companies to implement "communication" policies, aimed at increasing workers' identification with their objectives and problems. But again, our cases show, such policies are not generally viewed as an alternative to traditional industrial relations, except when they are directed to professional groups, such as technicians or administrative staff, who are not traditionally part of the trade union constituency. In fact, the greater propensity by the company management to establish direct relationships with their employees is due primarily to the increased importance of human resources, and to the diversification of individual interests and needs. It is the greater importance of workers' concern with quality; the more crucial role played by their skills; as well as the differentiation of their expectations in terms of pay, training, and career; which lead managers to try to involve them more directly in a company-defined horizon of problems and goals. As we will see, in some companies, especially in the Spanish ones, this individualization of work relations may pursue the objective of bypassing the mediating role of the unions as well; but, even in these cases, this is an additional objective, which should not obscure the more general reasons behind the change in managerial attitudes toward the work force.

The range of issues on which managers look for some degree of cooperation and involvement is fairly consistent in all the companies studied. Among the specific aspects of the work relationship that are usually negotiated or dealt with consensually, we find not only pay, but also work shifts, overtime, company welfare programs, and the management of redundancies. Other aspects are instead the object of unilateral decisions in all cases: These are the organization of production, technological innovation, and recruitment. But on many other issues, ranging from training to internal mobility, to incentives, to promotions, there are wide differences among the companies studied.

Another trend that can be observed in all the cases studied is a growing autonomy of the industrial relations actors at the company level. This trend stems partly from the more general process of decentralization of industrial relations, which, in the 1980s, accompanied the redistribution of corporate authority, and which was favored by both management and labor, in some cases limited to the level of the holding while in others extended to the level of individual businesses or profit centers. In addition to this, personnel management functions are growing everywhere, either because they incorporate some training functions or because of the "communication campaigns" mentioned above. Far from confirming the loss of autonomy of industrial relations functions that was expected only a few years ago (Piore & Sabel, 1984), our cases show a process of functional differentiation from the management of production.

Finally, the increase in autonomy of the local actors is helped by the loss of confidence in collective action taking place outside the workplace, which is shown by the minor role played by external trade unions and employers' associations in the management of company-level industrial relations.

Differences in Patterns of Human Resource Management and Industrial Relations

The elements of the work relationship that may be structured according to different rules and practices are many. They range from entry of the work force into the company and departure from it, to pay systems and fringe benefits (including company welfare systems), to job assignment and internal mobility, to the organization of working time, to the recognition and development of skills through career patterns and training schemes. In regulating each of these elements of the work relationship, many European employers have, as we have seen, increasingly tried to secure some consensus from their work force, not only to solve the general problem of industrial order but also, and especially, to improve company performance. However, even when they value such consensus highly, they still have different options available to try to achieve it. Basically, they may offer their workers substantive advantages in the solutions they give to each of these elements; and/or they may to some extent involve workers' representatives in the decision-making process, that is, in the mode of regulation of such elements.

When the re-regulation of specific, individual aspects of the work relationship is the main problem employers are confronted with, it is quite possible that on any such aspect—say, internal mobility—the company management tries to interact with individual workers; while on another—say, the organization of working time—it decides to involve the unions. In the example given, this may be so, for instance, because trade unions share an interest in flexible arrangements as far as the latter case is concerned, while they do not as regards the former. (In fact, unions can either constrain or facilitate change, given their own uncertainty on how to face managerial initiatives, and their declining but still relevant power to oppose them.) In other words, given the plurality of dimensions of the work relationship, the most convenient (to management) way of dealing with change in one dimension may well prove less convenient when another dimension is concerned. In a period of rapid change, especially when the critical problems in the organization of work are faced one by one as they emerge, managers are more interested in finding satisfactory, though possibly inconsistent, solutions, rather than in reaffirming the general principles that guide their style of management.

The roots of some major differences in the patterns of human resource management and industrial relations among European companies can, therefore, be traced to what has been called "the uncertainty of management in the management of uncertainty" (Streeck, 1987), or to the "pragmatic eclecticism," which is likely to prevail in any period of rapid and profound change (Regini, 1991).

The first definition of the current situation sees two basic alternatives for managers in the regulation of work: to stress either contract or status, that is, the contractual elements of the work relationship versus the aspects that foster the workers' identification with the company as a community. Yet, in all the companies we studied, we found some indicators of both strategies. If we take as indicators of the two strategies the use of internal versus external labor markets to fill vacancies, the involvement of workers in issues of production through such means as Quality Circles versus the hierarchical control of work, the existence of identity incentives versus selective ones, the degree of development of company welfare, and the extent of internal retraining, we may conclude that neither strategy was used consistently by any of the companies studied, apparently for no other reason than the "pragmatic eclecticism" noted above. This means that one source of the differences observed is simply to be found in the lack of a "model" that is widely shared and serves as a point of reference for managers when they have to decide on how individual aspects of the work relationship should be re-regulated. In this case we have differences without consistencies, that is, two (ideal-type) patterns of regulation that are used in nonsystematic ways by companies.

Other differences, however, suggest clearer alternatives companies face and to which they give more systematically contrasting answers. In what follows, I will briefly illustrate three types of choices they have to make. The first concerns the extension of the involvement of workers' representatives in decisions, or the strength of labor-management relations, as well as the degree of institutionalization and formalization of these relations. The second has to do with the use of direct relationships with individual workers— which, as we saw, are growing everywhere—as an attempt to bypass the unions or simply as a new method to increase overall information and communication. Finally, the third alternative regards the degree of homogeneity in the management of human resources, in which some rules and advantages may apply to either the whole labor force or some professional (and possibly age or gender) groups only.

THE DEGREE OF UNION PARTICIPATION
IN LABOR REGULATION

It is not easy to measure the extent and intensity of the involvement of workers' representatives in managerial decisions. The number of formal and informal meetings is not a good indicator; and the fact that in one company a few aspects of the work relation (say, redundancies, training, overtime, and shift work) are subject to consensual decisions, while in another there may be a few more aspects, is even less indicative, as this may depend on a number of reasons. Also, the actors' perceptions of either the "social climate" in the company or the degree of their respective influence may be misleading. The nature of their relationship is at times conceptualized as consultation, at others as information, and at others still as negotiation. But, to take the first concept, a closer look at the companies studied reveals that in a few cases what is seen as consultation is a relationship that effectively influences management decisions; while in others it is no more than information on what will be decided anyway, and acceptance of it. The difficulty is even greater when one compares different countries with a different industrial relations culture. To give just one example, while in all the British companies we studied the trade unions were perceived to have a far greater influence on decisions than the company management is ready to acknowledge, in the French firms the reverse is true: All managers stress the cooperative nature of their relations with the unions, while the latter insist that managers decide almost everything unilaterally.

In spite of these difficulties, it is clear that union involvement in the regulation of work is far more extensive, constant, and effective in some of the companies studied than in others. To some extent, were it not for the methodological warnings expressed above, it would seem possible to draw distinctions between countries, or national styles. Our companies, in fact, confirm the rather obvious expectation that in Germany the workers' representatives are far more deeply involved in various aspects of labor regulation than in France and Spain. Even so, not all the findings could be easily anticipated.

One that could not be anticipated is the fact that the legal rights of information, consultation, or negotiation do not seem to play a major role. In the next section, I will go back to this observation to detect potentially contradictory effects of these rights on the extension of cooperative relations. For the time being, suffice it to observe that the three countries I mentioned are the ones in which such rights (though of a different nature and to varying degrees) are more extensively and formally stated, while in Britain and Italy the law plays a minor role in this respect. Yet, the companies of the latter countries are definitely closer to the German ones, in terms of cooperative relations and union involvement in the regulation of work, than they are to the Spanish, and especially to the French.

A similar observation can be made if one takes into account the degree of formality of labor-management meetings and relations in general, a feature that is partly a consequence of how industrial relations are regulated by the law, and partly depends on the more general culture of the actors. Most agreements, meetings, and so on seem to follow fixed rules, timing, and procedures in both the German and Spanish companies, while in Italy and Britain an important part of decentralized relations takes place in highly informal ways. Again, this does not seem to have clear consequences on the extent and stability of union participation in the regulation of work.

A second finding is that the intensity of cooperation is not necessarily correlated with each actor's readiness to adapt to the views of the other. To take the example of labor flexibility, in some German companies, where labor-management cooperation is in a sense built in to the system and therefore very high, negotiation on working time has gone on for years, with neither partner trying too hard to force an agreement upon the other; while in the British companies we studied, where cooperation is more limited and depends on calculations that may rapidly change, and where an "economistic" tradition prevails, the unions were ready to "sell" labor flexibility, or better to "give up their veto powers" in exchange for wage increases.

A third finding is that, in all countries, the extension and intensity of involvement of the workers' representatives varies widely, depending on the industries concerned. Here, our data show some regularities that can hardly be interpreted as casual. The engineering sector (which employs a relatively skilled labor force) shows consistently higher levels of union participation in labor regulation than the chemical and the food processing industries.

Here, the main distinction is between companies with a rather segmented internal labor market and companies with a relatively homogeneous labor force. To be sure, the degree of segmentation depends primarily on economic-productive reasons. Where production has a strong seasonal character, for instance, such as in the food processing industry, the extent to which companies make use of whatever instruments of external flexibility are available to them is always likely to be greater than in industries characterized by market stability. It is no accident that almost all the food processing companies in our sample make extensive use of seasonal or temporary work, and that these groups within the labor force enjoy poorer contractual conditions than the permanent workers. But the fact that the German food processing company does not share this pattern to the same extent, on the one hand; and that in all the Spanish companies this division between temporary and permanent workers was recently reinforced, on the other, should alert us to the likelihood that other factors are at work. Here, the type of legislation, the power of the trade unions, and the length of their tradition as class-oriented representative institutions seem to make a difference. I will come back to these factors as explanatory variables, in the last section.

The segmentation between permanent and temporary workers is not the only line of division in the ways the company management regulates the work relation. In some companies, production workers are treated differently from the other workers. In others, incentives are specifically directed to technicians and white-collar workers. But in this case, it is even more difficult to trace causal links between the choices made and the features of the company. Here we are probably in the realm of the "pragmatic eclecticism" I discussed at the beginning of this section.

The Main Factors
of the Differences Observed

One obvious group of factors to examine, when trying to explain the differences in human resource management and industrial relations among companies, is that pertaining to their organizational-technological features. Much recent literature has explored this type of relationship. When setting forth the hypotheses for comparative research, I myself have assumed that the degree of technological innovation and the organizational features of the firms studied might explain the extent to which managers seek labor's consensus:

> Where a search for pragmatic and limited cooperation on specific aspects of the
> work relationship becomes the rule, the extent of labor's involvement is given

by the number of such aspects which are re-regulated consensually, as opposed to those which are not; it is, therefore, more the outcome of a series of pragmatic decisions on which dimensions of the work contract should be changed and how, than of a general policy style. If this is so, the rate of innovation and the technological-economic features of the company are likely to be the main explanatory factors. The more a company innovates, the more the various aspects of the organization of work must be re-regulated. And, the more the company depends on its labor force (on its willingness to cooperate by taking on responsibilities, initiative, concern for deadlines and product quality, etc.) for efficiently running the production process and for economic performance, the more the management will try to involve workers in such re-regulation. (Regini, 1991, p. 22)

However, the research findings only partly allow us to test such a hypothesis, as almost all the companies studied have recently undergone some major technological-organizational change. To be sure, innovation is quite different from case to case, and sometimes runs in opposite directions. But it is impossible to say whether change is greater in a firm that has introduced computerized numerical control equipment, or in one that has recently resorted to "traditional" production lines. Apart from these difficulties, anyway, our data show that, far from being constrained by commonly shared conditions of technological innovation and market competition, even companies that look alike in this respect tend to adopt variable solutions to the problem of the type of cooperation to seek in labor re-regulation, whether through direct relationships with some groups of employees or via the mediation of their representatives.

If the role of technological-organizational factors is difficult to assess, it is, however, quite clear that institutional factors are of major importance in explaining differences in human resource management and industrial relations. Because of space constraints, I will briefly comment on just two aspects: the role of legal rights to information, consultation, and negotiation in different national contexts, and the type of workers' representatives that are present in the companies.

1. I have already mentioned above that extensive legislation on the rights of workers' representatives to be informed, consulted, and so on, on a series of issues, does not, per se, determine a high degree of actual union participation in management decisions. While the existence of codetermination laws in Germany could lead one to such a conclusion, our data show that, on the other hand, the degree of union involvement is certainly higher in the Italian and British firms than in the Spanish and French ones, in spite of the greater role played by union-supportive legislation in the latter countries.

On a closer look, however, we may detect two major, though contradictory, effects of union rights legislation on the type of interaction between management and unions. On the one hand, the right to information, to consultation, or to participation in joint committees on a number of issues increases the technical content of the task of workers' representatives, and it may lead them, therefore, to cooperate with management or to oppose it on specific aspects and details, rather than on the basis of general slogans. This, however, seems to be the case only in the German firms, where the *Betriebsrate* are strong and the management is forced to take their points of view into account; while the weakness of the French and Spanish unions does not give them the power to actually influence the way work is regulated, hence they are not led to conceive of their task in more technical terms, and they even resent being overwhelmed with information they cannot control.

On the other hand, while the legislation on information and consultation rights expands the functions of the workers' representatives on a number of issues, and may avoid conflict on such issues, it also has the effect of freezing, so to speak, the boundaries between unilateral and consensual regulation. If companies abide by the law, as is basically the case in all the firms we studied, the workers' representatives have less incentive to ask for consensual regulation of more issues, and the management itself is content with the degree of participation offered to unions and does not feel under pressure to extend the area of their involvement. In other words, the extent and intensity of information, consultation, and negotiation become issues that are effectively removed from the industrial relations agenda and no longer perform the function of symbolically measuring the degree of cooperation in the relationships between management and unions. Paradoxically, then, the area of de facto participation may advance further in countries like Italy, in which legally defined rights are fewer, than in countries like France or Spain, with more extensive legal regulation of management-union interaction.

2. During the 1980s, in all European countries, the unionized companies trying to adapt their human resource strategies to the new market constraints, and evolving production patterns were confronted with growing cross-pressures. On the one hand, new factors—besides the traditional ones—seemed to push them to avoid involving unions in the re-regulation of work. The very weakening of the unions, in terms of their ability to represent workers' demands as well as of organizational resources, was of course a tempting opportunity for employers, who in many countries had suffered a "decade of union power," to exclude them. The lesser political and institutional support enjoyed by unions had the same effect. Also, the grow-

ing competition in world markets made employers less tolerant of rules and practices that acted as constraints or "rigidities."

On the other hand, employers were exposed to counter-pressures toward a greater, rather than a lesser, involvement of unions in the re-regulation of work. In the first place, in several countries trade unions had in the meanwhile become moderate enough, and had internalized the company needs for flexibility to such an extent, that their action was no longer necessarily a constraint to change. At the same time, for rapid and constant innovation to be successful, it clearly appeared important to control resistance to it, and this could be done more easily with the unions' support, rather than going against them. Last but not least, companies that were undergoing major processes of restructuring were especially vulnerable and, therefore, needed alliances (to get financial and political support on the one hand, and to manage the problem of the losers in such processes, on the other): In this perspective, trade unions, which maintained a fair amount of social legitimacy, could still be used to the employers' advantage.

The outcome of these cross-pressures was the widespread "pragmatic eclecticism" in human resource management and industrial relations strategies that I referred to above. Our data, however, show that the significant differences among companies in their responses to these cross-pressures are fundamentally due to the type of unions and workers' representatives that managers face. It is rather obvious that where unions are organizationally strong and nonmilitant, employers are more reluctant to fight them, and more ready to involve them in decisions, than where they are weak and/or conflictual. All the companies we studied, however, have relatively (at least compared to national figures) strong and nonmilitant unions, yet their behavior toward them differs, as we saw, rather significantly.

This seems to depend on the attitudes that unions have developed toward company needs, which are of a pragmatic nature in some cases, and more ideological—as they stress a clear distinction of functions—in others. In the former case, employers find it useful to consider unions as a resource in the management of labor, and they establish intense, though often informal, relationships with them. In the latter, employers are instead inclined not to exceed the degree of involvement that is forced upon them by law or by tradition. As the interviews for our research show clearly, managers' values and ideas do not matter greatly in this respect. Even the former type of behavior, in fact, stems from an opportunistic recognition of the unions' potentially positive role in the re-regulation of labor, and not from greater ideological sympathy toward them.

This explains why the boundaries of pragmatic-cooperative behavior, within which trade unions may be considered a resource by management, are rather strict. Cooperation must produce a form of micro-corporatism, that is, within the corporation borders, even at the expense of weakening the ties between workers' representatives in the workplace and external trade unions. The unions must focus on advancing the interests of the core labor force, accepting de facto a segmentation that hinders their ability to represent both the "higher" (technicians and administrative staff) and the "marginal" (e.g., the seasonal) groups of workers. They are confronted with a systematic division between daily decisions concerning the organization of work, in which they are invited to participate, and strategic decisions from which they are generally excluded. More generally, employers are ready to consider paying the economic cost for the slower and slightly modified decision-making process that results from union participation, but not to consider the possibility of substantially modifying their decisions.

Note

1. The research team included Paolo Perulli and Ida Regalia (Italy), Alain Lipietz (France), Bruno Cattero (Germany), Paul Marginson (Great Britain), and Fausto Miguelez (Spain).

References

Boyer, R. (Ed.). (1986). *La flexibilite du travail en Europe* [Labor flexibility in Europe]. Paris: La Decouverte.

Dore, R. (1986). *Flexible rigidities: Industrial policy and structural adjustment in the Japanese economy 1970-1980*. Stanford, CA: Stanford University Press.

Kern, H., & Schumann, M. (1984). Das ende der arbeitsteilung? [The end of the division of labor?]. Munich: Beck.

Piore, M., & Sabel, C. (1984). *The second industrial divide*. New York: Basic Books.

Regini, M. (1991, September 23-26). *Employers' reactions to the productivity drive: The search for labour consensus*. Paper presented at the IIRA 3rd European Regional Congress, Bari-Naples.

Streeck, W. (1987). The uncertainties of management in the management of uncertainty. *International Journal of Political Economy, 17*(3), 57-87.

16 \ The Take-Up of Human Resource Management by Mainstream Companies: Key Lessons From Research

JOHN STOREY

Debate about the degree and type of change in industrial relations has been a common occurrence in many parts of the world in the past few years. In the English-speaking countries in particular, there has been talk of "transformation" (Kochan, Katz, & McKersie, 1986), "personnel management in transition" (Sisson, 1989), "innovating to compete" (Walton, 1987), "Japanization" (Oliver & Wilkinson, 1990), and of a "new industrial relations" (The new industrial relations? 1991). But of all the concepts used to capture the array of changes, one in particular has made a remarkable, albeit controversial, impact: that is, Human Resource Management, or HRM. This topic has attracted intense speculation in North America, Australia, and Britain. Apparently, the issue has also surfaced in many other countries, but systematic data about this aspect are hard to trace.

The broad nature of the HRM phenomenon at the philosophical level has been extensively discussed (see Storey, 1989) and it is not my intention to rehearse these features again here. Rather, the purpose of this chapter is to

AUTHOR'S NOTE: This chapter reports results of a study conducted by the author while he was a Principal Research Fellow in the Industrial Relations Research Unit at the University of Warwick. The author would like to acknowledge the support of IRRU and ESRC and to acknowledge the constructive comments on the first draft of this report by John Purcell, David Buchanan, and Keith Sisson.

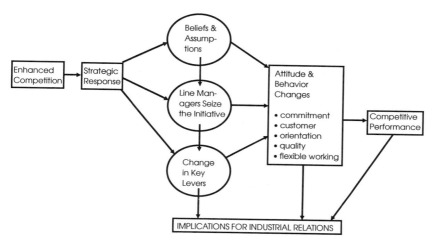

Figure 16.1. A Model of the Shift to Human Resource Management

As is made clear in Table 16.1, the 27 points constituting the checklist can be grouped into four main categories: (a) Beliefs and Assumptions; (b) Strategic Aspects; (c) the increased significance of Line Managers; (d) the utilization of a set of "levers" that are different from those to which managers previously had recourse. It is possible to summarize these aspects in a general model as shown in Figure 16.1.

In essence, the model highlights several key features of the new state of affairs—or new paradigm. Thus, the trigger is shown as the increased level of competition in product markets (in contrast, for example, to a new set of legislative requirements). The second feature is the alleged strategic nature of the corporate response to this new competition. This has two aspects: a definitive linkage between employment policies and the corporate plan to win competitive advantage, and a novel degree of integration between the various elements constituting those employment policies. The third high-lighted feature shown by the model is the threefold span of the HRM arena of action. This not only encompasses the *personnel* levers of selection, communications, training, and the like, but also brings in *cultural strategies* through working on beliefs and assumptions (of managers and other employees) and the *structural strategy* of projecting line managers to the fore. The model then shows how there is an assumed link to changed attitudes and behaviors and how these, in tandem with the new priority areas for action taken by managers (i.e., the aforementioned threefold span of HRM), can be expected to impact on industrial relations.

HRM AS A UNIVERSAL PRESCRIPTION?

Many of the tenets of HRM, as derived from American literature linking business strategy and HR (Beer, Spector, Lawrence, Mills, & Walton, 1985; Dertouzos, Solow, & Lester, 1989; Devanna, Fombrun, & Tichy, 1984; Kanter, 1984; Schuler & Jackson, 1987), have more than a passing resemblance to organizational models derived from the "Japanization" literature (e.g., Oliver & Wilkinson, 1990), and both of these can be seen to have much in common with the current orthodoxy in corporate strategy. The latter genre emphasizes organizational approaches to "corporate rejuvenation," which are characterized by organizational learning, commitment to the long term, and the nurturing of "intangible assets" (Pettigrew & Whipp, forthcoming; Stopford & Baden-Fuller, 1990). What seems to be emerging therefore is a formula of apparent near-universal application. There are many angles to this that require close attention. However, in this chapter, two issues are selected for discussion: The first is the degree of take-up of this sort of model by "non-exceptional cases"; and the second is the implications for industrial relations that seem to flow from the degree of take-up of HRM in these sorts of companies.

USING EMPIRICAL EVIDENCE

The purpose of this chapter, then, is to examine the changing employment management practices of a sample of *mainstream* British organizations. This term perhaps requires some explanation. The set of cases was not randomly selected. The core 15 cases upon which this report concentrates are all large and their names are generally familiar: In a commonsense way they are all arguably exceptional. But in the kind of industrial relations classification that Purcell and Sisson (1983) have constructed, the selected cases could be appropriately seen as mainstream. They were all unionized, were not occupying special greenfield sites, and had well-developed procedures in industrial relations. They were decidedly not part of the well-rehearsed litany of allegedly "lead" cases, such as IBM, Nissan, Toshiba, and BA, which have figured so prominently in so many discussions about new forms (e.g., Bassett, 1986; Trevor, 1988; Wickens, 1987). The 15 core cases were studied intensively during the period 1986-1988. Semistructured interviews were conducted at nearly all management levels in these organizations. These ranged from senior executives just below main board level, through divisional MDs, down to unit general managers, departmental managers, and frontline supervision. A listing of these cases follows:

The Core Cases

1. Austin Rover
2. British Rail
3. Bradford Metropolitan Council
4. Eaton Ltd.
5. Ford of Britain
6. ICI
7. Jaguar
8. Lucas
9. Massey Ferguson UK
10. The National Health Service
11. Peugeot-Talbot
12. Plessey (Naval Systems)
13. Rolls-Royce Aero Engines
14. Smith & Nephew
15. Whitbread Breweries

Mainstream Companies in Transition

In this section, the four categories noted above (Beliefs and Assumptions; Strategic Aspects; Line Managers; and Key Levers) will be used to order and analyze the data. The broad results from the case studies are summarized in these terms in Table 16.2. A more detailed presentation of the results from each case company, using the full 27-item checklist, is then shown in Table 16.3. In the paragraphs that follow, the emerging patterns from these results are identified and discussed.

The summary of results in Tables 16.2 and 16.3 inevitably oversimplify a more complex reality. Two particular problems in devising the figures should be given special note. The first is the problem of continuity, or rather lack of continuity. In many of these cases there would be a particular period of time when one or more of these 27 features were clearly being given paramount attention. A year later the emphasis might well have shifted to a new initiative. For example, at Bradford Metropolitan Council, an elaborated "Social Strategy" was embarked upon under a Labour party administration that embraced many of these elements. Following local elections a Conservative administration revamped the package in a radical way and emphasized a rather different set of these initiatives. Or to give another example, in 1987 Austin Rover was placing major emphasis upon the policy of harmonization;

TABLE 16.2 Summary of Results Using the Four Grouped Dimensions

	A Beliefs & Assumptions	B Strategic Aspects	C Line Management	D Key Levers
Austin Rover	✓	✓	✓	?
British Rail	?	?	✓	?
Bradford Metropolitan Council	✓	✓	✓	✓
Eaton Ltd.	✓	✓	✓	?
Ford of Britain	?	?	?	?
ICI	?	✓	?	?
Jaguar	✓	✓	?	?
Lucas	✓	?	✓	?
Massey Ferguson UK	✓	?	✓	?
The National Health Service	✓	✓	✓	?
Peugeot–Talbot	?	?	✓	?
Plessey (Naval Systems)	✓	?	?	✗
Rolls–Royce Aero Engines	?	?	✗	✗
Smith & Nephew	?	?	?	✗
Whitbread Breweries	✓	✓	✓	✓

a year later it was in retreat on this policy and a Total Quality initiative was being prepared. In Table 16.3, a tick is recorded where the criterion in question was, at some period during the research, being given clear emphasis. It does not mean the particular item necessarily persisted as a key feature of an organization's human resource approach.

The second difficulty in summarizing the findings in this way is that initiatives may be directed at one part of the work force and not another. Initiatives were indeed often unevenly applied. For example, many of these companies had launched into individual contracts and performance-related pay for their managerial staffs. In such instances the practice adopted in constructing this table was to record an "in part" score (denoted by a question

TABLE 16.3 Full Summary of Results

	The Fifteen Case Organizations														
Dimension	1	2	3	4	5	6	7	8	9	10	11	12	13	14	15
Aim to go "beyond" contract	✓	?	✓	✓	✓	✓	✓	✓	✓	✓	?	✓	?	?	✓
Impatience with rules	✓	✓	✓	✓	?	✓	✓	✓	✓	?	?	✓	?	?	✓
Prime guide to action: "business need"	✓	✓	✓	?	✓	✓	✓	✓	✓	?	✓	✓	✓	✓	✓
Values/mission	✓	?	✓									?	?	?	✓
Nurturing orientation	?	✗	?	?	?	?	?	?	?	?	?	?	?	?	?
Unitarist	?	?	✗	✗	✗	?	?	✗	?	✗	✗	✓		✗	✓
Conflict de-emphasized rather than institutionalized	✓	?	✓	?	?	✓	?	✗	?	?	?	✓		?	✓
Customer orientation to fore	✓				?	✓				?	?	✓			
Integrated initiatives	✓		✓		?	?	?	?	?	?	?	✗	✗	✗	✓
Corporate plan central	✓	?	✓		?	?	?	?	?	✗	?	✗	?	?	✓
Speedy decision making	✓		?	✗	?	?	?	?	?	✗	✗	?	✗	✗	✓
Transformational leadership	✓		?	?	?	?	?	✓			?	?	?	?	?
General/business/line managers to fore	✓														
Direct communication	?	✓													
Standardization/parity not emphasized	✓	?	✓		?	✓	?	✓		✗	?	✓	✗	✗	
Facilitative management	✓						?	✓	?	?	?	✗	?		✓
Selection integrated	✓									?	✓		?	✗	

(Continued)

mark). This is done where initiatives had been applied to at least several tiers of management, and to cases where there was evidence of an intent to roll out the policy to other grades.

As Table 16.3 shows, certain initiatives were more universally popular than others. Thus, all of the cases had in common a new emphasis upon the standing of line and general managers in the handling of "people issues." Likewise, communicating directly to employees had become the norm, and

TABLE 16.3 (Continued)

Dimension	1	2	3	4	5	6	7	8	9	10	11	12	13	14	15
Performance-related pay	✓	?	?	?	x	x	x	?	?	?	?	?	x	?	?
Harmonization	✓	?	?	x	x	x	?	x	x	x	?	?	x	x	?
Toward individual contracts	?	✓	?	x	x	x	?	?	?	?	?	✓	?	x	✓
Marginalization of stewards	✓	?	?	?	x	?	✓	✓	✓	✓	✓	✓	?	?	✓
Fewer job categories	?	?	?	?	✓	✓	?	?	✓	x	?	✓	x	x	✓
Increased flow of communication	✓	✓	✓	✓	✓	✓	✓	✓	✓	✓	✓	✓	✓	✓	✓
Teamworking	?	?	✓	✓	✓	✓	✓	✓	✓	✓	?	✓	✓	?	✓
Conflict reduction through culture change	✓	?	✓	✓	✓	✓	✓	✓	✓	✓	?	✓	?	?	✓
Learning companies/heavy emphasis on training	✓	?	✓	x	?	?	✓	✓	✓	?	?	?	✓	?	?
Wide-ranging cultural, structural, and personal strategies	✓	✓	✓	?	✓	✓	✓	✓	✓	✓	✓	✓	?	?	✓

KEY: ✓ = yes (existed or were significant moves toward)
        x = no
        ? = in parts

there had been an increased flow of communications. A number of items, such as the aim to "go beyond contract" and the adoption of an innovative posture with regard to employment practices, were indicative of notable departure from the erstwhile touchstone, in labor relations, of having recourse to procedure.

The item that is logged least frequently, however, is the idea of a unitary approach. This is significant, given the theme of this chapter, which is concerned with the implications for industrial relations. All of the cases were unionized and hardly any of them appeared to be taking clear steps to de-unionize. Given the extent to which they had pursued other elements of the HRM model, this particular finding might be read as an encouraging sign that human resource management and trade unionism are not as incompatible as some influential commentators have suspected (see Guest, 1989). As the table shows, however, seven of the companies had marginalized the trade unions to such an extent that their commitment to pluralism appeared highly dubious. This point is discussed in more detail later, in the section on industrial relations.

The freeing up of line managers to utilize the human resource to its full potential can thus be interpreted as aimed as much at sloughing off the restrictions imposed by staff specialists as it is at the disengagement from collective labor rules of agreements, custom and practice, understandings, and the like. In this sense, HRM could indeed be interpreted as a reassertion of managerial prerogative—but on a very different basis from earlier attempts, which were spearheaded by deskilling, fragmentation, and the ideology of property rights and managerial rights (see Storey, 1983, for an analysis of the various bases of the management proprogative idea). These concepts were still very current in the early 1980s (witness the debate about "macho management"), but by the end of that decade, concern with rights and principle had given way to the idea of managing change to survive in a continually uncertain environment. To what extent was this shift reflected down through the managerial ranks?

In fact this was one of the most remarkable and consistent findings of the study. There were clear signs of a newfound confidence among a significant proportion of them; they were involved in personal development programs and were typically *au fait* with the logic and mechanisms of the new approaches. Part of this new outlook and confidence was an espoused belief in the possibilities of transformational leadership, as distinct from transactional leadership. That is, many of the line managers in the sample had embraced the more ambitious goal of gaining their subordinates' commitment to the mission of their part of the enterprise, rather than the more limited goal of simply securing consent via some temporary trade-off. That said, the evidence of achievement in this regard was far less convincing than the apparent willingness to embrace this task by the line managers.

KEY LEVERS

Activity with regard to many of the key levers of HR, as listed in Table 16.1 and Table 16.3, was readily apparent in most of the case organizations. New initiatives were under way in the shape of enhanced communications, teamwork experiments, performance-related pay, harmonization, and training and development. This much is clear from the results shown in Table 16.3.

Selection, for example, was being treated more systematically, and most of these organizations were experimenting with standardized tests of one sort or another. The most notable development was the increased utilization of psychometric testing—especially for managers but also for supervisors and to an extent even for shop-floor operatives. Among managerial grades a number of these mainstream companies, for example Austin Rover and Lucas, had even subjected their existing management stock to the psychometric treatment. In addition, other devices to audit the extant managerial stock had been deployed. The results of these measures were used to sort and sift, and even displace, managers. These interventions, as with similar ones in the realm of appraisal, are very much in tune with the philosophy of HRM in that they not only suggest a dispassionate weighing and resorting of this resource; but in addition the devices display a marked bias toward an emphasis on attitudinal and behavioral characteristics, quite apart from any technical capabilities that may or may not be present.

Having briefly identified and explained the types of changes found to be occurring in the 15 mainstream organizations, the next task is to explore the implications of these developments for industrial relations as conventionally conceived.

Industrial Relations and Trade Unions

A number of commentators on the British scene have emphasized the remarkable continuity in IR machinery throughout the difficult period of the 1980s (Batstone, 1984, 1988; Legge, 1988; MacInnes, 1987). It is notable that these commentaries typically draw upon survey data. Case study research tends to paint a rather different picture (Morris & Wood, 1991; Storey, 1992).

The main changes in industrial relations can usefully be viewed in summary form before the details are discussed:

The Marginalization of Trade Unions
and Industrial Relations

The majority of managers—most especially personnel managers—made a point of stressing how IR had come to assume a very low position in their list of concerns and priorities.

Changes to Collective Bargaining

These changes affected both the content of bargaining and its form. Regarding content, it appeared that the scope of issues covered by joint regulation had narrowed considerably. Concerning the form of bargaining, there was a tendency for it to become increasingly similar to joint consultation. The shift in power had been such that management was able to bring issues to the table for "information." Comment was invited from the unions, but their opportunity to exercise a veto had been drastically reduced.

Proceduralism

There was a notable shift away from IR procedural devices, such as job evaluation and negotiated pay categories, and toward individualized contracts and performance-related pay.

Workplace Representatives

Shop stewards had seen their numbers and influence reduced. Facilities for shop stewards had been eroded and so too the amount of training for trade union duties.

Discussion

Given that the new human resource initiatives carry a considerable element of individualism, as opposed to collectivism, in their composition, there is clearly plenty of scope for tension between the two paradigms. How would this be worked through and accommodated? Four main scenarios seemed possible: (a) The unions and the joint procedure arrangements might be directly attacked, to leave an open field for the new approaches; (b) they might simply be ignored in a way that is tantamount to de-recognition; (c) the established and the new approaches might be run in parallel; (d) the joint arrangements might be integrated into the overall new approach.

The evidence accumulated suggested it was the third path that was followed by most of the case companies. In other words, the British mainstream organizations were operating dual arrangements.

Four basic questions can usefully be asked of the mainstream cases, with regard to industrial relations and trade unions:

1. What stance had management taken with regard to trade unions (i.e., in terms of the grade of recognition or moves to de-recognition; what action had been taken in relation to shop stewards)?

2. Irrespective of the institutional security of trade unions and their representatives, what stance had these managers adopted concerning collective bargaining?

3. To what extent were trade unions treated as partners in the process of managing change?

4. What impact did the new management initiatives, which placed the accent on relating to the labor force on an individualistic rather than collectivistic basis (e.g., through direct employee communication devices, performance appraisal, and task-level involvement), have on trade unions and industrial relations?

The Institutional Integrity of Trade Unions
Under the Change Programs

There had been few outright assaults in these case companies on trade unions. The highly publicized cases of complete or partial de-recognition have in fact occurred in only a few specific areas, most notably at GCHQ, the government security service, and parts of newspaper publishing and shipping. In general terms, personnel managers in the rest of the economy, especially in large established companies, tended to make reassuring noises with regard to official policies toward trade unions. There is little new in that. But behind the public face, a rather more complicated picture was unfolding.

In some cases there has been the targeting of particular groups or levels of management. Hence, in British Rail, the shift to individual contracts for certain management grades was accompanied by a simultaneous withdrawal from collective negotiations for these groups. In other cases, managers began to scrutinize membership levels among marginal groups, such as sales staff, with a view toward giving notice of withdrawal of bargaining rights.

Among the manufacturing group of cases covered by this research, one might have expected that, at the very least, the place of the manual and technical unions would have been secure. But in fact there was one particular case where there was a definite plan to withdraw recognition from all the unions in a cluster of sites. It is relevant to note that, in the case in question, membership levels were struggling at the 50% level, and the unions appeared to offer little effective challenge. The variables at play appeared to be both sheer vulnerability and the fact that the personnel director happened to be using, as his prime point of reference, certain nonunion sites in the vicinity. Among the 15 cases this was the only one where a clear, unambiguous policy intent to de-recognize the main unions both existed and was admitted to. More common was a generally more aggressive stance toward the unions, but without any apparent agenda (hidden or otherwise) to displace them. Thus, at Massey Ferguson, for example, the new initiatives on direct communication and human resources were accompanied by an adamant managerial stance that the number of shop stewards had to be reduced. On this and a host of other issues, the company took the fight to the unions, who found themselves, for the first time in some while, simply responding to management's agenda.

In other cases too, such as Lucas and Jaguar, the state of relations with the trade unions during this period was by no means harmonious. On the contrary, they were generally conflictive. But what was especially notable was the fact that management, during this period, evidently did not have rectifying that state of affairs on its list of priorities. Rather, the aim was to keep up the pressure and wrest areas of control out of the hands of the stewards' committee. To what extent was this part and parcel of the new human resource set of policies and practices? The fact that there was an alternative set of measures might be thought of as contributing to the hardline attitude. However, the balance of evidence was that such a linkage should be regarded as unlikely. First, this was because the managers responsible for the industrial relations approach were quite separate from the group sponsoring the human resource management initiatives, and not just separate but, in some considerable measure, in conflict with each other. Second, given the straitened product market circumstances, it seems highly probable that this fairly aggressive line with the stewards' organization would have been adopted irrespective of the existence, or no existence, of a set of human resource management policies.

Policies and Practices
Relating to Collective Bargaining

There was a widespread move to decentralize collective bargaining. One prime rationale for this was to take advantage of local labor market conditions. Another important reason was that it was seen to fit with the idea of distinct profit centers and other appurtenances of devolved management.

A point that should be noted, when comparing and contrasting cases, is that even among unionized companies, the variety of practices concerning collective bargaining was extensive. Thus, while plant representatives in some organizations were meeting with management as frequently as twice a week for relatively formal talks about various disputes, grievances, and procedural matters (e.g., at the Austin Rover Longbridge site in Birmingham), in other cases, collective meetings were held very rarely.

Overall, the most notable aspect with regard to collective bargaining was that there was now far less emphasis upon achieving productivity gains through the once ubiquitous mechanism of productivity bargaining. Ahlstrand (1990) has demonstrated the long-standing attachment to this device at the Fawley refinery even though, at the rational level, there was little evidence of any success with the method. Significantly, these mainstream companies, with a few notable exceptions, had seemingly begun to place their own faith less in the continued pursuit of detailed productivity agreements in the Esso mode, and rather more in the wide span of initiatives that extended beyond collective bargaining. To this extent at least, the balance between industrial relations and the new human resource approaches had therefore shown signs of adjustment.

Trade Unions as Partners or Outsiders
in the Process of Change

In the main, trade union leaders, both at national and workplace levels, were left on the sidelines of most of the managerial initiatives during this period. Halfhearted attempts were sometimes made to involve them. As one senior personnel manager at Austin Rover was fond of saying: "The unions were invited to the party but they didn't seem to want to come. So, the party went ahead without them."

Equally, it must be remembered that the internal politics of change were such that the people issuing the "invitations" were in any case rarely the main drivers of change. The major change programs were frequently devised outside the specialist personnel and industrial relations function. In consequence, by the time this branch of management got a hold on the change package, its shape was fairly well settled. As personnel were still widely regarded as the chief mediators with the unions, this inevitably meant late involvement by the unions.

Because personnel were themselves often marginal to the change process, this branch of management was itself frequently ambivalent about the new initiatives. The Austin Rover industrial relations managers, for example, were especially critical of the comprehensive package and program of change in that company, which carried the label "Working With Pride." This being the case, it was natural that the circumstances were inauspicious for progressing the idea of a social partnership at company level between management, workers, and trade unions.

The idea was also hampered for another reason. In those workplaces where agreements about change programs had been struck with the domestic steward organization, there was often subsequent tension with representatives from other sites—especially where there was inter-plant competition for work. Sometimes the deals were also at odds with official union policy.

The Impact of HR Policies and Practices
on Trade Unions and Collective Bargaining

It is difficult to disentangle the effects of human resource management type initiatives on trade unions and collective bargaining from the whole array of other changes occurring at this time. It has to be remembered that the unions were in an already weak position as a result of adverse political and economic conditions. But if these other factors are stripped away to focus on the battery of HR innovations relating to selection, appraisal, direct communication, task-level participation, training, culture change campaigns, and other similar initiatives, then the impact, though mixed, can generally be said to be adverse from the unions' viewpoint. The reasons for this were not always direct and obvious. In part, it resulted from the distraction of management to issues other than union relations. The unions could be seen as crowded out by other managerial concerns.

However, another factor was also at play. Each of the main elements of the human resource initiatives, such as more rigorous and systematic selection techniques, the extension of appraisal to all levels of the work force, direct communication to all employees, and job-level participation programs, tended to be viewed suspiciously by trade union representatives. This did not come as a surprise to most managers. On the contrary, they normally anticipated a hostile reaction. Even in those few cases where approaches were made to the unions to give some endorsement to the new systems, these solicitations were usually very halfhearted and token. The shape of the initiatives was invariably drawn up before the unions were invited to join the deliberations.

Managerial approaches to trade unions and industrial relations in these organizations, which were at once both traditional and yet also, at the time of the research, at least partly experimental, reveal the dilemmas and uncertainties surrounding the whole enterprise of human resource management in the British context. Perhaps not surprisingly, there was little evidence of any forthright move to abandon pluralism in favor of a wholehearted commitment to an individualistically based human resource program. Instead, the general tendency was to maintain the previous machinery while experimenting much more enthusiastically with policies and approaches that signaled a direction toward new priorities.

This dual approach to the management of labor was embodied in the operation of separate and distinct specialists (and even departments) responsible, respectively, for industrial relations and human resource management. Such arrangements were found, for example, at Massey Ferguson, Jaguar, and Ford. In such cases, the human resource management type of approach could be seen as running alongside, rather than supplanting, the ongoing industrial relations departments.

Across the variety of approaches, one startling fact stood out: While the old-style industrial relations "fire fighting" was disavowed and even scorned, there was hardly an instance where anything approaching a strategic stance toward unions and industrial relations could be readily discerned as having taken its place. It would appear that identifying clear managerial policies toward trade unions and collective bargaining is as difficult to do now, if not indeed more difficult, than it was 20 to 30 years ago, when the lack of policy on such matters was frequently berated (CIR, 1973; Cuthbert & Hawkins, 1973; Donovan, 1968; Hawkins, 1978; McCarthy & Ellis, 1973).

In a key regard there was perhaps little that was entirely new in this. Flanders had complained 30 years earlier that British managers "preferred to have as little as possible to do with labour relations [which was looked upon as] a nuisance, a disturbance diverting their energies away from what they regard as the more important aspects of their work" (1964, p. 251). In the intervening period, however, there had been very considerable attention paid to industrial relations as they became identified as the root cause of economic under-performance. Arguably, managers in the 1980s were therefore merely reverting to type. It is suggested here, however, that there was rather more to it than that—namely, that the new neglect of trade unions and industrial relations was a studied neglect. It carried a symbolic message: Managers are in the driver's seat, unions and industrial relations have to be demonstrated as relatively secondary and incidental to meeting market priorities, and secondary also to the newly rediscovered alternative ways of managing the labor (human) resource.

One of the crucial limiting factors in the attainment of such a clear message, however, was the relatively undeveloped nature of the HR function. Even in those cases where it had a separate institutional presence, there was a tendency for the function to be skeletally staffed, and for the unit's specialists to concentrate their efforts on the managerial grades. The extension of initiatives into the rest of the work force tended to be piecemeal and somewhat haphazard. The state of affairs was sometimes akin to having an HR department to handle the personnel management of managers, and an industrial relations/personnel department to look after the remainder. HR professionals were seen as an intellectual elite who enjoyed easy access to the higher reaches of corporate management, but who lacked a certain shop-floor credibility. In consequence, the legitimacy of initiatives formulated in the one setting for extension into the domain of the other was a source of tension. This again served to hamper the implementation of a coherent HR/IR policy. It is interesting to compare this with the point made by Purcell in *Beyond the Workplace* (Marginson, Edwards, Martin, Purcell, & Sisson, 1988). Coming at the issue from the other direction, he observed the paradox that large, well-established corporate personnel departments, heavily engaged in managing the institutional framework of industrial relations, tended to be "isolated from wider fundamental decisions in strategic management. As such they function more as the managers of constraints, not opportunities" (1988, p. 79).

The generalizable proposition that might deservedly be made, with regard to most of the mainstream companies during this period, is that marginalization of unions and industrial relations carried a powerful symbolic message about the new order. More pressing priorities were being signaled, and there was at least an implied viability in the alternative devices of direct employee communication and job-level participation, close appraisal and performance-related rewards. How much of this was bluff and how much stemmed from deep-seated belief (or even misconception) was hard to gauge. In any case, the halfhearted way in which the distancing of the trade unions was being handled at least afforded a certain comfort that a pragmatic reversal might be steered, should changed circumstances suggest such a need.

Conclusions

Mainstream employing organizations in Britain have, since about the mid-1980s, been characterized by a flurry of managerial initiatives that, either by design or secondary consequence, impact upon the practice of industrial relations. The sheer number of initiatives was unusual. Using a checklist of 27 dimensions, it was shown that managerial activity had been evident across most headings.

The nature of these initiatives shows some considerable commonality across different organizations and across industry sectors and the public/private ownership divide. A considerable amount of emulation has evidently been occurring. However, it is probably fair to say that the mainstream organizations have not rigorously and consciously pursued "Japanization," Human Resource Management, or any other coherent model. But what they have done is begin to install a whole array of measures, which, in effect, mark a significant departure from the proceduralist orthodoxy or formula, which for most of them characterized the post-Second World War period.

The scope of these managerial initiatives has also been unusually wide-ranging. They have involved not only changes to organizational and managerial structures, beliefs and values, but also a whole panoply of measures directed at redrawing the employment relationship. Many of them were devised and driven from outside personnel departments. Indeed, personnel specialists were among the least enthusiastic in their support for these initiatives.

The extent to which the range of initiatives were mutually reinforcing was cast into doubt. In many instances schemes appeared to have been launched independently of each other. Nonetheless, there was often a kind of underlying logic to them, so that, although not fully planned in relation to each other, the separate initiatives could be construed as pushing relations along in the same general direction.

When viewed as a totality, these initiatives have impacted upon the conventional practice of industrial relations and, in a more subtle fashion, have changed the very nature of those relations—at least during the period in question. Given the uneven character of the new approaches, as manifested in the phenomenon of dualism in particular, the future continuity of the model can by no means be assured. This issue is worth pursuing as a final point of discussion. Were the developments described in this chapter a transient phenomenon, characteristic only of the period of the research?

The research period (1986-1988) was characterized by certain distinctive features. It was a high point of Thatcherism, and a period of rapidly rising real incomes. Deregulation was being vigorously pursued; experimentation and novelty had become cultural norms. In other words the developments obviously occurred within a particular context.

Nonetheless, it can be noted that tendencies of a similar kind were being reported in many other countries. Furthermore, there has been little subsequent evidence to suggest any significant abandonment of the policies described here, the wholesale substitution of some alternative model, or the reinstitution of the preexisting one. Continuing contact with a number of these case organizations leads this researcher to believe that, at least at the time of writing (mid-1991), the broad character of the managerial orientations, policies, and actions described here has persisted. Future stability is far less certain—not only because of possible political changes and the repercussions of EEC regulation, but also because, as the paper makes clear, the initiatives, albeit impressive in their number, were not firmly grounded. It might be argued that while the easy part (the high-profile awareness programs, the launch of new direct communication channels and the like) has now been done, the next phase (consolidation and embedding the new ways deep into these organizations) has yet to be convincingly demonstrated. As argued here, the failure to work out a coherent policy that embraces human resource management and industrial relations is surely a sign of potential instability.[1]

Note

1. This issue forms the basis of a new ESRC project (1992-1994), titled "Managerial and Union Perceptions of Individualism and Collectivism in the 1990s," being undertaken at the University of Loughborough.

References

Ahlstrand, B. (1990). *The quest for productivity: A case study of Fawley after Flanders.* Cambridge: Cambridge University Press.
Bassett, P. (1986). *Strike free.* London: Macmillan.

PART V

Industrial Relations
and Political Transformation

17 \ Myth and Reality: Trade Unions and Industrial Relations in the Transition to Democracy

AMIRA GALIN

Over the past few years the world has witnessed a massive transformation in the political and industrial relations scene. The political transformation has been mainly one of change from nondemocratic regimes, be they authoritarian, totalitarian, or military, to democracies. In many cases this process has either influenced, or has been influenced by, the industrial relations system, and has changed the status of the trade unions vis-à-vis government and employers. Because political changes have taken place so rapidly, we still do not have a very clear picture of the relationship between political transformation and industrial relations, let alone any explanatory theories of the relationship.

Be that as it may, the relationship between political transformation and industrial relations may be considered in two dimensions: First, the myth, a complex image, tightly interwoven with expectations, aspirations, and conceptual evaluations. Second, the reality, which consists of genuine observations, and manifests itself in a complex of new and unfamiliar processes, generating conclusions and actions. The main question in this context is whether the relationship between political transformation and industrial relations lives up to expectations, or, by some quirk of irony, ends up producing the opposite effect. In other words, does the reality fit the myth?

AUTHOR'S NOTE: The author wishes to thank Professors Yoram Zeira and Ehud Harari for helpful comments on an earlier draft of this chapter.

On this question I found the national reports on political change and industrial relations both illuminating and puzzling. They were illuminating in that they helped me develop a broad conceptual framework of the complex relationship between recent political changes and industrial relations, and puzzling because they indicated an odd contradiction between myth and reality.

It has been widely accepted (Adams, 1989) that in most nondemocratic regimes (whether in Eastern Europe, Africa, Latin America, or other parts of the world) governments used to be the dominant actor, while trade unions were at best tolerated, closely controlled, and often repressed. The myth of a strong government, inevitably being accompanied by weak, repressed trade unions, has prevailed. It has been alleged that in many nondemocratic states industrial relations, as known in Western democracies, did not exist because of the resistance of the ruling elite to the rise of strong and independent union movements (Fashoyin, 1989). However, the national reports clearly show that these allegedly weak and ineffective trade unions played a most important role in stimulating the transition to democracy in many authoritarian states. Could it be that the main issue has not been the formal definition of a government as nondemocratic and repressive, but its real ability to exert authority over trade unions and other social groups? Could the myth of a strong nondemocratic government and weak, repressed trade unions have been ill-founded (Migdal, 1987, 1988)?

Even more puzzling is the gap between myth and reality after the political transformation. According to the myth, in countries of Eastern Europe and a number of African and Latin American countries, political transformation is inducing a complete overhaul of the industrial relations: "There is movement towards free trade unionism, towards genuine collective bargaining and decentralized and carefully considered dispute resolution procedures" (Gladstone, 1992, p. 1). Free trade unions, which have finally become legal partners to collective bargaining, are expected to be strong and vigorous. However, there is an indication in the national reports that once the political system has begun the transition toward democracy, trade unions may suffer an abrupt setback in their status. This is expressed in many cases in limitations on their ability to pursue political goals, and at times even economic goals. Such a setback in the unions' status, in a relatively democratic environment, negates the myth of the strengthening impact of democracy on trade unions. The myth has recently been shaken, to a certain extent, even in Western democracies, the cradle of free trade unionism and democratic industrial relations, where some of the traditionally democratic governments have clearly followed the strategy of weakening the status and integrity of organized labor (Keller, 1989).

How can we explain this setback in the unions' status as the environment moves toward democracy? The setback in the unions' status is even more puzzling, considering the expectations of, and requirements for free, strong unions, expressed by some Western governments and international institutions that have become, with the disintegration of the Soviet Union, the only source of assistance to many governments going through the process of political transformation.

It is the aim of this chapter to discuss the contradiction between myth and reality in the status of the trade unions and the industrial relations systems in the transition to democracy. The discussion will include an investigation of trade union status under nondemocratic regimes, examination of the formal and informal changes in trade union status in the transition to democracy, and a rundown of the factors at the root of the accepted misconceptions.

Of course, industrial relations systems in general, and trade unions in particular, vary from continent to continent and from country to country. The mode of transition to democracy may also vary in its character, pace, and results. However, in the effort to explain the relationship between political transformation and industrial relations, it is essential to combine certain common variables and to elaborate upon an explanatory conceptual framework. The conceptual framework offered in this chapter is based mainly on the reported experience of several countries, as presented to the Ninth World Congress of the International Industrial Relations Association. The experience of the majority of African countries is reported by Mesfin G. Michael, and the experience in South Africa is reported in Clive Thompson's paper. The experience in Eastern Europe is reported by Ludwik Florek, Lajos Héthy, and Bogdan Kavcic. The experience of Chile is reported by Emilio Morgado Valenzuela, and that of Hong Kong by David A. Levin and Stephen Chiu.

Though the following conceptual framework stems from a comparison of national experiences as presented in these papers, it may nevertheless indicate trends in other countries facing political transformation as well.

Strong Governments—Weak Trade Unions

DOES THE MYTH MATCH THE REALITY?

Trade unions tend to play a major role in the struggle against nondemocratic (colonial, military authoritarian, and totalitarian) regimes. The pattern of unions defying bans on independent political activities, to join and even assume political leadership, is repeating itself in the struggle for political change in many African countries, in the struggle against apartheid in South Africa, and in the struggle against Communist regimes in some East European countries.

Thus, history shows that in many African countries, despite restrictions and repressive measures imposed by the colonial regimes, trade unions enjoyed privileged positions and formed alliances with nationalist movements. Gradually after independence, however, almost all African countries established a one-party system or a military dictatorship, which co-opted the trade unions under the control of the party apparatus or within the framework of imposed labor legislation. Despite these measures, unions in African countries often organized mass demonstrations and strikes in order to compel their governments to accept their economic and political demands. The same trend of union activity has been noted in South Africa as well. Here, during the 5-year state of emergency of 1985 to 1990, the unions attacked the political status quo, while other political opposition groups were largely pushed underground. South African unions were the most organized opposition active in the country. The substantial differences notwithstanding, similar patterns can be found in South America. One example is Chile, where, despite the repression of trade unionism under the military regime of 1973 to 1990, trade unions played a key role in fighting the regime. In a way the experience of neighboring Argentina is similar. The military regime that began in 1976 was unable to suppress the alliance mounted by the trade unions, which articulated the political aspirations of the vast majority of the population and led to the return of civilian rule in 1983 (Munck, 1988, p. 140). But perhaps the most famous example is Poland, where the impact of the Solidarity trade union movement on political change was simply not to be ignored. Solidarity emerged not only as a trade union but also as an independent political power that forced, both legally and later also through underground activity, a complete reform of the political system in Poland. Undoubtedly, the waves of illegal strikes (especially the one of 1989) directly caused of the termination of the Communist system in Poland.

An example to the contrary is Hong Kong. Here, the colonial regime did not generate strong, militant trade unions pressuring for democratic rights, as was the case in many other colonial regimes. The unions rarely challenged the power structure in Hong Kong, nor did they pressure for improved labor legislation or redistribution of resources to the workers. Because of differences over ideology, goals, and strategies, they also found it difficult to cooperate with one another.

This exception only proves the rule, as the nature of the colonial regime in Hong Kong is substantially different from that elsewhere. The colonial government in Hong Kong exhibits certain democratic features and does not impose itself on an established local community, as did most other colonial regimes. It provides for a stable political and legal framework, with minimal intervention and state control. The Chinese community, for its part, accepts the British rule voluntarily and willingly. Up until the 1990 agreement between China and Britain, trade unions in Hong Kong were rather divided and weak. Their weakness was demonstrated in the fact that, despite their involvement in the bodies set up for the drafting of the Basic Law, which will determine the structure of Hong Kong's future legislature, their overall influence on the Basic Law was marginal. Thus, the transformation in Hong Kong is not from an authoritarian regime to democracy, as was the case in many other colonial regimes, but rather from partial democracy to an unknown entity. This may result in a reverse development trend—from weak unions to stronger, politically involved unions. Indeed, this can already be detected in the current growing political activism of the trade unions in Hong Kong.

Several attributes strengthen trade unions' status under nondemocratic governments and enable them to promote their activity, despite close government control and even repressive measures at times.

1. The Unions' Capability to Unite and Organize Different Parts of Society: In the absence of organized political parties in a nondemocratic regime, trade unions are the social organizations that can cross ethnic and religious borders and represent the interests of workers, as well as those of the community in which they operate. Thus, under nondemocratic governments, unions often demand not only better wages and working conditions, but also other social-political benefits, such as freedom of the press and human rights.

2. The Unions' Economic Control over Key Sectors of the Economy: In contrast to political opposition, which is based on political power alone, trade unions usually have an economic power base as well. They may be protected from the ruling elite by their ability to influence workers in key sectors of the economy, and by the economic weapon of strikes. Also, in many nondemocratic regimes, employer organizations hardly exist, or when they do exist they are often integrated into the ruling party, closely controlled and co-opted into carrying out the national economic policy. In the absence of independent employer opposition, unions can strengthen their economic grip on key sectors of the economy.

3. The Support Advantage: Surprisingly enough, despite possible sanctions, trade unions enjoy substantial support under nondemocratic regimes. Since trade unions are often the only organization that can protest and remain relatively inviolate under nondemocratic governments, they tend to act as a magnet for vast circles of opposition. They also have a broad appeal to the workers, who see them as their spokesman, not only in providing the solutions to their day-to-day problems and fulfilling their needs, but also in forging democratization and other political changes. In some instances, the increased union membership serves as another "safety belt" to shield unions from the repressive measures of nondemocratic governments.

4. *International Pressure:* The demand for full freedom of association is customarily a criterion for international support. As threats to the survival of nondemocratic governments and their leaders come not only from their own societies but in many cases also from international sources, even the most nondemocratic governments are hesitant to risk international criticism and sanctions for repressing trade union activity.

Thus, the myth of weak unions under strong, nondemocratic governments should be considered critically. If the measure of a union's strength is its capability to recruit a large number of supporters, to present the supporters' interests, and to achieve economic and political demands despite a hostile government, then unions such as Solidarity in Communist Poland, unions in African countries, and black unions under the apartheid government of South Africa must be viewed as possessing substantial strength.

The Aftermath
of Political Transformation

THE DEMOCRATIC ENVIRONMENT
AND TRADE UNION PERFORMANCE

The introduction of multiparty democracy in countries with a nondemocratic background often means reconstruction of the union movements. At times, it means complete separation of trade unions from governmental or party institutions, and in many instances also the separation of employer organizations. Trade unions become independent entities, often under a new legal code, which abolishes the old legal barriers on the right of association and free collective bargaining, and introduces recognition of the right to strike in particular and the right to collective dispute in general.

Thus, despite the differences in culture, history, and circumstances, the similarities in the impact of the political transformation in various countries and continents are amazing.

In Eastern Europe, the new industrial relations environment has come about largely due to the separation of the trade unions from government and party control, and the competition between the old and the newly formed trade unions. For example, in Hungary in the period between 1988 and 1990, a new industrial system emerged after the final separation of government, trade unions, and employer associations. Under this new system, all legal bans on free collective bargaining and strike activity were lifted, and seven trade union confederations (most of them based on their traditional structures and former leadership, but some newly formed) were established. Similarly, in Poland, the new industrial relations environment, which emerged after the establishment of the democratic government in 1989, has been characterized by two centers of trade unionism—the post-Communist trade unions (the "All-Poland Trade Union Alliance," which is now free of one-party control) and Solidarity. All the unions attained the right to represent workers' interests in collective disputes and also to influence the labor and social legislation process, including its interpretation and application. In Yugoslavia, too, where the political future is still by no means clear, the traditional trade unions have been reorganized to resemble the trade unions of Western countries, and some new trade unions have been established. With the new legislature of 1990-1991, collective bargaining was introduced for the regulation of labor relations, and the right to strike has been attained and used.

In Chile, as a typical example of Latin America, the transformation to democracy, in March 1990, has also influenced the most important representative organizations of workers, the CUT (The Unitary Workers Central) and the employer organizations, the CPC (The Confederation of Production and Commerce). Both unions and employer organizations have become more autonomous, and new channels for collective agreements between them have opened.

Despite the differences, the transformation of the many African countries, willingly or unwillingly, to multiparty democracies has resulted in the emergence of a new form of the industrial relations system. This has included the separation of the unions from the single ruling party, as well as the declaration of independence from any direct government control on the unions' administration. It has also included the lifting of bans on the right to organize workers and has eased the requirements for trade union recognition. The legal changes and newly emerging freedom of activities were expected to produce a strengthening of the unions. However, a close look at the reality, as reflected in the national reports, reveals that despite expectations to the contrary, the status of the trade unions has in fact weakened, not strengthened, as a result of democratization. True, the new legislation and rules often accord many powers to the trade unions—they may legally organize labor, they can represent labor interests within free collective bargaining, they can play an important part in the process of dispute resolutions, and they are easily able to gain recognition. However, there is still the question of whether these powers can be effectively utilized. The limited success of many unions in exercising their new rights suggests that the contribution of democratization to the power of the trade unions is not great.

The Unions' Difficulties
After Political Transformation

DOES REALITY REFLECT THE MYTH?

As a result of the political transformation to democracy, many external constraints on trade union activities are often lifted, and the freedom to negotiate and bargain with employers and government agencies is achieved. However, the serious internal problems that begin to build up, following the political change, tend to undermine the trade unions from within and even threaten to blow them apart. Thus, almost paradoxically, most of the factors that contribute to enhancing the powers of the unions under nondemocratic governments tend to disappear in the transition to democracy. Some of the reasons for this phenomenon are as follows.

1. The Unions' Capability to Unite Different Parts of the Society Tend to Fade. A democratic environment encourages pluralism, and internal division within and among trade unions. This usually results in rivalry between the unions and other interest groups, as well as among the various unions themselves.

Even in a country such as Poland, which is assumed to be home to a strong active union, a change in the status of Solidarity is apparent. Solidarity, the same trade union that played such a decisive role in bringing about democratization, has changed and weakened for several reasons: It has lost its attractiveness as a force for uniting opposition, as it has become only one of the many forces pushing for democracy; it has suffered internal division, which split the union into several factions; and it finds it hard to compete for membership with other trade unions, which can support workers' demands more effectively, as they are in opposition to the government. Comparable trends can also be traced in most East European countries, where pluralism and internal division (Héthy, 1991, pp. 17-19) have a negative impact on trade union status in the eyes of the people.

2. The Unions' Economic and Political Grasp Is Substantially Reduced. The divisions among and within the trade unions also act to reduce the unions' control over key sectors of the economy: The rivalry among factions of organized labor has been effectively exploited by both governments and employers to weaken the economic status of the unions.

Thus, for example, there is evidence that in some African countries the weakening of trade unions was encouraged by the new relatively democratic governments. In these countries, governments have deliberately used the demand for freedom of association to weaken trade union solidarity by encouraging the formation of many rival trade union centers. Similar developments are typical of certain countries in Eastern Europe (Héthy, 1991, p. 17). In Hungary, the acute conflict between the traditional unions and the newly formed unions led to fresh political intervention, in the form of two trade union acts that were passed in July 1991. In Yugoslavia, during the reestablishment phase, none of the unions had much power because their organizational structure and experience did not fit the new social conditions. Some of the trade unions were affiliated with political parties, transferring the rivalry among the political parties to the trade union arena. The central government quickly learned to take advantage of the unions' weakness and simply ignored them for the most part.

Another development that contributes to the reduction in union status following democratization is the expansion of the private sector, including the promotion of free employer organizations. These employer organizations oppose trade unions and do their best (not without success) to weaken their influence on the economy. Privatization increases the volume of the private sector and thus the power of the private employers and employer organizations. As privatization is a central demand of international institutions and Western countries for providing economic aid, reducing the economic hold of the trade unions becomes almost inevitable. This process is evident in many African countries as well as in East European countries.

3. There Is a Reduction in Support for Union Activities. As trade unions cease to be the opposition spokesman and return to focus on typical trade union problems, certain structural changes occur. Various opposition groups, which needed the "umbrella" of the union under nondemocratic governments, now form their own political centers and no longer need the union movement to represent them. This process, in conjunction with the development of union rivalry, has at times a further impact on reducing the level of unionization.

Further, the privatization process, the growth of small and medium-size undertakings, and at times the development of atypical work patterns tend to reduce union support among workers who work under these free market conditions. At times the result is even a reduction in the level of unionization. Thus, for example, in Poland the level of unionization was reduced drastically after the political change (45% in 1990, as compared to 95% before the political change), and the same process has also been taking place in many other countries in Eastern Europe (Héthy, 1991, p. 19).

4. There Is a Loss of International Support. International pressure, which generally encourages and protects union activity under nondemocratic regimes, usually disappears after political transformation, assuming that the goal of the change has been achieved. Once unions have gained their independence and bargaining rights following the democratic change, international support is suspended and weak unions are left without the international encouragement to which they had been accustomed in the past.

Conclusion

The gap between myth and reality may result in disillusionment and disappointment with the performance of trade unions in the transition to democracy. How can we account for this gap?

To understand the problem of losing power in the transition to democracy, two levels of union activity should be identified. The first is the external arena, in which the union officials interact with representatives of such other entities as governments and employers. The other is the internal, informal arena, in which union officials interact with the constituency they wish to represent, and with representatives of other unions.

Under nondemocratic government, union leaders face formal constraints in the external arena, such as on the right to negotiate and bargain with employers and government agencies. After political transformation, these formal constraints are often lifted, and freedom of external interaction is achieved. However, it would be a grave mistake to assume that the formal right of interaction with external agencies in itself determines the unions' capabilities in the new political environment. While it is true that legislation and agreements provide trade unions with various formal rights, the question of whether these rights can be effectively exercised still remains. In many cases, unions are not able to use these rights effectively because of new external pressures from employer organizations and the new government and, more important, because of serious internal problems.

The second arena within which the unions operate, that of the internal organization, is the one that to a large extent will reshape and determine the unions' capabilities and modes of interaction with other groups and organizations. If severe internal problems begin to build up, they may weaken and even threaten the unions' survival from within, thus negating the effectiveness and efficiency of their new formal rights.

The myth of weak unions under nondemocratic governments, and strong unions in the transition to democracy, stems from a limited inquiry into the internal facets of trade unions' performance, and from preoccupation with the formulation of formal institutions (collective bargaining, dispute resolution, and so on) rather than with their effectiveness and efficiency. Understanding reality should go below the surface of these formal external dimensions and enter into the analysis and understanding of the informal aspects and internal processes within and among trade unions.

Formal external rights or agreements do not help unions face three new problems in the transition to democracy. The first is the reduction of the union's internal power. This expresses itself in the loss of support for the union, and consequent reduction in its membership (such as Solidarity losing its solidarity), impairment of the union's capabilities to resolve conflicts among its own interests groups, and the union's struggle to ensure its own survival in the face of the new competition from other unions. The second is the problem of powerful emerging employer organizations, bent on minimizing the union's power and in many instances gaining government support in their struggle. The third is the problem of union-government relations: This concerns the union's power to influence government's priorities, legislation, and methods of intervention between labor and capital.

Against the background of the disintegration of old forms of union control, many unions find themselves, at least temporarily, with only a limited ability to solve these problems. Thus, despite their new formal rights, the reality is that, in the transition to democracy, strong unions have been a rarity.

References

Adams, R. (1989). Recent trends in industrial relations studies and theory—General report. *Proceedings—International Industrial Relations Association 8th World Congress*, 3-7.

Fashoyin, T. (1989). Recent trends in industrial relations research and theory in developing countries. *Proceedings—International Industrial Relations Association 8th World Congress*, 129.

Florek, L. (1992). The impact of industrial relations on political transformation in Poland. *Proceedings of the Ninth World Congress of the International Industrial Relations Association*. Sydney: IIRA.

Gladstone, A. (1992). Introduction. In A. Gladstone, H. Wheeler, J. Rojot, F. Eyraud, & R. Ben-Israel (Eds.), *Labour relations in changing environment* (pp. 1-13). Berlin: de Gruyter.

Héthy, L. (1991, September). *Changing labour relations in Eastern (Central) Europe*. Paper prepared for the 3rd European Regional Congress of the IIRA, Bari, Italy.

Héthy, L. (1992). Political changes and transformation of industrial relations in Hungary. *Proceedings of the Ninth World Congress of the International Industrial Relations Association*. Sydney: IIRA.

Kavcic, B. (1992). Industrial relations in post-socialist Yugoslavia. *Proceedings of the Ninth World Congress of the International Industrial Relations Association*. Sydney: IIRA.

Keller, B. K. (1989). The role of the state as corporate actor in industrial relations systems. *Proceedings—International Industrial Relations Association 8th World Congress*, 53-67.

Levin, D. A., & Chiu, S. (1992). Decolonization without independence: Political change and trade unionism in Hong Kong. *Proceedings of the Ninth World Congress of the International Industrial Relations Association*. Sydney: IIRA.

Michael, M. G. (1992). Perestroika: Its effects on labor relations in Africa. *Proceedings of the Ninth World Congress of the International Industrial Relations Association*. Sydney: IIRA.

Migdal, J. S. (1987). Strong states, weak states: Power and accommodation. In M. Weiner & S. P. Huntington (Eds.), *Understanding political development*. Boston: Little, Brown.

Migdal, J. S. (1988). *Strong societies and weak states*. Princeton, NJ: Princeton University Press.

Morgado, E. (1992). Labor relations in the transition to democracy: The case of Chile. *Proceedings of the Ninth World Congress of the International Industrial Relations Association*. Sydney: IIRA.

Munck, R. (1988). Capital restructuring and labour recomposition under military regime: Argentina (1976-1983). In R. Southhall (Ed.), *Trade unions and the new industrialization of the third world* (pp. 121-141). Pittsburgh: University of Pittsburgh Press.

Thompson, C. (1992). Strategy and opportunism: Trade unions as agents for change in South Africa. *Proceedings of the Ninth World Congress of the International Industrial Relations Association*. Sydney: IIRA.

18 \ The Impact of Industrial Relations on Political Transformation in Poland

LUDWIK FLOREK

The role of industrial relations on political changes in Poland differed between the period of struggling for the dismantling of the Communist system, and that of the period after the establishment of a democratic government. The previous period is connected first of all with the emergence of Solidarity in August 1980 and its legal and (after the imposition of martial law in December 1981) underground activity. This period ended with the creation of the first democratic Government in September 1989. Some features of the first period, however, existed earlier since Solidarity was a continuation of the tradition of the Polish work force fighting against low wages and poor conditions of life and work resulting from the centrally planned economy and the totalitarian Communist system. (There were waves of strikes in 1956, 1970, and 1976.)

This chapter examines the impact of trade unions, collective labor disputes and strikes, and workers' participation on political transformation. As regards collective agreements, they have not been concluded for many years. The absence of collective bargaining resulted from the lack of a real market and of genuine employers in the state sector. Another reason is that the imperfect legislation on collective bargaining of 1986 (see Florek, 1987, pp. 81-98) has not been changed so far.

The role of Polish industrial relations is in some respects similar to that in other East European countries for at least two reasons. First, before the establishment of Solidarity in 1980, all of these countries, including Poland, had similar labor relations[1] shaped along the Soviet model (which was a result of the dominant role of the state, ruled by the Communist Party, and state ownership of industry). Second, though they are diversified now, all post-Communist countries are experiencing comparable difficulties in transforming political systems. They are also all taking similar steps to solve their political and economic problems (see "Industrial Relations," 1990; "Sweeping Economic and Labour Reforms," 1990).

But the Polish case also has some specific features. Poland, as distinct from other countries of this group, took over the pre-1939 legal system[2] assuring only the modifications and interpretations necessary to become consistent with the needs and goals of a Communist system (Matey, 1988a, p. 191). Second, Poland began earlier (about 7 years earlier[3] than any other East European country) to search for a new model of labor relations.[4] It also has the greatest amount of positive and negative experience in this field. This resulted among other things from the fact that the Polish economic crises began earlier than in other Communist countries of Eastern Europe and, what is more important, the impact on income and living standards has been greater.[5] Third, Polish labor relations played a more important role in the dismantling of communism than industrial relations in other East European countries. Fourth, the changes in Poland influenced to a large extent (along with Soviet *perestroika*) political developments in the whole of Central and Eastern Europe.

The Period Before 1989

TRADE UNIONS

In this period the impact of industrial relations on political changes seems to be one of the most evident in modern history. This was because "Solidarity," as an independent trade union, played a decisive role in political transformations. Solidarity was the first independent political power in Poland and in the Communist bloc. The significance of its role, however, also resulted from the fact that Solidarity was a trade union. The emergence of an independent political power in the form of a trade union can be explained by many reasons. First, a certain prewar tradition of free trade unions existed in Poland. Second, in a totalitarian state, an independent trade union could be established more easily than an opposition political party. Owing to the lack of different political and social organizations, plant work forces were the only organized social groups able to protest. Thanks to the fact that they were in great numbers, the various work forces were protected against sanctions that would have been applied against individuals or small political parties. Third, under Polish conditions an independent trade union was supported by vast numbers of workers, more than any opposition political movement, because the union demanded higher wages and better terms of employment, not just political change. Fourth, as a trade union, Solidarity could very quickly establish its sections in almost all enterprises and public institutions (like the previously existing trade unions). Fifth, the fact that the Polish opposition had the form of a trade union permitted international pressure for the observance by Poland of its international obligations arising from ratified human rights covenants and International Labor Organization Conventions.[6] On the other hand, "Solidarity," as the only independent force at the time of its emergence, attracted all the opposition forces (among others, the Roman Catholic Church and intellectual groups) that actively supported the activity of the trade union.

Since the story of Solidarity is well known, I would like only to point out a few basic aspects of its role in political transformations in Poland:

1. Solidarity was not merely demanding higher wages and better conditions, the normal trade unions' concerns, but the wholesale reform of the political system.

2. Its demands such as, for example, independent trade unions, freedom of the press, print and publications,[7] release of political prisoners, meant the abolition of the previous totalitarian system.

3. Solidarity brought about changes in political attitudes in the vast circles of Polish society[8] that opposed Communist rule and supported democratic transformations to an extent that finally forced the Communist regime to give up power.

4. In 1989 Solidarity won a partially free election, gaining 35% of the seats in the Sejm (the Lower House of the Polish Parliament) and 99% in the Senate and, afterward, created the first non-Communist government.

COLLECTIVE DISPUTES AND STRIKES

The impact of Solidarity on political transformation is strongly connected with collective disputes and strikes. Through many decades of Communist rule, strikes were banned (though there was no explicit legal prohibition) and when they broke out they were fought by political means (e.g., anti-strike propaganda) and their leaders were often repressed.[9] In August 1980 strikes were recognized de facto in the Gdansk Agreement,[10] but prohibited again after the imposition of martial law on December 13, 1981. The 1982 Trade Union Act provided for the first time in a Communist country the right to strike.[11] The exercise of this right was subjected to many conditions specified in the Act (among others, a quite long procedure for the settlement of collective disputes that had to precede a strike). The law also contained a very long list of public employees and essential services for whom strikes were not permitted. In addition, the 1986 Amendment to the Labor Code prohibited strikes during collective bargaining.[12] As a result, almost all the strikes in the 1980s were unlawful because it was very difficult to strike legally.[13]

This nonobservance of law in the past can be, however, considered positive from the political point of view. Illegal strikes exercised a strong pressure on the Communist government. The right to strike was used especially in 1980-1981 to introduce political changes, because workers were very often demanding not only an increase in wages but also the restructuring of the state authorities or the dismissal of local party or administration functionaries. Strikes were also one of the reasons for giving up power by Communists. In particular, the wave of illegal strikes in Poland in May 1988 was the direct cause of the Round Table Talks,[14] leading to the dismantling of the Communist system.

WORKERS' PARTICIPATION

Another item of industrial relations influencing political transformation was workers' participation. The introduction of workers' councils[15] after 1956 was supposedly to serve in the democratization of labor relations and the entire political system. Afterward this idea was supplemented with the necessity of socializing the means of production (which were in fact more state than social property). In fact, workers' participation in the past contributed to a certain limited independence of enterprises. For example, workers' councils often supported managers when they were in conflict with the state administration (especially when managers demanded a change in the plan imposed on an enterprise, or an increase in wages). On the other hand, workers' councils were controlled to a large extent by enterprise party organizations. Their role was also limited because enterprises were dependent on the state administration.[16]

In 1981 new legislation (still in force) on workers' participation in decision making in undertakings[17] was adopted and increased the role of workers' participation in the 1980s.[18] In particular, since 1981 (except for the martial law period) workers' councils have been participating in the appointment of enterprise directors. This had different forms, ranging from expressing views concerning the candidates or organizing a competition procedure (connected with the interviewing of candidates by a workers' council), to the election of a manager. As a result, workers' participation weakened in the 1980s, a personnel policy of the Party known throughout the world as *nomenklatura,* and meant a certain democratization of both economic and political power.

8. It is worth mentioning that even the Communist Party was democratized to a large extent, and this strongly affected later political transformation, in particular the peaceful transmission of power in 1989. Moreover, the previous official trade unions changed their structure and character.

9. Although the law was silent as to participation in strikes, there was a tendency to treat such action as a breach of work discipline, thereby justifying summary dismissal. In some cases, even more rigorous measures against strikers were adopted. See Szubert (1990, p. 63).

10. Concluded between the Solidarity strike committee and the government.

11. Articles 43-52 of the Trade Union Act.

12. See Article 241, para. 7 of the Labor Code (Decree of June 26, 1974, Journal of Laws, No. 24, item No. 141 with further amendments). An English translation: The Labor Code of the Polish People's Republic, Warsaw, 1979. See also the amendment of the Labor Code on collective agreements of November 26, 1986 (Journal of Laws, No. 42, item No. 201).

13. Wildcat strikes also continued after the recognition of Solidarity unions in 1988; despite their illegal character, sanctions were not applied on the strikers because the general political climate of the country did not permit the rigid application of the law. See Szubert (1990, p. 68).

14. The Round Table Talks were a round of political negotiations held in the spring of 1989 between the last Communist government and Solidarity together with some other opposition groups, resulting in a partially free Parliament election.

15. A characteristic feature of the Polish system of industrial relations in the state sector is the coexistence, at the undertaking level, of two mechanisms of workers' representations: elected workers' councils and trade union representatives. Both bodies negotiate with the management, and although their respective functions and attributions are spelled out in detailed legislation, there are problems of coordination. On the other hand, the interests of the workers' representatives, from the very nature of things, run parallel to the interests of the trade union. As a result, workers' participation partially overlaps trade union action.

16. See, for example, Sewerynski (1985, pp. 103-109), which presents the evolution of workers' participation in Poland.

17. The Act of September 25, 1981, on the State Enterprise (Unified text: Journal of Laws, No. 35, item No. 201) and the Act of September 25, 1981, on the Employees' Self-Government in State Enterprises (Journal of Laws, No. 24, item No. 123).

18. For more details on the competence of workers' councils, see, for example, Florek (1983, pp. 38-39).

19. Matey (1988b, p. 318) even put forward the view that "with their embattled attitude to economic and social matters they increasingly gained the confidence of Polish society." Actually this was not confirmed later, when none of the candidates of these trade unions won in the 1989 Parliament election.

20. Polls show that a large portion of workers are against privatization and a free market economy; this could also slow down political changes.

21. See Articles 19-23 of the Trade Union Act of May 23, 1991 (Journal of Laws, No. 55, item No. 234).

22. See the Act on Employers' Organizations of May 23, 1991 (Journal of Laws, No. 55, item No. 235).

23. See Articles 1 and 17 of the Act of May 23, 1991, on the Settlement of Collective Labor Disputes (Journal of Laws, No. 55, item No. 236).

24. The state administration has consistently blocked these increases by a special drastic remuneration tax.

25. See Article 1, Section 12, of the Amendment of the Act on the State Enterprises (Journal of Laws, 1990, No. 17, item No. 99).

26. It is anticipated, however, that workers' councils will be kept in state enterprises, or enterprises which will be transferred to workers' ownership (which is possible if the staff buys all the assets of an enterprise).

27. Article 17, Section 1, of the Act on State Enterprises Privatization of July 13, 1990 (Journal of Laws, No. 51, item No. 298).

28. The problem of political compensation for workers of state enterprises is of great importance under Polish conditions. Most of them supported Solidarity and its struggle for political change. Now, in the period of transformation to a market economy, they will lose a large part of the social benefits and privileges that existed in a centrally planned system. It especially concerns job security because, since the beginning of 1990, the unemployment rate has grown from zero to 10% of the Polish work force, and further mass redundancies are expected.

29. Article 24, Section 1, of the above Act.

30. Article 5, Section 1.

31. Since freedom of association is a substantial element of political democracy, it is included in the 1966 International Covenant on Civil and Political Rights (Article 22, para. 1) and is also sometimes guaranteed in constitutions of various countries. See Ziskind (1976, p. 205). See also Javillier: in *Manuel de droit du travail,* Paris, 1986, at 25: ". . . la possibilité d'expression des divergences d'interets entre employeurs et salaries, entre patronat et syndicats, constitue un element essentiel de la democratie politique . . . ."

References

Florek, L. (1983). Fragen des polnischen Arbeitsrechts. *Recht der Arbeit, 36,* 38-39.

Florek, L. (1987). Le neuveau droit de conventions collectives de travail. *Droit Polonais Contemporain,* 81-98.

ILO (International Labor Organization). (1989a). *Social and Labor Bulletin,* 128, 243.

ILO. (1989b). *World Labor Report* (Vol. 4, p. 18). Geneva: Author.

Industrial relations: Today and tomorrow. (1990). *Social and Labor Bulletin* (ILO), 13-14.

Javillier, J. C. (1986). In *Manuel de droit du travail.*

Matey, M. (1988a). Essential traits of socialist labour codes. *Comparative Labour Law, 2,* 191.

Matey, M. (1988b). Labour law and industrial relations in Poland. In R. Blanpain (Ed.), *International encyclopedia for labour law and industrial relations.* The Netherlands: Kluwer.

Sewerynski, M. (1985). La participation des travailleurs a la gestion de l'enterprise en droit polonais. *Droit de travail dans l'enterprise, Folia Iuridica* (Kodz), *19,* 103-109.

Sweeping economic and labor reforms. (1990). *Social and Labor Bulletin* (ILO), 229-230.

Szubert, W. (1990). New trends in Polish labour relations. *Comparative Labour Law, 12,* 62-64.

Ziskind, D. (1976). Labour law in 143 constitutions. *Comparative Labour Law, 1,* 205.

19 \ Political Changes
and the Transformation of
Industrial Relations in Hungary

LAJOS HÉTHY

The transformation of Hungary's industrial relations system started as early as the 1970s—as a follow-up to the Economic Reform of 1968—and gained impetus in 1988-1990.[1]

The New Industrial Relations System
as It Emerged in 1988–1990

In 1988-1990—in the period when Hungary's last communist government (headed by Prime Minister Miklós Németh) achieved a remarkable record in facilitating a smooth and peaceful alteration of both the economic and political systems—new perspectives opened up for changes in industrial relations. These included: (a) the exclusion of the Communist party (and any political parties) as an actor in industrial relations; (b) the final separation of government, trade unions, and employers' organizations, the latter appearing on the scene as autonomous actors dependent on their membership; (c) the lifting of the legal barriers imposed on free collective bargaining (by the Labor Code amendments of 1989) and efforts to build up a multilevel mechanism of bargaining; (d) the recognition of collective labor disputes, including those over interests (a Strike Act was adopted in 1989); (e) the establishment of a national tripartite institution of social consultation (the

National Council for the Reconciliation of Interests, NCRI); and (f) the adaptation of the earlier schemes of workers' participation to the conditions of privatization and a market economy (1989).

The tripartite National Council for the Reconciliation of Interests (NCRI)[2] was set up at the end of 1988, with the participation of the government, the National Council of Hungarian Trade Unions (SZOT),[3] and the then-existing employers' organizations (the Chamber of Economy, the National Association of Entrepreneurs, the cooperative organizations, the organizations of small craftsmen and retail traders). Its major functions (in the new liberal wage determination system, introduced in January 1989) were first to take decisions (as to guaranteed minimum wages, exemptions from taxation on wage increases, and so on) and second, to make recommendations for enterprises as to minimum and maximum wage increases. The three sides—the government, the trade unions, and the employers—were equal; three major partners (the government, SZOT, the Chamber of Economy) having a right of veto. The NCRI had no foundation in legislation; the government simply transferred a part of its own authority in wage determination to it.

The above changes in the industrial relations system were conceived in the double conviction that: (a) The industrial relations system (its major actors and institutions) is an integrated part of the (coming) market economy and multiparty democracy, and its development is needed by the ongoing reform; and (b) it may contribute to the alleviation of tensions, to the prevention and solution of conflicts arising from economic transformation and macroeconomic stabilizations. The changes, primarily the establishment of the National Council for the Reconciliation of Interests, reflected, beyond any doubt, a kind of neo-corporatist approach toward industrial relations on the part of the last Communist government and its social partners.

The effective functioning of institutions like the NCRI presupposes the existence of strong and unified social partners on both the workers' and employers' side. In Hungary, as a heritage of the past, none of the social partners were really strong (autonomous, independent, dependent on their membership), although their reshaping contained promise in this respect. In addition, as a result of the pluralization in this period, the social partners, especially the trade unions, became more and more divided.

In 1989-1990 new (independent, alternative) trade unions were established (the Democratic League of Independent Trade Unions and the Workers Councils) and the traditional unions were subject to major changes: (a) The representation of workers' interests (and the defense of workers' rights) emerged as a top priority in action; (b) the separation of trade unions and state institutions as well as the Communist party was completed; (c) there was a shift toward confederative (i.e., decentralized) organizational structures and a democratization of internal administration; and (d) pluralization took place within the traditional unions as well.

The National Council of Hungarian Trade Unions (SZOT) had been constituted by 19 sectoral federations. These federations were composed of 73 trade federations, most of which joined to form the National Confederation of Hungarian Trade Unions, MSZOSZ, at a congress in March 1990. Some past member organizations of SZOT (e.g., the Chemical Workers Federation), however, did not join MSZOSZ.

For the transformation of trade unions, three alternative (or partly complementary) alleys opened up in the region: (a) the Polish way, at least as it looked around 1980, that is, the newly formed independent union(s) taking over the workers' organizations; (b) the traditional unions being transformed into autonomous workers' organizations under the control of their membership; (c) the traditional unions being dissolved, as a result of the political revolution, and replaced by (at least in principle) new workers' organizations (the Czechoslovak way). In Hungary, due to the peaceful political transition and their voluntary transformation, the traditional unions have survived, are part of the present reality, and will probably have to be taken into account in the future.

The 1989-1990 transformation resulted in seven trade union confederations. Most of them were based on the traditional structures and retained their earlier leaders; some of them were newly formed. These confederations, including their reported membership figures as of April 1991, were as follows: (a) MSZOSZ, National Confederation of Hungarian Trade Unions, 2.6 million; (b) SZEF, Trade Unions' Cooperation Forum, 557,000; (c) Autonomous Workers, 374,000; (d) Democratic League of Independent Unions, 130,000; (e) National Alliance of Workers Councils, 160,000; (f) ÉSZT, Intellectuals' Trade Union Association, 63,000; (g) Solidarity, 75,000.

Employers' organizations were subject to a similar process of reshaping. Newly formed organizations of private entrepreneurs (National Association of Entrepreneurs, VOSZ; Hungarian Manufacturers' Association, GYOSZ) appeared on the scene and traditional ones (the Chamber of Economy) were reorganized.[4]

The Economic and Political Stage
for Industrial Relations in 1990–1991

The 1990 spring parliamentary elections were won by the opposition, and a new Center-Right government was formed (by Prime Minister József Antall).

The Antall government is based on the coalition of three parties: the Hungarian Democratic Forum (MDF), the Independent Smallholders and Citizens Party (FKGP), and the Christian Democratic People's Party (KNDP). The opposition parties in the Parliament are the Alliance of Free Democrats (SZDSZ), the Young Democrats (FIDESZ), both of which are liberal, and the Hungarian Socialist Party (MSZP), Social Democrat, a successor to the past Communist party (MSZMP).

The Antall government's main objective, as laid down in its Program for National Renewal, is to establish a strong "social market economy," in which private property is to dominate but where the vulnerable social groups are entitled to the protection of a "social safety net." The new government has inherited from its predecessors the difficult (and unaccomplished) task of macroeconomic stabilization: that is, the restoration of a balanced budget and the maintenance of the country's ability to fulfill its heavy international debt service. This task, by its nature unpopular, calls for the contraction of internal expenditure and personal consumption and a reduction of personal real income and real wages. The result is growing unemployment and poverty and relatively high level (2-digit) inflation. Such an economic situation (and macro-stabilization policies) are setting the stage for industrial relations at the beginning of the 1990s.

The major indicators of economic crisis (and of stabilization) for 1990 in Hungary were as follows: (a) The GDP declined by 4.3%; (b) internal expenditure and personal consumption decreased by 5.3% and 4.5%, respectively; (c) real wages declined by 5.1% (following a long period of gradual decline of 12% in 1978-1988); (d) inflation (consumer price index rose to 28.9%); (e) the number of unemployed rose by 100,000 (2%); (f) the number of those living under the official subsistence minimum was estimated at 10% to 17% of the population (1.2 million to 1.8 million people) as early as 1987. Forecasts for 1991 are even more negative: The decline of GDP, internal expenditure, and consumption is to continue; inflation is expected to be 33% to 35% (OECD, 1991). Unemployment is dramatically increasing; the number of unemployed was 294,000 (6.1%) in September.

Although the above figures appear to be frightening, they do not necessarily reflect realistic processes (as for their consequences for the workers) due to the great, and growing, importance of the secondary economy and related (often clandestine) employment and invisible income in Hungary, only partly covered by statistics (see, e.g., Ladó, Szalai, & Sziráczky, 1991) That is why it is difficult to forecast what the real risks are of a "social explosion" in Hungary, and what is (and can be) the role of institutionalized industrial relations, primarily of NCRI, in alleviating social tensions.

In industrial relations the Antall government when elected was faced with the existing (inherited) institutions and actors (trade unions and employers' organizations). It had to find answers to very practical and sensitive questions:

1. How to define its own role in industrial relations; should it withdraw (and leave most of the field to the workers' and employers' organizations), or should it try to maintain the predominance of its predecessors?

2. How should it define its relationship to the workers' organizations, to the traditional unions, on the one hand, and to the newly formed unions, on the other hand?

3. What should it do with the existing institutions of industrial relations, primarily with those that after all are manifestations of definite (neo-corporatist) industrial relations and (reform Communist or Social Democrat) political philosophies (first of all, the NCRI)?

The major difficulty that hindered the government in finding proper answers to these questions was that none of the governing coalition parties, and most of the opposition parties, had a clear industrial relations philosophy; there existed no definite ideas about the preferable future shape of the industrial relations system, except for scraps:

1. A nostalgia for the Workers Councils of 1956 as "genuine forms of worker representation" in the coalition parties. Ironically, these short-lived bodies were typical manifestations of socialist self-management (Héthy & Csuhaj, 1990).

2. A hostility to the traditional trade unions: Most parties, including the Free Democrats and Young Democrats in the opposition, questioned their legitimacy and looked upon them as the "last bulwarks of past communism."[5]

3. Doubts as to the legitimacy of the past employers, that is, the management of the enterprises in the state sector.[6]

4. A suspicion about the National Council for the Reconciliation of Interests: It was thought that its functioning curtailed the government's and Parliament's rights while offering an opportunity for the successor organizations of the party state (e.g., traditional unions) to have their influence felt.

These scraps, however, have not been composed into industrial relations philosophy(ies) harmonized with the essential political philosophies of the coalition. One should remember, the Center-Right coalition advocates, according to its own declarations, a mix of conservative and liberal values and appeals for support primarily to the intellectuals and peasantry and to a future middle class of owners. No industrial relations philosophies have emerged on the side of the liberal opposition, either. Workers are under-represented in the Parliament, but the newly formed unions appear to have close—political—links with the major parliamentary parties: The League seems to have the support of the Free Democrats, while the Workers' Councils seem to be affiliated with the governing Hungarian Democratic Forum. (The traditional unions, namely MSZOSZ, as a matter of course have recently resumed contacts with the socialists.)

The Survival of the Neo-Corporatist Governmental Approach in 1990–1991

The Antall government kept hesitating in 1990-1991 on how to define its role in industrial relations, its relationship to the existing partners (primarily the trade unions) and institutions (primarily the NCRI). For one year it accepted the existing social partners and institutions. It did not take any initiatives in legislation to carry through further changes to complete or alter the transformation carried out by the last Communist government. The first new pieces of legislation in this field were the two Trade Union Acts (passed in July 1991) and the Labor Code (submitted to the Parliament in September 1991). These seem to settle important problems related to the unions, but evade critical industrial relations issues (e.g., that of national-level tripartite consultations and the future of the NCRI).

As for the government's role in industrial relations, it soon became obvious that, despite its conservative and liberal political philosophies, it is to continue the neo-corporatist (in a sense, party state) traditions of its predecessor. This could be attributed to both objective and subjective reasons:

1. The government has adopted an interventionist ideology and practice as to the economy; in the conditions of economic crisis (and macroeconomic stabilization) it has not left wage determination for free bargaining between workers and employers, because it involves dangers for the delicate balances of the economy; its social partners (trade unions, employers) are in a phase of transformation, in which the government, willingly or unwillingly, gets involved (e.g., in trade union conflict); until privatization makes progress the government remains the major employer in the economy and retains this position in the surviving state sector, and so on.
2. The government (and the state administration), lacking a new model to follow, has tended to keep to the methods and techniques of their predecessors: Central regulations have retained their importance; negotiations and bargaining could fit into the existing (inherited) decision-making procedures with great difficulties.

The government's continuing predominance in the guidance of the economy and in industrial relations appears to function also as a means of the representation of political (party) interests in securing political power.

Concerning the National Council for the Reconciliation of Interests (NCRI), the new government had the choice among three alternative courses of action: (a) to confirm it and to make negotiations substantial; (b) to eliminate it; and (c) to keep it but to limit its authority and influence. All these courses of actions involved traps. On the one hand, the institutionalized tripartite dialogue offered a tacit recognition and legitimation to all partners—the unions and employers' organizations—regardless of whether they were representative and legitimate, and had or had not the support of their membership. If they had not, the agreements achieved would be of little or no value for the government, as they could not function as proper guarantees of social peace. On the other hand, a neglect of dialogue with the trade unions and employers might have added to the present and future social and political tensions and conflicts. In addition, the new government's commitment to institutionalized tripartism was considered as important for its international image (at the ILO and other international organizations).

After brief hesitation Hungary's new government revitalized this tripartite body (renamed Council for the Reconciliation of Interests) in the summer of 1990:

- The CRI's formal competence was widened (it was transformed into a consultative body on labor, social, and economic policy);
- participation was broadened (on the workers' side—beyond MSZOSZ—all the newly emerged trade union confederations, including the newly formed trade unions, were invited to join);
- its organizational structure was modernized (beyond its plenary session, it has specialized committees and also an administrative secretariat) and extended regionally;
- an institutional relationship was established between the CRI and the government (the government appointed a liaison person who sits in the meetings).

The CRI has repeatedly increased guaranteed minimum wages; has had intensive discussions on various issues of wage, employment, and training policy, as well as labor legislation; and, in a somewhat exceptional role, settled the taxi driver blockade in October 1990.

If they were not to lose their membership and were to partly regain credibility, the trade unions had no other choice but to stand up against the most critical austerity measures of the government. The government, cornered by the problems of the economy and still convinced that it was able to set out the inevitable "one best way," however, was often reluctant to enter into negotiations about its most critical measures (e.g., the raising of the administered prices of gasoline and energy) touching severely upon both wage earners and employers. Tensions necessarily mounted and were reflected in a movement of public disobedience (the taxi driver blockade in October 1990) and a political (antigovernment) strike threat (in June 1991). At the same time the minimal preconditions of cooperation were provided by the fact that even the trade unions recognized the necessity of stabilization, were not opposed to privatization, accepted unemployment, and so on.

The CRI, however, is faced with grave difficulties:

- It has not been given a say in issues of essential importance for workers, employers, and industrial relations (e.g., in the formulation of the government's privatization program);
- its legal foundations have continued to be missing, although one of its subcommittees was given legal status by the Employment Act, 1991;
- the veto right of the major workers' and employers' partners has ceased (de facto) to exist; the government has retained its right to act in the absence of consensus;
- its institutional (legal) relationship to the government (and Parliament) is still not clarified.

The Relationship Between the Government and the Trade Unions

The relationship between the government and the trade unions appears to be an issue of key importance for the present and future of Hungary's industrial relations system.

When Hungary's new government revived the Council for the Reconciliation of Interests in the summer of 1990, it tacitly (a) recognized the legitimacy and representativeness of all the seven trade union confederations, and (b) demonstrated that it would not discriminate among them on the basis of their past or present political affiliation.[7]

Since the appearance of the newly formed unions, pluralism and beyond that—most unfortunately—division have prevailed among the workers' organizations. The major issues of debates among traditional (successor) and newly formed unions are legitimacy and representativeness. On the one hand, it is argued that traditional unions have an inherited membership that joined them under political pressure, and they can rely on inherited wealth (assets) partly created by earlier state subsidies. On the other hand, it is emphasized that newly formed unions have not proved to be attractive enough for the working people, while traditional unions, after the phase of organizational modernization and democratization, could retain most of their members, even in a for them "unfriendly" political climate (i.e., when the successor organizations of the party state are looked upon with suspicion or even hostility by the new government and parliamentary parties).

The most thorny problem is that of trade union assets. Such assets (vacation homes, office buildings, and the like) put traditional unions in an advantageous position, while the lack of such assets is a definite handicap for the new unions.

The conflicts among the trade unions were smoothed over for 1990 (all of them joined the CRI and cooperated within its framework). During the year, however, they could not find a negotiated solution for their problems, primarily that of the distribution of assets. On the contrary their relations became worse and even their institutional contacts (in the framework of the so-called Trade Union Round Table) came to an end in early 1991. (While in the period of the taxi driver blockade of October 1990, MSZOSZ and the League were united against the government, they took opposite positions in June 1991: MSZOSZ was for a general strike, and the League was against it.)

In case of conflicts among trade union confederations, the government may choose among three possible alternative courses of actions. It can: (a) assume a neutral passive role; (b) try to play a catalyst role, that is, mediate in order to find negotiated solutions; or (c) intervene and impose a solution on the parties. The government seemed to follow the first course of action for a one-year period (from summer 1990 to summer 1991.) It was after the trade union conflict had become acute that the government—in fact, the Parliament—intervened. It passed two trade union Acts in July 1991.[8]

The first act obliged the unions to report on their assets, sequestered those assets, blocked union funds, and established a body (VIKSZ) as provisional caretaker of such assets and funds. At the same time the act envisaged trade union elections, the results of which would serve as a basis for the redistribution of assets.

The second act required that check-off authorizations by union members be confirmed by those members. (Traditional unions mostly applied this method to collect their membership fees.)

The new acts were welcomed by the newly formed unions. But the traditional unions protested sharply. They labeled the acts as unconstitutional and politically discriminatory.[9] Complaints against the new acts were made by several trade union confederations, and the Socialists, before the Constitutional Court. MSZOSZ—until a decision is taken by the court (some time in autumn)—refused openly to comply with the new legislation. This led its political opponents to say that it tacitly questioned the legitimacy of the Parliament.

At the same time the traditional unions energetically embarked on a campaign to secure the confirmation of check-off authorizations by their members.

In autumn 1991 the trade union "war" appears to have arrived at a standstill, or cease-fire. The traditional unions suffered certain losses in membership, but the process of check-off confirmation did not lead, as it had been expected, to a restructuring in favor of the newly formed unions. MSZOSZ retained 2 million of its earlier 2.6 million members (among the 2 million, 1.1 million signed the check-off authorizations and another 900,000, it is reported, paid their fees directly).

The League reports increasing membership (250,000 in September); while that of the Workers' Councils somewhat declined (*Héti Világgazdaság*, 1991). These workers' organizations do not make use of the check-off system.

The trade unions' inability to find a negotiated solution without outside intervention involves risks for the future of the trade union movement itself. Privatization, economic and technological restructuring, the growth of small and medium-size enterprises, the spread of atypical work, and the flourishing secondary or informal economy are all menaces for all the unions. There is a danger that, while the unions devote vast energies to their internal quarrels, unionization keeps sinking. This weakens their positions in relation to the government and the newly emerging private owners, and has a negative impact on the protection of workers' interests in a very critical phase of economic and political transformation.

In addition, in a period when political intervention by the past Communist party has ended, it is unfortunate to provoke a precedent for a new type of political intervention—even if it is probably constitutional and by a freely elected government and Parliament.

Hungary is on its way toward parliamentary democracy and a market economy, as are its industrial relations system and the major institutions and partners—workers' and employers' organizations as well as the government.

In 1990-1991 the industrial relations system—as reformed by the last Communist government—remained basically unchanged, although its functioning was burdened by the trade union conflict.

The government's attitude (political behavior, legislation) was characterized by a basic contradiction. It adopted a neo-corporatist approach to the industrial relations system (by maintaining the CRI, by enforcing national and sectoral bargaining and agreements, and so on). It imposed, however, a scenario on the trade unions' transformation that caused acute conflicts between the government and most of the unions. Neo-corporatism "is founded on the principle of integration rather than separation of the political, economic and social aspects of life resulting in a superior, rather than subordinate, position for the ideological objectives contained in the political system relative to the operation of the economic system" (Salamon, 1987, p. 11). Both the new Center-Right government and the formerly Communist trade unions appear to be in favor of the corporatist or interventionist ideology, but in the service of differing ideological objectives. Perhaps this difference offers an explanation for the above contradiction.

The transformation of industrial relations is not easy. It is burdened by political and ideological debates, by struggles between traditional pressure groups trying to survive and new ones looking for a foothold. It is also impeded by a general lack of vision and of a clear, coherent, and global concept of what is to be done to either establish or correct the new institutional and legislative framework. Developments are often based on isolated interventions, motivated by the pressure to find solutions for new problems or simply by the urge to follow models in the rest of Europe. It will take, most probably, a longer period of time until a model of industrial relations appears that fits well into the tissue of the new emerging political and economic system and, at the same time, is based on the historical and cultural traditions of the country.

Notes

1. For a description of the historical development of Hungary's industrial relations system, see Héthy and Csuhaj (1990).

2. The activities of NCRI (and later of CRI) can be defined as a form of "social concertation" (LaFlamme, 1987).

3. The central trade union organization of the party/state.

4. Ongoing privatization is to basically change the structure of employers and their organizations. The state's present 90% share in ownership in industry and trade is to be reduced below 50% by 1994.

5. As early as the summer of 1990 draft acts had been submitted to the Parliament, initiating the testing of trade union membership and the freezing of trade union assets, but they were not put on the agenda for one year. MSZOSZ reacted nervously. At the 77th session of the International Labor Conference (June 1990) its president, Dr. S. Nagy, spoke of "a genuine danger in Hungary that the Government and the Parliament take decisions affecting the rights of workers, without including the trade unions in decision making . . . an attempt is being made to infringe the provision concerning freedom of association and to make the situation of the National Confederation of Hungarian Trade Unions impossible—an organization vital for our country— by making workers belong to so-called independent unions" (Minutes of the conference).

6. Most enterprises in Hungary's state sector function under the control of Enterprise Councils, composed of the representatives of workers and management, and are entitled to elect the enterprise's director. The government, in August 1990, ordered a re-election of these bodies and of directors. In industry, surprisingly about 80% of past directors were re-elected.

7. It should be noted that among the new confederations only MSZOSZ covers most of the economy. The center of gravity of the Autonomous Workers is in the chemical industry, and that

of SZEF in public services; the League and Workers' Councils have sporadic organizations all over the country.

8. Acts XXVIII and XXIX, 1991. Magyar Közlöny, Budapest, July 17, 1991. Legislation was initiated by three MPs (a Free Democrat, a Young Democrat, and an MP of the governing Democratic Forum, the latter being the president of the Workers' Councils).

9. The traditional unions raised objections, for example, to the composition of the VIKSZ. In the four-member body, one position each was reserved for the League and the Workers' Councils and one each for MSZOSZ and the rest of the confederations.

References

Héthy, L., & Csuhaj, V. I. (1990). *Labour relations in Hungary.* Budapest: Institute of Labour Research.

Heti Világgazdaság. (1991, September 14). Budapest.

Ladó, M., Szalai, J., & Sziráczky, G. (1991, September). *Labour market and social policy implications of structural change in Central and Eastern Europe.* ILO-OECD-CCEET Conference, Paris.

LaFlamme, G. (1987). Concertation: Nature, questions and conditions. *Labour and Society, 3.*

Népszava. (1991, April 10). Budapest.

OECD. (1991). *Economic survey.* Paris: Author.

Salamon, M. (1987). *Industrial relations. Theory and practice.* Englewood Cliffs, NJ: Prentice-Hall.

20 \ Decolonization Without Independence: Political Change and Trade Unionism in Hong Kong

DAVID A. LEVIN

STEPHEN CHIU

During the 1980s, three major political events affected Hong Kong: (a) the restructuring of Hong Kong's Legislative Council to include some seats filled by elections; (b) the 1984 Sino-British joint declaration on the future of Hong Kong, under which Hong Kong will become a Special Administrative Region under the sovereignty of the People's Republic of China from July 1, 1997; and (c) China's drafting of the Basic Law as the mini-constitution under which Hong Kong will be governed after China resumes sovereignty. These events are part of the process by which Britain and China have designed Hong Kong's political future in the form of decolonization without independence (S. K. Lau, 1990). While they have posed new issues and challenges for all industrial relations actors, it is arguably the union movement that has faced the most acute dilemmas of choice regarding what strategy it should pursue to realize its objectives in a changing political environment.

Our first aim in this chapter is to describe how the Hong Kong union movement has responded to the changing political environment of the 1980s, but to do so we need to establish a historical frame of reference by reviewing how the movement defined its relationship to the political system prior to the 1980s. Our second aim is to identify the influences on the movement's past and presently evolving lines of action vis-à-vis the political arena. In this respect, our chapter is intended as a contribution to theoretical discussions of the circumstances under which union movements in developing countries adopt a political strategy, and the determinants of the nature of this strategy.[1] Our general arguments are as follows. First, while historical conditions were conducive to the adoption of a political strategy by the union movement, such a strategy did not materialize except briefly. Second, political events of the 1980s have stimulated the adoption of a political strategy by the union movement, but these events should be viewed as reinforcing more fundamental forces working in the same direction. Third, how the union movement has responded to the events of the 1980s has been shaped as much by organizational processes as by environmental factors. The latter two arguments are elaborated in the concluding section.

The Pursuit of a Political Strategy:
A Theoretical Overview

As a benchmark for assessing the historical construction of Hong Kong trade union political strategies, we start with three efforts to theorize about the conditions under which union movements in developing countries are likely to employ a political strategy for pursuing objectives. The first, advanced by Kerr, Dunlop, Harbison, and Myers (1973), stresses that movement strategies at the early stages of industrialization will reflect the composition and associated strategies of different types of industrializing elites. Colonial administrators constitute one of these types and Kerr et al. expect this type to produce a labor movement oriented to political action and guided by a strong anticolonial ideology.

A second line of theorizing is Sturmthal's (1967, 1973) writings on the rationality of movement choices between economic and political action. His argument is that given three conditions—a labor market situation of excess supplies of labor, a substantial proportion of unskilled and semiskilled workers in the employment structure, and a "strong resentment over the class society"—a labor movement that seeks to be all-inclusive will rationally choose a political strategy that may include acts "ranging from violence to the organization of, or at the least participation in, a large political movement" for advancing workers' interests (1973, p. 17).

A more recent line of theorizing about movement strategies is Lipset's (1983) comparative analysis of sources of diversity in the character of working-class movements in industrial societies, in particular the conditions under which radical or reformist working-class politics will emerge. Lipset's approach may be viewed as an attempt to theorize sociologically about the conditions under which what Sturmthal called the "resentment over the class society" is likely to dominate in the formation of a movement's political character. This depends in Lipset's view on two main factors. The first is the nature of the social-class system prior to industrialization. The more rigid this system is, the greater the resentment of the class society is likely to be, and hence the more likely the emergence of a radical labor movement that will adopt a political strategy as a primary means of action. The second factor is the response of economic and political elites to the demands of workers for the right to participate in the polity and the economy. If elites resist granting full political and economic citizenship to the working class, then labor movements are more likely to pursue revolutionary goals through a political strategy of action.[2]

Despite their differences, all three theories lead to the same historical expectation, namely that the Hong Kong union movement should have adopted a political strategy. It follows in Kerr et al.'s case from having colonial administrators as an industrializing elite; in Sturmthal's case from the historical situation of excess supplies of labor and an employment structure with substantial numbers of unskilled and later semiskilled workers (cf. England, 1980); and in Lipset's case from the status distinctions between colonizers and colonized, plus the absence of full political and economic citizenship for the Hong Kong Chinese. However, historical reality did not fully conform to this scenario.

The Historical Construction of Trade Union Political Action

The Hong Kong union movement has defined its relationship to the colonial political system in different ways historically. We highlight these differences for three periods—the 1920s, the immediate post-World War II years, and the 1950s to the late 1970s—before turning to the 1980s.

THE 1920s: STATE REPRESSION OF POLITICAL ACTION

The first major trade union growth wave in Hong Kong occurred in the 1920s in the context of an entrepôt economy, a colonial regime relatively tolerant of union organization, prior worker experience in guild organizations, and the immediate threat to workers' livelihood posed by sharp price increases. Initially, major trade unions, such as the Chinese Engineers' Institute and the Chinese Seamen's Union, waged industrial action for improvements in terms of employment, a model followed by many other unions formed in the early 1920s (Chan, 1984, p. 209). However, this economic strategy was soon overtaken by the mass participation in the 1925-1926 Canton-Hong Kong strike-boycott, essentially a political protest directed at British commercial interests and colonial rule, sparked largely by British actions in China. The demands made by a strike organizing committee to the colonial authorities for civil and political equality of Chinese with Europeans in Hong Kong, and for the 8-hour day, a minimum wage, collective bargaining, the abolition of the labor subcontracting system, and workers' insurance, are suggestive of the strong underlying latent resentments of the inferior political, economic, and social position of Chinese labor under British colonial rule (Chesneaux, 1968, p. 291).

Colonial authorities viewed these demands as a product of Communist influence over the Hong Kong working class and a threat to their own survival. They closed ranks with Chinese elites to mobilize countermeasures to undermine the strike-boycott. To suppress future political action, the authorities enacted the 1927 Illegal Strikes and Lock-Outs Ordinance, which made political strikes unlawful and which imposed stricter controls on unions' external organizational linkages and their use of union funds. The principal radical unions were banned.

1945–1951: THE FAILURE OF AN ECONOMIC STRATEGY

Trade unions, many of prewar origins, rapidly reemerged following the end of Japanese occupation in 1945. The union movement faced once again the dilemma of how to define its relationship to the state (as well as employers) in a context similar in major respects to that of the 1920s—a burgeoning supply of labor due to a vast influx of refugees, a high rate of inflation, and a bureaucratic colonial regime that was reinstituted in its prewar form. Another similarity was the alignment of unions along lines of external political loyalties. Both the Hong Kong Federation of Trade Unions (FTU), which supported the policies of the Chinese Communist party, and the Hong Kong and Kowloon Trade Union Council (TUC), which supported the policies of the Kuomintang (KMT), were formed in the late 1940s. A small number of unions remained politically autonomous.

As in the 1920s the initial strategy of major unions was to adopt economic action, encouraged by the problems of livelihood in the immediate postwar period and by the relatively high degree of coordination among major European employers in setting wage levels at that time. The rudimentary elements of a collective bargaining system seemed to be emerging (England & Rear, 1981, p. 190). However, the aggressive confrontation by some FTU-affiliated unions with large (often British) employers entailed costs— withdrawal of company recognition, dismissal of union leaders, a loss of membership—which became apparent, for example, in the 1949-1950 industrial action by the FTU-affiliated Tramways Union (Tsang, 1988, pp. 127-129). From the early 1950s the use of economic action declined, as indicated by the subsequent sharp drop in days lost due to strikes (Turner et. al., 1980, pp. 89-91).[3]

1950s–1970s: POLITICAL QUIESCENCE

Changes in the structure of the economy and the labor market during the 1950s and 1960s further undermined the potential effectiveness of economic action. Previous union strongholds in shipbuilding and repairing declined, and along with them the basis for economic unionism. As small-scale firms proliferated in the new, export-oriented light industries, organizing their workers into unions grew difficult. A new generation of Chinese industrial entrepreneurs emerged who employed personal and paternal strategies of labor control, invoking the imagery of a benevolent patriarch in managing their firms and disciplining their work force (Djao, 1981; King & Leung, 1975; S. L. Wong, 1988, pp. 92-97, 134-136).

Hong Kong's form of industrialization also sustained a set of individual and familial strategies of market behavior that weakened class formation. As demand for labor soared in the labor-intensive manufacturing sector, from the late 1950s, and competition for labor intensified, workers discovered that they could get higher pay through individual action via exit or the threat of exit (England & Rear, 1981, p. 49). The tight labor market, combined with what S. K. Lau (1982, p. 72) calls "utilitarianistic familism," enabled the working-class family to pursue a strategy of survival and mobility by pooling family resources. The patriarchal arrangements in the Chinese family allowed working-class families to appropriate the income of their unmarried working daughters, who filled the growing number of semiskilled jobs (Salaff, 1981).

THE EMERGENCE OF "RHETORICAL" POLITICS

Yet these changes also created a situation increasingly ripe for a shift to a strategy of political action. As the size of the working class grew, and especially the weight of the semiskilled, political action appeared to be the most effective route for the labor movement to advance the welfare of the working class (cf. Sturmthal, 1967, p. 59). Political action would also have been a rational strategy to compensate for the weakness of organized labor at the workplace level.

In one respect, union strategy did become political. The behavior of both the FTU and the TUC had strong political overtones in the 1950s and 1960s, with respect to the prominence of their allegiances to the two Chinese political parties, their participation in the propaganda war between the Taiwanese and Mainland Chinese governments, and their involvement in Left-Right clashes in Hong Kong (Leung, 1986a, 1986b). But such behavior was of an "extrovert" nature and political primarily on a symbolic level since it did not entail taking action against colonial authorities. Except for participation in mass disturbances in 1967, influenced by the Cultural Revolution then under way in China, the FTU rarely challenged the existing power structure in Hong Kong, demanded an end to colonial rule, or pressured the state for improvements in labor legislation and redistribution of resources to the working class.

Two developments within the labor movement after 1968 were subsequently to impact on union movement strategies. The first was a new trade union growth wave, mainly in the civil and public services.[4] The bulk of these new unions were not affiliated with either the FTU or TUC and thus are usually described in political terms as "independent" or "neutral." The second development was the increasingly active role of the Hong Kong Christian Industrial Committee (CIC), which, while not a trade union, engaged in quasi-trade union activities, encouraged the formation of independent unions in the private sector, and was to play a key role in forging coalitions to protest against policies of the Hong Kong government.

The 1980s:
Toward a Political Strategy of Action

Since the late 1970s the union movement has become much more prominent in the domestic political arena, as indicated by its involvement in social protest campaigns, in formal political institutions, and in struggles over the Basic Law.

PARTICIPATION IN SOCIAL PROTEST

Trade union participation in social protest actions was in some cases aimed at seeking specific reforms in labor legislation or in opposing specific government policies. In other cases, representatives of trade unions and other labor organizations joined with community groups in protest campaigns over matters of general community concern. Examples include the Coalition Against Bus Fare Increase (1981), the Coalition for the Monitoring of Public Utility Companies (1982), the campaign against revision of Japanese textbooks (1982), and the Joint Conference for the shelving of the Daya Bay Nuclear Plant (1986) (Chiu, 1986, pp. 58-65; Tso, 1983, pp. 24-36).

While it was mainly independent trade unionists who participated in these protest movements, the FTU, in a major departure from past policy, also became involved in a few of these campaigns. This reflected a major reorientation of the FTU's strategy following the downfall of the Gang of Four, and China's new policy of the four modernizations. Instead of focusing on political issues in China, the FTU became increasingly concerned with local issues.[5] However, sustaining inter-union cooperation between independent unions and the FTU proved difficult due to differences over ideology, goals, and strategies of action.

PARTICIPATION IN FORMAL POLITICAL INSTITUTIONS

Once it became clear in the early 1980s that British rule over Hong Kong would come to an end, the Hong Kong government began to institute a series of structural changes in the political system. In 1982 it opened to direct election some positions on the Urban Council and District Boards. In 1985 it implemented changes in the structure of the Legislative Council (LEGCO), not however by introducing direct elections, but by creating a system of indirect elections based on regional and corporate (officially called "functional") constituencies for a limited number of seats.[6] One of the nine functional constituencies was the Labour constituency, which was allocated two seats. While this granted the union movement a recognized political status and opened a new institutional channel for participation in the making of public policy, the influence of trade unionists on LEGCO has been structurally limited since they are far outnumbered by legislative councillors from the government and the business and professional sectors.[7]

The union movement acted quickly to take advantage of the new political opportunities. The FTU, the TUC, and some independent trade unions participated actively in the 1985 District Board elections by encouraging members to register as voters, drawing up lists of candidates whom members were asked to support, and sponsoring their own members as candidates. The FTU claimed 10 candidates were from member unions, of whom 5 were elected; while the TUC reportedly put up 7, with 2 elected. Another major player was the Hong Kong Professional Teachers Union (PTU) whose members reportedly won 24 seats on the District Boards (Miners, 1988, p. 45). The first election in 1985 for the two LEGCO seats from the Labour functional constituency turned out to be noncompetitive since only two candidates were nominated, one from the FTU and the other from the TUC.[8]

THE BASIC LAW

Following the Sino-British agreement in 1984 on the transfer of sovereignty over Hong Kong to China in 1997, the Standing Committee of China's National People's Congress (NPC) established the Basic Law Drafting Committee (BLDC) to formulate a draft set of proposals by 1988 and a final

Basic Law by 1990.[9] An especially contentious issue in the drafting of the Basic Law was the structure of Hong Kong's future legislature. Within Hong Kong, a major division emerged between those who advocated a faster pace of democratization and those who opposed major changes on the grounds that rapid democratization would threaten Hong Kong's stability and prosperity. Prominent business elites supported the latter position and they were backed by China's leaders, who made it clear that any changes in the political system during the transitional period would have to converge with the Basic Law (R. Wong, 1990, p. xxii).

The union movement was split along similar lines.[10] The FTU supported moderation in the pace and degree of democratization, in line with China's position that the primary task was to maintain Hong Kong's stability and prosperity during the transitional period.[11] The more outspoken independent unions generally favored a more democratic political framework for the future SAR, with a higher proportion of representatives elected by universal suffrage. Both groups concurred, however, in calling for inclusion of such labor rights as organization, collective bargaining, and social security in the Basic Law.

The structure of the future legislature continued to be a contentious issue until China and Britain reached agreement, in February 1990, on the structure of the future legislature. From 1995 to the year 2007, representatives elected from functional constituencies are to occupy one-half of the 60 LEGCO seats. The number filled by direct elections will rise from 20 seats in 1995-1999 to one-half for the 2003-2007 legislative session. This proposal was immediately approved by the BLDC, and the final Basic Law was promulgated by the NPC in April 1990. Trade union reactions to the final draft of the Basic Law varied. The FTU considered the future political framework under the Basic Law to be acceptable as "doing justice to the interests of all circles." Independents were disappointed with the outcome, while the TUC remained silent.

Although trade unionists were involved in the bodies set up for the drafting of the Basic Law, their overall influence was relatively marginal, partly because they lacked a unified position but mainly because they did not have political clout comparable to the capitalist elite where it mattered most, that is, with China's leaders. The dominant players in negotiations over Hong Kong's future were China, the British government, and the capitalist class in Hong Kong (Lo, 1989). There were only 2 Hong Kong trade unionists among the 23 appointed Hong Kong members of the BLDC, and unionists had a relatively small number of representatives on the Basic Law Consultative Committee, established by the Hong Kong members of the BLDC to collect local opinions on the draft basic law. While the right to strike and the right to participate in trade unions are included in the Basic Law, as is reference to legal protection of "welfare benefits and retirement security of the labour force" (Basic Law: Ch. 2, Art. 27, 36), demands by both the FTU and independent unions for the right of collective bargaining were not included in the Basic Law. On this score, even the FTU leaders have expressed reservations about the Basic Law.

The Future of Political Action

In late 1989 a series of labor disputes involving bus drivers, airline caterers, and civil service groups, all from the relatively "advantaged" sector of the work force, erupted over issues of pay and conditions of work (Ng, 1990, p. 295). Some viewed this as a consequence of post-Tiananmen anxieties and the collapse of confidence in a future under Chinese sovereignty. It led to predictions that "Hong Kong would become less and less governable as more and more interest groups felt compelled to risk a showdown because of a shortened horizon" (R. Wong, 1990, p. xx). Yet it seems unlikely that the union movement as a whole will shift its emphasis to a strategy of economic action. Labor unrest may simmer in the civil service, and disputes may break out in the more sheltered sectors of the economy, but any spillover into the competitive sector seems a remote possibility as long as trade unions remain weak there. The slackening pace of economic growth also creates an unfavorable environment for economic actions, since employers typically become more cost-conscious in bad times.

On the other hand, the growing political activism of the trade unions over the past decade will likely continue. With the future structure of LEGCO set by the Basic Law, the Hong Kong government quickly approved a new political structure to dovetail with future arrangements. The principal change was the creation of 18 seats to be filled by direct election in September 1991. In anticipation of direct elections, a number of political parties had already formed and geared up for the elections. Because of their membership, organizational skills, and links with the grass roots, trade union support will be sought by candidates competing for direct election. Moreover, trade unions have a general stake in the outcome of the direct elections since it will impact on the future composition of LEGCO, and hence public policy with regard to issues important to labor. However, it appears that the independent unions and the FTU will support different candidates.

As the number and weight of independent trade unions in the union movement have grown, they have come to recognize their common interests in promoting democratization and preserving civil rights and freedoms, and also in serving as a counterweight to the FTU now that the TUC has become marginalized. In early 1990 the Hong Kong Confederation of Trade Unions

(CTU), with 21 independent unions and a combined membership of 80,000, was formed, making it the second-largest union federation after the FTU.

Both the FTU and the CTU have denied any intention of forming political parties, but they have aligned themselves to different political groupings. The FTU, one of a network of pro-China organizations in Hong Kong, has mounted a registration drive among its members and is officially backing one of its vice-chairpersons to run for direct election in a district where it believes its chances of winning are good ("Voter Registration Drive," 1991). The CTU, by contrast, is loosely associated with the United Democrats of Hong Kong (UDHK), a political party whose leaders are keen to safeguard Hong Kong's autonomy, civil rights, and freedoms from interference by China after 1997. The chairman of the CTU, who is also an executive committee member of the UDHK, recently announced that he will run for direct election (in his capacity as director of the Christian Industrial Committee, but with support from the UDHK) in the same district as the vice-chairperson from the FTU. This will be one major test of the relative grass-roots strength of the FTU and the independent union movement. It is part of the broader competition in the coming direct elections between a loose coalition of parties that are sometimes referred to as the "democracy lobby," two pro-business parties, and a network of so-called patriotic organizations.[12] The outcome will be closely watched as an indication of whom voters trust to best represent Hong Kong's interests in the run-up to 1997.

The Union Movement and Political Action: Theory and Reality

The Hong Kong union movement, like its counterparts elsewhere, faced historically the problem of defining its relationship to the political order. Historical conditions during the formative period of the movement bore strong resemblance to those of other developing countries: a dependent economy, a colonial regime overtly biased toward business interests, and status discrimination against the indigenous Chinese. On the basis of experience elsewhere, as well as the theories reviewed earlier, one might have expected a "rational" labor movement to capitalize on this situation by creating an inclusive working-class movement, appealing to workers' experience of class deprivations and anticolonial resentments, and by pursuing democratic rights for workers in industry and the polity.

Reality did conform briefly, in the 1920s, to these expectations, but this was an isolated episode. When the union movement reemerged after World War II, it did not adopt a long-run political strategy for advancing workers' interests. Its "political" character entailed manipulating political rhetoric and symbols, rather than seeking to alter Hong Kong's political or economic framework. In this respect the Hong Kong union movement appears to be a deviant case (cf. Turner et al., 1980, p. 145). However, changing union behavior in the 1980s pointed to a growing "convergence" with a Third World model, as Hong Kong unions turned to the political arena by participating in and leading social protest movements, pressuring the government to reform the political system, and engaging (albeit in a peripheral role) in the drafting of the future constitutional framework.

The shift in Hong Kong union movement strategies, from a deviant to a more conventional pattern, can perhaps be of value in clarifying some assumptions underlying existing theories. In this concluding section, we attempt to draw out the broader implications of the Hong Kong case for theories of union political behavior in developing countries, by focusing on how four sets of variables—the form of Hong Kong's industrialization, status identities, colonialism and political culture, and organizational processes—contributed to both the historical depoliticization of movement strategies and the recent shift toward a more active political strategy.

The Form of Industrialization

An emerging body of literature on the newly industrializing countries of Asia suggests that the structure and dynamics of the economic environment in these countries shape movement strategies along different lines from those of the earlier industrializers (Deyo, 1987, 1989; Deyo, Haggard, & Koo, 1987; Siddique, 1989). This literature stresses that the postwar pattern of export-led labor-intensive industrialization, most evident in the East Asian region, has created an unstable, atomized "hyperproletariat," composed of substantial numbers of women and migrants working under diverse labor control systems that have reduced their mobilization potential. If export-led labor-intensive industrialization in Hong Kong diminished the potential effectiveness of union economic action, it also made mobilization for political action equally difficult. In other words, the viability of both forms of union actions, as collective actions, has been constrained by the economic structural context.

Over the past two decades the Hong Kong economy has grown rapidly and has become more diversified with the expansion of the tertiary sector, including the civil and public services, and business and financial services (Scott, 1989, pp. 220-232; Sit & Wong, 1989, pp. 12-21). The economy increasingly resembles a postindustrial society, with a shift away from labor-intensive to more informative-intensive economic activities (So & Kwitko, 1990, p. 384). Accompanying the diversification of the economy is a more diversified social structure, including a substantial new middle class, much of it linked to the growth of the tertiary sector (Scott, 1989, pp. 232-236). One consequence of this structural change has been the proliferation of white-collar and professional unions, which has transformed the composition and the character of the union movement. These new unions are more capable of waging collective actions and are less averse to employing political means to realize their ends. Furthermore, the rise of the new middle class has created the social basis for the emergence of a nucleus of political activists in the pro-democracy movement who are also eager to solicit the support of unions.

Social Status and Movement Character

Status identities and groupings have also contributed to the shaping of union movement character in Hong Kong, but in ways that differ from the experience of Western societies. In the so-called East Asian "Confucian" societies, family and kinship groupings have constituted the primary source of corporate identity for individuals. Whereas pre-industrial status systems in Western societies led to cohesive local communities and strong occupational identities that served as bases for working-class mobilization, family and kinship groupings in Hong Kong were poorly suited for this purpose. The social architecture of Hong Kong society, comprised of a multitude of small familial groups anxious to defend and advance their interests, made mobilization along class lines for political action difficult.

Moreover, it is important not to overlook the way in which pre-industrial and industrial status systems interact to affect the mobilization potential of the working class. While industrial workers became numerically the dominant segment of the Hong Kong working class after World War II, a substantial proportion were women in semiskilled jobs, who were among the lowest paid stratum of the working class (Salaff, 1981, pp. 19-23; Turner et al., 1980, pp. 74-75). The union movement came to represent the somewhat better paid male stratum of the labor force, to the relative neglect of the interests of women in industry (Turner et al., 1980, p. 149). Hong Kong's industrialization thus generated new status distinctions (skilled/semiskilled) that reinforced pre-industrial ones (male/female), weakening rather than augmenting the potential for collective action.

By the 1980s new status groupings were clearly emerging, based on such identities as residence, occupation, and consumption. Status politics, in the sense of the mobilization along status lines to defend sectional interests, has become a common phenomenon in Hong Kong's political scene (Cheung, Lui, Chan, & Wong, 1988). While this may not help the development of a more unified union movement, it certainly has contributed to the politicization of unions, as occupationally based status groups have come to recognize the value of unions in achieving their objectives in both the economic and the political spheres.

The Changing Context of Colonialism

Existing literature has suggested that the Third World context of political dependency structures the relationship between the union movement and the political arena in different ways from that found in Western societies. Colonialism, for example, has been regarded as the principal cause of the politicization of labor movements in developing countries (Siddique, 1989; Sturmthal, 1973, pp. 24-25; Yesufu, 1966, pp. 104-105). Differences in labor policy among colonial powers have also been noted as sources of divergence in the character of labor movements among Third World countries (Roberts & De Bellecombe, 1966). Moreover, how political dependency interacts with political culture, that is, the normative orientations held toward the state and political participation, may also vary among developing countries.

While historically British colonial rule in Hong Kong was a politically exclusionary regime so far as the mass of Chinese were concerned, this did not generate the mass resentment of a class and colonial society that one might have anticipated.[13] One reason may be that Hong Kong was not a case of a colonial regime imposing itself historically on a well-established society. Rather, Chinese came to Hong Kong to "subject themselves voluntarily under the rule of an alien colonial administration" (S. K. Lau, 1982, p. 7). The acceptance of this British colonial rule rested on what might be termed an implicit social compact between the British colonial rulers and the Chinese society. The Chinese society expected the colonial government to provide a stable political and legal framework within which economic livelihood could be pursued with minimal state controls over, and intervention into, their lives. In exchange, the Chinese society tolerated the economic deprivations of capitalism and the political deprivations of colonialism.[14] Thus, for a majority of Hong Kong Chinese, colonial rule was not perceived as a "problem" that needed to be solved, and the ostensible rigid status distinctions and discrimination (which diminished in the postwar period) between the colonizers and the colonized did not fuel the growth of an anticolonial political movement.

If this characterization of political culture is valid, then it casts some doubt on the assumption implicit in theories reviewed earlier that an emergent working class will inevitably develop strong political interests in seeking democratic rights in the economy and polity when these are denied. Hong

Kong Chinese had strong political interests, but these did not take the form of seeking rights. S. K. Lau's (1982, p. 160) generalization seems apt, at least up to the 1970s, when he points out that for the Hong Kong Chinese political freedom "does not mean freedom to participate in political decision-making but freedom from political oppression." In this respect, the avoidance of political action by the trade union movement may have fit the political culture of the Hong Kong Chinese, who did not look to either the union movement or the state as institutions to be used for securing class benefits.

By the 1980s, however, politics was no longer avoided for two reasons. First, the social character of the population has changed in ways that impact on its normative and behavioral orientations toward political action. The general level of education has increased substantially since the 1960s, and with rising levels of education have come better knowledge and awareness of rights, as well as capabilities of acting to secure these rights (Cheung & Louie, 1991, p. 1). As the proportion of the population locally born has grown, the sense of a distinct Hong Kong identity has strengthened, and with it a concern about the quality of life (Lau & Kuan, 1988, pp. 178-186). There is evidence that the ethos of "utilitarianistic familism" has been eroding and that the "unconditional abhorrence and a fear of politics has abated among the Hong Kong Chinese" (Lau & Kuan, 1988, pp. 70-71).

Second, the colonial regime has itself undergone a gradual transformation. Of enormous political importance has been the growing role of the colonial state in the provision of collective benefits in areas of public housing, education, transport, welfare, and health, as well as in the upgrading of standards of employment and workplace safety.[15] The "growing sense of dependence on the government for a variety of things related to daily living makes it well-nigh impossible for people to avoid politics" (Lau & Kuan, 1988, p. 72). As the state has become an increasingly important provider of these benefits, it has attracted the formation of pressure groups attempting to influence state policies through petitions, protest rallies, signature campaigns, press conferences, opinion surveys, and occasionally violent confrontation with state authorities (Cheung & Louie, 1991, p. 22).

Organizational Processes

Finally, while the structural context of Hong Kong's development explains in part the trajectory of union movement strategies, these structural effects have been mediated by organizational processes.[16] Several organizational theorists have argued that an organization's character is initially shaped by the historical conditions at the time of its founding, and that once formed, this character is likely to continue to exert a profound influence on subsequent behavior (Aldrich & Auster, 1986; Stinchcombe, 1969).[17] In this respect, the hesitancy of the FTU in pursuing a full-blown political strategy historically may be partially explained by the external political loyalties, established during its formative period, that constrained its ability to capitalize on the "objective" situation of political opportunities. For example, after 1949, the FTU may have felt constrained from using a political strategy because of possible detrimental effects upon China, which depended on Hong Kong for a substantial proportion of foreign exchange earnings. The FTU may also have been constrained by its anticolonial ideology, since using political channels to pressure colonial authorities for action favorable to the working class could be taken to imply acceptance of the legitimacy of colonial rule, hence the boycott from 1950 of the elections to the Labor Advisory Board. This strategy of avoiding interaction with the colonial regime precluded the FTU's formulation of a consistent strategy of pushing for workers' rights in the political arena. In these respects, it can be argued that the "institutionalized myth" (patriotism toward China, and anticolonialism) embedded in the FTU (and, with a different content, also in the TUC) from its formative period tended to produce conservatism in organizational behavior (cf. Meyer & Rowan, 1977).

Intra-organizational processes reinforced this tendency. The militancy of FTU affiliates in the late 1940s backfired when members and affiliate unions broke away from the FTU, forming their own independent unions or simply defecting to the TUC camp (Carton, 1971, p. 143). To arrest the breakaway movement and to maintain a reasonable level of loyalties within the organization, the FTU and its affiliates altered their strategy in the 1950s, from militant industrial actions and confrontational tactics to one that stressed the provision of welfare services and mutual aid.

Taking this argument a step further, we can also identify an organizational dimension to the union movement's recent repoliticization. Organizational processes can be observed to mediate between the impinging environmental forces and the growing emphasis on political action. For instance, the CTU was largely formed out of an amalgam of unions, formed in the 1970s and the 1980s, in the civil service, the white-collar occupations, and the service sector. Individually, they lacked a political agenda, as they were formed primarily for the purpose of pursuing sectional interests. The CTU has, however, demonstrated a clear inclination to employ political means to achieve its objectives. The role of the CIC as the linking pin in forging a coalition of independent unions, and in the formation of the CTU, was critical in effecting this "conversion."[18] The broader vision of social and economic justice embodied in the organization of the CTU, and the readiness to enter into the political arena to achieve its objectives, should be attributed in part to the organizational influence of the CIC.

Organizational processes are also responsible for the FTU's revived interest in the political sphere. Due to its historical ties to the PRC, the FTU has supported the Chinese government's policy of maintaining the "stability and prosperity" of Hong Kong during the transitional period. If the FTU were to adopt a militant shop-floor strategy of pushing strenuously for collective bargaining rights and wage claims, this would be regarded as challenging the prerogatives of capital and inimical to investors' confidence. Hence, a strategy of demanding moderate improvements in labor legislation enables the FTU to display publicly its commitment to labor's interests without appearing overly threatening to business interests. Furthermore, since the PRC has been critical of the policies of the Hong Kong colonial government, challenging the lame-duck colonial establishment is also consistent with the FTU's patriotic orientation. For the FTU, institutional politics satisfy the dual demands of maintaining organizational legitimacy and loyalties, and conforming to the patriotic norms embedded in its organizational principle.

Thus, if we are to understand how political transformations impact on trade union political behavior in developing countries, we first need to grasp the ways in which historical specificities of the economic structure and sociopolitical configurations of these countries have influenced movement character. We also need to complement such analysis with much greater attention to the mediating effects of organizational processes.

Notes

1. All union movements face problems of defining their objectives and deciding whether to pursue these objectives in the economic arena, the political arena, or both. While in a broad sense all decisions about objectives and the context of action may be construed as political, we limit the use of political strategy to refer to all forms of movement action aimed at the state and its policies.

2. Lipset also stresses the enduring effects of formative experiences on subsequent movement character, that is, ideology, structure, and strategies of action (1983, p. 16). This is an advance over previous theories since variations in the character of union movements in industrial societies often defy explanation based solely on a logic of capitalism, industrialism, or the labor market (cf. Gallie, 1983, p. 22). We shall return to this point in our conclusions.

3. Postwar state policy toward trade unions was embodied in the 1948 Trade Unions and Trade Disputes Ordinance, which replaced the 1927 Illegal Strikes and Lock-Outs Ordinance. The 1948 ordinance made trade union registration compulsory in order to enable the state to regulate union objects and internal administration. There was initially resistance by some unions to complying with the provisions of the ordinance. While all unions had registered by the early 1950s, achieving their conformity with other provisions of the ordinance continued to be a problem for the government throughout the 1950s and early 1960s (Yiu, 1980, pp. 26, 38).

4. Over the period 1967-1968 to 1979-1980, the number of registered trade unions in the civil service rose from 34 to 122, and declared membership of civil service unions increased from about 17,400 to 60,700 (Lam, 1988, p. 158). This wave continued in the 1980s as the

number of civil service unions increased to 173 by 1989. Union membership in public administration and social and related community services accounted for 45% of total union membership in 1989 (Registrar of Trade Unions, 1990, p. 86).

5. As part of its changing strategy, the FTU affiliates began from the early 1980s to participate in the election of worker representatives to the Labor Advisory Board (LAB). As a result, union participation rates in LAB elections increased substantially (Chiu, 1986, p. 37).

6. Scott (1989, p. 269) argues that the creation of functional constituencies was a strategy for dealing with "problems arising from the deepening crisis of legitimacy" and the need to seek "a consensus to support the Hong Kong government's policies in the transitional period and to enable power to be transferred in 1997 from one strong executive government to another."

7. The electorate for the Labour functional constituency is the same as for the LAB—all registered employee trade unions—with each union that registers as an elector entitled to one vote.

8. Since the FTU and TUC can vote en bloc, the candidates they sponsor have a considerable advantage in the Labour constituency election. One other trade unionist, the president of the PTU, one of the largest unions in Hong Kong, ran successfully for election from the Education constituency.

9. Hong Kong as a Special Administrative Region (SAR) of China is supposed to enjoy a high degree of autonomy after 1997, except on matters concerning foreign affairs and defense. The government of the PRC, in an elaboration of its basic policies regarding Hong Kong, stated that Hong Kong's capitalist system and life-style would remain unchanged for 50 years after 1997, and that existing rights and freedoms—including those of speech, assembly, association, strikes, and choice of occupations—would be incorporated into a Basic Law. On the paradoxes of the Basic Law, see Ghai (1991, pp. 27-28).

10. On the conflict between the FTU and independent unions over the process of selecting the seven labor representatives to serve on the Basic Law Consultative Committee, see E. Lau (1988, pp. 99-100).

11. For details on how the FTU's position on the structure of the future SAR legislature changed after the Tiananmen massacre, in June 1989, see Levin and Chiu (forthcoming, a).

12. On the parties associated with the democracy lobby, see Tsim (1989, p. xxxiii). For discussions of the problems of these parties and their leaders, see S. K. Lau (1990), Lee (1990), and So and Kwitko (1990).

13. While Kerr et al. predicted that colonial elites would generate a politically oriented union movement, they also suggested that colonial regimes differ in their mode of rule, thus implying that variable political consequences may follow. Of their three subtypes of colonial regimes, British colonial rule in Hong Kong most closely approximated that of "segmental colonialism," which they consider to be "the lightest form of colonialism" and which "seldom has severe political repercussions" (1973, pp. 68-69).

14. This does not mean the working class was always politically passive. Even prior to the 1920s, resentments against the state led to mass protest, but these were sporadic and were frequently shaped as much by events in China as in Hong Kong.

15. For discussions of the expanded role of the state in the area of employment relationships after 1967, see England (1989) and Turner et al. (1980, pp. 103-117).

16. The working assumption is the primary existence of unions as organizations and the union movement as a network of organizations. The significance of the organizational variable in the study of industrial relations and labor movements has been emphasized in a number of recent studies. See, for example, Zeitlin (1987, 1989), Offe (1985), and Lembcke (1988). For discussion of the significance of the organizational variable in trade union growth waves in Hong Kong, see Levin and Chiu (forthcoming, b).

17. In this respect, movement strategies that are initially "isomorphic" with the environment may tend over time to become increasingly non-isomorphic (cf. Nelson, 1989).

18. One indicator of the CIC link to the CTU is that most of the CTU's full-time executives were or presently are CIC staff. A number of the CTU affiliates were in fact formed under the guidance of the CIC.

References

Aldrich, H., & Auster, E. R. (1986). Even dwarfs started small: Liabilities of age and size and their strategic implications. *Research in Organizational Behavior, 8.*

The basic law of the Hong Kong special administrative region of the People's Republic of China. (1990, April). Hong Kong: The Consultative Committee for the Basic Law of the Hong Kong Special Administrative Region of the People's Republic of China.

Carton, G. W. (1971). *China and Hong Kong, 1945-1967.* Unpublished doctoral dissertation, Harvard University.

Chan, M. K. (1984). *Labor and empire: The Chinese labor movement in the Canton delta, 1895-1927.* Ann Arbor, MI: University Microfilms International. (Original work published 1975)

Chesneaux, J. (1968). *The Chinese labor movement, 1919-1927.* Berkeley: University of California Press.

Cheung, B. L., Lui, T. L., Chan, T., & Wong, T. W. P. (1988). *Class and Hong Kong society.* Hong Kong: Twilight Books. (In Chinese)

Cheung, A. B. L., & Louie, K. S. (1991). *Social conflicts in Hong Kong, 1975-1986: Trends and implications* (Occasional Paper No. 3). Hong Kong: The Chinese University of Hong Kong, Hong Kong Institute of Asia-Pacific Studies.

Chiu, K. Y. P. (1986). *Labour organizations and political change in Hong Kong.* Unpublished master's dissertation, University of Hong Kong.

Deyo, F. C. (Ed.). (1987). *The political economy of the new Asian industrialism.* Ithaca: Cornell University Press.

Deyo, F. C. (1989). *Beneath the miracle: Labor subordination in the new Asian industrialism.* Berkeley: University of California Press.

Deyo, F. C., Haggard, S., & Koo, H. (1987). Labor in the political economy of east Asian industrialization. *Bulletin of Concerned Asian Scholars, 19,* 42-53.

Djao, W. (1981). "Traditional Chinese culture" in the small factory in Hong Kong. *Journal of Contemporary Asia 11,* 413-425.

England, J. (1980). Strategic factors in trade unionism and industrial disputes in Hong Kong. *Labour and Society, 5,* 267-289.

England, J. (1989). *Industrial relations and law in Hong Kong* (2d ed.). Hong Kong: Oxford University Press.

England, J., & Rear, J. (1981). *Industrial relations and law in Hong Kong.* Hong Kong: Oxford University Press.

Gallie, D. (1983). *Social inequality and class radicalism in France and Britain.* London: Cambridge University Press.

Ghai, Y. (1991). The past and the future of Hong Kong's constitution. An inaugural lecture from the Sir Y. K. Pao chair of public law [Supplement]. *Gazette, 38* (University of Hong Kong).

Kerr, C., Dunlop. J. T., Harbison, F. H., & Myers, C. A. (1973). *Industrialism and industrial man.* Harmondsworth, UK: Penguin.

King, A. Y. C., & Leung, D. H. K. (1975). *The Chinese touch in small industrial organizations.* Hong Kong: The Chinese University of Hong Kong, Social Research Centre.

Lam, W. H. (1988). Proliferation and consolidation of trade unionism in the public service. In Y. C. Jao et al. (Eds.), *Labour movement in a changing society: The experience of Hong Kong.* Hong Kong: University of Hong Kong, Centre of Asian Studies.

Lau, E. (1988). The early history of the drafting process. In P. Wesley-Smith & A. Chen (Eds.), *The basic law and Hong Kong's future.* Hong Kong: Butterworths.

Lau, S. K. (1982). *Society and politics in Hong Kong.* Hong Kong: The Chinese University Press.

Lau, S. K., & Kuan, H. C. (1988). *The ethos of the Hong Kong Chinese.* Hong Kong: The Chinese University Press.

Lau, S. K. (1990). *Decolonization without independence and the poverty of political leaders in Hong Kong* (Occasional Paper No. 1). Hong Kong: The Chinese University of Hong Kong, Institute of Asia-Pacific Studies.

Lee, M. K. (1990). Politicians. In R. Y. C. Wong & J. Y. S. Cheng (Eds.), *The other Hong Kong report 1990.* Hong Kong: The Chinese University Press.

Lembcke, J. (1988). *Capitalist development and class capacities: Marxist theory and union organization.* New York: Greenwood.

Leung, P. L. (1986a). A brief history of the federation of trade unions. In M. K. Chan et al. (Eds.), *Dimensions of the Chinese and Hong Kong labor movement.* Hong Kong: Hong Kong Christian Industrial Committee. (In Chinese)

Leung, P. L. (1986b). A brief history of the trade union council. In M. K. Chan et al. (Eds.), *Dimensions of the Chinese and Hong Kong labor movement.* Hong Kong: Hong Kong Christian Industrial Committee. (In Chinese)

Levin, D. A., & Chiu, S. (forthcoming, a). Dependent capitalism, colonial state and marginal unions: The case of Hong Kong. In S. Frenkel (Ed.), *Trade Unions and the new Asian industrialization.*

Levin, D. A., & Chiu, S. (forthcoming, b). Trade union growth waves in Hong Kong: Strategies and problems of organizational development. In H. A. Yun (Ed.), *Work, organisation and industry: The Asian experience.*

Lipset, S. M. (1983). Radicalism or reformism: The sources of working-class politics. *American Political Science Review, 7,* 1-18.

Lo, S. H. (1989). Colonial policy-makers, capitalist class and China: Determinants of electoral reform in Hong Kong's and Macau's legislatures. *Pacific Affairs, 62,* 204-218.

Meyer, J. W., & Rowan, B. (1977). Institutionalized organizations: Formal structure as myth and ceremony. *American Journal of Sociology, 83,* 340-363.

Miners, N. (1988). The representation and participation of trade unions in the Hong Kong government. In Y. C. Jao et al. (Eds.), *Labour movement in a changing society.* Hong Kong: University of Hong Kong, Centre of Asian Studies.

Nelson, R. E. (1989). Organization-environment isomorphism, rejection, and substitution in Brazilian Protestantism. *Organization Studies, 10,* 207-224.

Ng, S. H. (1990). Labour and employment. In R. Y. C. Wong & J. Y. S. Cheng (Eds.), *The other Hong Kong report 1990.* Hong Kong: The Chinese University Press.

Offe, C. (1985). Two logics of collective action. In C. Offe, *Disorganized capitalism.* Cambridge: Polity Press.

Registrar of Trade Unions, Hong Kong. (1990). *Annual departmental report.* Hong Kong: Government Printer.

Roberts, B. C., & De Bellecombe, L. G. (1966). Development of collective bargaining in former British and French African countries. In A. M. Ross (Ed.), *Industrial relations and economic development.* London: Macmillan.

Salaff, J. (1981). *Working daughters of Hong Kong: Filial piety or power in the family?* Cambridge: Cambridge University Press.

Scott, I. (1989). *Political change and the crisis of legitimacy in Hong Kong.* Hong Kong: Oxford University Press.

Siddique, S. A. (1989). Industrial relations in a third world setting: A possible model. *The Journal of Industrial Relations, 31,* 385-401.

Sit, V. F. S., & Wong, S. L. (1989). *Small and medium industries in an export-oriented economy: The case of Hong Kong.* Hong Kong: University of Hong Kong, Centre of Asian Studies.

So, A. Y., & Kwitko, L. (1990). The new middle class and the democratic movement in Hong Kong. *Journal of Contemporary Asia, 20,* 384-398.

Stinchcombe, A. L. (1969). Social structure and the invention of organizational forms. In T. Burns (Ed.), *Industrial man.* Harmondsworth, UK: Penguin.

Sturmthal, A. (1967). Industrialization and the labor movement: A set of research hypotheses. *Labor relations in the Asian countries.* Tokyo: The Japan Institute of Labor.

Sturmthal, A. (1973). Industrial relations strategies. In A. Sturmthal and J. G. Scoville (Eds.), *The international labor movement in transition.* Urbana: University of Illinois Press.

Tsang, S. Y. S. (1988). *Democracy shelved.* Hong Kong: Oxford University Press.

Tsim, T. L. (1989). Introduction. In T. L. Tsim & B. H. K. Luk (Eds.), *The other Hong Kong report.* Hong Kong: The Chinese University Press.

Tso, M. T. T. (1983). *Civil service unions as a social force in Hong Kong.* Unpublished master's dissertation, University of Hong Kong.

Turner, H. A., Fosh, P., Gardner, M., Hart, K., Morris, R., Ng, S. H., Quinlan, M., & Yerbury, D. (1980). *The last colony: But whose?* Cambridge: Cambridge University Press.

Voter registration drive by union. (1991, June 3). *South China Morning Post,* p. 6.

Wong, S. L. (1988). *Emigrant entrepreneurs: Shanghai industrialists in Hong Kong.* Hong Kong: Oxford University Press.

Wong, R. Y. C. (1990). Introduction. In R. Y. C. Wong & Joseph Y. S. Cheng (Eds.), *The other Hong Kong report 1990.* Hong Kong: The Chinese University Press.

Yesufu, T. M. (1966). The state and industrial relations in developing countries. In A. M. Ross (Ed.), *Industrial relations and economic development.* London: Macmillan.

Yiu, Y. N. (1980). *Trade union policy and the trade union movement in Hong Kong.* Unpublished master's dissertation, University of Hong Kong.

Zeitlin, J. (1987). From labour history to the history of industrial relations. *Economic History Review* (2d Series, 40), 159-184.

Zeitlin, J. (1989). "Rank and filism" in British labour history: A critique. *International Review of Social History, 34,* 42-61.

21 \ Strategy and Opportunism: Trade Unions as Agents for Change in South Africa

CLIVE THOMPSON

Apartheid in South Africa has represented a special case of twentieth-century authoritarianism. Although the outside world may have seen a racial oligarchy wielding power and enjoying privilege by virtue of classically blunt instruments, the truth has been more complex. While the political, social, and economic segmentation of South African society has been guaranteed, often unsparingly, by brute force at critical junctures, the maintenance of the system has principally been a matter of divisive and oppressive administration (see Adam, 1971). Even then, control over the society has been uneven and punctuated by pockets of both institutional and chancing opposition. However, as long as the domestic economy could be driven by the gold and maize couplet, and serviced by cheap and acquiescent labor, the racial center could hold.

In the event, demographic factors, an open economy (imports and exports have amounted to more than 40% of the annual Gross Domestic Product for most of this century: Nattrass, 1981, p. 268), and the imperative to develop skilled labor drawn from the disenfranchised populace, converted earlier social ambiguities into clear contradictions as a process of transformation took root within a largely uncomprehending society in the early seventies.

The year 1973 was a dramatic one in recent South African labor history. Some 10 years after the black liberation movements had been banned, their internal leaders jailed, and the union movement suppressed, a spontaneous strike among textile workers in the province of Natal ballooned into protracted mass action by more than 100,000 workers in the region. The action abated, but among its consequences was a forgathering of worker leaders, academics, and students, and the creation of forums and structures, which would yield a new union movement and a formidable challenge to the status quo.

Social Change:
Some Key Concepts

In their provocative study series, O'Donnell and Schmitter (1986) have identified certain key concepts and features that illuminate the process of transition from authoritarian rule. Of necessity they first give attention to the notion of transition itself, by which they mean the interval between one political regime and another. They note that the early phase of transition is characterized by *liberalization*—a process that begins when the incumbent rulers, usually to protect their perceived interests, begin to modify their own rules by extending first-generation rights, such as freedom of expression, of association, and the like—to individuals and groups. Implicit in their analysis is an acknowledgment that liberalization is a reaction rather than an initiative: It is perhaps an article of faith as much as an empirical observation that those burdened will strain against the yoke. The neutralization and co-optation of dissent are the presumed objectives of the newly flexible rulers but, as the authors stress and as the South African case, among others, demonstrates, the creation of space entails a dynamic of unintended, even unimagined, consequences. The social process is "underdetermined."

Liberalization may deliver *democratization:* the advent of a society based on constitutionalism, full citizenship, and political pluralism. While reiterating that all progress is precarious and all processes reversible, O'Donnell and Schmitter postulate (1986, p. 12) that the transition to political democracy sets up the possibility for another:

> At the risk of confusing the term with other uses in the social sciences, we have called this "second" transition "socialization." It also involves a double stream, two independent but inter-related processes. The one, which some label "social democracy" consists of making the workers in factories, the students at schools and universities, the members of interest associations, the supporters of political parties, the clients of state agencies, even the faithful of churches, the consumers of products, the clients of professionals, the patients in hospitals, the users of parks, the children of families, etc., ad infinitum, into citizens— actors with equal rights and obligations to decide what actions these institu-

tions should take. The other process, at times associated with the term "economic democracy," relates to providing equal benefits to the population from the goods and services generated by society: wealth, income, education, health, housing, information, leisure time, even autonomy, prestige, respect and self-development.

The authors state candidly that the focus of their enquiry is political democracy, so that the dynamics of the "second transition" are left largely unexplored. Socialization is of course a matter of a particular moment to labor movements, and this aspect will be pursued further within the context of South Africa (see also Valenzuela, 1989).

The O'Donnell and Schmitter framework can perhaps more fruitfully be deployed, and some of its indeterminacy filtered out, if the process of transition is viewed against the backdrop of the more fundamental process of transformation in a particular society. As Price (1991, p. 4) puts it:

The foundation upon which the formal political order rests can be thought of as a "substructure" of domination—social interactions, cultural norms, economic activities, and informal power relationships that create the basis for compliance with the prescriptions of the ruling group. Changes in this underlying structure are often the precursor and condition for alteration in the political system's "superstructure," the formal system of power. Basic alterations in the former, the substructure of power, can be thought of as involving political *transformation,* and can be distinguished from political *transition,* the movement from one formal arrangement of power to another. Transformation prepares the way for transition.

Industrial relations has figured as a fundamental component of transformation in South Africa. Its shaping antecedents help both to explain recent developments and to suggest what is possible, and perhaps probable, as the country proceeds with its sea change.

Trade Unions and
Transformation in South Africa

The minority government's social scheme was disturbed by a number of developments in the seventies. Black workers had shown their hand dramatically in 1973, and in 1976 it was the turn of the angry youth. The Sowetan revolts of that year shook the system of "Bantu education" and signaled the start of a campaign against black local authorities that was to be sustained without let-up into the nineties. While the workers and youth were demanding political rights and economic advancement, the modernizing and internationally exposed economy was being stunted by shortages of skilled labor. A statutory job color bar prevented Africans,[1] in particular, from being selected and trained for promotion. The first serious rumblings of trade sanctions and disinvestment were being heard, and the severing or curtailment of the country's diplomatic, sporting, and cultural ties with the international community was proceeding apace. The exiled African National Congress with its armed wing, Umkhonto we Sizwe, threatened the status quo still further.

All of these developments entailed immediate social costs to the rulers and their constituents, and the extent of future damage remained uncertain. There were other cracks of historic origin in the edifice of white supremacy. Diverse institutions in South Africa have enjoyed definite, if restricted, space in which to challenge prevailing orthodoxies. Sections of the relatively free press were at large to attack the government's social policies, as were certain universities and churches. Again, a largely independent judiciary could be relied upon to produce unsettling judgments on sensitive issues.

It was within the more or less darker recesses of the factories, however, that working-class elements were stumbling their way toward an organizational recipe that would, in time, not only transform economic relations but also play an instrumental part in the demise of the whole apartheid order. In a distinct departure from the patterns and practices of the past, the emerging worker leadership decided to abandon mass recruiting and to direct all its resources at consolidating union membership at a modest number of factories within selected areas and industries (Baskin, 1991, p. 21; Friedman, 1987, p. 87). Not only did the tactic prove to be viable in a hostile environment, but it also provided a template for making future strategic choices and ultimately become a building block for industrial unionism.

The approach expressed itself in terms of a slowly expanding circle of recognition disputes at plant level. Effectively excluded from statutory protections, and with no assistance from the common law, unions were left to win recognition through industrial action. Many employers responded by dismissing en masse, making use of statutory "influx control" measures to deport striking black workers from the cities to rural "homelands."

While unskilled workers could be readily replaced in an economy plagued by high levels of structural unemployment, the costs of victimizing semi-skilled and skilled workers escalated with each passing year. Furthermore, a number of recognition disputes were centered around multinationals whose international vulnerability impelled them toward negotiated solutions. Although in absolute terms union density remained low during the seventies, the unionized plants—which numbered in the hundreds by the close of the decade—projected a powerful demonstration effect in key sectors, such as the motor, metal, clothing, textile, and chemical industries.

In the latter half of the seventies the state responded to the arc of pressures ranged against it with a two-pronged strategy of repression and reform. The new prime minister, P. W. Botha, who later arrogated to himself the office and centralized powers of state president, announced to his supporters, in a celebrated 1979 speech, that apartheid was a "recipe for permanent conflict" and that white South Africans should "adapt or die." His administration saw the rise of a new cadre of functionary, the securocrats, who developed what was termed the "total national strategy" to combat the "total onslaught," ostensibly Communist-inspired, against the country. A central body, the State Security Council, was introduced to coordinate both repression of internal dissidents and the destabilization of neighboring states (Cloete, 1991, p. 32; Price, 1991, p. 85).

The militarization attendant upon the adaptive process was counterbalanced by imposed, technocratic reform or, as became known in the domestic idiom, reform by stealth. The dualistic policy was conceived and executed with the intention of dictating both the direction and the pace of change. Its objective was to modernize racial domination in pragmatic, self-interested fashion (Adam, 1971), by a controlled process of incorporating and accommodating previously excluded groups. It represented, however, a move toward process politics, and a clear deviation from the confident end-product dogma that had informed the social engineering of earlier grand apartheid architects. Although an element of uncertainty must have been factored into the equation, a sense of power—false security, in the event—emboldened the securocrats to proceed with their plans.

There were principally two areas of application for the reform arm of the total strategy: labor and politics. Control over the process, a sufficient level of acceptance by the targeted constituencies, and a rough parity of development in industrial and political relations were essential if the policy were to unfold as intended. None of these prerequisites was realized, but the imperious reformers persevered regardless. Their headstrong social engineering and, ironically, given their claims, their lack of adaptability, undermined their game plan, intensified social conflict, and finally precipitated accelerated change of a different order. It was the asymmetry of the response—something which ought to have been predicted—that confounded the government. The labor reforms were seized upon and manipulated, while the political initiatives were rejected and resisted.

Trade unions were equipped to negotiate, not only because of their immediate history but because terms could, in fact, not be dictated to them. A true exchange was possible, the outcome of which would depend on which party could exploit the looming indeterminacy to best advantage. A mobile adversary faced a lumbering one. On the other hand, the niceties of negotiation held no attraction for the government's political opponents. They had no operational or effective power base, and the only prospect that beckoned was absorption in another's system.

The antithetical reception of the reform package caught the P. W. Botha administration off balance. Thereafter and until its demise, its policies remained reactive.

During May 1977 the government appointed a commission, chaired by a university professor, Nic Wiehahn, to reappraise the country's labor laws. As in other quarters of South African life, industrial relations had hitherto been a segregated affair. White, colored, and Asian workers were regulated by a relatively advanced system of labor laws, incorporating self-governing bipartite bodies called industrial councils. African workers were excluded from mainstream legislation, and the sum total of their legal rights was contained in whatever (contractually enforceable) recognition agreements their unions could bargain with employers.

The Wiehahn Commission advocated a radically different dispensation: that labor legislation should be deracialized, freedom of association recognized, and an industrial court with sweeping unfair labor practice powers introduced. The recommendations were made on the basis that they represented a sophisticated strategy to regulate the emerging black unions through co-optation. These unions, the commission noted, should be brought within the "protective and stabilizing elements of the system [with its] essential discipline and control" (*South African Labour Bulletin*, 1987, p. 141).

In the face of serious misgivings from elements within the South Africa cabinet, the recommendations were enacted in 1979. The *verligtes* (the enlightened thinkers) had triumphed over the *verkramptes* (the hardliners). Now it was the turn of the labor leaders to equivocate. Unionists had paid a heavy price for their activities through the seventies and they would continue to suffer grievously under both official security measures and clandestine groupings in the eighties. Many had been banned, several had died while in detention. A vigorous, even acrimonious, debate, over the merits and demerits of participation in statutory structures, was triggered in union circles.

The very intensity of the debate probably served to inoculate the union movement against any enervating consequences that participation might have entailed: Both hardliners and softliners pinned their colors firmly to the mast of labor movement autonomy. Those who favored participation eventually won the day, and by the mid-eighties the advantages of participation had turned even skeptics. One analysis (Fine, De Clercq, & Innes, 1987, pp. 198-200, 202) in 1981 was particularly persuasive and prescient:

> It is characteristic of the state to present its reforms both as a recognition of the rights of its citizens and as an optimum form of control over them. The temptation facing the state's critics is to reject the soft language of rights as no more

than an illusory veil, while accepting the hard language of control as a true mirror of reality. But neither side of the coin is correct. On the one hand, it cannot be assumed that rights are merely a veil for power or a mystification which hides the brutal realities of class domination. The existence of rights constitutes a vital resource for the oppressed and an inhibition of the power of the oppressors. That is why the winning of rights from the state has been a vital part of all labour movements. . . .

[O]ur response to these innovations cannot be determined by the state's intentions; rather we must make our own assessment of the real effects of registration [of trade unions]. For between the state's intentions and their realization in practice falls a shadow: the struggle of workers. Whether the new forms of labour control will serve as a stimulus for its development (as the state fears) cannot be gauged by studying the state's intentions alone.

The vital task of black workers is to reach for means whereby they can take hold of the instruments which the state seeks to use against them and turn them around to their own advantage. . . .

The risk from the perspective of the rulers is that whatever concessions or rights it offers will be used by black workers in ways that were never intended: to consolidate, broaden and strengthen the union movement. This is the weak underbelly of the government's strategy. Our argument is that by making a principal out of a boycott the opportunity to exploit this weakness is lost.

Three features of the emerging black unions' strategy stood out in the first half of the eighties: Organization building generally followed the pattern of factory-by-factory recruitment and consolidation; the spaces afforded by the new labor laws were aggressively exploited; and union autonomy was asserted in the face of calls for broader political involvement.

The open texture of the labor laws proved to be a major Achilles' heel for the authoritarian reformers. Lacking a coherent blueprint for labor's rights and duties, and endeavoring to be all things to all people, the government effectively delegated legislative powers to the new industrial court. The judicial officers in turn were unsure of their role and, after initial hesitation, sought guidance in the beacons provided by the Conventions and Recommendations of the International Labor Organization and comparative law generally. The result was the rapid creation of a jurisprudence of individual unfair dismissal, negotiating rights, and protection for strikers (Thompson, 1988, p. 347). The initial reluctance of unions to use the courts dissipated once the trend of the judgments became clear (see Table 21.1). With victimization outlawed, the unions were able to step up their recruitment campaigns, and their membership figures grew rapidly throughout the eighties (see Table 21.2). Recognition disputes and their associated hazards became less prevalent as the industrial court established the precedent that employers were under an obligation to negotiate with representative unions. The leverage that

TABLE 21.1 Cases Brought to the Industrial Court, 1979–1990

Year	Case Load
1979	4
1980	15
1981	30
1982	41
1983	168
1984	399
1985	801
1986	2,000
1987	3,500
1988	3,800
1989	4,500
1990	6,400

SOURCE: Annual Reports of the Department of Manpower.
NOTE: Unions and employees were the applicants in the vast majority of cases.

TABLE 21.2 Membership of Registered Trade Unions, 1979–1990

Year	Membership (all races)
1979	727,000
1980	781,000
1981	1,054,000
1982	1,226,000
1983	1,288,000
1984	1,406,000
1985	1,391,000
1986	1,698,000
1987	1,879,000
1988	2,084,000
1989	2,130,000
1990	2,459,000

SOURCE: Annual Reports of the Department of Manpower.
NOTE: There were 2.08 million members in trade unions in 1988 and an estimated 338,000 members in unregistered unions, representing about 42% of the workforce falling under the Labor Relations Act or, 22% of the economically active population (excluding the "independent" homelands). Whereas there were 292,000 Africans who were members of registered unions in 1980, some 956,969 Africans belonged to registered unions in 1988 (Race Relations Survey 1988/89, South African Institute of Race Relations, Johannesburg: 1990).

unions could exact in interest disputes was bolstered further when the court determined that the expedient of mass dismissals was an unfair response to procedural strike action.

The new body of law created by the industrial court not only provided swords and shields to the unions, but also legitimated a different system of labor relations, one that was essentially universalistic, pluralistic, and relatively libertarian in character. A perplexed business community was forced to adapt or die. The new industrial relations regime spawned a further Trojan horse: the industrial relations manager who believed in the premises of the new system. A number of corporate figures emerged who played major roles in facilitating the adoption of novel procedural and substantive norms. As a group, they formed a bridgehead for new thinking in the company boardroom.

The impact of a persuasive IR managerial lobby within the largest South African mining house—the Anglo American Corporation—accounts in significant measure for the spectacular recruiting success of the National Union of Mineworkers. Black workers remained nonunionized within the mining industry for more than a century, up until 1982. At the end of that year, an astute union leader rejected the established wisdom of incremental recruitment and negotiated an access agreement to the tightly regimented compounds of mines in the Anglo American stable. Within 3 short years 250,000 black mineworkers had been signed up—a union density of some 40% in the entire industry.

Labor relations, though highly adversarial (see Table 21.3), began to assume the proportions of a negotiated enclave within a broader system of political repression. The adaptive capability of the business establishment was enhanced, while the disjunction between the economy and the polity became increasingly acute.

Broadly speaking, the emerging unions maintained an abstentionist position on national politics for the first decade of their existence (Hindson, 1987, p. 209). It was the product of a learning experience, a survival and growth strategy that worked. Their longer term goals of achieving a Socialist transformation could best be promoted by insinuating themselves into the economy, rather than exposing themselves in politics. The working-class interests of the labor movement, it was reckoned, could best be protected through independence from extraneous forces (Foster, 1987, pp. 219, 228).

The government's model for constitutional reform in the political arena, in contrast, not only generated direct popular resistance, but also forced the unions to change their workerist modus operandi. In 1983 the new tricameral constitution was endorsed in a referendum of white voters and then adopted by Parliament. In essence, the formerly white Parliament was enlarged to accommodate two further chambers, one for those classified as "colored"

TABLE 21.3 Strikes, 1979–1990

Year	No. of Strikes	Total Workers Involved	Total Workdays Lost
1979	101	22,803	67,099
1980	207	61,785	174,614
1981	342	92,842	226,554
1982	394	141,571	365,337
1983	336	64,469	124,596
1984	469	181,942	379,712
1985	389	239,816	678,273
1986	798	424,340	1,308,958
1987	1,148	591,421	5,825,231
1988	1,025	161,679	914,388
1989	855	—	1,238,686
1990	948	—	2,973,921

SOURCE: Annual Reports of the Department of Manpower.

and one for those classified as Indian. There was, however, no room for blacks in the renovated Houses of Parliament. For whites nurtured on a diet of racism, the new constitution meant nothing less than the adoption on a completely new mindset; the deliberately unarticulated premise was that the system would in time evolve to include Africans, and that relative numbers would loom large at that stage. In other words, notwithstanding the obvious defensive expediency inherent in tricameralism, the specter of majority rule was for the first time visible on the horizon.

Events showed that the government could control neither the contours nor the pace of political reform. A broad alliance, the United Democratic Front, was created to resist the new constitution, and civil unrest on a scale unprecedented in South Africa's history was unleashed in August 1984. The government was not deflected from its constitutional path but responded instinctively with a panoply of repressive measures. Troops occupied black townships, fatalities ensued, and many activists were detained. Then a new factor was introduced: Urban youths called upon the trade union movement to support them in a stayaway planned for November 1984. After some debate, the unions broke with their 10-year strategy, and on November 5 and 6, some 500,000 workers and 400,000 scholars engaged in a stayaway in the target area of the Transvaal province (Labour Monitoring Group, 1987, p. 259).

The downward spiral of dissent and repression continued. In mid-1985 a state of emergency was declared, which would remain in force for 5 years.

Tens of thousands of activists and innocents were detained, the United Democratic Front and other political movements were banned, meetings of the extra-parliamentary opposition were prohibited, and the press was heavily censored. Aggression turned inward as well, with the emergence of factional violence within black communities. Although labor action in support of political demands continued throughout the state of emergency, the unions generally maintained a definite organizational distance from the political movements. By 1988 the leadership of the extra-parliamentary political opposition had been all but decimated, while the unions remained largely intact, shielded by their entrenched presence in thousands of sites in the economy, including by then the statutory industrial councils, and by the threat of a weapon that security measures could not neutralize—a protracted general strike (cf. Valenzuela, 1989, p. 447). As it was, the incidence of strike action climbed dramatically from 1984, to reach nearly 6 million lost working days in 1987 (see Table 21.2). The territory that labor relations had carved out for itself stood relatively firm. From a legal point of view, emergency measures could not be brought to bear against trade unions—the enabling security legislation, framed for a different generation of labor actors, disallowed any direct attacks on union activities, including procedural industrial action, as the government discovered to its cost in litigation on the first and last occasion on which it transgressed its own laws. While many trade unionists were detained without trial for alleged political transgressions, the top leadership of the labor movement generally remained free to operate.

Appreciating that labor could not be accosted in a frontal assault, the government attempted a more circuitous route: It amended the Labor Relations Act (LRA) in 1988, so as to give the labor courts more latitude in outlawing and penalizing strike action (*South African Labour News*, 1991, p. 1). This development was manna for the unions. The state of emergency had effectively eclipsed the political opposition, and had unnerved a union leadership, trained to eschew political adventurism and who sensed that rank-and-file membership was weary of solidarity stayaways. Now the unions could mobilize around issues that impacted upon their members directly; under the guise of protecting their industrial interests, they could destabilize the oppressive state. They would be operating on home ground. For 2 years the unions rallied their supporters in an anti-LRA campaign that produced the largest labor stayaways in recent history. To compound matters, some labor judges and arbitrators began to brand as unfair the dismissal of workers who stayed away from work in protest against the legislative amendments [Cameron, 1990, p. 93; *Gana & others v Building Materials Manufacturers Ltd* (1990) 11 *ILJ* 335 (IC); *Samancor Ltd and National Union of Metalworkers of SA* (1991) 12 *ILJ* 431 (ARB)].

But for a society on the threshold of transition, the enduring significance of the LRA campaign lay not in the unions' capacity to strike, but to negotiate. Even as the stayaways proceeded, the principal but rival federations of black workers, the Congress of South African Trade Unions (COSATU) and the National Council of Trade Unions (NACTU), joined forces to open discussions with the main employer confederation in the country, the South African Consultative Committee on Labor Affairs (SACCOLA), with the object of settling the terms of new labor legislation. The employers were amenable and, in May 1990, shortly after the new state president announced the government's break with the apartheid past at the opening of Parliament, the employer and union bodies signed an accord on proposals for amended labor laws.

Trade Unions and Transition

There were many factors that forced president F. W. De Klerk's hand in unbanning the African National Congress and the Pan Africanist Congress, on February 2, 1990, and setting in motion real democratic reform. Most were hemorrhaging in nature: The war in Namibia and Angola had drained the national fiscus, the weapons boycott meant that South Africa's air supremacy on the subcontinent had been lost to Cuban MiGs, military reversals occurred and more appeared imminent; the brain drain continued relentlessly; many white graduates were opting for emigration rather than 2 years' military service fighting an unwinnable war on foreign soil; disinvestment and sanctions had bled the economy for 5 years, and the burgeoning pool of unemployed translated into still more social unrest. The abolition of influx control in 1986—itself a forced step—had accelerated the flow of humanity from the impoverished rural areas into the cities; the third world was visibly and massively encamped around the first.

These factors combined with the more structural changes: the unions' established but adversarial place in the economy, and the disenfranchised community's steadfast resistance to any imposed political arrangement. Their political resilience was demonstrated by the diverse campaigns—from hunger strikes to mass marches—which sprang into life the moment the application of the emergency regulations was relaxed, following state president P. W. Botha's incapacitation in February 1989.

The transition literature places great store on pact formation by pragmatic elements within the contending leadership groups (O'Donnell & Schmitter, 1986, p. 37; Valenzuela, 1989, p. 445). Within this context the industrial relations community has already played and will continue to play a special role in the process of change. At the level of declared ideology, a large chasm separates the union Socialists and Communists from business's free market-eers. The actual record of transactions between unions and employers demonstrates something different: pragmatism. While industrial unrest may have attracted the headlines over the years, the fundamental change in economic relations between labor and management has been wrought through sustained negotiations and evermore encompassing agreements. In the seventies, procedural and substantive contracts at the level of the plant represented the high-water mark of institutionalized relations. By the mid-eighties, the major parties were utilizing the centerpiece of the deracialized legislative scheme, industrial councils, to strike industry-wide deals. At the height of the state of emergency and in the wake of the retrogressive 1988 labor statute amendments, some unions had bargained sweeping agreements with a number of key multinationals and domestic corporations, in terms of which the parties not only rejected any recourse to the statutory labor regime, but also undertook to combat the effects of apartheid's social and security legislation. These "contracting out" agreements were underpinned by a further voluntarist development, independent arbitration and mediation.

But it was the controversy surrounding the 1988 legislation itself that was to provide the impetus for the most remarkable, and generalized, exemplar of pact formation. Mention has already been made of the restitution accord entered into between the apex employer and union bodies in May 1990. In September of the same year, that accord, in modified form, was endorsed by the South African cabinet following an exhaustive series of negotiations. The terms of what has become known as the 1990 Laboria Minute were far-reaching indeed. The state agreed, first, to purge the labor laws of all the contested 1988 features. It also undertook to extend the scope of those laws to include public sector workers, farmworkers, and domestic servants. In return, the unions agreed to abandon further planned labor action on the issue. However, it was the other aspect of the Minute that had the greatest transitional significance: The unions agreed to become members of the central statutory body charged with the developing of labor policy, the National Manpower Commission (NMC). This step was contingent upon that body's being reconstituted along more representative lines, something that the state bound itself to do. In return for participation, the state agreed to submit no further labor legislation to Parliament unless or until it had been processed by the NMC.

An extraordinary event had occurred. COSATU, in alliance with the ANC, and NACTU, in alliance with the PAC, had in effect agreed to serve in a form of interim industrial government. The state had agreed to restrict procedurally, and in effect substantively, its own law-making powers. All this had occurred at a time when the ANC and the government were demonstrably at odds over the preconditions to bargaining in the political sphere, and when the PAC was still formally engaged in an armed struggle with the minority regime.

The explanation for this striking incongruency lies in the respective histories of the labor and political actors. For the unions, the employers, and the state labor department, well acquainted with one another's power bases and conditioned by 15 years of intensive brokering, the Laboria Minute was merely a progression, albeit a singularly important one, of the established logic of negotiation. The political protagonists, on the other hand, were novices, uncertain of both their own capacities and those of their adversaries. In the political arena, a settling-out process must first run its laborious course before the real business of negotiations over interim arrangements, and an eventual constitution, can be undertaken (see Van Zyl Slabbert, 1991, p. 6). Upon assuming office, the civilian F. W. De Klerk decided to engage in the future at a point where, for all of its beleaguered status, the minority government still held much more power than its principal opponent, thé African National Congress—a further factor accounting for the discrepancy in bargaining confidence between that organization and its union alliance partner.

Unlike most other authoritarian societies subject to the forces of liberalization and democratization, South Africa seems set to experience a protracted period of transition. What is more, the society-in-transition is likely to shade incrementally, rather than switch epochally into the post-apartheid era. On this assumption, the unions have much to exploit. They are the most organized of the opposition power brokers active in the country and, crucially, have initiated a process of high-level engagement at the time when others are still ensnared in preliminaries.

It has long been an expressed hope of the white business community that, with sufficient redirection of resources, the modest group of black entrepreneurs could grow into a sizable middle class that would stabilize the entire society. It is a much safer bet that the business community and perhaps the state could, and may well, achieve the same result through a robust partnership with the employed working class. The bulwark effect vis-à-vis the third of the economically active population who cannot be absorbed into employment by the formal sector is likely to be more secure. *Realpolitik* suggests that it is better to strike deals with the exploited than the neglected. That said, the viability of any social market plan that treats those in employment as an elite will remain a volatile issue for the foreseeable future (see Lewis, 1991, pp. 261-266).

The central debate in South Africa is not about the defining qualities of a post-apartheid constitution—in fact, the model drafts of the main political rivals have a marked family resemblance—but about the socioeconomic choices that will need to be made if the basic needs of the country's citizens

PART VI

Labor Market
Policies and Practices

22 \ The Macro/Micro Interface in Labor Market Policy and Practice

ENG FONG PANG

This chapter summarizes the main points of the six papers prepared for Theme 5, The Micro/Macro Interface in Labor Market Policy and Practice, of the Ninth World Congress of the International Industrial Relations Association. It then discusses some policy and empirical issues raised by these papers, and examines aspects of the macro/micro interface in developing countries.

Perspectives on the Macro/Micro Interface

The six papers submitted for Theme 5 (see references) interpret the macro/micro interface in labor market policy and practice differently. All of them are concerned with the experiences of industrialized countries, one of them from a gender perspective. Together they suggest three ways to look at the broad theme of the macro/micro interface in labor market policy and practice. The first way is to examine how key macroeconomic variables—growth, inflation, employment—affect and are affected by labor market policies and institutions. This perspective of the interface has attracted considerable policy and research attention in recent years because of the divergent macroeconomic responses of industrial countries to common external shocks in the 1970s and 1980s. This divergence has led to growing interest in comparative macroeconomic institutions, particularly labor market institutions, and macroeconomic performance.

369

Two of the papers prepared for Theme 5 deal with this perspective of the interface. The paper by Carlo Dell'Aringa and Manuela Samek Lodovici on industrial relations and labor policies in European countries discusses how labor market policies "enter into the relationship between industrial relations and economic performance." More specifically, it considers how variations in labor market policies and industrial relations influence the level and pattern of unemployment and the unemployment-inflation trade-off. The Dell'Aringa-Lodovici paper recognizes the macroeconomic benefits, namely, lower unemployment and inflation of an active labor market policy and a coordinated, consensus-based industrial relations system of the kind found in Nordic countries, but it also draws attention to the mixed evidence on the cost-effectiveness of active labor market policies, and the difficulty of reshaping national labor market institutions.

The paper also suggests that the emergence of an interdependent world economy has reduced the effectiveness of national macroeconomic policies including labor market policies. The Swedish experience provides a fine example. In the 1960s, the Swedish model, characterized by a solidaristic wage system, active labor market policies, social harmony, and a highly developed welfare system, worked well, producing strong growth, full employment, low inflation, cyclical stability, and no structural imbalances. By the 1970s, however, it was clear the model was losing its effectiveness, in part because of the economy's vulnerability to external shocks. The scope for expansionary stabilization policies was limited because Sweden was suffering from budget deficits. Moreover, it had to follow the restrictive policies of other countries also adjusting to the shocks. Environmental concerns also weakened the policy commitment to strong growth. There was increased emphasis on job protection and resistance to labor mobility. And the public sector began to lead the way in wage changes, untying the connection between productivity growth and wage increases. By the late 1980s, the Swedish economy was growing slower than in most other OECD countries, but the unemployment rate remained far below that of most other countries, thanks in part to active labor market policies. In the past few years, Sweden has introduced tax reforms, reduced public sector spending, and accepted the need for unemployment to rise. But the effect of these changes on the country's international competitiveness is still not clear. What is clear, however, is that the political and economic conditions that underlie the success of the Swedish model have changed drastically, and that solidaristic wage and active labor market policies are not enough to ensure fast growth with an acceptable unemployment inflation trade-off.

The contribution by Janet Walsh and William Brown (1992), on corporate pay policies and the internationalization of markets, analyzes the relationship between bargaining structures and macroeconomic performance in a range of OECD countries. The thrust of their argument is that increasing international competition is diminishing the benefits of a national employer solidarity strategy based on wage restraint, and that to maintain their competitive position in an interdependent global economy, employers must focus on productivity growth and cooperate to develop common training systems that support productivity gains. In their view, the policy attention given to the advantages of a centralized or coordinated bargaining structure is misplaced, because it rests too heavily on wage restraint as a strategy when the real challenge for employers increasingly exposed to global competition is to develop common strategies to promote productivity and training.

A second way to examine the interface is to analyze how national economic changes and labor market policy and institutions affect wage developments at the industry and enterprise levels. The papers by Bob Gregory and Anne Daly (1992), on the determinants of relative wages in Australia and the United States, and by Isik Urla Zeytinoglu (1992), on nonstandard forms of employment and their appropriateness for women, may be said to reflect this view of the interface. Employing a human capital model, the Gregory-Daly paper compares the effects of many variables on wages in Australia and the United States, two countries that have very different labor market institutions. The authors find, among other things, that in both countries, formal education explains only a part of the variation in earnings, and that the industry of employment was also a significant determinant of earnings. The competitive model therefore does not fully explain wage formation. The authors suggest that the large inter-industry variation in wages is probably not due to unobserved differences in training or worker quality, because the same large variation is observed in unskilled workers. One explanation—not easily tested—is that high wages promote efficiency. Another is that there are significant product market differences among industries and that, for some reason, employers in these countries are forced to, or find it necessary to, share their rents with workers.

Gregory and Daly also report that in Australia, which has a centralized wage-fixing system, the earnings distribution is narrower than that in the United States, which has a highly decentralized labor market. Their results provide additional evidence that Australian labor market institutions, in pursuit of equity goals, have reduced the dispersion of relative earnings, an outcome that may have weakened labor flexibility and contributed to the poorer macroeconomic performance of Australia relative to the United States, in the 1980s.

The paper by Zeytinoglu is not concerned with comparative macroeconomics, but rather examines how economic and social conditions—growing competition, the need of employers for a flexible work force, pressures to contain wage costs, the changing and constrained choices of new labor force entrants, particularly women—have led to the rise of nonstandard (and less esteemed) forms of employment. Zeytinoglu finds that women are more likely to be involved in nonstandard forms of employment and have fewer opportunities than men working full-time for job or career advancement. She argues that the micro choices of work and family that women make will continue to be limited, in the absence of progressive changes in macro social institutions that would bring about a more equal sharing of responsibilities between men and women, and greater social value being attached to nonstandard forms of employment.

A third and related way to consider the macro/micro interface is to analyze how a firm's policies on labor are influenced or shaped by external conditions. This is the perspective Jacques Belanger and Gilles Breton (1992) take in their paper on economic restructuring and work management. Their paper argues that in responding to increasing international competition, employers have two choices: a strategy of constraint that emphasises managerial control, specialization, and Taylorist modes of production; and a strategy of voluntary consent that relies on the creativity and participation of workers to ensure a firm's competitiveness. They illustrate the effectiveness of the second strategy, with a case study of a Canadian engineering factory where workers were given autonomy and maintained productivity high enough to assure the factory's international competitiveness.

The paper by Francois Eyraud (1992) comments on the rapport between the firm and the market in work force management. Eyraud draws attention to the limitations of the neo-classical standard theory of the firm in explaining the wage structure of firms, and the need for a strategic perspective to understand the behavior of firms and their interactions with the external market. In the standard model, product markets determine not only the range of products firms make but also the technology they use. Technology conditions the choice of work organization, which in turn determines wage levels and structures. In this deterministic view, institutions, job protection, and work organization rules are seen as barriers obstructing the operation of free markets, and hence bad for efficiency. A different perspective sees skills and work organization shaping technology, and technology in turn determining a firm's range of products. The standard view encourages firms to adjust to competition through prices and rationalization, the second through training and upgrading. To illustrate this difference, Eyraud mentions the contrasting behavior of U.S. firms and Japanese firms. U.S. firms operate on the basis of specialization, individual contracts, vertical coordination, and optimization—practices that reflect American individualist values. As a consequence, external labor markets are flexible, workers mobile, and mutual commitment between workers and firms weak. In such a system, firms maximize narrowly defined goals, paying particular attention to cost control and treating labor as a variable cost. Their individual behavior is rational, but collectively their actions may hurt the economy. Consider the example of enterprise investment in worker training. Individually, it makes sense for firms to shy away from investing in worker training because of potential labor mobility. When a large number of them follows this individual logic, there is underinvestment in training and a smaller supply of trained workers, which affects the productivity and competitiveness of all firms in the economy.

In contrast to U.S. firms, Japanese firms—at least the large ones—are believed to operate on different principles. They practice horizontal coordination rather than vertical coordination—there is cooperation and sharing of information across departments and functions. Workers are paid according to rank, rather than specific jobs, and so can be more flexibly deployed and retrained. Planning and implementation are not separated, as in U.S. firms, but are highly integrated, a practice that consumes time and resources, but also allow firms to learn and adjust quickly to changing technological and market conditions. This contrast between U.S. and Japanese firms can be overdone, however. Also, organizational forms are not immutably fixed by history, tradition, or culture. Organizations can be redesigned. In recent years, U.S. firms have begun to adopt some of the organizational forms and practices of successful Japanese firms. They have shown greater commitment to workers and have given them more autonomy and power to solve problems. On their part, Japanese firms are shifting from seniority and emphasizing merit as a promotion criterion, and devising incentives to ensure that small groups do not pursue their own interests at the expense of organizational objectives. They have also modified the practice of lifetime employment, and have resorted increasingly to hiring workers for mid-level and other non-entry positions. In brief, a convergence in organizational form and practice between the United States (and other industrialized countries) and Japan is occurring, driven in large part by competitive pressures facing all firms in an interdependent world economy. This convergence may well lead to the development of a new model of the firm that suggests richer insights in how a firm relates and responds to its environment.

International Competition
and Domestic Labor Markets

In discussing the macro/micro interface in labor market policy and practice, the powerful influence of the international economy on the national economy must be recognized. In the past 30 years, there have been significant structural changes in the world economy as well as in national economies. In the industrialized countries, there has been a decline in mass-production work, and a shift to services and flexible production. Recent years have seen the emergence of a new system of industrial organization, based on flexible specialization that takes advantage of microelectronics to develop new products and processes. This new system has drastically changed the job structure in OECD countries, especially the United States. Its rise has paralleled the globalization of competition and markets. Product cycles have shortened, and firms are increasingly rationalizing production on a global scale, both to spread R&D and other costs and to maintain their competitive position. One consequence of this development is to reduce the scope of action for national unions.

When markets are national, the benefits of coordinated or centralized bargaining are clear. Both employers and unions are aware of the externalities of their wage bargaining behavior. This awareness encourages wage moderation and thus promotes employment expansion. However, with increasing global competition, employers have come under increasing pressure to stay competitive. They cannot pass the cost of wage increases to their buyers because of international competition. To drive costs down, they have to move operations abroad to lower cost countries, a move that weakens their commitment to national employer solidarity and industry-wide bargaining. Workers who are largely confined to national labor markets cannot follow internationalizing firms. Nor is it easy for their unions to join together internationally to bargain collectively with multinational employers. The rise of internationalized product markets not only diminishes the traditional powers of unions, but also reduces the effectiveness of national macroeconomic policies to influence the labor market.

International competition also drives a wedge between the interests of multinational employers and the interests of the countries in which they are headquartered. The global interests of a multinational company are not necessarily identical to those of a country. This divergence between corporate and national interests has to be taken into account in policies to improve the macro/micro interface in labor market policy and practice. It suggests that policies to stimulate aggregate employment and improve the employment-inflation trade-off are likely to be ineffective unless they are matched by policies to promote long-term productivity growth and human resource development in the national economy. Governments have an important role to play in creating an environment and providing the incentives that encourage firms to invest in their workers and plants. Their labor market policies should focus less on costly job protection and pay more attention to expanding the capacity of firms to compete and create new employment opportunities.

The Macro/Micro Interface
in Developing Countries

Because the six papers did not consider the macro/micro interface in developing countries, a brief discussion may be useful. As in industrial countries, there is a wide range of labor market institutions and experiences in developing countries. In recent years, many developing countries have had to follow structural adjustment programs, which have had significant labor market effects. In most of them, however, the macro/micro institutional links are weak; workers are not well organized, and bargaining structures are underdeveloped. Very few countries have centralized or coordinated bargaining systems. In the East and Southeast Asian region, decentralized wage-fixing is the rule. In South Korea, state influence on wage settlements was strong before 1987. Since then, the lifting of controls and the rapid growth of unions have led to rapid increases in wages. But a coordinated bargaining structure has yet to emerge. In Taiwan and Hong Kong, the market has been the major determinant of wages, with government labor market policy having only a small direct impact on industry wage and employment patterns. The larger ASEAN countries—Indonesia, Malaysia, Thailand, and the Philippines— have yet to reach full employment, although the economic progress several of them have achieved since the mid-1980s has been impressive. In these countries, macro policies creating a more open and liberal economy have played a significant part in expanding manufacturing employment and creating new full-time employment opportunities for women.

Apart from Japan, which may be said to have a decentralized but coordinated bargaining structure, Singapore is the only country in the region that has experience with coordinated bargaining. Until the late 1980s, unions and employers in Singapore participated with the government in a tripartite wages council to develop annual wage guidelines. In the 1970s and early 1980s, the guidelines were followed closely, but the achievement of full employment led eventually to wage drift, a phenomenon common among countries with consensus bargaining systems and full employment. Since the late 1980s, wage bargaining has become more decentralized, although there continues to be a high level of coordination in wage matters on the union as well as the employer side. Government policy has also focused on wage reforms, to make wages more flexible by reducing the fixed annual negotiated component of wage increases in collective agreements, and tying bonus payments more closely to economic performance. This type of labor market policy to strengthen the macro/micro link is more easily practiced by small countries that have many large enterprises and a history of tripartite cooperation. In Singapore the unions, which represent less than 20% of the work force and are highly supportive of government policy to restructure the economy, realize the macro consequences of wage demands on the island's open economy. Their key strategy to raise real wages has been to work with employers to improve productivity and skills, a strategy that has contributed to Singapore's record of full employment and low inflation in the past two decades.

In most developing countries, except for a few in the East and Southeast Asian region, the impact of structural adjustment programs on employment and incomes has been severe. In many East and Southeast Asian developing countries, job restructuring has been facilitated by sustained and high economic growth. Significant changes have occurred in the labor market. Wages have risen rapidly and wage differentials widened, reflecting the shortage of skills. Manufacturing and services employment have expanded quickly, as have the number of full-time jobs and women in the work force. This experience contrasts with that of slower-growing industrialized countries, where industrial restructuring has eliminated many full-time jobs while creating many new, less well-paid secondary or peripheral jobs. In these countries, the thrust of macro policies and of micro industry and firm policies has been essentially defensive rather than anticipatory. In the faster-growing Asian countries, rapid growth and the relative absence of institutional rigidities have smoothed the adjustment process. If they are to continue to enjoy strong growth through continuous adjustment, they will need to avoid the macro and micro policies that have sapped the ability of firms in many industrial countries to meet the never-ending challenge of international competition.

References

Belanger, J., & Breton, G. (1992). Restructuration economique et regulation du Travail au Canada. *Proceedings of the Ninth World Congress of the International Industrial Relations Association.* Sydney: IIRA.

Dell'Aringa, C., & Lodovici, M. S. (1992). Industrial relations and labour policies in European countries. *Proceedings of the Ninth World Congress of the International Industrial Relations Association.* Sydney: IIRA.

Eyraud, F. (1992). Remarques sur le rapport entre entreprise et marche dans L'evaluation des qualifications (perspective comparative). *Proceedings of the Ninth World Congress of the International Industrial Relations Association.* Sydney: IIRA.

Gregory, B., & Daly, A. (1992). Who gets what? Institutions, human capital and black boxes as determinants of relative wages in Australia and the U.S. *Proceedings of the Ninth World Congress of the International Industrial Relations Association.* Sydney: IIRA.

Walsh, J., & Brown, W. (1992). Corporate pay policies and the internationalisation of markets. *Proceedings of the Ninth World Congress of the International Industrial Relations Association.* Sydney: IIRA.

Zeytinoglu, I. A. (1992). Part-time and other non-standard forms of employment: Why are they considered appropriate for women? *Proceedings of the Ninth World Congress of the International Industrial Relations Association.* Sydney: IIRA.

23 \ Corporate Pay Policies and the Internationalization of Markets

WILLIAM BROWN

JANET WALSH

The bearer of good news can be forgiven for being dismayed if only half the message is understood. Industrial relations specialists can similarly be forgiven for disquiet that the recently acquired enthusiasm of many economists for the importance of national wage bargaining structures is based upon a limited understanding of the issues involved. This belated interest is to be welcomed. But if economic policy is to benefit from the insights of industrial relations research, it will be necessary to clarify what that research implies.

Our discussion starts with the importance attributed by macro-economists to the inflationary implications of different countries' wage-fixing institutions. Our criticism will concentrate upon their neglect of the microeconomic processes whereby employers elicit productivity from their employees. For this, it is necessary to discuss the pay strategies adopted by individual companies. Our analysis questions the undue simplicity of the prescription that governments should encourage nationally coordinated pay bargaining. Instead we draw attention to the implications of different bargaining structures for the effective management of labor. The feasibility of national bargaining arrangements is reduced by the remorseless advance of international competition, undermining institutions that are confined by the frontiers of single nations.

The Macroeconomic Problem

Those concerned with economic policy within their own countries have long been uncomfortably aware that the control of national unit labor costs is influenced in some complicated way by their country's structure of wage bargaining. The first systematic comparative study that drew the issue to the attention of macro-economists was that of Bruno and Sachs (1985), in which they examined the varied success of different OECD economies in coping with the worldwide shock of oil price increases in the 1970s. A key feature of the countries who managed to control domestic inflation without unduly high levels of unemployment, they concluded, was the extent to which they had centralized wage bargaining.

This analysis was developed by Calmfors and Driffil (1988), who supported a theoretical argument with empirical evidence that there is a hump-shaped relationship between the degree of centralization and the unemployment level. Low unemployment is associated with both decentralized systems (as in Japan and Switzerland) and those that are highly centralized (such as Austria and Sweden), while intermediate countries (such as Italy and Belgium) tend to have high unemployment.

Their theoretical explanation was based upon Olson's (1982) notion of "encompassing organizations." Employment is relatively high, the argument goes, in economies where bargaining is conducted by a few organizations. Because they are large, such organizations cannot easily pass on the cost of their actions to others, and thus the scope for free riding is limited. They are therefore forced to internalize the external effects of wage increases, which encourages moderation in wage demands and a consequently high level of employment. But employment can also be expected to be high in economies where bargaining is conducted by many small unions or representatives at the level of the single firm. It is not in the interest of an individual union bargainer to achieve a relatively high wage increase, because the firm in question is likely to pass it on in a price increase that might lead to a fall in its employment. Under single-employer bargaining, the argument implies, wages are disciplined by product market competition.

The worst case, on this theory, is the intermediate position of industry-level, multiemployer bargaining. Here bargaining is dominated by a range of medium-size organizations. They possess some market power and, in contrast to national level organizations, are able to pass on most of the costs of their actions to others. This is because the degree of substitutability between the products of different industries is small, so that the influence of product market competition on wages is blunted. Higher wages and price increases at the industry level will result in a relatively limited fall in demand and employment. Each organization will thus seek to free ride on the others by driving up wages, and this will lead to higher prices and lower wages at the aggregate level.

Subsequent reformulations by Layard (1990) and Soskice (1990) have introduced greater awareness of the industrial relations realities of bargaining. Layard argues that the option of extreme decentralization is not realistic in countries with widespread collective bargaining. The wage increases of one group influence the aspirations of others. In particular, problems arise when decentralized bargainers link increases in wages to increases in productivity. Decentralized bargaining is likely to encourage firms experiencing relatively high productivity growth (perhaps because of rapid technical progress) to give larger wage increases. These are likely to be propagated to other firms in the same product market, and beyond, through comparability claims, leading to industrial unrest and the risk of a wage-price spiral. Under centralized bargaining, by contrast, wage increases overall are more likely to follow the productivity rise of the whole economy, and firms benefiting from higher than average productivity growth are better able to pass the gains on to the whole economy, in reduced prices or increased employment.

Both Layard and Soskice recognize that the extent of centralization of formal national bargaining structures may be a misleading guide to the extent to which bargaining is coordinated in practice. Unlike Calmfors and Driffil, their analyses try to take account of the existence of powerful employer or trade union organizations that informally coordinate ostensibly separate bargaining units. Layard compares 20 OECD countries to conclude that those with more centralized bargaining, including those informally coordinated, have a more favorable unemployment/inflation trade-off. Soskice introduces two important refinements. The first is to take account of the "local pushfulness" that the unions of a particular country are given, both by their scope for local autonomy in collective bargaining and by the extent to which they have short-term issues (such as wages and job control), rather than long-term issues (such as training and job security), to bargain over. His second important refinement is to define the degree of coordination not as the average of both employer and union coordination, but as the degree of coordination of the stronger partner. This interpretation allows Japan to be classified as strongly coordinated in recognition of Japanese employer solidarity, despite a relatively disunited union movement. Like Clegg (1975), Brown (1986), Sisson (1987), and others, Soskice emphasizes the crucial importance of national employer solidarity in containing unit wage costs under collective bargaining.

The Neglect of Productivity

This reawakening of institutional awareness among economists can only be welcomed. Adam Smith, Karl Marx, and John Commons are among those who will sleep easier in their graves as a result. But the application of quantitative analyses should not conceal the impressionistic way in which the salient institutional characteristics are defined, assessed, and quantified or scaled. This is largely unavoidable. Comparative typologies of labor market institutions necessarily involve subjective judgments. Other economists such as Freeman (1988) and Rowthorn (1988) have made use of more quantifiable measures, such as wage dispersion and union density. One difficulty with the intriguing relationships, which their studies establish, lies in interpreting whether and how the measures that are used reflect the underlying labor market institutions.

There is a much more fundamental difficulty with this macroeconomic quest for the institutional basis for an improved trade-off between real wages and unemployment. It lies in its central preoccupation with wage restraint. More specifically, it lies in the consequent neglect of the issue of labor productivity. Changes in unit labor costs are logically no less a consequence of changes in labor productivity than of changes in wage levels. An exclusive pursuit of wage restraint not only overlooks the potential for productivity improvement, but it is actually likely to hinder it.

In part this can be explained in terms familiar to economists rather than industrial relations specialists. It is an essentially short-run view that sees wages as primarily a cost of production and considers wage restraint to be sufficient to reduce unemployment. Quite apart from the important role of wages in the growth of economic demand, wage levels also influence employers' investment decisions with regard to both human and fixed capital. Thus a rise in a firm's real wage levels relative to other firms will encourage the employer to consider a move toward more capital-intensive production techniques, and will increase the incentive to employ a more highly trained labor force. As Landesmann and Vartiainen (1989) point out, if the secret of the success of the "social corporatist" Nordic economies over the past 30 years had simply been wage restraint, they would have become low-wage economies relying on labor intensive techniques, which has not happened.

Indeed Landesmann (1990) argues that the pattern of causation is quite different. It is the ability of social corporatist countries to restructure their economies, with active retraining policies and with the encouragement of technological innovation, which has enabled them to combine relatively full employment with increasing living standards. On this argument, it is investment policy, not wages policy, that is the key to keeping real wage growth at acceptable levels, and sufficiently in step with productivity growth that inflation is controlled. Coordinated bargaining aimed at wage restraint alone, so often called for in times of inflationary crisis, can never achieve rising wages and employment growth in the long run. As a crisis measure it may be unavoidable, but it certainly should not be the guiding principle of long-term institutional reform.

These criticisms should certainly not be taken to imply that economists are blind to the crucial importance of labor productivity as a policy problem. Far from it. Among British economists both Layard and Soskice have played an outstanding role in stimulating debate and research on training policy. The point at issue is how far, taking into account what is known about industrial relations processes, it makes any sense at all to consider wage policy in isolation from other policy measures (including training) intended to raise labor productivity. How far can industrial relations research findings cast light on this, and so inform the emerging economic debate and its policy prescriptions?

The Fragmentation of
National Bargaining Structures

All markets operate within an institutional context, and owe much of their success or failure, in delivering socially desirable results, to that context. The foregoing economic debate implies that national labor markets are less likely to fail to deliver internationally competitive unit wage costs when bargaining is nationally coordinated. So far we have suggested that the debate unduly emphasizes institutions of wage restraint. Before pursuing this criticism further we shall add another, which is that, as a basis for policy prescription, it offers more than it can deliver. Irrespective of the policy intentions of governments, there appears to be an international tendency for national bargaining structures to become more fragmented. Whatever the economic rationale of nationally coordinated bargaining, the institutional tide seems to be flowing against it. Before inquiring into the underlying forces, we shall establish this empirical point by sketching the recent experience of a number of developed countries on which data are available.

New Zealand and Australia are two countries whose formative labor legislation gave them highly centralized bargaining structures based upon industrial agreements. In recent decades both countries saw the growth of informal single-employer bargaining known, respectively, as "second-tier" and "over-award" bargaining. In New Zealand a government policy of weakening the arbitration system culminated in 1987 legislation, which seeks to eliminate second-tier bargaining by forcing a choice between multiemployer and single-employer agreements (Brosnan, Smith, & Walsh, 1990). In Australia, by contrast, the Accord policy of the government of the 1980s has reinvigorated the centralized system of pay determination. In spite of this, however, Australia has seen a continued shift away from multiemployer and toward single-employer awards (Rimmer, 1988).

At the other extreme, the United States has never had tendencies (or, in peacetime, official policies) toward centralized bargaining structures, and single-employer bargaining has always been strong, accounting in 1980 for 60% of the major collective agreements that cover 1,000 or more workers. The remaining 40% of major agreements were the result of multiemployer negotiation based upon local or regional product markets. During the 1980s this picture was transformed. As Flanagan (1990) reports:

> The most dramatic change in official bargaining structures is the shift from multi-employer to single plant bargaining. In non-manufacturing, multi-employer bargaining determined employment conditions in about two-thirds of major bargaining units in 1980 but in a little over one-third of the units in 1988. Multi-employer bargaining virtually disappeared from the manufacturing sector. In both sectors and in virtually all industries, single-plant bargaining increased substantially. . . . Effective multi-employer bargaining also declined as many pattern bargaining arrangements broke up in favor of single-employer bargaining.

In Canada the structure of bargaining was relatively stable, at least between 1965 and 1982, when available data suggests that single-employer bargaining units rose only slightly, from 81% to 85% of all units (Anderson, Gunderson, & Ponak, 1989). Davies (1986) noted a shift to greater coordination of bargaining within, rather than between, firms. He argued that the relative stability of multiemployer arrangements would not survive the changing context of competition. Confirming this, Thompson (1989) suggests that fragmentation accelerated subsequently, with industrial agreements at the provincial level coming under attack, and many provincial employer associations losing their bargaining authority under the pressure of industrial concentration, a growing nonunion sector, and free trade with the United States.

Many European countries have strong traditions of employer solidarity and have developed a variety of forms of coordinated bargaining over several decades. The Dutch experience has been especially interesting. The concentration of industrial ownership in Holland in the 1970s has weakened its strong system of industrial bargaining, allowing the emergence of single-employer bargaining and the integration of bargaining units within large corporations. But Huiskamp (1986) argues that this has not prevented the pursuit of macroeconomic objectives:

In Holland, the large corporation as a new focus for the development of interorganizational relationships between unions and employers fits in very well indeed with the centralized and comprehensive nature of Dutch national industrial relations. One could say the large corporation as a non-voluntary hierarchy of companies has replaced the employers' association as a voluntary arrangement.

Sweden's centralized bargaining system had been under increasing strain for many years when, in 1990, contrary to the government's wishes, the national employers' confederation decided to cease national bargaining on wages and conditions, leaving it up to industrial federations alone. Among other factors the pressure from large companies, especially in the engineering industry, for greater autonomy had become too great. The confederation's director predicts further decentralization of bargaining in future (Myrdal, 1991).

Finally, there is the experience of Britain, with one of the weakest traditions of employer solidarity in Europe. The comprehensive system of industrial agreements that dominated bargaining until the 1950s has fallen apart. Multiemployer agreements, which were the principal means of pay-fixing for perhaps four private sector employees out of five in 1950, had declined in coverage to one in five by the mid-1980s, and there has been further substantial decline subsequently. An additional aspect of fragmentation became apparent as single-employer bargaining developed in the 1980s. There was an increasing tendency for large multidivisional and multiplant firms to decentralize their internal bargaining structures. At the same time fewer and fewer firms engaged in the practice of "two-tier" bargaining, whereby they would top up multiemployer rates with single-employer additions. They were generally opting unequivocally for one or the other (Brown & Walsh, 1991). Since the 1960s the transformation of the bargaining structure of the British private sector has received official encouragement, both from a royal commission of inquiry of 1968, which gave its blessing to single-employer bargaining, and later, in the 1980s, from a government that has been actively opposed to multiemployer agreements. But no legislative steps have been taken to hasten the change. The driving force has been the strategy of the employers themselves.

Two conclusions are suggested by this brief survey of selected international experience. The first is that the rise of single-employer bargaining is an international phenomenon. Employer solidarity, at least along its traditional contours of single industries within national frontiers, is in general decline. The second conclusion is that this appears to have been happening regardless of whether particular national governments are in favor of it, largely independent of statutory intervention. Whatever the supposed macroeconomic advantages of more centralized wage bargaining, international experience offers little encouragement to those who hope that direct government action might bring it about.

The Management of Productivity

Why is it, when economists identify such substantial benefits in greater centralization of bargaining, that the employers of the world seem to be moving in the opposite direction? Our studies of British companies suggest reasons of sufficient generality that they are likely to be echoed in other countries.

Both single-employer bargaining and the decentralization of bargaining within firms are partly by-products of long-term changes in the internal organization of large firms, most notably the widespread adoption of multidivisional or devolved corporate structures. Williamson (1975) argues that, in response to increasing size and diversity of corporate activities, such structures economize on the transaction costs arising from the hierarchical growth of the firm and the associated problems of internal control. It becomes easier to separate strategic and operational decision making. Long-term corporate planning becomes the responsibility of top-level management, while operating decisions are decentralized to lower levels of business.

Decentralized wage bargaining—to divisional or site level—is partly a by-product of organizational devolution, as employers have sought to reshape bargaining units around the contours of profit-related business centers. Single-employer, intra-firm wage fixing enables employers to act autonomously and to gear pay settlements and wage structures to their particular competitive circumstances, independently of the pay policies of other companies. They generally seek to blur the significance of internal comparisons between intra-firm bargaining units by altering pay settlement dates, dispersing negotiations over the annual pay round, reshaping pay structures, and differentiating employment conditions.

The consequence is not, however, complete fragmentation. The autonomy of local management in fixing pay within these decentralized bargaining structures is generally circumscribed by a variety of mechanisms, ranging from consultation with higher level management to the imposition of pay guidelines or financial limits (Marginson, Edwards, Martin, Purcell, & Sisson, 1989). Ostensibly decentralized firms generally have a high degree of tacit pay coordination.

At the same time as the managerial scope for more finely focused single-employer bargaining has been growing, the potential benefits of multiemployer bargaining have been diminishing with the internationalization of product markets. Industrial relations systems are generally nation-specific, bound together by national systems of labor law and national trade union and employer organizations. Because labor markets, like nations, are spatially coherent, employers have been able to use national solidarity as a device for controlling some fairly crude and observable dimensions of labor costs, most notably wage rates and hours of work.

Even at its purest this multiemployer control of wage rates and hours of work was rarely tight. Countries with relatively strong industrial agreements, such as Sweden and Australia, had substantial wage drift. In countries with apparently strong industrial agreements on hours of work, such as Belgium and France, overtime working could get badly out of control. More seriously, such agreements obliged employers to deny themselves the discretion to use pay positively and flexibly as part of a broader structure of firm-specific motivating devices. There was thus an implicit choice or trade-off. Industrial agreements obliged employers to metaphorically manage labor with one managerial hand tied behind their backs. But at least some stability was given to wage levels and to hours worked.

Studies of bargaining structure (e.g., Weber, 1967) have long noted the tendency for multiemployer bargaining arrangements to try to encompass whole product markets. For both employers and unions this has the advantage of assisting them to pass the cost of wage increases on in price increases. Multiemployer agreements, in the time-honored phrase, "take wages out of competition" within the national product market and at the same time, by constraining managerial discretion within the firm, limit the scope for competition between firms based upon unit labor costs. But this multiemployer collusion is increasingly difficult when product markets become less spatially specific, as they inevitably do with increased international trade. For the past 40 years the rate of growth of international trade in manufactures has been approximately one-and-a-half times as fast as the growth in world production of manufactures. There is no long-term prospect of this slackening. The internationalization of product markets has been a profoundly influential force for change.

Employer collusion across frontiers is difficult to sustain; trade union collusion across frontiers has proved all but impossible. With steadily falling transport costs, and with capital investment being managed on an ever-more global scale, the benefits of multiemployer bargaining thus tend to diminish. They diminish especially for those companies that are themselves multinational, and thus do not have all their production eggs within the same national basket. Both foreign-owned companies and indigenous companies with a strong foreign presence show less commitment to domestic multiemployer arrangements than exclusively indigenous companies. Whether in Britain, or Sweden, or Australia, or wherever, they show a greater inclination for single-employer bargaining (Deaton & Beaumont, 1980; Enderwick & Buckley, 1983). Once firms with strong international interests break ranks, it is usually difficult for those firms with more parochial interests, who seek to remain in the multiemployer agreement, to maintain its effectiveness.

It is important to emphasize that even when multiemployer bargaining is at its most effective, for those participating it still presents some serious impediments to efficient labor management. The price of an effective industry-wide structure of wage rates is usually a set of job descriptions that are crudely defined and technologically rigid. The employees who hold these job descriptions have every reason to be suspicious of technical change. They are also provided with the clearest linguistic lever for comparisons with holders of the same job description in other firms. This facilitates coercive comparisons, not just on pay and hours (which the agreement may be able keep in check), but also on issues such as job content, manning levels, and non-wage conditions on which it may be dumb.

A multiemployer strategy thus has considerable inherent defects. Its strengths relate primarily to the two components of labor cost that are relatively visible and quantifiable and, in the context of this discussion, particularly conspicuous to orthodox economic analysis: wage rates and hours of work.

The alternative single-employer strategy has the defect that it invites unions to "whipsaw" through the product market, picking off employers one by one on these relatively visible components. But steps can be taken against this. The fact that employers do not bargain together does not prevent their acting in solidarity against organized labor (as in Japan) or having joint strike insurance schemes (although these are generally associated with multiemployer bargaining, as in Sweden). Furthermore, where skill acquisition is internal to the firm, idiosyncratic job descriptions tend to confuse interfirm comparisons.

The advantages of the single-employer strategy overlap with those of what is sometimes called "organizational" as opposed to "market" relationships with labor, or what Okun (1981) contrasted as "career" and "casual" approaches to labor, or, in a slightly different context, utilizing the internal labor market as opposed to the external labor market. They are particularly important to questions concerning labor productivity. This applies, for example, when the main means of skill acquisition is informal experiential learning, when carefully tailored career structures and stable and predictable internal salary structures are of major importance in encouraging employees through the long learning process. It applies in the large tracts of employment, where labor productivity growth depends primarily upon labor adapting to frequent, incremental technological change. This requires considerable fluidity of job titles, with employees metaphorically having to intermittently unpack and repack their toolbox of competencies. It fits in with the more individualistic treatment of employees, which is associated with the decline of manual employment, and with a more enterprise-related approach to collective bargaining.

Thus, it is not only the way in which firms structure and control themselves that encourages single-employer bargaining, it is also the fact that the more potent means of competing in unit costs is through the promotion of labor productivity, rather than the restraint of wages. The main means of labor productivity growth in the long run is not getting employees to work harder; it is technological innovation. What is demanded of employees is that they adapt smoothly to the usually incremental and spasmodic demands of the changing technologies. The human side of this is generally better managed through firm-specific motivating mechanisms, of which the pay structure is a part.

This argument has to be qualified with the important observation that, for some countries, a major basis of productivity growth may be a comprehensive system of industrial training. Such a system is likely to bolster the fading rationale for multiemployer organization. Employers are generally reluctant to undertake the costs of training unless they can be confident that, once trained, their labor will not be "poached" by rival employers who have spent nothing on training. As an alternative to tightly controlled internal labor markets, industry-wide training arrangements, preferably with statutory support, can provide an effective guard against free riding employers and inadequately trained labor. Countries that have such arrangements, such as Germany, provide their employers with both the organization and the incentive to cooperate on pay fixing as well as training. Countries with inadequate training programs, such as Britain, may feel obliged to rekindle employer solidarity in order to catch up. The reform of national training arrangements may thus stimulate greater national coordination of pay fixing as a benign side effect. It is, however, likely to be at a higher level than that of individual industries, and to take the form of loose collusion between the major employers of a country irrespective of their product market.

Conclusion

Recent macroeconomic research has produced a powerful argument for the greater coordination of pay bargaining as a policy priority. Paradoxically, however, most industrialized countries appear to be set firmly on a course of dismantling their industry-wide arrangements and fragmenting their bargaining structures. This chapter has sought to explain the paradox in the light of the increasing internationalization of product markets, and changes in the internal organization of firms. It has argued that the economists' analysis has over-emphasized policies for wage restraint, to the neglect of the way in which employers manage labor productivity. Unless they take account of this, and thereby win the support of employers, policy prescriptions intended to improve countries' employment and real wage performance will fail.

References

Brosnan, P., Smith, D. F., & Walsh, P. (1990). *The dynamics of New Zealand industrial relations.* New York: John Wiley.

Brown, W. A. (1986). Facing up to incomes policy. In P. Nolan & S. Paine (Eds.), *Rethinking socialist economics.* Cambridge: Polity Press.

Brown, W. A., & Walsh, J. (1991). Pay determination in Britain in the 1980s; The anatomy of decentralisation. *Oxford Review of Economic Policy, 7*(1).

Bruno, M., & Sachs, J. (1985). *The economics of worldwide stagflation.* Oxford: Blackwell.

Calmfors, L., & Driffil, J. (1988, April). Centralization of wage bargaining. *Economic Policy.*

Clegg, H. A. (1975). *Trade unions under collective bargaining.* Oxford: Blackwell.

Davies, R. J. (1986). The structure of collective bargaining in Canada. In W. C. Riddell (Ed.), *Canadian labour relations.* Toronto: University of Toronto Press.

Deaton, D., & Beaumont, P. (1980). The determinants of bargaining structure. *British Journal of Industrial Relations, 18.*

Enderwick, P., & Buckley, P. J. (1983). A comparative analysis of foreign- and domestically-owned firms. *Labour and Society, 8*(4).

Flanagan, R. J. (1990). *Union labor adjusts to a change in the climate* (Mimeo). Stanford, CA: Stanford University.

Freeman, R. (1988, April). Labour markets. *Economic Policy.*

Landesmann, M. (1990). *Industrial policies and social corporatism* (DAE Working Paper No. 9009).

Landesmann, M., & Vartiainen, J. (1989). *Social corporatism and long-term economic performance* (DAE Working Paper No. 9010).

Layard, R. (1990). *Wage bargaining and incomes policy: Possible lessons for Eastern Europe* (DP No. 2). London: London School of Economics, Centre for Economic Performance.

Marginson, P., Edwards, P. K., Martin, R., Purcell, J., & Sisson, K. (1989). *Beyond the workplace: Managing industrial relations in the multi-establishment enterprise.* Oxford: Blackwell.

Okun, A. (1981). *Prices and quantities.* Washington, DC: Brookings Institution.

Olson, M. (1982). *The rise and decline of nations.* New Haven, CT: Yale University Press.

Rimmer, M. (1988). Enterprise and industry awards. In *Enterprise-based bargaining units.* Business Council of Australia.

Rowthorn, B. (1988). *Wage dispersion and employment: Theories and evidence* (DAE Working Paper No. 9001).

Sisson, K. F. (1987). *The management of collective bargaining.* Oxford: Blackwell.

Soskice, D. (1990). Wage determination: The changing role of institutions in advanced industrialized countries. *Oxford Review of Economic Policy, 6*(4).

Weber, A. R. (1967). Stability and change in the structure of collective bargaining. In L. Ulman (Ed.), *Challenges to collective bargaining.* Englewood Cliffs, NJ: Prentice-Hall.

Williamson, O. E. (1975). *Markets and hierarchies.* New York: Free Press.

24 \ Industrial Relations and Labor Policies in European Countries

CARLO DELL'ARINGA

MANUELA SAMEK LODOVICI

With the oil shocks of the early 1970s and 1980s, the economic growth rates of industrialized countries slowed, and inflation and unemployment rose. Since 1983 these countries have recovered from inflation and low economic growth, but unemployment rates have remained generally high. However, the degree of both deterioration in the 1970s and early 1980s, and recovery in the 1980s, differed greatly from country to country, especially regarding trends in inflation and unemployment.

Table 24.1 shows that EEC countries experienced the worst performance in the labor market in both periods, while the best performance in terms of unemployment is found in the Scandinavian countries, Switzerland, Austria, and Japan.

It is currently acknowledged that this unemployment record can be attributed largely to supply-side shocks. The effects of these shocks were intensified in many countries by different institutional features: The characteristics of the labor market; and the way labor policies and industrial relations operate in different countries portray important explanations of these diverse trends.

The two main aspects usually considered in the most recent literature on the subject are:

TABLE 24.1 Unemployment and Inflation 1974-1990: An International Comparison (Period Average and Average Percentage Changes from Previous Year)

Countries	Unemployment Rates*		Consumer Prices		Variation in Performance (1983–1990)—(1974–1982)		
					Unemployment Inflation Misery Index (un.+infl.)		
	1974– 1982	1983– 1990	1974– 1982	1983– 1990			
Non-EEC Europe (avg.)	2.21	2.90	8.63	4.96	.68	−3.67	−2.99
Austria	2.07	3.51	6.29	2.87	1.44	−3.42	−1.98
Norway	1.91	3.31	9.79	6.45	1.40	−3.34	−1.94
Sweden	2.10	2.31	10.33	6.94	.21	−3.39	−3.18
Finland	4.68	4.65	12.26	5.76	−0.03	−6.50	−6.53
Switzerland	.31	.71	4.48	2.76	.40	−1.72	−1.32
EEC (avg.)	6.10	10.42	13.51	7.06	4.32	−6.45	−2.13
Denmark	6.53	9.07	10.97	4.70	2.54	−6.27	−3.73
Germany	3.63	6.44	5.01	1.84	2.81	−3.17	−0.36
Netherlands	6.14	9.86	6.92	1.50	3.72	−5.42	−1.70
Belgium	7.79	10.40	8.19	3.69	2.61	−4.50	−1.89
Great Britain	6.37	9.91	14.74	5.69	3.54	−9.05	−5.51
France	5.44	9.69	11.47	4.79	4.25	−6.68	−2.43
Italy	7.123	10.12	16.92	7.85	2.99	−9.07	−6.08
Spain	6.21	18.82	17.18	8.07	12.61	−9.11	3.50
Portugal	6.96	6.95	22.39	16.35	−0.01	−6.04	−6.05
Greece	2.70	7.67	18.63	18.11	4.97	−0.52	4.45
Ireland	8.20	15.65	16.23	5.12	7.45	−11.11	−3.66
Non-European Countries (avg.)	5.56	6.61	9.74	4.39	1.06	−5.35	−4.30
United States	7.12	6.62	9.01	3.86	−0.50	−5.15	−5.65
Japan	2.03	2.55	8.52	1.56	.52	−6.96	−6.44
Australia	5.43	7.90	11.54	7.56	2.47	−3.98	−1.51
Canada	7.64	9.37	9.87	4.56	1.73	−5.31	−3.58

SOURCE: OECD, *Economic Outlook,* July, 1991c.
NOTE: *Standardized unemployment rates, except for Switzerland, Denmark, Greece, Austria, Portugal, Ireland for the period 1974–1982.

1. The greater rigidity of labor markets and higher unionization rates in the European countries, relative to non-European countries (especially North America), may explain the greater difficulty in recovering from high inflation levels without incurring high increases in unemployment rates. Employment protection and high levels of unionization lead to a system of wage determination, where the employed labor force (insiders) set wages at very high levels, while the unemployed (especially the long-term unemployed) have little influence.

2. The better unemployment performance of Scandinavian countries, and their lower unemployment-inflation trade-off, are generally explained by the way

labor policies operate in these countries and by the greater coordination in their industrial relations systems.

It is currently acknowledged that a policy especially oriented toward income maintenance for the unemployed may increase the unemployment rate and the duration of unemployment. On the other hand, active labor market policies aimed at improving the supply-side of the labor market by giving the unemployed incentive to get a job may have a positive effect both on unemployment and on the unemployment-inflation trade-off.

The different orientation of labor market policies in European countries helps to explain the particular characteristics of unemployment, as shown in Table 24.2. In EEC countries unemployment lasts longer, with a greater rate of long-term unemployment (more than 12 months) and very low outflow rates from unemployment.

The two countries that present the lowest incidence of long-term unemployment are Sweden and the United States, two countries very different in terms of the way the labor market, industrial relations, and labor policies operate.

A high rate of long-term unemployment is particularly negative in both the short and the long term. Long-term unemployment exerts very little downward pressure on wage inflation: Those unemployed for a long time do not compete with the employed in the labor market because their reemployment probabilities are very low, given that they are regarded poorly by employers, and their skills get more obsolete the longer they are unemployed. The obsolescence of skills moreover implies a waste of labor potential in the long run.

Looking at the empirical cross-country evidence and recent literature, the aim of this chapter is to discuss how labor market policies enter into the relationship between industrial relations and economic performance.

The attention of European countries in this debate has grown in recent years for two main reasons:

1. The increasing problems with skill shortages and labor mismatches faced by European countries have increased the focus on structural active labor market policies as instruments to accompany macroeconomic policies, with the role of improving macroeconomic performance by expanding potential growth and removing inflationary bottlenecks.

2. Moreover, Eastern European countries are facing an increasing level of unemployment, now hidden in the public sector, and have to evaluate which mix of measures is the best suited to tackle the problem. A critical evaluation of the Swedish model and its feasibility in different social and political situations is now under way in these countries (Lehmann, 1991).

TABLE 24.2 Unemployment Characteristics and Employment Growth: An International Comparison

	Unemployment Characteristics Flows in/out of U Inflows/Outflows (% of source pop.[a])		Percentage of Long- Term U	Employment Growth Average Annual % Rates of Change	
	1988		1989	1974–1982[b]	1983–1990
Non-EEC Europe (avg.)	.86	30.35	9.43	.63	.59
Switzerland	na	na	na	−.28	.49
Austria	na	na	12.70	0.21	.52
Norway	.79	30.30	11.60	1.81	.67
Sweden	.40	30.40	6.50	.83	.81
Finland	1.39	39.50	6.90	.56	.47
EEC (avg.)	.28	4.78	52.97	−.01	.80
Denmark	.44	8.30	25.90	.07	.72
Germany	.26	6.30	49.00	−.49	.79
Netherlands	.23	na	49.90	−.18	.99
Belgium	.10	2.70	76.30	−.37	.54
Great Britain	.68	9.50	40.80	−.57	1.71
France	.33	5.70	43.90	.19	.24
Italy	.18	2.30	70.40	.76	.50
Spain	.12	1.30	58.50	−1.45	1.40
Portugal	.07	3.20	48.30	.08	1.55
Greece	.28	5.30	52.40	1.06	.62
Ireland	.37	3.20	67.30	.84	−.30
Non-European Countries (avg.)	1.29	27.98	13.55	1.47	2.03
United States	1.98	45.70	5.70	1.79	2.14
Japan	.37	17.20	18.70	.77	1.29
Australia	.92	18.20	23.00	1.09	2.56
Canada	1.89	30.80	6.80	2.21	2.14

SOURCE: OECD, *Employment Outlook*, July 1990 and July 1991b, 1991c, for the unemployment data; and OECD, *Economic Outlook*, July 1991b, 1991c, for the employment growth data.
NOTES: a. Working age population less the unemployed for inflows; total unemployment for outflows.
b. Standardized unemployment rates except for Switzerland, Denmark, Greece, Austria, Portugal, Ireland for the period 1974–1982.

The Positive Experiences

As we have seen, there are countries that outperform EEC countries in terms of labor market conditions: within Europe, the Scandinavian countries, Austria, and Switzerland; outside Europe, Japan and the United States.

Table 24.3 presents some indicators of the way labor market policies operate in the different countries being analyzed.

TABLE 24.3 Labor Market Policies in OECD Countries

	Unemployment Rates		Public Expenditure on Active Measures				U Benefits (1980)	
			in % of GDP (Period Avg. 1985–1990)	% of Active Policies Over Total		per Unemployed as % of Output Per Person (1990)	Average Repl. Ratio	Maximum Duration (in months)
	1983	1990		1985	1990–1991			
Non-EEC Europe (avg.)	3.36	2.80	.78	.45	.49	37.88	51.40	15.12
Switzerland	.80	.60	.17	.37	.57	28.33	70*	12
Austria	3.70	3.30	.31	.23	.24	9.09	41*	7
Norway	3.40	5.20	.64	.56	.46	19.04	43	18.60
Sweden	3.50	1.50	1.82	.71	.70	105.30	56	14
Finland	5.40	3.40	.96	.40	.46	27.65	47	24
EEC (avg.)	10.74	8.92	.87	.28	.38	10.83	38.60	18.20
Denmark	10.40	9.60	1.18	.21	.23	14.06	55	30
Germany	7.70	5.10	.97	.36	.47	20.00	49	12
Netherlands	12.00	7.50	1.09	.25	.31	13.89	60	36
Belgium	12.10	7.90	1.22	.26	.29	14.18	43	indef.
United Kingdom	12.40	6.90	.73	.26	.39	8.55	31	12
France	8.30	9.00	.75	.22	.27	8.11	49	30
Italy	8.80	9.90	.68	.30	.53	8.08	15*	6
Spain	17.00	15.90	.65	.11	.25	5.03	41	24
Portugal	7.90	4.60	.48	.51	.62	11.30	36	12
Greece	7.80	7.70	.32	.33	.48	5.45	14	5
Ireland	13.70	14.00	1.51	.29	.34	10.50	32	15
Non-European Countries (avg.).	8.45	5.63	.33	.28	.25	4.94	24.50	8.30
United States	9.50	5.40	.27	.33	.29	4.63	17	6
Japan	2.60	2.10	.17	.29	.29	6.19	15	7
Australia	9.90	6.90	.31	.23	.19	2.52	24	indef.
Canada	11.80	8.10	.56	.25	.24	6.42	42	12

SOURCES: Unemployment: OECD, *Economic Outlook*, 49, July 1991b, 1991c. Public expenditures on labor market programs as a % of GDP and unemployment benefits data: OECD, *Employment Outlook*, July 1991. Active labor market measures include: Public Employment Services and Administration, Labor Market Training; Youth Measures; Subsidized Employment and Measures for the Disabled.
NOTE: *Initial gross replacement rates.

JAPAN AND SWITZERLAND:
THE CONCORDANCE COUNTRIES

Japan and Switzerland show a very peculiar situation in terms of their industrial relations and social systems. Industrial relations are rather decentralized and levels of unionization are low; however, the informal system of coordinating and managing consensus is highly articulated, and as such, interest groups are integrated at a central level, and industrial conflict is rare. Thus, in a corporatist ranking these two countries should be at the top, but in a very different position with respect to truly corporatist countries, because the way consensus is reached is different.

In these countries, the way full employment is maintained during years of crisis is also different: The strongest groups in the labor force remain employed, while the adjustment process falls almost entirely on the marginal labor force (women, the elderly, and small-business employees in Japan; foreign workers and women in Switzerland).

The "employment principle"—where the key objective is to find work for the unemployed—is applied mainly through incentiving labor hoarding for the core labor force and through training in the private sector. On the other hand, full employment has been maintained in the corporatist countries primarily through employment growth in the public sector, active employment policies (especially in Sweden), and moderately expansive fiscal and monetary policies (in Austria and Norway especially). The different methods with which the concordance countries and highly corporatist countries have been able to curb unemployment can be seen by looking at employment trends (Table 24.2) and at data on public expenditures on active labor market programs (Table 24.3). Compared to the other countries under examination, Japan and Switzerland display a sharp slowdown in employment in the crisis years (1974-1982), but no increase in unemployment. A rise in inflation did not accompany the pursuit of full employment policies during the crisis years. The average annual rate of inflation is much lower in these countries than the others and this has been possible thanks to the consensus-based and informally coordinated system of industrial relations and wage negotiation.

THE SCANDINAVIAN COUNTRIES AND AUSTRIA:
CORPORATISM AND ACTIVE LABOR MARKET PROGRAMS

Austria, Norway, Sweden, and recently Finland represent the more truly neo-corporatist countries. Neo-corporatist economies are characterized by large interest groups representing substantial parts of society. There are usually institutional structures (committees, joint committees) that serve in tripartite consultation and in mediating interests, and which permit an effective application of income policies based on consensus. Conflict is generally low, and negotiations occur primarily at a centralized level.

The advantages associated with these systems of industrial relations can be synthesized as follows:

1. There is a higher likelihood that the negative social effects of their own behavior are internalized by the large interest coalitions. Trade unions and employers are, therefore, sensitive to macroeconomic constraints stemming from wage increases.
2. Centralized bargaining allows for simultaneous negotiation, thereby reducing the risk of upward wage spirals.

In these countries, the main employee and employer organizations collaborate with the government in defining income and labor policies. There is generally consensus on the objectives of maintaining the lowest possible level of unemployment and pursuing solidaristic policies. The principal associations represent wide segments of society and all social groups, meaning problems typical to this type of negotiating (prisoner's dilemma and free riding) can be overcome, and cooperative agreements can be reached.

Industrial relations based on corporatism, centralized wage setting, and solidaristic policies allow wage moderation and reduce the risks of an upward wage spiral. Active labor programs are an important element within this framework: Their role is to reduce unemployment and its persistence by preventing unemployment inflows and incentiving unemployment outflows. Their aim is to improve the supply side of the economy, thus making it possible to reduce the inflationary potential of a full-employment policy. Sweden is the best example of this policy. The objective of full employment has been given high priority, but there is a significant amount of flexibility in the Swedish labor market, as compared with other European countries. As a result, contrary to what occurred in most OECD countries, unemployment rates in Sweden did not rise significantly after the two oil price shocks. The characteristics of unemployment are also different from those prevalent in most countries: The unemployment rates of both females and males are similarly low; the share of long-term unemployment is also relatively low: only 6.5% of total unemployment, as compared to an average of 53% for EEC countries. The low rates of unemployment and the much lower persistence of unemployment are obtained by very strong intervention of public authority in the labor market. Placement in labor market programs and relief work prevent entry into long-term unemployment, while training the unemployed and attending to employers' needs keep up the flow of vacancies. High unemployment outflows are obtained by integrating a severe regime of unemployment benefits (relatively low replacement rates, limited duration of benefits and, above all, strict controls over benefit recipients' search behavior), and by active programs aimed at finding job or training opportunities for all those unemployed for more than a year. The main measures include employment services, such as providing information, guidance, or financial support to assist the unemployed in finding a job; labor market training; direct job creation; and employment subsidies. Sweden is the country that spends the most on these kinds of programs. More than two-thirds of the labor market policy budget is spent on "active" measures, as compared to an average of 38% for EEC countries and 28% for the major non-European countries.

Low unemployment implies a tight labor market situation and is usually accompanied by strong inflationary pressures. Indeed, inflation in Sweden has been higher than OECD average inflation for some time, but the trade-off between inflation and unemployment is one of the best among Western countries. In the late 1970s and early 1980s, in contrast with most other OECD countries, Sweden's inflation-unemployment trade-off did not deteriorate. Labor market policies may have helped this outcome by preventing the rise in unemployment and the development of a hysteresis phenomenon (OECD, 1989).

The interrelation between the industrial relations system and labor programs has thus brought about interesting results in terms of the labor market performance:

1. In corporatist countries, and especially in Sweden, wages are highly sensitive to unemployment levels, even in low-rate ranges. Sweden has the best unemployment-inflation trade-off of all industrialized countries: "[T]he NAIRU was recently estimated at below 2% and an increase in unemployment from 1.5% to 2.5% would bring down wage inflation by around 3 percentage points within a year" (OECD, 1990, p. 102).

2. Unemployment hysteresis and job-matching problems are solved better than in other countries. In Sweden the relationship between labor demand and supply was stable during the 1970s and 1980s, contrary to most OECD countries, which experienced an increased mismatch between labor demand and supply (a shift out of the Beveridge curve).

3. The sectoral reallocation of labor in Sweden is not through price (wage) signals, but through quantity signals and direct policy intervention, given the pursuit of solidaristic policies (Pissarides & Moghadam, 1989). Labor measures can thus be viewed also as a way to correct the distorted signals coming from the compressed wage structure determined by solidaristic wage policies (OECD, 1989).

According to some authors (Jackman, 1989, Jackman, Pissarides, & Savouri, 1990), active labor market policies "have been at least as important as the wage setting process in accounting for the low unemployment rates of the Nordic economies" (Jackman, 1989, p. 4).

The sharp rise in Sweden's inflation in the late 1980s doesn't indicate that labor market policies are flawed. The problem seems to be that these policies were overworked: The unemployment rate was pushed too low. At an unemployment rate of 1.4% in 1989, the Swedish labor market was overheated; this occurred together with a weakening of the corporatist credo in industrial relations. The wage-bargaining system is increasingly fragmented in Sweden and other Scandinavian countries and wage drift is increasing, putting to debate the solidaristic policy pursued by central unions up to now (Dell'Aringa & Samek Lodovici, 1991; OECD, 1990). This is a policy that has brought about high wage compression and is one that is considered partially responsible for the skill shortage problems that are characterizing the Swedish labor market today.

A cross-country comparison still underlines the importance of the Swedish "employment principle": Because of the efficiency of the Swedish labor market and its labor policies, an unemployment rate of just 3% to 4% should be enough to keep Sweden's inflation rate down to that of its main trading partners.

THE UNITED STATES: THE MARKET ECONOMY

The U.S. labor market is characterized by competitive markets, low employment protection, weak interest groups, and fragmented wage negotiations occurring mainly at the firm level. In this country, wage moderation is imposed by market mechanisms. In the 1970s and 1980s, the United States showed wage moderation and relatively good performance regarding inflation and employment growth, even if it was somewhat less positive with respect to unemployment than the corporatist countries.

Labor market policies traditionally have a more limited scope in the United States, as compared to Sweden and other Scandinavian countries. Even in the years of the "Great Society," under the Johnson administration, manpower policies were confined to public sector job creation and training, with a view toward assisting disadvantaged groups in getting reintegrated into the labor market (OECD, 1990). In the 1980s the accent was shifted from public intervention to private intervention, and to measures aimed mainly at improving the flexibility of the labor market.

Together with Sweden, the United States is another country that presents a relatively low incidence of long-term unemployment. As in Sweden, the rates of outflow from unemployment are relatively high, and this allows for reducing unemployment persistence. The way in which these outflows are obtained is however very different: In the United States this occurs through a very flexible and unprotected labor market, as can also be seen from the relatively high rates of inflow into unemployment.

Which Lessons for Europe?

The EEC countries experienced the largest surge in unemployment in the years following the oil crises. Their industrial relations systems are also the most conflictive and difficult since they include union organizations powerful enough to impose their interests, but too numerous and not encompassing enough to internalize the results. There are differences, however, that can be related to the different level of consensus and cohesion in the industrial relations and social systems, and to the different policies being pursued. We can roughly distinguish two groups: countries with a certain level of consensus and coordination in the wage determination process (Central European countries); and countries with a lower level of coordination and higher level of conflict such as Italy, France, the United Kingdom, and Southern Europe (Spain, Greece, and Portugal). The latter group of countries is in the worst situation: Interest organizations are strong enough to impose their conditions in the negotiating process, but are not encompassing enough to significantly sustain the social costs of their actions. These countries are characterized by a fragmented and unstable system of industrial relations, a relatively high level of unionization (with the exception of France), and many unions that are divided along ideological and political lines, making the coordination and co-option on effective income policies very difficult to implement. In these countries, bargaining occurs at various levels that are not coordinated among themselves; systems for regulating the settlement of conflict usually do not exist; nor are there formal or informal controls over the bargaining process.

Labor policies in EEC countries have traditionally been centered around income maintenance for the unemployed (Table 24.3). The forms are different (unemployment insurance, unemployment assistance, guaranteed minimum income, social welfare), but the benefits usually are relatively high and are provided for a long time, while there is little control over the search behavior of the unemployed. In those countries where benefits for long-term unemployment are limited, such as southern Europe, other forms of income assistance usually prevail (such as the system of *Cassa Integrazione Guadagni* [Income Integration Fund] in Italy), together with a very strong system of employment protection.

Finally, as Layard (1989) and Jackman et al. (1990) point out, active labor policies, by preventing the unemployed from dropping out of the labor force, may increase competition for jobs and thus restrain wages. This positive effect is prevalent in the long run and is especially relevant for those measures more explicitly targeted on the long-term unemployed and those related to training. Indeed, besides reduction of the unemployment rate, Calmfors and Nymoen do not consider other important long-run goals of active labour programs; that is, to help a more efficient job-matching and a reduction of skill shortages through training measures. This different aim of labor policies may well become the most important one in the 1990s, because demographic trends will reduce the supply of labor in the Western countries (OECD, 1991a).

Conclusions

As we all know, the labor market is not like other markets. The allocation of labor resources has to meet efficiency criteria, but the allocative function of the labor market is strongly conditioned by the prevailing societal consensus on social standards and norms of equity. Any deregulation or change that touches these consensus-based provisions has to be built on a new consensus, something very difficult to achieve, especially in the short run. For this reason it is very difficult to impose a radical shift in the way the labor market and industrial relations operate in each country. However, something can be learned from other countries' experiences, and gradual change may be implemented, especially through policy measures.

We have seen that in Europe the most positive experiences in terms of labor market performance are those of Switzerland, Austria, and the Nordic countries. Relative to EEC countries, all these countries present a system of consensus-based, coordinated industrial relations and labor policies, inspired by the "employment principle": to assist the unemployed to return to work, rather than paying them to remain unemployed.

The industrial relations systems of EEC countries are difficult to change. At least for the foreseeable future, most European countries will have to live with the problems created by fragmented unions, as well as lack of both consensus and social cohesion. Moreover, bargaining at the firm level is certainly going to have greater weight, but sectoral bargaining will generally maintain its present level of importance. However, if coordination at a transnational level is to evolve, it must concern national coverage unions, as only these organizations will be able to put their action into effect at a European level. Social dialogue should consider this as one of the most urgent goals to be achieved.

More can be done on the labor policies side. The Swedish "employment principle" is gaining attention and favor, in EEC and Eastern European countries, as a way to obtain and maintain a favorable unemployment to inflation trade-off. It is also a way to tackle the increasing problems of shortages of skilled labor and job mismatches faced by European countries. However, a greater analysis and the pursuit of a well-designed evaluation procedure are required to further address some issues related to the cost-effectiveness of labor policies, as well as to study the relationship between active programs and wage determination.

References

Bjorklund, A. (1991). Evaluation of labour market policy in Sweden. In OECD, *Evaluation of labour market and social programmes*. Paris: OECD.

Calmfors, L., & Nymoen, R. (1990, October). Real wage adjustment and employment policies in the Nordic countries. *Economic Policy*.

Dell'Aringa, C., & Samek Lodovici, M. (1991). Industrial relations and economic performance. In T. Treu (Ed.), *Participation in public policy making*. De Gruyter.

Jackman, R. (1989, January). *Wage formation in Nordic countries viewed from an international perspective* (Discussion Paper No. 335). London, London School of Economics, Centre for Labour Economics.

Jackman, R., Pissarides, C., & Savouri, S. (1990, October). Labour market policies and unemployment in the OECD. *Economic Policy*.

Layard, R. (1989). *European unemployment—Causes and cure?* (Discussion Paper No. 368). London: London School of Economics, Centre for Labour Economics.

Layard, R. (1990a, May). *Wage bargaining and incomes policy: Possible lessons for Eastern Europe* (Discussion Paper No. 2). London: London School of Economics, Centre for Economic Performance.

Layard, R. (1990b, May). *Understanding unemployment* (Discussion Paper No. 4). London: London School of Economics, Centre for Economic Performance.

Lehmann, H. (1991, June 13-14). *Economies in transition, unemployment and the role of labour market policies: The case of Poland*. Paper presented at the International Conference on "The Restructuring of Labour Market in Eastern Countries," Milan.

OECD. (1989, March). *OECD economic survey of Sweden*. Paris: OECD.

OECD. (1990, December). *OECD economic survey of Sweden*. Paris: OECD.

OECD. (1991a). *Labour market policies for the 1990s*. Paris: OECD

OECD. (1991b). *Employment outlook, July 1991*. Paris: OECD.

OECD. (1991c). *OECD economic outlook, July 1991*. Paris: OECD.

Pissarides, C., & Moghadam, R. (1989, January). *Relative wage flexibility in four countries* (Discussion Paper No. 331). London: London School of Economics, Centre for Labour Economics.

Rodseth, A. (1991, June). *Are employment policies counterproductive when wage setting is centralized?* (Discussion Paper No. 28). London: London School of Economics, Centre for Economic Performance.

25 \ Who Gets What? Institutions, Human Capital, and Black Boxes as Determinants of Relative Wages in Australia and the United States

ROBERT GREGORY

ANNE DALY

Australia has a unique combination of labor market institutions. There is a high degree of trade union coverage, predominantly organized along craft lines, which extends across enterprises and is often national in scope; as of June 1985, 63% of male employees and 47% of female employees were members. The union structure is similar to the United Kingdom but different from many other countries, such as Japan and the United States, where unions are usually organized on an enterprise basis. The unusual feature, however, is that for each occupation, minimum wage rates are determined by state and federal tribunals, so that the pay of university professors is fixed along with those of bus drivers, laborers, fitters and turners, storemen, and so on. As of May 1983, these award rates of pay, which number many thousands, covered 83.6% of male and 89.7% of female employees. They are legally enforceable minimums, so the opportunity exists for over-award payments, but most

AUTHORS' NOTE: We are grateful to George Fane, Barry Hughes, Brian Easton, Glenn Withers, Bruce Chapman, Richard Harris, Steve Dowrick, and Robin Pope for helpful comments. An earlier version of this chapter was presented at the Annual Political Economy lecture at the University of Newcastle.

workers receive the award rate of pay for the job.[1] Finally, the combination of craft unions and award rates of pay, which are mainly national in coverage, leads to a considerable degree of centralization of the wage fixing system. Occasionally this degree of centralization is almost complete, for example during the Accord period, 1983-1990, when most wage increases occurred in response to federal tribunal judgments to increase all wages by a given percentage. At other times there is less centralization, for example, during the 1979-1982 period, when individual negotiations between employers and trade unions were more common. It is widely believed that the tribunal system strengthens and widens the influence of trade union attitudes toward wage fixing and wage relativities (for a fuller discussion of the institutional framework, see Niland, 1986).

Most Australians believe that their labor market institutions exert a significant impact on wage outcomes, and are not just a veil behind which the laws of demand and supply inexorably exert their influence. This belief has never been stronger than today. There is, however, no unity of views as to the nature of this impact. Some labor market observers believe that the behavior of Australian institutions enables the achievement of desirable equity goals, such as a more equal distribution of earnings, with little or no efficiency cost. Others believe the behavior of these institutions impedes economic growth, diminishes labor mobility, reduces income levels, creates unemployment, and generates high rates of wage inflation.

Over the past few years both supporters and opponents of the current shape of institutions have argued for some change. Much of the focus has been upon the determinants of wage relativities, and we will confine our attention to this issue. The radical view is that wage rates should be tied more to establishment profitability and productivity performance, and tied less to a craft union structure and national productivity and consumer price increases. The Business Council of Australia, for example, has been arguing for greater wage flexibility, to be achieved by a new institutional structure of smaller unions based on the enterprise or establishment. The leadership of the Australian Council of Trade Unions has also been arguing for change. It wants larger unions and more flexibility in wage relativities.

How might we provide evidence as to the impact of institutions on wage relativities, and to judge the merits of these different arguments? It is quite a difficult task. The first requirement is a theory to predict wage outcomes under different institutional arrangements. The second requirement is a method to estimate the quantitative significance of the theoretical predictions. One approach, which has been used to measure the impact of incomes policies, is to fit wage regression equations to data from epochs in which institutional structures are different, and include a series of dummy variables for each epoch to estimate the impact of institutional change (Chapman &

Gruen, 1990). This option is not available to us because we are discussing a more radical change in the institutional framework, one for which previous Australian experience does not provide an adequate guide. We need a different approach.

First, we adopt the human capital model as a framework for our analysis of wage relativities. This is the dominant paradigm in the published economic literature, both on a world scale and in Australia. It seeks to explain different wage relativities by different stocks of human capital (Oaxaca, 1973). The empirical applications of the model have been widely used within countries to help explain wage relativities of men and women, native and foreign-born workers, and blacks and whites in the United States. The logic of the model, however, enables it to be used to explain cross-country differences in relative wages (Gregory & Daly, 1990). The model suggests that countries with a wide spread of relative earnings have a wide spread of human capital endowments.

Second, we proceed on the basis that we can measure the impact of institutions by comparing estimates of Australian parameters of the human capital model—generated within a labor market in which union attitudes are strongly reinforced by Australian tribunals—with estimates of U.S. parameters—generated in a labor market where there are no centralized wage fixing procedures, there are few union members, and unions are organized along enterprise lines.[2] The U.S. labor market therefore will be treated as counterfactual to the present set of Australian institutions. Of course this may not be the ideal comparison, but we will show that Australian and U.S. labor markets are very similar in terms of labor force quality and other work force characteristics that are most likely to affect wage relativities. As a result, it may be reasonable to attribute difference in model parameters to institutional structures. Another advantage of a U.S.-Australian comparison is that those most opposed to the current set of Australian institutions seem to see the U.S. labor market as the goal toward which Australia should move.

Therefore, we are adopting a simple broad-brush methodology that seems to us to be ideal and to provide rich insights at the beginning of this new field of research; but as we learn more about differences in earnings relativities across countries, the gains from narrowing the focus of analysis and increasing its complexity will increase. The broad-brush methodology, however, suggests two caveats be kept in mind. One caveat is that by influencing returns to different types of human capital, the institutional framework may trigger second-round responses affecting the accumulation and dispersion of human capital among the labor force, and, if so, institutional effects may spread well beyond their direct first-round influence on parameter values.[3] Furthermore, these second-round effects in turn may affect parameter values. The other caveat is potentially more important. Human capital parameters may be affected by institutions other than those we have identified, and by factors other than institutions. With this in mind, some readers may prefer to interpret parameter differences across countries as a measure of the extent of our ignorance of what is causing different patterns of earnings relativities. However, to strengthen our suggestion that a significant part of parameter differences is determined by the different institutional framework of each country, we show that many of our results conform with parameter differences in the U.S. labor market when the human capital model is fitted to separate samples of union and nonunion members. Our two country samples, and the fact that one sample is drawn from a heavily unionized country and the other is not, will be analyzed in much the same way as two samples of union and nonunion members within a country. The U.S. work on earnings relativities between union and nonunion samples is one source that generates our priors.[4]

We are not the first to assess the impact of Australian labor market institutions by comparing Australian earnings relativities with those of another country. The seminal paper is that of Hughes (1973), which by comparing earnings relativities for 63 and 69 industries in manufacturing in the United Kingdom and the United States, respectively, concludes that relative to the United Kingdom in the early sixties "the Australian arbitration framework did not at that time exert much of an equalizing effect on the industrial wage structure" (p. 161) but, relative to U.S. earnings, the Australian dispersion was significantly narrower. Subsequent work on Australian-U.K. comparisons by Norris (1977) and Australian-U.S. comparisons by Mitchell (1984) has supported these conclusions.[5] Finally, a series of papers, Gregory and Duncan (1981), Gregory, Daly, and Ho (1986), and Gregory and Daly (1990), have documented the importance of labor market institutions in changing women's pay relative to that of men.

We build on this earlier work in three ways. First, we place the influence of the Australian institutional structure firmly within the context of a human capital model. Earlier authors did not fully account for differences in human capital endowments of the work forces of different countries. Our method of analysis enables us to isolate model parameters that generate similarities and differences in pay relativities across countries, and to conjecture on the role of human capital endowments under different labor market institutions. Second, we explore in depth the influence of four contributing factors to the dispersion of earnings relativities—levels of education, the length of work force experience, sex of the worker, and industry of employment. Third, there are a number of interesting new findings that subsequent work needs to explain. We mention just two. The first is that, relative to a 25-year-old male, the earnings of older men in the United States are about 30% greater than their Australian counterparts. This is a very substantial difference, which may reinforce the current policy concern that wage relativities generated by the Australian institutional structure discourage the accumulation of human capital and on-the-job training. The second is that after accounting for human capital endowments, industry of employment exerts a similar and substantial effect on relative earnings in both countries. This effect is largely unexplained by economic theory and seems to be very much of a black box.

The Effect of Human Capital on Earnings

THE THEORETICAL FRAMEWORK

We do not discuss in depth the derivation of the human capital model. A fuller development is discussed in Mincer (1974) but, very briefly, the model explains individual earnings in terms of formal education, labor force experience, and family attributes. When undertaking formal education the student foregoes contemporaneous earnings in the labor market, which is thought of as an investment that subsequently receives a rate of return. It is the return to this investment that leads to higher income for workers with higher education levels. With respect to the relationship between earnings and labor force experience, workers are also thought of as investing in on-the-job training for which they receive lower wages when they are young; the gap between the lower wage during on-the-job training and the alternative market wage is further investment in human capital. Older workers receive higher wages than the young, part of which is a return on earlier investment. On-the-job training leads to a positive slope of the age-earnings profile until the depreciation of human capital begins to dominate the returns on investment, and the age-earnings profile peaks and then declines. Finally, family variables are usually included in the model, such as marital status and number of children. The link between these variables and human capital is not usually spelled out in any detail. They can be thought of as reflecting motivation in the labor market, willingness to invest in on-the-job training (which is typically not measured in these data sets), and as proxies for interrupted labor force experience (which is also not measured in these data sets).

To estimate the model, we add male and female earnings equations together as:

$$E_i = \sum_{j=1}^{n} B_j \, X_{ij} + \sum_{j=1}^{n} G^{F_j} \, X^{F}_{ij} + U_i \tag{1}$$

where E_i is the log of the earnings of the ith person and X_j are formal education, labor force experience, and family variables. The superscript, $F,$

refers to female individuals. Consequently, male workers earn B_j for each attribute, and female workers $(B_j + G_j)$. U_i is an error term.

Once an earnings equation such as (1) is fitted to the data, we can proceed in two steps. First, we can compare parameter estimates across countries. For example, does obtaining a degree in the United States increase earnings as much as in Australia? If not, can we conjecture as to whether this parameter difference is the outcome of different institutional frameworks? This procedure can be undertaken for as many variables as are included in the earnings equation. Second, we can take earnings of various groups of workers in each country, for example, 45-year-old males, and explain their earnings relative to other groups in terms of different attributes, such as average education levels, and different parameter estimates attached to each attribute.

RESULTS FROM THE HUMAN CAPITAL MODEL

Our samples of earnings and individual characteristics of U.S. and Australian employees are restricted to average weekly earnings of full-time wage and salary earners. We use weekly earnings because Australian data do not provide good estimates of hourly earnings. In each country, a full-time worker is employed 35 hours or more per week. The Australian data, for workers 15 to 54 years old, are drawn from the *1981 Households Sample File* of the Australian Bureau of Statistics' Census of Population and Housing. The U.S. data is obtained from the March 1982 *Current Population Survey* and refer to the labor force state of individuals in 1981. There are 16,641 Australian and 16,198 U.S. observations.

A summary of the earnings data is presented in Table 25.1, which lists the proportion of those earning less than 55% and more than 128% of average earnings of full-time wage and salary earners. Columns 1 and 2 are standardized by average full-time earnings of men and women in aggregate, and Columns 3 to 6 by average male earnings in each country. The distribution of earnings is more compact in Australia because fewer wage and salary earners fall into the extreme income earning groups. This is particularly so for women. In the United States, 52.4% earn less than 55% of average male earnings. The proportion in Australia is 24.6%, less than half that of the United States. The question before us, therefore, is whether the more compact earnings distribution in Australia can be explained by human capital variables, or as the outcome of decisions from our unusual institutional structure.

The results of fitting equation (1) are given in equations 1 and 2 of Table 25.2. The constant term measures the average log of weekly earnings of an unqualified male who did not complete high school, of urban residence,

TABLE 25.2A Coefficients on Industry Variables from Equations 3 and 4 Reported in Table 25.2

	Males		Females	
	Australia	United States	Australia	United States
1. Agriculture	−0.306	−0.623	−0.076	0.165
	(−9.66)	(−12.58)	(−1.07)	(1.69)
2. Gas, electricity, and water	−0.037	0.131	0.191	0.089
	(−1.27)	(2.85)	(2.50)	(0.95)
3. Coal	0.283	0.394	−0.233	0.000
	(6.84)	(4.31)	(−1.43)	(0.00)
4. Oil and gas extraction	0.343	0.429	−0.154	0.578
	(2.23)	(4.97)	(−0.14)	(1.69)
5. Mineral mining	0.162	0.203	0.004	0.512
	(4.41)	(2.34)	(0.04)	(2.23)
6. Stone, clay, and glass	−0.059	0.036	0.056	0.088
	(−1.63)	(0.65)	(0.55)	(0.70)
7. Metal manufacture	−0.030	0.259	0.144	−0.044
	(−0.99)	(5.89)	(1.64)	(−0.48)
8. Chemicals	−0.003	0.175	0.072	0.063
	(−0.09)	(3.91)	(0.97)	(0.77)
9. Metal goods	−0.178	0.079	0.124	0.109
	(−5.76)	(1.85)	(1.81)	(1.42)
10. Vehicles	−0.127	0.231	0.082	0.132
	(−4.24)	(5.77)	(1.22)	(1.69)
11. Electrical machinery	−0.097	0.088	0.050	0.029
	(−2.80)	(2.10)	(0.76)	(0.43)
12. Other machinery	−0.115	0.130	0.078	0.054
	(−3.43)	(3.41)	(0.94)	(0.79)
13. Prof. and photog. equip.	0.033	0.172	0.023	0.006
	(−0.45)	(3.08)	(0.15)	(0.06)
14. Food	−0.120	0.062	0.092	0.053
	(−4.11)	(1.45)	(1.58)	(0.71)
15. Textiles	−0.154	−0.135	0.076	0.099
	(−3.36)	(−1.93)	(0.99)	(0.92)
16. Clothing	−0.091	−0.310	−0.120	0.104
	(−1.72)	(−4.24)	(−1.68)	(1.12)
17. Wood products	−0.176	−0.132	0.185	0.058
	(−5.36)	(−2.57)	(2.41)	(0.58)
18. Paper	−0.005	0.091	−0.082	−0.134
	(−0.10)	(1.75)	(−0.77)	(−1.48)
19. Printing	—	—	—	—
20. Rubber	−0.078	0.005	−0.047	0.040
	(−1.92)	(0.09)	(−0.60)	(0.45)
21. Leather	−0.255	−0.207	0.225	0.065
	(−2.20)	(−2.16)	(1.34)	(0.59)
22. Miscellaneous mfg.	−0.118	0.064	0.073	−0.076
	(−1.86)	(1.09)	(0.62)	(−0.85)
23. Construction	−0.085	0.028	0.042	−0.008
	(−3.16)	(0.77)	(0.66)	(−0.10)
24. Wholesale trade	−0.049	0.058	0.070	−0.051
	(−1.84)	(1.51)	(1.30)	(−0.76)
25. Retail trade	−0.143	−0.154	0.037	0.031
	(−5.32)	(−4.18)	(0.72)	(0.51)

(Continued)

TABLE 25.2A (Continued)

	Males		Females	
	Australia	United States	Australia	United States
26. Repair shops	−0.214	−0.165	0.137	−0.205
	(−5.04)	(−3.41)	(0.91)	(−1.61)
27. Restaurants	−0.172	−0.404	0.059	−0.027
	(−4.90)	(−8.81)	(0.95)	(−0.41)
28. Transport	−0.045	0.125	0.118	−0.015
	(−1.65)	(3.26)	(2.00)	(−0.20)
29. Communication	−0.032	0.189	0.119	0.132
	(−1.08)	(3.97)	(1.99)	(1.76)
30. Banking and finance	0.046	0.085	0.003	−0.054
	(1.50)	(1.80)	(0.06)	(−0.78)
31. Insurance	0.021	0.054	0.055	0.024
	(0.54)	(1.12)	(0.83)	(0.32)
32. Real estate	−0.007	−0.160	0.095	0.067
	(−0.16)	(−2.71)	(1.22)	(0.74)
33. Business administration	0.010	−0.109	0.024	0.057
	(0.34)	(−2.41)	(0.44)	(0.79)
34. Public administration	0.0004	0.043	0.110	0.089
	(0.01)	(1.14)	(2.203)	(1.40)
35. Health	−0.075	−0.096	0.087	0.107
	(−2.37)	(−2.33)	(1.59)	(1.74)
36. Education	−0.068	−0.2092	0.147	0.131
	(−2.24)	(−5.20)	(2.66)	(2.16)
37. Welfare	−0.502	−0.358	0.259	0.194
	(−0.97)	(−7.19)	(3.44)	(2.61)
38. Other services	0.098	−0.012	−0.054	0.055
	(3.11)	(−0.24)	(−0.82)	(0.73)
39. Entertainment	−0.100	−0.264	0.164	0.092
	(−2.00)	(−3.72)	(1.96)	(0.75)
40. Personal services	−0.333	−0.345	0.108	−0.253
	(−5.15)	(−4.93)	(1.25)	(−2.77)

TABLE 25.3 Full-Time Weekly Earnings by Age, Australia and the United States, 1981. Earnings of Men Age 25 = 100

	Actual Earnings Men Age 25 = 100		Predicted Earnings		$\frac{(1)-(2)}{(1)}$
Age	Aust. (1)	U.S. (2)	Aust. with U.S. Coefficients (3)	U.S. with Aust. Coefficients (4)	(5)
16	41	31	51	38	24
25	100	100	100	100	0
35	127	140	137	130	−10
45	113	142	133	125	−26
55	110	143	128	117	−30
64	105	113	119	98	−8

SOURCE: A. Daly, *The Labour Market in Three Countries: An International Comparison of Relative Earnings in Australia, Great Britain and the United States*. Doctoral thesis, Australian National University.

counterpart, a result consistent with the union earnings gap literature. From 16 years of age the age-earnings profile in the United States increases more quickly than in Australia until the gap between the countries is a substantial 30% by 55 years of age and then falls. This U-shaped earnings gap between the two countries is also consistent with studies of the earnings of union and nonunion members. The difference in the age-earnings profiles, however, may be attributable either to different estimated parameter values in each country or to different endowment mixes for each age group, and it is only the former that should be attributed to the institutional framework.

The simplest way to allocate the gap to these two sources is to proceed as follows. We take the Australian endowments and combine them with the U.S. experience coefficients. A comparison of this series, Column 3 with the original Australian series, Column 1, will reveal the contribution of coefficient differences across the two countries. The new series calculated for Australia is much steeper but is still flatter than the original U.S. series, indicating that some of the steeper profile in the United States is generated by the differences across countries in the resource endowments of each age group. It is difficult to be precise, but about three-quarters of the gap between Australia and the United States may be the result of differences in coefficients.

The exercise can be repeated for U.S. endowments combined with Australian coefficients, Column 4. The U.S. profile is flattened quite considerably but is still steeper than that of Australia, reinforcing the result that about three-quarters of the gap between the countries stems from coefficient differences and one quarter from resource endowments.[8]

It is clear that Australian coefficients flatten age-earnings profiles relative to the United States, and the parallels between the cross-country comparison and findings from union and nonunion studies are very close. The evidence is consistent, therefore, with the view that Australian institutions compress earnings relativities generated by age-earnings profiles.

Men and Women

There are also systematic parameter differences between the earnings equations for men and women that are consistent across countries. All estimated female education parameters to adjust the male education parameters are negative, and 6 of the 8 statistically significant at conventional levels. The lower average weekly earnings for women within each education category, *ceteris paribus,* is between 6% and 8% in each country (Table 25.2).

Family variables are also important and seem to exert much the same impact in each country. Unqualified married women earn significantly less than unqualified married men; 20% less in Australia and 25% less in the

POLICIES AND PRACTICES

TABLE 25.4 Explaining the Female-Male Earnings Ratio Between Countries, Australia and the United States, 1981

	Earnings Ratio F/M	Residual Gap to Be Explained	Other Country Endowments	Difference Not Explained by Endowment Differences
U.S. Pay Structure	0.63	0.14	0.63	0.14
Australian Pay Structure	0.77	0.14	0.76	0.13

SOURCE: Gregory and Daly (1990).

United States. The presence of a child under the age of 18 also substantially reduces earnings for women; 17% in Australia and 10% in the United States.

The literature on U.S. union wage differentials seems to show that, relative to nonunion members, women union members receive much the same wage benefits as union men, and there is no noticeable sex bias in the union effect. It is clear from Table 25.2 that women in both countries earn less than men, but the extent of the aggregate difference is not immediately obvious because of difficulties of combining so many female coefficients. To overcome this problem we adopt the same methodology as the previous section. First, we calculate the female-male earnings ratio for each country from equations 1 and 2, Table 25.2. The predicted earnings ratio is 63% in the United States and 77% in Australia. There is a predicted 14 percentage point earnings gap in favor of Australian women.

The first row of Table 25.4 lists calculated earnings ratios, using coefficients from the U.S. earnings equation. Similarly, calculations listed in the second row are derived from Australian coefficients. Table 25.4 indicates that only a very small fraction of the large gap between the female-male earnings ratios can be explained by combined differences in human capital variables in each country. This is illustrated by the similar magnitude of the earnings ratios along each row. For example, proceeding along Row 1, if workers with average Australian human capital endowments were paid according to the U.S. pay structure, the earnings ratio would be 63.0% (Column 3), the same as the predicted ratio using U.S. endowments (Column 1). Likewise, if male and female workers with average U.S. human capital endowments were paid according to the Australian pay structure, they would receive an earnings ratio of 76.0% (Row 2, Column 3); one percentage point less than the Australian earnings ratio (Row 2, Column 1).

Therefore, the difference in the female-male earnings ratio in each country is almost fully attributable to estimated parameters, which we attribute to the labor market institutions. This gap is of the order of 22% and is similar in magnitude to the largest difference in the male age-earnings profile between 45 and 54 years.

The narrower female-male earnings gap in Australia is not in accord with the U.S. union wage gap literature, and therefore cannot easily be attributed to larger union membership in Australia. In this instance, it is important to make a distinction between the tribunal and award wage system on the one hand, and union coverage on the other. Although Australian unions have usually endorsed the concept of equal pay, very little was done until 1969. During the 1950s and 1960s U.S. and Australian women received similar pay levels relative to men. In other papers we have explained the mechanism by which Australian labor market institutions changed the earnings relativity (Gregory & Daly, 1990). Very briefly, in three important judgments over the 1969-1974 period, "equal pay for equal work" in 1969, "equal pay for work of equal value" in 1972, and the extension of the male basic wage to females in 1974, the Australian federal tribunal increased female pay relative to males by 30%. As far as we can tell the extensive award wage system carried the change to all workers. As a result, a large earnings gap opened up between the U.S. and Australian female-male earnings differential and has been maintained. This gap is a clear example of the way in which it is sometimes important to distinguish between the tribunal and unions, a distinction that has not seemed important in earlier sections. The tribunal and extensive award coverage was able to initiate a quick and effective change that has been slow to come in the United States, where federal and various state initiatives are exerting their influence slowly. The male-female differential is a good example of the way in which labor market institutions can be used to affect relative earnings.

Industry of Employment

Many recent suggestions for change in labor market institutions argue that there should be more relative wage variation across enterprises. An important report to the Business Council of Australia recommended that "Remuneration must reflect more enterprise-specific factors so that a competitive and productive culture is encouraged" (Business Council of Australia, 1989, p. 9). Unfortunately, because of confidentiality requirements imposed on government statistical agencies, it is difficult to access enterprise data. As with previous researchers, therefore, we have recourse to industry data and ask, is there any evidence that the craft union structure and tribunal system significantly affect industry wage relativities?[9] This was the original question posed by Hughes (1973).

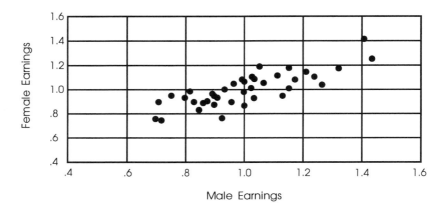

Figure 25.1. Male and Female Earnings by Industry, Australia, 1981

There is no clear guide as to what to expect from the union wage gap literature. If unions are concentrated in what would otherwise be high-paying industries, then they will appear to widen the dispersion of earnings. If they are concentrated in what would otherwise have been low-paying industries, the opposite will be true. The presumption that Australian institutions narrow the industry wage differential has usually flowed from the fact that unions are organized along craft lines, and therefore extend across industries. Given the extensive award wage system, some equalizing effects might be expected.

Figures 25.1 and 25.2 present earnings data for 39 industries standardized by mean earnings in each country. Earnings vary significantly by industry in both countries, and there is a strong positive correlation between male and female earnings. For men and women in both countries, average weekly earnings in the three highest paying industries are more than twice that in the three lowest paying industries. There is also a strong positive correlation between the wage distribution across the two countries (Figures 25.3 and 25.4). This strong association prompts two important sets of questions, equivalent to those posed in each of the previous sections:

1. What is the relationship between industry relative wages and human capital variables? Can earnings variation by industry be explained with high-paying industries employing workers with above average human capital, and low-paying industries employing workers with below average human capital?
2. Is there an industry effect independent of human capital influences, and if so, do Australian institutions generate a different pattern of industry effects than institutions in the United States?

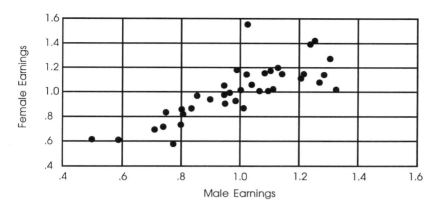

Figure 25.2. Male and Female Earnings by Industry, United States, 1981

The Relationship Between Industry Wages and Worker Quality as Measured by Human Capital Variables. To standardize the variations of relative wages across industries for human capital effects, we add industry variables to equations 1 and 2 of Table 25.2, and present the coefficients of the human capital variables in Columns 3 and 4 of Table 25.2, and the industry coefficients in Table 25.2A. All estimated industry effects are measured relative to the printing industry, which is close to the middle of the earnings distribution in each country. We adopt the same methodology as before. There are two additional sets of dummy variables, one to capture the industry effect on male earnings, and another to capture the adjustment required to the estimated male coefficients to derive the industry effect on female earnings. The constant term now incorporates the additional restriction that it refers to male earnings for an unqualified worker in the printing industry. All male industry coefficients are therefore relative to this group. The interpretation of the female industry coefficient is a little more complex. The earnings gap for unqualified females in each industry, relative to that of unqualified males, is given by the addition of the female industry coefficient plus the coefficient of the unqualified female education category.

Industry of employment obviously brings new information to the explanation of individual earnings, adding 11% to the R^2 for Australia and 25% for the United States, where industry influences seem stronger. Each coefficient attached to a dummy variable, such as education, marital status, and children, needs now to be interpreted as applying to the printing industry, and this has led to small changes in coefficients. For example, the penalties attached to each female education group seem to be greater for this industry.

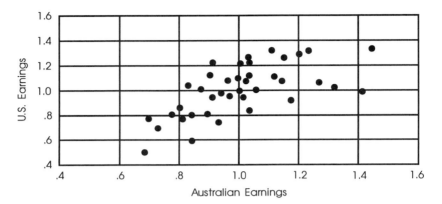

Figure 25.3. Male Earnings by Industry, Australia and the United States, 1981

However, the addition of industry variables does not disturb any of the basic human capital relationships, and male coefficients seem largely unaffected.

Industry effects are quite substantial and are as important as educational qualifications. In Australia, the earnings gap for men between the three highest paying and the three lowest paying industries, after adjustment for worker attributes, is about the same as additional earnings associated with a degree relative to not completing high school. For Australian females, the gap is a little less, about 40%. In the United States, the industry gap is even greater, approximately 80% for both males and females, exceeding by about 16 to 20

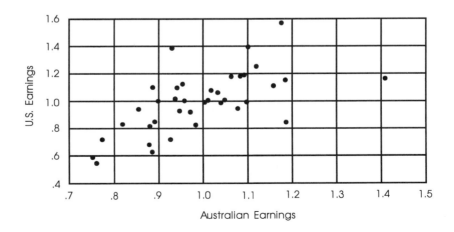

Figure 25.4. Female Earnings by Industry, Australia and the United States, 1981

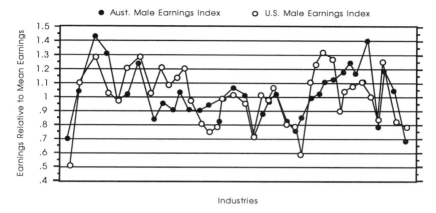

Figure 25.9. Male Earnings by Industry, United States and Australia, 1981

produces a relative average wage that is 10% less for males in the United States. There are similar effects for women, relative to average female wages. In this instance those in the 10 lowest paying industries in the United States receive about 30% less than their Australian counterparts. In the 10 highest paying industries, U.S. women receive about 10% more. This industry effect spreads evenly across all education groups, and the range of industry effects for the educated and uneducated is greater in the United States.

Third, although the important conclusion is the high degree of correlation of industry effects across the two countries, there are systematic differences by sector, which are evident in Figures 25.9 and 25.10. The industry coeffi-

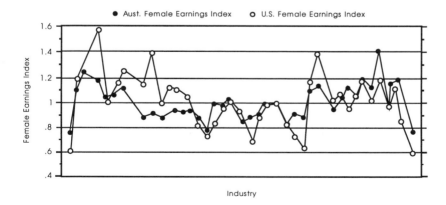

Figure 25.10. Female Earnings by Industry, United States and Australia, 1981

cients are arranged for each country, from left to right in the usual ASIC order, beginning with agriculture, mining, manufacturing, then through the service sector to government.[10] The most important difference, evident for men and women, is that manufacturing wages are low in Australia relative to the United States. The Australian manufacturing work force on average is paid about 20% less relative to other sectors. The gap seems to be largest in the metal and machinery sectors. This is a particularly interesting result, given Australia's history at the beginning of the century, which linked tariffs and newly created labor market institutions together in an attempt to increase relative wages of manufacturing workers. There is no obvious association between relative wages and industries highly protected by the tariff; in relative terms the highly protected motor vehicle industry pays at least 20% less than in the United States, but the highly protected clothing industry pays men relatively more but women about the same. Manufacturing is the heartland of unionism, and yet it does relatively less well in Australia, perhaps suggesting that our centralized wage system has held the strong back, relative to the United States? In any event, it is not clear that deregulating the labor market to move wage relativities toward the U.S. system will lead to relative wage decreases in those parts of the economy that need to compete internationally. Other noticeable differences are that men and women are paid relatively well in the Australian business service sector (banking and finance, insurance, real estate, and business services), and that Australian women are relatively well paid in wholesale and retail trade, repair shops, and restaurants.

Concluding Remarks

The first conclusion to emphasize is that, despite differences in institutional structures, the pattern of wage relativities generated in each labor market is broadly similar. The qualitative outcomes of human capital model on relative wages are common to both countries. A quick assessment might suggest that there were few differences between the two countries.

The second conclusion, however, is that a closer assessment of the pattern of wage relativities suggests a number of differences, all of which can be considered as part of the same general conclusion that the dispersion of relative earnings is narrower in Australia. In order of quantitative significance, the more important differences between Australia and the United States are the following:

1. The female-male earnings gap is narrower in Australia. In 1981 Australian women, relative to men, were about 25% better off than their U.S. counterparts.

This earnings advantage of Australian women extends to all classes, married, single, highly educated and less educated women. As demonstrated more fully elsewhere, the narrower earnings gap in Australia stems from the ability of Australian institutions to change earnings relativities quickly (Gregory & Daly, 1990). The different relative earnings of women across the countries cannot be explained by human capital variables as measured.

2. The difference in the earnings gap between men of different ages across the two countries can be as large as the difference in the male-female earnings gap. The age-earnings profile peaks earlier and is flatter in Australia. Relative to a 25-year-old, a 55-year-old male in the United States earns 30% more than his Australian counterpart. About half of this gap can be explained by human capital variables. The flatter profiles in Australia extend to all education groups.

3. Although the industry effect is strong and positively correlated across the two countries, the earnings relativities attributed to the industry effects are compressed in Australia. The 10 lowest-paying industries in Australia, relative to average earnings, pay about 10% more for men and 20% more for women than their counterparts on the earnings ranking in the United States.

4. Finally, earnings relativities for formal education also seem compressed in Australia when account is taken of the relative size of each education group.

All the results in this paper support the commonly expressed view that Australian labor market institutions, relative to those of the United States, have been a force for reducing the dispersion of relative earnings, and increasing relative earnings for those employed full-time on the bottom of the earnings distribution. The effects of Australian institutions are similar to the general effects of unions on earning relativities in the United States.

A third set of conclusions relates to the power and similarity of the industry effect in both countries. Industry effects are as large as human capital effects, and knowing the industry in which someone works is as good an income predictor as knowing only their education level or age. The industry effect is strongly correlated across countries, sexes, and education levels, but the source has not been satisfactorily identified and, as it is a mystery, we have referred to it as a black box. Of course there is no shortage of possible theories. One set relates to inadequate measurement of human capital variables. Thus, it could be argued that industry effects may be proxies for different levels of on-the-job training across industries, or that our measure of formal training may be too blunt in that the best trained go to high-paying industries, and the worst to low-paying industries. Another set of theories relates to variables that are not a part of human capital theory but relate to product conditions or technology, such as product monopoly power or, to mention another black box, the impact of firm size on individual earnings. The contribution of our results is to show that a theory must be able to encompass industry effects that are similar in different countries, similar for men and women, and similar for different education levels. Hence the argument that industry effects measure the earnings impact of on-the-job training does not explain why women share in industry effects when it is well known that their access to on-the-job training is limited. Likewise, the argument that a better measure of formal training quality would remove industry effects does not explain why the unskilled also share in the phenomenon. These remarks are not meant to discount each of these possibilities, but to indicate that searching for one answer is unlikely to be successful and to indicate that there is a need to widen the database to include more variables (for further discussion of industry effects, see the debate between Krueger & Summers, 1988, and Murphy & Topel, 1990).

To conclude, we make four general points by way of caveats. The first is the obvious point that comparisons at different periods of time may give different results. Perhaps Australian earning relativities were affected by the long period of wage indexation that went before 1981 and the beginning of the wage break out that is just caught up in our data? Our judgment is that all results are sufficiently robust that they will not be significantly affected by such events. Perhaps we should not be too hasty, as there is some evidence in the United States that age-earnings profiles and returns to education do vary significantly through time.

The second point is that the comparison of earnings relativities across countries consists of two parts; first, documenting the different outcomes of the two labor markets, and second, attributing differences to institutions. The second step is conjecture, which we attempt to support by showing the similarity between Australian and U.S. country comparisons with those of union and nonunion earnings relativities within the United States. We have attempted to account for other factors that we believe will affect wage outcomes, but the problem with residual techniques, such as the one we have used, is that all relevant factors may not be fully accounted for.[11]

Third, our results should not necessarily be interpreted to mean that any change that moves Australian labor market institutions more toward those prevailing in the U.S. labor market will automatically produce U.S. relative earnings outcomes. It will obviously depend on the extent of the change. Finally, the broad-brush methodology adopted here cannot be expected to answer all the questions raised. It should serve as a framework within which a range of new interesting questions can be pursued.

Notes

1. For the economy as a whole, over-award payments are about 2% to 3% of ordinary time pay for male employees, and 1% to 2% for female employees. Over-award payments are larger in the private sector, however, and can be quite substantial for individual industries and firms.

2. In 1981, our year of comparison, union membership in the United States extended to 28% of male and 16% of female wage and salary earners.

3. As an example of what we have in mind, the institutions may flatten the slope of the age-earnings profile. If this reduces on-the-job training and the accumulation of human capital, the age-earnings profile will be further flattened.

4. Even though award coverage in Australia is so extensive, Mulvey (1986) found union differentials similar to the United States after standardizing for education, experience, occupation, sex, and nationality. There is a narrower spread of earnings among union members across education and age categories. The mechanisms generating this result are not known.

5. With regard to the comparison with the United Kingdom, Norris (1977) suggests "the evidence does not, in general, support the proposition that compulsory arbitration brings about a more egalitarian wage structure. We have identified, however, some specific instances where low-paid workers do seem to have fared better under the Australian system" (p. 263). For the comparison with the United States, Mitchell (1984) suggests that "the arbitration system can push wages up. It can compress the wage structure by pushing up the wages of those on the bottom" (p. 187).

6. The unqualified comprise 30% of full-time employees in Australia, and 17% in the United States. Those with degrees are 12% in Australia, and 22% in the United States.

7. We share this data limitation with many other studies (Blau & Beller, 1988; Johnson & Solon, 1986; Sorensen, 1989). for some purposes, however, this may not be a serious problem. The combination of variables—potential experience, married, and children—may provide a reasonable measure of actual labor force experience for women and ensure that there is no bias in other estimated coefficients of the regression equations of Table 25.2.

8. Despite trying a wide range of functional forms, there are still difficulties in finding a good fit to the data at each end of the age-earnings profile. This is noticeable at 16 years of age when we construct the predicted series for each country.

9. It has been well known for some time that there is a relationship between industry of employment and average wages (for the United States, Wachtel & Betsey, 1972; for Australia, see Chapman & Miller, 1983; Hughes, 1973), and yet it is quite unusual to include industry as an explanatory variable in the human capital model, presumably because human capital theory has been unable to incorporate an adequate explanation for industry effects. Recently, however, industry effects have again attracted interest. Krueger and Summers (1988) find important industry wage effects in the United States (see also Johnson & Solon, 1986; Sorensen, 1989), and questions naturally arise as to whether, after standardizing for human capital variables, industry of employment has a similar effect on wages in Australia, despite the difference in institutions. A series of papers looking at industry effects in Australia has been written by Borland and Sen (1989, 1990).

10. See Table 25.2A for industry order. We have omitted industry 4—Oil and gas extraction—from Figures 25.9 and 25.10 to make the scale more manageable.

11. It would be interesting to extend the Australian analysis to distinguish between award and over-award rates of pay, and the impact of industry effects on rates of pay per hour and the number of hours worked. Our data do not allow us to do this.

References

Blau, F. D., & Beller, A. H. (1988). Trends in earnings differential by gender, 1971-1981. *Industrial and Labor Relations Review, 41*(4), 513-529.

Borland, J., & Sen, A. (1989). Inter-industry wage differentials: How much can human capital explain? (Mimeo). University of Melbourne.

Borland, J., & Sen, A. (1990). *The sources of inter-industry wage differences in Australia.* Paper presented to the Australian Labor Markets Research Program Workshop, Centre for Economic Policy Research, Australian National University.

Business Council of Australia. (1989 July). *Enterprise-based bargaining units: A better way of working* (Vol. 1). Melbourne: Author.

Chapman, B. J., & Gruen, F. H. (1990, January). *An analysis of the Australian consensual incomes policy; the prices and incomes accord* (Discussion Paper No. 221). Australian National University, Centre for Economic Policy Research.

Chapman, B. J., & Miller, P. (1983). Determination of earnings in Australia: An analysis of the 1976 census. In K. Hancock, Y. Sano, B. Chapman, & P. Fayle (Eds.), *Japanese and Australian labour markets: A comparative study.* Canberra: Australian-Japan Research Center.

Gregory, R. G., & Daly, A. (1990, February). *Can economic theory explain why Australian women are so well paid relative to their U.S. counterparts?* (Discussion Paper No. 226). Australian National University, Centre for Economic Policy Research.

Gregory, R. G., & Duncan, R. C. (1981, Spring). Segmented labor market theories and the Australian experience of equal pay for women. *Journal of Post Keynesian Economics, 2*(3), 403-428.

Gregory, R. G., Daly, A., & Ho, V. (1986, August). *A tale of two countries: Equal pay for women in Australia and Britain* (Discussion Paper No. 147). Australian National University, Centre for Economic Policy Research.

Hughes, B. (1973). The wages of the strong and the weak. *Journal of Industrial Relations, 15*(1), 1-24.

Johnson, G., & Solon, G. (1986). Estimates of the direct effects of comparable worth. *American Economic Review, 76*(5), 1117-1125.

Katz, L., & Summers, L. H. (1989). Industry rents: Evidence and implications. In M. N. Baily & C. Winston (Eds.), *Brookings papers on economic activity: Microeconomics* (pp. 209-275). Washington, DC: Brookings Institution.

Krueger, A. B., & Summers, L. H. (1988). Efficiency wages and the inter-industry wage structure. *Econometrica, 56*(2), 259-293.

Lewis, H. G. (1986). The union relative wage effect. In O. C. Ashenfelter & R. Layard (Eds.), *Handbook of labour economics* (Ch. 20). North Holland: Amsterdam.

Mincer, J. (1974). *Schooling, experience and earnings.* New York: National Bureau of Economic Research.

Mitchell, D. (1984). The Australian labour market. In R. E. Caves & L. B. Krause (Eds.), *The Australia economy, a view from the north.* Sydney: Allen & Unwin.

Mulvey, C. (1986). Wage levels: Do unions make a difference? In J. Niland (Ed.), *Wage fixation in Australia.* Sydney: Allen & Unwin.

Murphy, K. M., & Topel, R. H. (1990). Efficiency wages reconsidered: Theory and evidence. In Y. Wiess & G. Fishelson (Eds.), *Advances in the theory and measurement of unemployment.* London: Macmillan.

Niland, J. R. (Ed.). (1986). *Wage fixation in Australia.* Sydney: Allen & Unwin.

Norris, K. (1977). The dispersion of earnings in Australia. *The Economic Record, 53*(144), 475-489.

Oaxaca, J. R. (1973). Male female wage differentials in urban labor markets. *International Economic Review, 14,* 693-709.

Sorensen, E. (1989). Measuring the effect of occupational sex and race compositions on earnings. In R. T. Michael, H. I. Hartmann, & B. O'Farell (Eds.), *Pay equity empirical inquiries.* Washington, DC: National Research Council, National Academy Press.

Wachtel, J. M., & Betsey, C. (1972), Employment at low wages. *Review of Economics and Statistics, 54*(2), 121-129.

APPENDIX   Definition of Variables Used in the Regression Equations

AUSTRALIA

Education Variables

Unqualified	Age on leaving school was less than or equal to 15; no further qualifications.
High School	Age on leaving school was greater or equal to 16, but the person had no postsecondary qualifications.
Postsecondary	Trade certificate or other postsecondary certificate.
University Degree	Completion of a bachelor's degree.

Experience

Age minus years of schooling minus 6. Estimated coefficients have been multiplied by 100.

Children

A dummy variable taking the value of 1 if children under the age of 18 were present in the household and were the responsibility of the head of the household or spouse.

Area

Rural	Those living in a community of less than 1,000 people.
Urban	Those living in a community of more than 1,000 people.

433

Marital Status

Spouse Present	Currently married and living with spouse.
Other Marital Status	Widowed, separated, or divorced individuals.
Single	Never married.

UNITED STATES

Education Variables

Unqualified	Completed less than 4 years of high school.
High School	Completed 4 years of high school.
Postsecondary	Completed 1 to 3 years of college.
University Degree	Completed 4 years of college.

Experience

Age minus years of schooling minus 6.

Children

A dummy variable taking the value of 1 if children under the age of 18 were present in the household and were the responsibility of the head of the household or spouse.

Area

Rural	Those living in a community of less than 1 million people.
Urban	Those living in central cities or other communities of more than 1 million people.

Marital Status

Spouse Present	Currently married and living with spouse.
Other Marital Status	Widowed, separated, or divorced individuals.
Single	Never married.

26 \ Part-Time and Other Nonstandard Forms of Employment: Why Are They Considered Appropriate for Women?

ISIK URLA ZEYTINOGLU

One of the most important trademarks of the 1980s has been the increased use of part-time and other nonstandard forms of employment in the developed market-economy countries of the United States, Canada, among European Community members, Australia, and even in the presumed heaven of lifetime employment, Japan (Kahne, 1992; Komiya, 1991; Köhl, 1990; Lever-Tracy, 1988; Nye, 1988; Meulders & Tytgat, 1989; Tilly, 1991; Zeytinoglu, 1987). While academic and practitioner-oriented studies all show an increase in the number of workers employed in part-time and other nonstandard forms of employment, there seems to be little debate on why these employment forms are almost universally applied to female workers. In this chapter, my purposes are first, to discuss the relationship between macroeconomic conditions and the increase in part-time and other nonstandard forms of employment, and second, to initiate the debate on why part-time and other nonstandard forms of employment are created primarily for the female work force rather than the male work force. Arguments in this study are based on my accumulated knowledge on this topic and my survey of part-time work in unionized organizations in Ontario, Canada (Zeytinoglu, 1989a).

AUTHOR'S NOTE: This research was partially supported by the Arts Research Board of McMaster University.

Nonstandard Employment Forms

There are a variety of terminologies used synonymously for nonstandard employment forms. *Atypical, peripheral, marginal, secondary,* and *contingent* employment are the most common ones. In this study I use the term *nonstandard,* which, to me, is the closest to a neutral terminology and the least demeaning of all.

Any employment other than full-time indefinite contract falls under the nonstandard employment category. The terminology broadly refers to the following groups of employees (Belous, 1989; EIRR, 1990; Kassalow, 1989; Nye, 1988; Meulders & Tytgat, 1989):

1. Part-time workers who are employed less than full-time hours but on a regular (permanent, retention) basis and have indefinite contracts. This is the fastest-growing employment type within the nonstandard employment category (Thurman & Trah, 1990; Zeytinoglu, 1991a).

2. Temporary workers who are hired only when they are needed to perform specific, short-term jobs or when an immediate need arises. Temporary workers can be "casual part-time workers," who work less than full-time hours and on an on-call basis; "the company's temporary pool workers," who are employed by the company and can work full-time or part-time hours, depending on the need, but do not have a fixed employment and who move around the company, depending on the need in each department; "agency workers," who are hired on a temporary basis from an employment agency; "fixed-term contract workers," who are employed only for the duration of the contract; and "seasonal workers," who are employed only during a specified time of the year, such as during the summer or holidays.

3. Job-sharing is an employment form where two permanent part-time employees share one full-time job on a part-time basis.

4. Home-based or tele-workers are either considered self-employed or are on the company's payroll. Work is conducted at home, on a continuous, piecework basis, and for an indefinite period.

5. Subcontracting refers to work that is performed either in the firm or outside the firm, but by another company's employees.

Typical Characteristics of Part-Time and Nonstandard Employment Forms

JOB CHARACTERISTICS

Although there is a great variety of nonstandard employment forms, there are some common characteristics of these jobs. The most specific characteristic of part-time and nonstandard employment forms is its peripheral position in the organization. Regardless of the personal characteristics and the skill level of the individual, anyone who is employed in a nonstandard job is considered secondary to the core full-time worker (Zeytinoglu, forthcoming-a). It is the full-time worker who is considered first in promotions and in access to training that leads to promotion possibilities. In layoffs, full-time workers are protected prior to part-time and other nonstandard employee groups. In addition, most part-time and other nonstandard jobs are low-paying and often give few benefits.

EMPLOYEE CHARACTERISTICS

The majority of the employees in part-time and other nonstandard employment forms are females and most have dependent children (CEC, 1990; Feldman, 1990; Meulders & Tytgat, 1989; Statistics Canada, annual; Thurman & Trah, 1990; Tilly, 1991). Some of these workers are voluntary part-time or nonstandard employees, but many are forced to choose these employment forms because of lack of facilities to care for their dependents. A second large group within the part-time and other nonstandard employee category is students. These students do not have the same concerns or the family responsibilities as the first group. Since they are transient in these jobs and do not foresee their future in such working conditions, they are unwilling to insist on changes to improve the working conditions in these jobs (Zeytinoglu, 1991a).

Part-time and nonstandard employment forms can be a good opportunity for the elderly population to continue to contribute to the work world. However, there are only a small number of retirees within the part-time and nonstandard employee group. This is partially because in North America (Kahne, 1985; Labour Canada, 1983) paid work after retirement is not economically feasible due to some legal complications in existing pension and unemployment laws.

Within the part-time and other nonstandard employee group, there is another section about which we should be particularly concerned. These are recent university or high school graduates employed in part-time and other nonstandard jobs on an involuntary basis. They are employed in these jobs while seeking full-time employment in the fields in which they are trained. However, many are unable to find employment in their specialization areas. These are well-rounded, intelligent, and highly motivated individuals who were led to, or who chose, fields that the business world in the 1980s and 1990s seemed to consider not necessarily relevant. I think it is important for us to discuss the mismatch of labor supply and demand and its impact on filling part-time and other nonstandard employment vacancies.

INDUSTRY CHARACTERISTICS

Most part-time and other nonstandard employment forms are in the service sector (Thurman & Trah, 1990; Zeytinoglu, 1987). At least in Canada, most projected new jobs will be in the service sector (Economic Council of Canada, 1991), so an increase in these nonstandard employment forms should be expected. Among various nonstandard employment forms, subcontracting seems to be about the only one that has a long tradition in the manufacturing sector.

In terms of employing part-time and other nonstandard employee groups, there seems to be no difference between private and public sector organizations (Hakim, 1990; Nye, 1988). For example, in Canada federal and provincial governments have their own temporary employee pools, as well as fixed-term contract (project) employees. Workers in these jobs are not permitted to join unions since they do not have permanent positions with the government.

UNIONIZATION RATE

A small percentage of part-time and other nonstandard workers are unionized. In Canada the percentage of unionized part-time workers is 19%, and with those covered by collective agreements, this figure reaches to 24%. Part-time workers in the public sector have a higher rate of unionization than their private sector counterparts (Zeytinoglu, 1991a).

Employer Views on Part-Time and Other Nonstandard Employees

Employers have different opinions about their full-time, part-time, and other nonstandard employees. As characterized in the literature (Labour Canada, 1983; Martin & Peterson, 1987; Osterman, 1987; Zeytinoglu, forthcoming-a), most employers perceive part-time and nonstandard employees as less committed, less efficient, and of having higher voluntary turnover (quitting) rates than their full-time counterparts. Other employers, however, perceive part-time employees as committed and efficient, if not better, than their full-time counterparts (Dombois & Osterland, 1987; Gallagher, Wetzel, & Ellis, 1989).

Perceptions of individuals are based on their lifelong experiences and influence their behavior. Thus employers' perceptions of their part-time and other nonstandard employees' commitment to work, efficiency, and stability influence these workers' employment and promotion possibilities. Studies show that the lower esteem in which employers hold part-time and other nonstandard employees limits their career opportunities (Belous, 1989; ILO, 1989; Zeytinoglu, forthcoming-a).

Employer reluctance to provide career opportunities to part-time and other nonstandard employees might be related to training costs, and the longer period that is needed to receive the payoff of that training from these workers, or the possibility of not receiving it at all. Simple economic theory dictates that for general training, such as the type needed for promotion to managerial or professional positions, the majority of the training costs should be incurred by the individual; and for job-specific training, the majority of the costs should be incurred by the employer. It is also an accepted fact that if employers were to share training expenses, then rational behavior would require them to choose full-time employees for training and subsequent promotion, since there is a shorter period of return. While these arguments are plausible, I do not believe that they are unchangeable facts. In pure monetary terms it might be more profitable to follow simple economic theory. However, if one considers the nonmonetary advantages of providing equal treatment to all groups of workers, the increase in employee loyalty, stability, motivation, and satisfaction might well be worthwhile to invest in for full-time, part-time, and other nonstandard employees. Of course this argument all depends on how employers perceive their workers. If part-time and nonstandard workers were seen as an expendable work force, then spending money on these individuals would be money wasted. I think it is important for us to discuss employment and career opportunities for nonstandard workers, and related to that, how the training expenses could be covered for these workers.

Macroeconomic Conditions
and the Increase in Nonstandard Work

The increase in part-time and nonstandard work is influenced by a number of interrelated demand and supply factors. Zeytinoglu's (forthcoming-b) study on unionized part-time workers showed that the demand for part-time workers is influenced by the flexibility the employers need in scheduling work, and some employees' preference to work part-time. That study also found that, unlike most of the literature on part-time work and workers, in unionized organizations savings in wages and benefits are factors of minor importance in hiring part-time workers covered by collective agreements.

In studying the demand for part-time and other nonstandard employees, other studies found that in addition to the above factors, macroeconomic conditions also influenced employment decisions taken in organizations

(Hagen & Jenson, 1988; Sengenberger, 1981). In particular, during economic recession, the demand for labor stagnates or declines, and the supply of labor exceeds available jobs, thus increasing the competition among workers to be employed in that limited number of jobs. Striving to take advantage of the labor surplus, employers introduce a variety of employment structures. In addition to the traditional full-time work, they introduce part-time, temporary, or subcontracted work (Sengenberger, 1981) for women workers who are docile and willing to accept lower wages, and have lower probability to unionize (Hagen & Jenson, 1988). Similarly, when the global economy is unstable, and when private sector organizations are seeing a decline in their profits, or when budgets are decreasing in public and semipublic organizations, employers tend to employ part-time and other nonstandard employees as a buffer against such an unfavorable macroeconomic environment (Osterman, 1988). Governments also relax protections in the labor legislation, permitting various nonstandard employment forms to function with either minimum or no legal protection (Vogelheim, 1988).

To give examples of the impact of the macroeconomic environment on part-time and nonstandard employment forms, we do not have to look far. I would recommend that we examine the institutions that most of us are employed in—universities. I will focus only on the Canadian university system and the increase in the number of part-time academics in these universities since the early 1980s. I am sure that most of you will be able to point out similar situations in universities in your countries.

In Canadian universities, the phenomenon of the part-time academic is inextricably linked to economic, social, and political developments in the country. In particular, two key factors—student enrollment and government funding—shape the employment possibilities of university faculty. In the 1950s and the 1960s, the federal and provincial governments' commitment to the excellence of Canadian universities—a commitment demonstrated in increased funding—strengthened the university faculty's position within the educational system. At this time, while student enrollment and government funding were increasing, many full-time faculty positions were created. However, in the mid-1970s and afterward, the government's goals shifted from excellence in education to increasing economic growth and controlling the rising inflation rate. As a result, university funds were cut back, while student enrollment continued to increase (OCUFA, 1989). University administrators started to adopt part-time and other nonstandard employment forms for academics (CAUT, 1989).

In implementing a variety of employment forms in their organizations, employers seek three major goals: flexibility, cost-effectiveness, and predictability (Osterman, 1987). Canadian universities attempted to achieve flexibility and cost-effectiveness through part-time and fixed-term contract faculty, while they ensured predictability through a core group of full-time faculty. Using part-time and fixed-term contract faculty is a short-term solution to major economic problems in universities. Although for the short term, university administrators are keeping their costs under control and providing services to an increasing number of students through employing part-time faculty, the long-term implications of using part-time faculty seem to be negative. Full-time positions are not created, and junior scholars are effectively forced to work in insecure, low-paying, and often low-status jobs (Zeytinoglu, 1989-b). After a certain time, many are forced to depart these unstable university careers, leaving behind their ambitions, goals, and struggles. This is investment in time and money lost for the society, not only for the individuals. As a result, in the late 1990s when a large number of university faculty will be reaching their retirement years, there will be a shortage of faculty to fill their places.

The universities' example applies to most other organizations, whether they are in the public or private sector. When organizations adopt hiring part-time and other nonstandard employees as their strategy, they may benefit in the short term in savings in labor costs and achieving flexibility. However, in the long term, organizations will lose a great deal. Since they are not investing in their human resources, when core full-time workers leave or retire, these organizations are left with a weak employee base because it consists mostly of workers whom employers considered peripheral and whom they did not invest in training.

Women and Part-Time and
Other Nonstandard Forms of Employment

Why most part-time and other nonstandard jobs exist in female-dominated occupations/sectors, rather than in male-dominated occupations/sectors, is the question that needs to be asked. The evidence shows that part-time and other nonstandard employment forms exist in the retail trade, hospitality, healthcare, and education (Zeytinoglu, 1991a), finance, and community/ government services sectors, where most women are employed. There are very few part-time or other nonstandard workers in primary industries, manufacturing, and construction, where most males work.

The interesting phenomenon is that, depending on the sex of the work force, employers introduce different employment strategies (Beechey & Perkins, 1987). In male-dominated bargaining units, workplaces, or industries, such as auto or steel industries, employers use multiskilling, robots, or other labor-saving technology to achieve flexibility and cost-effectiveness. Thus while they heavily invest in technology, they also decrease the labor input. Those few who continue to be employed in the company are employed as full-time workers. These workers earn high wages and benefits and enjoy relative job security. On the other hand, in female-dominated bargaining units, workplaces, or industries, such as healthcare or retail trade, employers also introduce new technology to achieve flexibility and cost-effectiveness, but it is introduced in such a way that most workers are employed on a part-time or nonstandard employment form. For the reasons of such a differential treatment among sexes, some employers say that men cannot work in part-time or other nonstandard jobs because they cannot earn the income for their family, and therefore, women are employed (Beechey & Perkins, 1987; ILO, 1989; Zeytinoglu, 1989a). I wonder how women earn their family's income on these nonstandard jobs. I think we should ask the question as to why employers consider it appropriate to use different flexibility strategies, depending on the sex of the individual.

In terms of occupation, if part-time and other nonstandard employees were to be found within each sector, they are almost always in female-dominated occupations, such as clerks, secretaries, cashiers, cleaning staff, or food servers. Let me take a manufacturing company, such as a steel company in North America, as an example. In this company most full-time jobs will be in production and will employ males. If there are any part-time, temporary, job-sharing, or subcontracted jobs, they will be filled mostly by women, and these jobs will generally be in typical female-dominated occupations. Let me give another example, but this time from a female-dominated industry and company. If we were to examine the retail trade sector, and in particular, a retail food store, what we will see is that most meat cutters are men working on a full-time basis, and cashiers are women working on a part-time or temporary basis. Even in professional occupations, part-time and other nonstandard employment forms exist in the female-dominated professions of nursing or elementary school teaching, rather than in male-dominated professions, such as engineering (Zeytinoglu, 1991b). In some professions where the percentage of women is increasing, in proportion to this increase, the percentage of part-time, agency workers, or job-sharers is also increasing. Lawyers (Loveman, 1990) and pharmacists in North America are typical examples of this phenomenon.

The Impact of Patriarchal Values

It is not a coincidence that the majority of part-time, temporary, job-sharing, home-based, tele-work, and subcontracted workers are women. Since it is presumed that females are subordinates in paid employment (Legge, 1987), earning the secondary income for the family, their careers

Belous, R. S. (1989). *The contingent economy: The growth of the temporary, part-time and subcontracted workforce.* Washington, DC: The National Planning Association.

CAUT (Canadian Association of University Teachers). (1989). Problems of peripheral academic [Problemes de l'universitaire-chercheur marginalise]. *CAUT Bulletin, 36*(1), 7.

CEC (Commission of the European Communities). (1990). *Proposal for a council directive on certain employment relationships with regard to working conditions* (Com(90) 228 final— SYN 280 & SYN 281).

Del Boca, D. (1988). Women in a changing workplace: Italy. In E. Hagen, J. Jenson, & C. Reddy (Eds.), *Feminization of the labor force: Paradoxes and promises.* Oxford University Press.

Delsen, L. (1990). European trade unions and the flexible workforce. *Industrial Relations Journal, 21*, 260-273.

Dombois, R., & Osterland, M. (1987). New forms of flexible utilization of labour: Part-time and contract work. In R. Tarling (Ed.), *Flexibility in labour markets* (pp. 225-243). London: Academic Press.

Economic Council of Canada. (1991). *Employment in the service economy.* Ottawa: Author.

EIRR (European Industrial Relations Review). (1990). Nonstandard forms of employment in Europe: part-time work, fixed term contracts and temporary work contracts. London: Eclipse.

Feldman, D. C. (1990). Reconceptualizing the nature and consequences of part-time work. *Academy of Management Review, 15*, 103-112.

Gallagher, D. G., Wetzel, K., & Ellis, R. (1989). *Part-time employment in the health care industry: Consequences for organizational commitment.* Paper presented at the 1989 Academy of Management Meeting, Washington, D.C.

Hagen, E., & Jenson, J. (1988). Paradoxes and promises: Work and politics in the postwar years. In E. Hagen, J. Jenson, & C. Reddy (Eds.), *Feminization of the labor force: Paradoxes and promises.* New York: Oxford University Press.

Hakim, C. (1990). Core and periphery in employers' workforce strategies: Evidence from the 1987 E.L.U.S. survey. *Work, Employment and Society, 4*, 157-188.

ILO (International Labor Organization). (1989). Part-time work. *Conditions of Work Digest, 8.*

Kahne, H. (1985). *Reconceiving part-time work: New perspectives for older workers and women.* Totowah, NJ: Rowman and Allanheld.

Kahne, H. (1992). Part-time work: A hope and a peril. In B. Warme & L. Lundy (for K. Lundy) (Eds.), *Part-time work: Opportunity or dead-end?* New York: Praeger.

Kassalow, E. (1989). Labour market flexibility and new employment patterns: The U.S. case in a comparative framework. In H. Wheeler (Ed.), *Labour market flexibility and new employment patterns: Proceedings of the eighth world congress of the IIRA* (pp. 75-98). Paris: ILO.

Köhl, J. (1990). New deal and new forms of employment. *Labour and Society, 15*, 237-255.

Komiya, F. (1991). Dismissal procedures and termination benefits in Japan. *Comparative Labor Law Journal, 12*, 151-164.

Labour Canada. (1983). *Part-time work in Canada: Report of the commission of inquiry into part-time work.* Ottawa: Government of Canada.

Lapidus, G. W. (1989). The interaction of women's work and family roles in the USSR. *Canadian Woman Studies [les cahiers de la femme], 10*, 41-45.

Legge, K. (1987). Women in personnel management: Uphill climb or downhill slide? In A. Spencer & D. Podmore (Eds.), *In a man's world: Essays on women in male-dominated professions.* London: Tavistock.

Lever-Tracy, C. (1988). The flexibility debate: Part-time work. *Labour & Industry, 1*, 210-241.

Loveman, G. W. (1990). The case of the part-time partner. *Harvard Business Review*, 12-29.

Martin, J. E., & Peterson, M. M. (1987). Two-tier wage structures: Implications for equity theory. *Academy of Management Journal, 30*, 297-315.

Meulders, D., & Tytgat, B. (1989). Atypical employment in EEC countries. *The International Journal of Comparative Labour Law and Industrial Relations, 5,* 61-81.

Mills, A. J. (1989). Gender, sexuality and organization theory. In J. Hearn, D. L. Sheppard, P. Tancred-Sheriff, & G. Burrell (Eds.), *The sexuality of organization* (pp. 29-44). London: Sage.

Nye, D. (1988). *Alternative staffing strategies.* Washington, DC: Bureau of National Research.

OCUFA. (1989). OCUA recommended 10.5% increase. *OCUFA Forum, 6*(9), 1.

Osterman, P. (1987). Choice of employment systems in internal labor markets. *Industrial Relations, 26,* 46-67.

Osterman, P. (1988). *Employment futures: Reorganization, dislocation and public policy.* New York: Oxford University Press.

Sengenberger, W. (1981). Labour market segmentation and the business cycle. In F. Williamson (Ed.), *The dynamics of labor market segmentation* (pp. 243-259). London: Academic Press.

Spencer, A., & Podmore, C. (1987). *In a man's world: Essays on women in male-dominated professions.* London: Tavistock.

Statistics Canada. (annual). *The labour force* (Catalogue 71-001).

Thurman, J. E., & Trah, G. (1990). Part-time work in international perspective. *International Labour Review, 129,* 23-40.

Tilly, C. (1991). Reasons for the continuing growth of part-time employment. *Monthly Labor Review, 114,* 10-18.

Vogelheim, E. (1988). Women in a changing workplace: Federal Republic of Germany. In E. Hagen, J. Jenson, & C. Reddy (Eds.), *Feminization of the labour force: Paradoxes and promises.* Oxford University Press.

Walby, S. (1986). *Patriarchy at work.* London: Polity Press.

Zeytinoglu, I. U. (1987). Part-time workers: Unionization and collective bargaining in Canada. *Proceedings of the Thirty-Ninth Annual Meeting* (IRRA Series), 487-495.

Zeytinoglu, I. U. (1989a). *Part-time workers and collective bargaining: A survey of employers and unions.* Technical report prepared for the Social Sciences and Humanities Research Council of Canada.

Zeytinoglu, I. U. (1989b). *Flexibility and the academic world: Part-time faculty in Canadian universities.* Paper presented at the UMIST/Aston Organization and Control of the Labour Process Conference.

Zeytinoglu, I. U. (1990). Part-time work in the education sector: A study of teachers in Ontario's elementary schools. *Journal of Collective Negotiations in the Public Sector, 19,* 319-337.

Zeytinoglu, I. U. (1991a). A sectoral study of part-time workers covered by collective agreements: Why do employers hire them? *Relations Industrielles [Industrial Relations], 46,* 401-418.

Zeytinoglu, I. U. (1991b). *Part-time professionals in female-dominated occupations: Why so few are progressing in their careers.* Paper presented at the Workshop on Gender and Economic Restructuring, Waterloo, Ontario.

Zeytinoglu, I. U. (forthcoming, a). Unionized part-time professionals and opportunities for filling full-time vacancies and training. *Relations Industrielles [Industrial Relations].*

Zeytinoglu, I. U. (forthcoming, b). Reasons for hiring part-time workers in unionized organizations. *Industrial Relations.*

PART VII

Change in an
International Context

forgiving: "An idea isn't responsible for the people who believe in it." And in an approach no doubt familiar to academics only too conscious of the imperative to publish or perish, Bronson Alcott observes that: "Ideas, when vended in a book, carry with them a kind of dignity and certainty which awe many into implicit belief." Journal editors, take note.

Perhaps the best-known observation about ideas, and one that underscores the uncomfortable linkage between the policy researcher and the political implementer, comes from John Maynard Keynes: "The power of vested interests is usually exaggerated when compared with the gradual encroachment of ideas. . . . Indeed, the world is ruled by little else. . . . Madmen in authority, who hear voices in the air, are distilling their frenzy from some academic scribbler of a few years back."

Ideas in industrial relations not only travel from one generation forward to another, but more important, they move back and forth between countries and cultures. Exchange occurs in a variety of ways, but most important in the international movement of industrial relations ideas are the scholarly journals, the leading half dozen of which in the past 20 years have published more than 500 articles with a distinct international flavor. Such internationalism might arise because the article is specifically focused on the experiences in one country and is published in a journal based in another country; or because there is a clear and specific comparison between the experiences of two countries; or because the article is theoretical or conceptual but cast toward a comparative goal.

A reading of this comparative literature suggests ideas in industrial relations move between countries and cultures for any of 10 primary (and sometimes overlapping) reasons:

1. to better understand industrial relations convergence and diversity (e.g., Niland & Clarke, 1991; Strauss, 1988).
2. to keep a finger on the research pulse (e.g., Capelli, 1985; Peterson, 1986; Strauss & Feuille, 1978).
3. to provide the basis for better theorizing (e.g., Capelli, 1985; Kochan, McKersie, & Capelli, 1984).
4. to sharpen domestic insights (e.g., Beaumont, 1988).
5. to better maintain relevance in a changing world order (e.g., Cochrane, 1976).
6. so a vested interest might gain a strategic advantage or insight.
7. to guard against unwelcome transplants or imports (e.g., Swan, 1980).
8. to help survive the paradigm shift (Dunn, 1990; Kochan, Katz, & McKersie, 1986; cf. Keenoy, 1991).
9. to facilitate and justify policy development (e.g., Dunlop, 1977; Hameed, 1971; Turner & Jackson, 1969; Whittingham & Towers, 1971).

10. to serve the scholars' urge to study and explain the whole, to bring order and insight to apparently chaotic reality (e.g., Craig, 1975; Dunlop, 1958; Goodman et al., 1975).

The international exchange of ideas in industrial relations has long been vital in building a mature discipline. The future role of such exchanges, particularly in the contemporary context of change, is the focus of this chapter, which also provides an opportunity to touch base with each of the themes of the Congress: the role of the state; the future of trade unionism; the rise of human resources management and its challenge to industrial relations teaching, research, and practice; the role of industrial relations in political transformation; and the bridges to be built between macro policy and micro implementation.

My argument is that in the 1990s the international dimension will become even more important because of what is happening to the discipline in an academic sense, and because of what is happening to industrial relations systems in a practical sense. I come to this conclusion after examining aspects of the two key contemporary challenges facing academics and practitioners: the need for policy and systems to maintain relevance in a changing world order as they seek greater flexibility and adaptability; and the need for the discipline to survive the paradigm shift generated by these changes.

Surviving the
Quest for Flexibility

The rise and fall of convergence theory, one of the more spectacular episodes in comparative international research, underscores the simple fact that in industrial relations diversity is pervasive (Cochrane, 1976). In the mid-1980s, for example, five key models could be identified for the OECD member countries.

Encompassing bargaining is found in countries such as Austria, Sweden, and Germany where "industrial relations have been based on bargaining structures with great breadth but little depth"; *job control bargaining,* found in the United States and Canada, included as key features a high degree of legalism, role making that covers a wide range of personnel practices, and a plant or enterprise focus; *enterprise bargaining,* found in Japan, developed strong bonds between the union and the company, with an understandable absence of horizontally solidaristic campaigns (Shunto notwithstanding); *fragmented bargaining,* as in France, the United Kingdom, and Italy, featured "widespread competition between unions, the existence of multiple and largely uncoordinated levels of bargaining and a lack of strong formal or informal controls on the collective bargaining process"; and finally, *fragmented bargaining with compulsory arbitration,* of which Australia has been the prime and perhaps only example, where tribunals strove to standardize wages and conditions between industries, with no attempt to distinguish between "interests" and "rights" regulation.

But will such diversity be so evident by the mid-1990s? Economic pressures on different countries and the general direction of their strategic industrial relations responses over the past decade are remarkably similar, allowing of course for the inevitable variation in detail, which reflects the rich array of cultures and institutional arrangements. Indeed, we may well be witnessing limited evidence for a particular version of the convergence thesis (see Treu, 1987), with instances of the fragmented bargaining model, the compulsory arbitration model, and perhaps also the job control model increasingly difficult to find. This is not to say that all bargaining systems are shifting to either a Japanese model of enterprise bargaining or a Swedish/German model of encompassing bargaining. But we are likely to see more countries fit one of these two models, while most of the rest will fit a third model, where potentially fragmented bargaining is coordinated or regulated, either through social compact, government executive action, or legislation— the *regulated bargaining* model.

Most countries with mature industrial relations systems have started to loosen regulatory controls in the labor market, relocating rule making toward the enterprise level. Some, naturally, have more scope for change and further to travel than others, given their initial starting point. But the goal of greater flexibility in the interests of efficiency, sometimes prompted by and sometimes translated into a more active and strategic stance by management in shaping industrial relations outcomes, is widespread if not endemic. A counterpart retreat in the power and influence of trade unions, although not inevitable, nonetheless has occurred. Governments, for their part, have generally been quite strategy-oriented and alert to the opportunities in fostering the transformation of industrial relations. In short, the period of the past decade has been anything but static; dynamics and change are the order of the day, with incomes policies, productivity bargaining, and worker participation regimes now the insignia of past decades. This raises some interesting issues that would benefit increasingly from consideration in an international context; the thinking and the action in other countries is always more relevant in times of change and heightened strategic choice, particularly where the shift is less than transitory. There is an understandable impulse both to avoid reinventing the wheel, and to avoid having it run you over.

TRANSITORY OR
PERMANENT DECENTRALIZATION?

Experience and casual observation should caution us against any presumption of permanence in social systems. But if we can establish that the quest for greater flexibility is likely to be with us throughout the 1990s, then there is greater value in the international exchange of ideas in industrial relations, for how others operate may point the way to a comparative advantage, even survival.

Indications are that the underlying forces for decentralism will persist, and that more and more the center of gravity will be located at the enterprise or operating unit level. The fundamental imperatives toward the enterprise focus include shifts in the nature of corporate share holding, the squeeze from third world manufacturing activity on developed country profits, micro-technology developments, and the side effects of a more highly interdependent world economy. As we shall see, none of these forces for change is a transitory phenomenon.

Irreversible changes in corporate share holding impel corporate management systems toward a lower locus. The emergence of managed funds and the growth in pension provisions over the past few decades have meant that significantly greater proportions of share holding are now in the hands of professionals, whose performance is closely monitored on a month-to-month, even week-to-week, basis. Fund managers are more likely to quickly off-load shares of companies judged not to be performing, and this starts a chain reaction in which share prices fall and the prospect of takeover looms larger than before. To "save" their company, the board of directors continue the chain reaction by pressuring their factory managers to attack inefficiencies and generally adopt a much tougher line in dealing with labor. The net effect is that corporate performance is evaluated within a much shorter time frame, and this contributes significantly to more aggressive management focused at the enterprise level, rather than the industry or national level. This can be expected to produce more flexible pay regimes, with an emphasis on bonuses and other forms of contingent remuneration. The rise in employee share ownership, while linked more to the search for employee loyalty and enterprise bonding, nonetheless serves to reinforce the decentralist theme.

A related force for further decentralism is the squeeze on profits and the pressures generated from third world manufacturing activity for OECD countries to pare labor costs through both relaxation of government-induced controls and workplace reorganization, including use of new technology. Developing countries have been more willing to experiment with innovative management systems and work organization techniques. This, together with competitive pressures on the established manufacturers, in turn intensified the international search in OECD countries for survival techniques, and industrial relations systems have come under particularly close scrutiny. Typical responses are tightened operations, the design of products more responsive to consumer preferences, greater quality assurance, new wave technology, and new management systems emphasizing devolution. The success of Japan led many to seek to emulate or assimilate certain of that country's management concepts and industrial relations practices. But on the whole, as Barkin argues, the developed countries "were slow to recognise that patchwork and temporary expedients could never recapture or hold positions. Producers had also to overcome smug attitudes of indifference, condescension and ignorance of the advances in foreign countries and to adopt them where possible" (1987, p. 18).

Training requirements, particularly those linked with the needs of micro technology, are another major factor in sustaining an enterprise focus. Hunter notes an increasing demand for more company-specific training: "the emphasis has swung from dependence on a general skill to be traded in the external market to reliance on skill acquisition in line with the technology and work organisation structure of the specific employer" (1991, p. 142). The enterprise thus becomes integral in the task of tackling youth unemployment, thereby providing a clear nexus between a macro policy concern and the micro delivery of a solution to that concern, issues focused on in Theme 5 of the Congress: The Micro/Macro Interface in Labor Market Policy and Practice. France provides an interesting parallel: Here the individual firm, "which according to traditional socialist doctrine was the root of all exploitation, was rehabilitated and became a job creating unit and a source of innovation" under the Mitterand Socialist government (Delamotte, 1991, p. 98). Mathews, commenting on the Australian experience, also sees the importance of the enterprise for: "the formulation of skills-based work and pay systems, the mechanisms and procedures governing workers' allocation to and progression through skills-based job classification systems, the tracing out of career paths and the conduct of skills audits and training programmes" (1992, p. 43). But he also reminds us that other issues, such as "skills standardisation, accreditation and portability of qualifications . . . can only be resolved at the trans-enterprise level."

Another factor reinforcing decentralism is the growing economic internationalization, and the boost this gives to awareness among countries about the relative effectiveness (or ineffectiveness) of their particular approach to industrial relations. With the globalization of the world economy, competition flows more freely between countries, with the result that domestic systems of industrial relations are not so insular as when high tariff walls protect productivity and work practice idiosyncrasies. Australia is a classic case in point.

With its unique system of industrial regulation based on tribunal involvement, Australian industrial relations for decades placed great emphasis on equity and uniformity of wage outcomes across industries and enterprises with vastly differing productivity. With highly favorable terms of trade in the 1950s and 1960s, Australia developed for itself the concept of being "a lucky country," in which wage outcomes were largely unrelated to productivity inputs, except in the most generalized way. However, as terms of trade deteriorated through the 1970s and 1980s, the luck started to run out, and the idiosyncrasies of the local industrial relations system came more and more under a microscope whose light source, so to speak, was the industrial relations experiences in Europe, particularly Austria (Dunkley, 1984). The past 5 years have seen a profound shift both in the center of gravity in the industrial relations system (from centralized to industry and on toward enterprise) and in the underlining process for rule making and dispute resolution (from tribunal arbitration toward collective bargaining) (Niland & Spooner, 1991).

These changes would have been impossible without the international experience and insights generated by those leading the reforms (ACTU/TDC, 1987). At the same time, the international exchange of ideas can serve a cautionary purpose. Whether the Australian reforms are taken further into the realms of deregulated labor markets and individual (rather than collective) bargained contracts depends on how the political process and the electorate will assess the radically transformed New Zealand industrial relations arrangements. In a similar vein, Swan examined the relevance of public sector bargaining regulations and practice in the United States, for those considering reform of the Canadian approach, and concluded:

> Canada and the U.S. are, in many ways, similar countries. But each has had to adapt public sector bargaining to meet the demands of their respective constitutional structures. Statutory bargaining models, unlike migratory geese, are not necessarily able to fly across the border and live happily on the other side. Some of the plumage is protective coloration designed to allow them to survive in one country or the other; across the border it may prove at best decorative and at worst unwelcome. (Swan, 1980, p. 290)

It is, of course, axiomatic that industrial relations arrangements reflect the culture, the institutions, and the legal framework of a particular country, and what may work well in one part of the world may fit very poorly with the institutions and infrastructures in another. Thus, while ideas might be internationally transportable, their translation operationally from one country to another is less certain, as the literature time and time again reminds us. Certainly one of the refrains in the public policy debate in Australia has been that collective bargaining is a foreign concept and not importable to antipodean traditions and tribunal arrangements.

This may be a reasonable proposition where the receiving environment is unreconstructed, but when public policy is strategy-oriented, the policymakers and the legislators are prepared to pave the way with institutional reform. The issue thus becomes not so much whether the idea is nonsense, because the home body will reject the transplant, but whether there are changes to domestic law and institutions that can and will be undertaken, where the idea is inherently worthwhile. The marvel of the transformation of industrial relations in Australia is both the international origins of the ideas underpinning the changes, and the fact that reforms were injected into the institutions and the legal framework to make those new ideas operational.

STRATEGIC CHOICES FOR THE KEY PLAYERS

Decentralism can be expected, on balance, to promote flexibility and enhance management power. The indications are thus that with more emphasis on enterprise-level activity, employers will control the agenda for change. Certainly, both Hunter (1991) and Kochan and Wever (1991) expect management to occupy the driver's seat in the foreseeable future. Yet there is the case of Australia, where unions rather than managers have led the push for innovation in work practices and flexibility, perhaps for the very reason that they don't have the upper hand, but do have a strong sense of the need to transform to survive. Also, even in countries such as the United Kingdom, France, the United States, and Germany, management's ability to take full advantage of the stronger enterprise locus will be limited without union cooperation.

Disquiet is evident among some British managers that, if economic or legislative factors further weaken established institutions, unions might feel pushed to a more militant, last-ditch resistance. The choice facing management is whether to continue with the tougher line, or begin to ease the pressure in search of "a more co-operative approach from responsible and representative unions . . . to contribute constructively to the adjustment process" (Hunter, 1991, p. 144). Streeck echoes this sentiment. Unions and employers can choose either antagonistic or cooperative strategies toward one another, and in the tradition of the classic prisoner's dilemma theorem, the welfare of each is influenced by how well they anticipate the other's eventual stance. Because of their enhanced power base through decentralism, the position of employers is probably less vulnerable. But it is also evident that, even in a context of considerable adversity and some hostility, the labor/management symbiosis survives (Streeck, 1991, p. 83).

The fate of trade unions, which is focused upon in Theme 2 of the Congress, rests on many factors. New technology, emphasizing much tighter orbits of control and small-scale production efficiencies, is changing the face of industrial relations by guaranteeing the decentralized unit a crucial role. Large smokestack complexes can be replaced by mini-mills, whose set-up costs are less than the capital maintenance bill on the industrial juggernauts they replace. As the patterns of basic production change, a transformed industry mix, in favor of service and finance and away from manufacturing, will affect basic industrial relations, as will customer-dedicated production runs; subcontracted outwork in the workers' homes; the rise of a much better educated work force, which is more inclined to insist on decision making closer to home; and the general drift toward white-collar work. These are all issues largely beyond the control of trade unions. Yet there are also areas where they do have discretion to affect their future, and two issues will be particularly significant.

One major challenge to trade unions will be the growing inclination of public opinion to mobilize against what are seen as exceedingly indulgent and self-serving stances. Delamotte refers to the impact of public opinion in forcing public sector unions, particularly in electricity and railways, to modify action that disrupts social and economic life (Delamotte, 1991, p. 109). The issue, however, runs deeper than just overt industrial conflict. As the OECD itself notes, "unions representing relatively small groups of workers, often enjoying regulatory job protection, have pressed wage claims with little regard for the cost in terms of employment opportunities for others." While this may be more typical of countries with the fragmented bargaining model, such elements also exist in countries whose industrial relations systems are cast in the other models. How trade unions handle the issues of dual labor markets, internal versus external orbits of job opportunity, and the rise of precarious employment will bear heavily on future public perceptions of trade unions. Lessons from the experience of other countries must be increasingly important.

In some countries, like Germany and Australia, the sheer intricacy of constitutional provisions and the general regulatory framework provide protection from employers and governments that might wish to tap public opinion to exert leverage on trade unions and weaken their standing. But even here, as in countries such as the United States, France, and the United Kingdom, where unions lack such protective infrastructure, their fate will be tied to how hardline they try to be in preserving (even enhancing) the benefits and protections of core workers over those in the peripheral labor force. The fact that women are heavily concentrated in this latter group, and that awareness is growing over equal employment opportunity values and practices, reinforces the seriousness of the challenges to be mounted against old-style unionism. It is also worth noting that no set of ideas has had a greater impact on work relationships in the past decade than those of EEO, and they have for the most part been internationally generated.

The second area where the future of unions lies largely in their own strategic stance arises from the growing emphasis on enterprise bargaining. Tensions between full-time officials operating at an industry or national level, and the lay officials or unionized worker representatives based within the enterprise are evident in quite a few countries (Niland & Clarke, 1991). The leadership and structural challenge is to both decentralize the power and authority needed to bargain at enterprise levels, and centralize the provisions of staff expertise and other resources needed to develop long-run strategies and advise local union entities on the increasingly complex array of technical, economic, and organizational issues that confront labor today. How this is eventually settled in each case will say much about the likely future relevance of trade unions in modern industrial society.

Also important will be whether management's bonding strategies simply seek to move full-time officials to an arm's-length relationship—or will it seek to engineer their complete demise? As Kochan and Wever see it, the more trade unions "cling to their traditional roles within the New Deal system, the more freedom and incentives management will have to pursue a union-avoidance strategy" (Kochan & Wever, 1991, p. 52). The alternative, taking Germany as an example, is for unions to provide management with assets they would find hard to generate on their own, such as "worker commitment, willingness to undergo training and retraining, governable organizational flexibility at the work place and active support for structural change." As Streeck observes, a credible offer of cooperation will reduce the attraction to employers of a test of strength, "even if this means foregoing present opportunities to restore managerial privilege and, in the longer run, deunionize important segments of the labour force" (Streeck, 1991). The position is probably little different in other OECD countries, especially the United Kingdom, with the prominent example there of the EEPTU (Electricians) offer of greater flexibility through their willingness to negotiate single-union agreements. Where unions must have some concern would be the management strategy of cooperation up to the point of relative advantage, and then a switch to a tougher stance to drive home an absolute advantage.

The general picture, then, is that management can be expected to bolster the trend toward decentralization of industrial relations processes, and this would be enhanced if unions chose to cooperate with an enterprise focus. This is not to say that unions will (or should) meekly accept decentralization on management's terms alone, or without negotiating a greater influence in the decision-making process. The scope for strategy analysis and considered action is now quite profound. To return to the classic prisoner's dilemma, by choosing cooperation with one another, unions and management can both be better off in the long run, although an antagonistic posture could well have a better pay-off for the initiator over the short run. This calls for great maturity, which is essentially an ability to choose a strategy of sustaining short-run costs for longer run gains. Here is perhaps the key role for governments in the next decade, a topic addressed in Theme 1 of the Congress: The Role of the State in Industrial Relations.

Governments can never guarantee that their legislation will change institutions and procedures in the planned manner, but their actions unquestionably fashion the industrial relations mood of a country in which day-to-day exchanges are played out. Unforeseen events with electoral implications understandably affect the stance of governments at any particular time. But over the longer run, the choices are not dissimilar to those in the prisoner's dilemma analogy and indeed will influence how the two industrial parties deport themselves in that same sense.

In one policy direction, governments can foster an industrial relations climate in which unions and management are each likely to opt for the shorter run maximization of their individual welfare. Here unions face the higher risk strategy of digging in and fighting all the way to oblivion, as they resist technology, industry restructuring, enterprise-focused bargaining, and efficiency campaigns. Their longer run chances of success are not good, although management's victories may well be Pyrrhic.

Alternatively, governments can encourage the type of climate in which labor and management develop sufficient trust with one another to focus on the longer run strategy, in which trade unions become the partner in managing change, accommodating new technology, supporting (even sponsoring) industry restructuring, and pursuing efficiency arrangements. One difficulty with this scenario is restraining the destabilizing hostilities of the extreme Left and the extreme Right. Another problem, naturally, will be the disjunction between electoral processes in the Western democratic model, which tend to require 3-to-4-year cycles, and the 5-to-10-year time frame implicit in the industrial relations transformation process. That is, maturity is no less required of governments than it is of unions and employers. "It has become increasingly obvious," as Kochan and Wever (1991) point out, "that widespread economic problems require solutions that depend critically on the active participation and cooperation of all three parties to the employment relationship."

Industrial relations systems (or environments) are never static, but the changes currently running are more profound, and probably more permanent in their fundamental impact, than anything witnessed since industrial relations has become an identifiable academic discipline. Given the close nexus between the discipline and the profession (the same cannot be said of sociology and philosophy, even physics and physiology), such a sea change is bound to have a major bearing on industrial relations as a field of study.

Surviving the Paradigm Shift

Industrial relations is a precarious field of study, for its demise in one or another part of the world is reportedly imminent from time to time. Strauss and Feuille (1978), for example, talk about a golden age of American industrial relations, a period in the 1920s and 1930s in which "industrial relations gradually increased its domain beyond the Wisconsin Group's original interests in labor law, collective bargaining, social insurance and labor history, and in so doing drew into the fold psychologists, sociologists and political scientists." Yet, by the 1970s some American scholars feared that this golden age had passed, at least in regard to research:

> British research is more exciting that ours [American]. It asks more funda-
> mental questions. Its research topics are less constrained by accepted
> orthodoxy. A vocal left wing makes complete acceptance of the status quo
> rather difficult . . . obviously cross-fertilisation between U.S. and British
> research would be useful . . . however, British scholars seem much more aware
> of U.S. research that we are of theirs, and this one sided awareness may be
> slow to change. (Strauss & Feuille, 1978, p. 273)

Now, with the human resource management (HRM) juggernaut moving out from the contemporary American experience, "a vocal left wing" has less inherent appeal, and more than a few British academics might feel that the really interesting ideas for the 1990s are being sourced on the other side of the Atlantic, or even further afield in multinational corporations. This is no ordinary new wave, for it has the potential to shift dramatically the under-lying power bases within the discipline. Among academics there is concern that responsibility for industrial relations is moving to the business schools, where a different paradigm operates. Among practitioners the concern is that the devolution approach and the techniques of HRM serve to mainline the industrial relations function, with the importance of the line manager grow-ing at the expense of the expert. It is not being overly dramatic to wonder whether the discipline will survive much beyond the year 2000. If it does, certainly it will look quite different by then, and a change of name would be only part of the story.

Fields of study and research exist because they have a home within universities, although the academic discipline may be organized differently from country to country. In countries such as Britain, the United States, Australia, Nigeria, Canada, and New Zealand (all predominantly English-speaking), we find separate departments of industrial relations, while in Europe industrial relations is more likely to be embodied within the cognate disciplines of economics, politics, law, psychology, sociology, and so on. Irrespective of its particular organizational form, the discipline will survive only if it is able to generate or garner sufficient resources, which in turn depends on student demand and on institutional politics, which themselves can be influenced by the moral and financial support coming from practitioners. In this respect the future of industrial relations as a field of study is no different from that of music or mathematics, accounting or astronomy, or physics and physiotherapy. The development of the academic discipline in Australia can be traced through three phases, elements of which are no doubt evident in many other countries.

First, the *foundation phase* ran through the 1950s and 1960s. Academics who had been appointed to the cognate disciplines began to explore the industrial relations issues in their field, to produce such subjects as industrial psychology, labor law, labor history, labor economics, and the like. Searching for a special identity, and often feeling marginalized from their own disciplinary mainstream, these academics formed distinct institutional groupings. Their efforts were bolstered by a growing interest among students and were supported by industry in specifically focused industrial relations programs. It mattered little that scholars in the more traditional disciplines worried about the lack of a theoretical framework for industrial relations and the absence of a clear body of research literature to support teaching. These would come in the next phase.

Second, the *growth and consolidation phase* ran throughout the 1970s and into the 1980s. During these years the student numbers grew extraordinarily. At the University of New South Wales, for example, while 10 undergraduate students graduated with a major in industrial relations in 1972, by 1978 this had grown more than fourfold to 45 (and was to fall back to fewer than 10 by 1990). Schools of industrial relations emerged, usually in close association with faculties of law or economics and, through an incredible surge in research output, a distinctively Australian body of material emerged. Interestingly, some of the cognate disciplines even courted the presence of industrial relations to help boost student numbers (and therefore their own resource base). Special research centers, funded through earmarked grants from government, became almost commonplace. The discipline may have been in the doldrums in the United States during this period, but for Australia a golden age of sorts had arrived.

It should be acknowledged that this probably had as much to do with the industrial relations traumas being reported daily, in a press given to hyperbole and colorful detail, as it did with any discovery of a new mother lode of truth to be taught and researched in the groves of academe. And herein probably lies the kernel of the problem.

Third, the *challenge and survival phase* presents itself as we enter the 1990s. We now see a rising skepticism about the relevance of industrial relations study among its main stakeholders: students, policymakers, practitioners, and funding bodies. The imperative to approach industrial relations through the portals of human resource management are, as elsewhere, strong in Australia and growing. Against this background the health and strength of the discipline would be at risk from two scenarios. One would arise if the industrial relations turmoil reached such a pitch that the community no longer accepted the traditional remedies offered by a discipline disinclined to change, and looked elsewhere for the holy grail—something analogous to the concern traditional medicine may direct toward the growing role of alternative medicine. The other scenario entails a successful application of change techniques by the traditional practitioners, such that the headlines (and therefore the student interest) fade. This outcome is analogous to the impact on dental practice of its professionals promoting the use of fluoride. However, to continue the analogy, dentists discovered that there were bigger and brighter professional challenges to meet in the time no longer devoted to such run-of-the-mill procedures as filling cavities, or, to put this into the industrial relations idiom, the constant fighting of brushfires.

The lesson of the past 40 years in Australia, as elsewhere, is clear: The shape of an academic discipline—indeed its very existence and survival—is intimately bound up with the institutional arrangements for its teaching and research. If the courses are not offered, the students can't enroll and the discipline can't be grown and ideas can't be transmitted into contemporary practice, nor can they be passed on down through succeeding generations of scholars. Research and the generation of ideas are dependent on sufficient student interest in a discipline (although, from time to time special support may be extended to keep the seed corn alive through a particularly bad patch). Much of this must be familiar to academics in other countries; reports are quite common of declining interest among students in traditional industrial relations courses, although as Purcell (1992) notes:

> It has not gone unnoticed in Britain that a number of academic stalwarts of the labour movement now find themselves holding professorships funded by major companies under the title "Human Resource Management." It is industrial relations by another name, like so many textbooks where the 2nd edition is simply retitled, or like the MBA elective in a major British university where numbers were falling until it was retitled "Human Resource Management" with little change of content.

No doubt these techniques are used from time to time, but they hardly amount to a longer run strategy for survival. As the user-pays principle and fee-charging practices extend beyond North America into other university systems, students can be expected to exercise greater voice over what they receive and how it is delivered. This effect will be reinforced by the growing support in government and corporate circles for competency-linked assessment of higher education performance. Also significant on the scene is the burgeoning presence of business schools and their proclivity for teaching industrial relations as human resource management, even as straight management strategy. Traditional industrial relations has been more about the established contours of bargaining and other rule making, whereas the focus of the 1990s seems to be much more about engendering change in the interests of greater flexibility. Thus, the fact that the business schools enroll adult age students at the graduate level is probably an advantage for them, given the greater maturity required to handle the ideas and practicalities of strategy and change management.

The irony is that industrial relations in the 1990s is facing from human resource management what the cognate disciplines faced from industrial relations itself a quarter of a century earlier. In both periods the old approach was seen to be out of touch with emerging reality.

Let me return to the growth and consolidation phase in the evolution of the discipline in Australia, and an exchange of ideas at a 1978 Conference on "Industrial Relations Teaching and Research in Australia and New Zealand." Howard (1978) argued that industrial relations academics collectively suffered an inferiority complex:

> Social scientists in general are afflicted with a heavy burden of cultural cringe, and economists who enjoy high status among social scientists certainly quail before even an applied, much less a pure, mathematician. Industrial relations stands well below economics . . . and this lowly status has, in Australia, inhibited the development of vigorous debate and enquiry in industrial relations theory. (p. 27)

The proposition was that industrial relations might embrace respectability through the pursuit of theory, perhaps even grand theory. However, Geare (1978) adopted a different stance:

> In my view, industrial relations courses tend *too much* to the theory and neglect the practice. Thus, essays written on the *theory* of collective bargaining get more weight, in most courses, than works on tactics and strategy in collective bargaining and actual role-playing of negotiations, and the preparation of cases get even less weight. This, I feel, is in part due to our low status and resulting

defensiveness. We do not wish to appear academically inferior by indulging in *practical* work. This ignores the fact that academically "superior" subjects like physics, chemistry and to an even greater extent medicine, spend a lot of time doing very basic practical work. (p. 53)

There is a certain timeless quality in this exchange about theory versus relevance. In the 1970s the issue for the discipline was how to gain respectability in the eyes of other social science scholars, and theory development was seen as a path toward legitimacy. The absence of a theoretical framework for HRM is often seen today as its Achilles' heel. In the 1970s those pushing industrial relations as a field of study emphasized its greater relevance over the disciplines from which it was emerging. Now in the 1990s, this issue of relevance is seen by the HRM aficionados as the Achilles of industrial relations. The question is whether industrial relations will learn from the lessons (even lesions) of its own origin.

One lesson with which it is difficult to quarrel is that species survive when they either repel invaders or adapt to changing circumstances. Great courage, and not a little foolhardiness, is needed to pursue the defensive strategy. The adaptive strategy, in which industrial relations seeks to better integrate itself with the world of human resource management, has a much greater appeal. Understandably, the relative attractiveness of one approach over the other may have something to do with age. Older academics, those whose careers have been forged over the years in the industrial relations dimension, feel both that they have more to defend and less to lose with a last-ditch stand. They are also more likely to have a deeper bond with the spirit of trade unionism. The younger academics, with careers still ahead of them, are likely to be much more adaptive. A lot of this has to do with what Dunn refers to as the "root metaphor" in industrial relations, and the act of faith necessary to embrace a paradigm shift.

For survival, an academic discipline needs clients and mentors. Just how the discipline projects itself to students and to practitioners is crucial and, in the 1990s, this will be bound up with the idea of the root metaphor. Dunn's argument is that the old industrial relations, focusing on trade unions, collective bargaining, strikes, and Dunlopian rule making, implies a trench warfare approach to life—an approach with a "nervous obsession with what 'the other side' is up to." Whether enacted or remembered, "it tends to foster paranoid melodrama . . . [which] can be discerned on both sides of the left and the right poles of industrial relations analysis" (Dunn, 1990, p. 10). In contrast, the new industrial relations, which is to say the HRM paradigm, is built on what Dunn calls the "becoming metaphor." While this entails "leaving a safe, familiar place . . . enduring privation, facing temptation and dangers," there is always the hope that the traveler will prevail over the travails and return home safely. This is inherent in the HRM orientation, where change and hopeful travel is the sine qua non. The journey is important, not the end point that tends never to arrive: "Arrival suggests the end of change, whereas the new industrial relations is about perpetual change" (Dunn, 1990, p. 21). This bears powerfully upon clients and mentors, who are not necessary fussed about a lack of intellectual rigor or theoretical respectability. More critical is a root metaphor that can sell hope:

> And who can blame the career-orientated student of the 1980s for not wishing to be trained as a managerial trench soldier when human resource management beckons? Worse, who can blame them if they identify those of us in the old industrial relations with our metaphor and come to see us as the ones in the trenches, peeping apprehensively over the sandbags as the tanks of the new paradigm roll unheedingly over our barbed wire? Who can blame colleagues in the new paradigm for seeing us as stuck with an idiom that closes off our options and holds us in a labyrinth of our own making, our research preoccupations confined and blinkered by the earthworks around us. Their metaphor is, after all, so much more open, expansive and even heroic. (Dunn, p. 17)

Conclusion

Times of great change, such as those we are witnessing these days, can threaten survival, or they can provide rare opportunities. The challenge facing industrial relations is to develop a discipline, which is at the one time intellectually satisfying to scholars—something more than the academic equivalent of ambulance chasing, but which is also useful to policy making and professional practice. These are not incompatible goals. By and large medicine, law, engineering, and a host of other fields of study have managed to capture the right symbiosis. Admittedly, there is one aspect that poses a greater challenge for industrial relations, and that is the fact that the major changes in our area—devolution and a focusing of energies at the enterprise level—draw more on the skills of the trained generalist than on those of the professional specialist. But given the key role in the nineties to be played by clients and mentors, the demand and therefore the resource base will be there, but only for the new industrial relations, not the old.

References

ACTU/TDC. (1987). *Australia council of trade unions and the trade development council, Australia reconstructed.* Report of the ACTU/TDC mission to Western Europe. Canberra, Australia: Australian Government Publishing Service.

Alden, J. (1982). A comparative analysis of moonlighting in Great Britain and the U.S.A. *Industrial Relations Journal, 13*(2), 21-31.

Bamber, G. J., & Lansbury, R. D. (1983). A comparative perspective on technological change and industrial relations *IRRA 36th Annual Proceedings*, 92-99.

Banks, R. F. (1969). The reform of British industrial relations: The Donovan report and the labour government's policy proposals. *Relations Industrielles/Industrial Relations, 24*(2), 333-378.

Barbash, J. (1980). Collective bargaining and the theory of conflict. *British Journal of Industrial Relations*, 82-91.

Barkin, S. (1971). Trade-unions in an age of pluralism and structural change. The response to the irrepressible demands of the common man. *Relations Industrielles/Industrial Relations, 26*(4), 801-826.

Barkin, S. (1980). European industrial relations. A resource for the reconstruction of the American system. *Relations Industrielles/Industrial Relations, 35*(3), 439-445.

Barkin, S. (1987). The flexibility debate in Western Europe: The current drive to restore management's rights over personnel and wages. *Relations Industrielles/Industrial Relations, 42*, 12-43.

Bartol, K. M., & Bartol, R. A. (1975). Women in managerial and professional positions: The United States and the Soviet Union. *Industrial and Labor Relations Review*, 524-534.

Beaumont, P. B. (1988). The Thatcher/Reagan administration approaches in labor relations. *IRRA 41st Annual Proceedings*, 342-350.

Belous, R. S. (1986). How flexible is flexible? The United States labor market versus Western Europe. *IRRA 39th Annual Proceedings*, 101-107.

Benson, J. (1982). Trade union attitudes to job-sharing in Australia and some lessons for the U.K. *Industrial Relations Journal, 13*(3), 13-19.

Blanpain, R. (1976). The impact of recent developments in the E.E.C. on national labour law systems. *Relations Industrielles/Industrial Relations, 31*(4), 509-519.

Bomers, G.B.J., & Peterson, R. B. (1977). Multinational corporations and industrial relations: The case of West Germany and the Netherlands. *British Journal of Industrial Relations, 15*(1), 45-62.

Bonenfant, J-C. (1970). The Woods and Donovan reports. *Relations Industrielles/Industrial Relations, 25*(1), 3-11.

Bray, M. (1982). Democracy from the inside: The British AUEW(ES) and the Australian AMWSU. *Industrial Relations Journal, 13*(4), 84-93.

Cameron, S. (1983). An international comparison of the volatility of strike behavior. *Relations Industrielles/Industrial Relations, 38*(4), 767-780.

Capelli, P. (1985). Theory construction in IR and some implications for research. *Industrial Relations* (Berkley), *24*(1), 37-61.

Cochrane, J. L. (1976). Industrialism and industrial man in retrospect: A preliminary analysis. *IRRA 29th Annual Proceedings*, 274-287.

Craig, C. (1977). Towards national job evaluation? Trends and attitudes in Britain and in the Netherlands. *Industrial Relations Journal, 8*(1), 23-36.

De Givry, J. (1974). Industrial relations: An international viewpoint. *Relations Industrielles/Industrial Relations, 29*(2), 268-271.

Delamotte, Y. (1991). France. In J. Niland & O. Clarke (Eds.), *Agenda for change: An international analysis of industrial relations in transition* (pp. 90-114). Sydney: Allen & Unwin.

Derber, M. (1982). Review symposium on Kochan's collective bargaining and industrial relations. *Industrial Relations, 21*(1).

Dunkley, G. (1984). Can Australia learn from Austria about incomes policies? *Journal of Industrial Relations, 26*(3), 365-384.

Dunlop, J. T. (1958). *Industrial relations systems.* New York: Holt.

Dunlop, J. T. (1977). Policy decisions and research in economics and industrial relations. *Industrial and Labor Relations Review, 30*(3), 275-282.

Dunn, S. (1990). Root metaphor in the old and new industrial relations. *British Journal of Industrial Relations, 28*(1), 1031.

Fajana, S. (1989). The systems approach as theory for multinational industrial relations in developing countries. *Relations Industrielles/Industrial Relations, 44*(3), 615-632.

Form, W. H. (1973). Job vs. political unions: A cross-national comparison. *Industrial Relations* (Berkley), *12*(2), 224-238.

Franke, W. (1987). Accommodating to change. Can IR learn from itself. *IRRA 40th Annual Proceedings,* 474-481.

Geare, A. J. (1978). Doctrine, theory and teaching in industrial relations. In D. J. Turkington (Ed.), *Industrial relations teaching and research in Australia and New Zealand* (pp. 54-57). Wellington, NZ: Victoria University of Wellington.

Goodman, J., Armstrong, E., Wagner, A., Davis, G., & Wood, S. (1975, Spring). Rules in industrial relations theory: A discussion. *Industrial Relations Journal.*

Gospel, H. F. (1983). Trade unions and the legal obligation to bargain: An American, Swedish and British comparison. *British Journal of Industrial Relations,* 343-357.

Gurdon, M. A. (1987). Divergent paths. Civil service employment relations in Australia and Canada. *Relations Industriellesi/Industrial Relations, 42*(3), 566-575.

Hameed, S. M. A. (1971). Extension and feasibility of the Woods report to the developing countries. *Relations Industrielles/Industrial Relations, 26*(3), 575-590.

Harrison, B. (1983). Comparing European and American experience with plant closing laws. *IRRA 36th Annual Proceedings,* 120-128.

Hartmann, G., Nicholas, I., Sorge, A., & Warner, M. Computerised machine-tools, manpower consequences and skill utilisation: A study of British and West German manufacturing firms. *British Journal of Industrial Relations,* 221-223.

Howard, W. A. (1978). Doctrine, theory and teaching in industrial relations. In D. J. Turkington (Ed.), *Industrial relations teaching and research in Australia and New Zealand* (pp. 25-48). Wellington, NZ: Victoria University of Wellington.

Hunter, L. (1991). Britain. In J. Niland & O. Clarke (Eds.), *Agenda for change: An international analysis of industrial relations in transition* (pp. 115-146). Sydney: Allen & Unwin.

Kassalow, E. M. (1984). The crisis in the world steel industry: Union-management responses in four countries. *IRRA 37th Annual Proceedings,* 341-351.

Keenoy, T. (1991). The roots of metaphor in the old and the new industrial relations. *British Journal of Industrial Relations, 29*(2), 313-328.

Kochan, T. A., Katz, H. C., & McKersie, R. B. (1986). *The transformation of American industrial relations.* New York: Basic Books.

Kochan, T. A., McKersie, R. B., & Capelli, P. (1984). Strategic choice and industrial relations theory. *Industrial Relations* (Berkley), *23*(1), f16-39.

Kochan, T. A., & Wever, K. R. (1991). United States of America. In J. Niland & O. Clarke (Eds.), *Agenda for change: An international analysis of industrial relations in transition* (pp. 19-52). Sydney: Allen & Unwin.

Levine, S. B. (1961). Our future industrial society: A global vision. *Industrial and Labor Relations Review* (Cornell), *14*, 548-555.

Marginson, P. (1991, September 23-26). *Bargaining in ECUS? European integration and transnational management-union relations in the enterprise* (Mimeo, pp. 1-18). Third European Regional Congress of the International Industrial Relations Association, Bari and Naples, Italy.

Mathews, J. (1992). The industrial relations of skills formation. *Proceedings of the Ninth World Congress of the International Industrial Relations Association.* Sydney: IIRA.

Maurice, M., & Sellier, F. (1979). Societal analysis of industrial relations: A comparison between France and West Germany. *British Journal of Industrial Relations,* 322-336.

Myers, C. A. (1962). The American system of industrial relations: Is it exportable? *Proceedings of the 15th Annual Meeting of the IRRA,* 2-14.

Niland, J., & Clarke, O. (Eds.). (1991). *Agenda for change: An international analysis of industrial relations in transition.* Sydney: Allen & Unwin.

Niland, J., & Spooner, K. (1991). Australia. In J. Niland & O. Clarke (Eds.), *Agenda for change: An international analysis of industrial relations in transition.* Sydney: Allen & Unwin.

Peterson, R. B. (1986). Research design issues in comparative industrial relations. *IRRA 39th Annual Proceedings,* 244-251.

Purcell, J. (1992). Human resource management—Implications for teaching, theory, research and practice in industrial relations. *Proceedings of the Ninth World Congress of the International Industrial Relations Research Association* (Vol.3 , pp. 1-12). Sydney: IIRA.

Rawson, D. W. (1983). British and Australian labour law: The background to the 1982 bills. *British Journal of Industrial Relations,* 161-180.

Rees, A. (1977). Policy decisions and research in economics and industrial relations: An exchange of views. *Industrial and Labor Relations Review, 31*(1), 3-17.

Rosenberg, R., & Resenstein, E. (1981). Operationalising workers' participation: A comparison of U.S. and Yugoslav models. *Industrial Relations Journal, 12*(2), 46-52.

Stieber, J. (1967). Implications of West European manpower programs for the United States. *IRRA Proceedings from the 20th Annual Meeting,* 297-306.

Strauss, G. (1988). Australian labor relations through American eyes. *Industrial Relations* (Berkley), *27*(2), 131-148.

Strauss, G., & Feuille, P. (1978). Industrial relations research: A critical analysis. *Industrial Relations* (Berkley), *17*(3), 259-277.

Streeck, W. (1991), The Federal Republic of Germany. In J. Niland & O. Clarke (Eds.), *Agenda for change: An international analysis of industrial relations in transition* (pp. 3-89). Sydney: Allen & Unwin.

Swan, K. P. (1980). Public bargaining in Canada and the U.S.: A legal view. *Industrial Relations* (Berkley), *19*(3), 272-291.

Thompson, M., & Roxborough, I. (1982). Union elections and democracy in Mexico: A comparative perspective. *British Journal of Industrial Relations,* 201-217.

Treu, T. (1987). *Public service labour relations: Recent trends and future prospects: A comparative survey of seven industrialised market economy countries.* Geneva: ILO.

Turner, L. (1989). The politics of work reorganization: Partnership and Conflict in the U.S. and West German auto industries. *IRRA 42nd Annual Proceedings,* 142-148.

Tzannatos, A. (1987). Equal pay in Greece and Britain. *Industrial Relations Journal, 18(4),* 275-283.

Verma, A., & Thompson, M. (1988). Managerial strategies in Canada and the U.S. in the 1980's. *IIRA 41st Annual Proceedings,* 257-264.

Whittingham, T. G., & Towers, B. (1971). The British industrial relations bill: An analysis. *Relations Industrielles/Industrial Relations, 26*(3), 620-638.

Author Index

About the Contributors

Roy J. Adams is Professor of Industrial Relations at McMaster University and Associate Member of the Center for Industrial Relations at the University of Toronto, Canada. He holds a Ph.D. from the University of Wisconsin and has published on a wide range of areas, including comparative industrial relations, trade unions, workers' participation in enterprise decision making, and industrial relations theory. He is the editor of two books: *Comparative Industrial Relations: Contemporary Research and Theory* (with Noah Meltz) and *Industrial Relations Theory: Its Nature, Scope and Pedagogy*.

Janice R. Bellace is Professor of Legal Studies and Management at the Wharton School of the University of Pennsylvania. She serves as Vice Dean of the Wharton School, and Director of the Wharton Undergraduate Division. She received her bachelor's and law degrees from the University of Pennsylvania, and she holds an MSc degree from the London School of Economics. She is the author of numerous books, chapters, articles, and papers, and is general editor of the *Comparative Labor Law Review*.

Gideon Ben-Israel is a member of the Executive Bureau of the Histadrut: the Federation of Labor in Israel. He holds a degree in Economics from the London School of Economics and a Law degree from the Hebrew University of Jerusalem, Israel. He has published widely on trade unions, labor law, and international and comparative industrial relations.

William Brown has been the Montague Burton Professor of Industrial Relations at the University of Cambridge since 1985, where he is currently Chair of the Faculty of Economics and Politics. Educated at Leeds Grammar School and Oxford University, he worked in the National Board for Prices and Incomes before moving to the University of Warwick in 1968. He was a founding member of the Industrial Relations Research Unit and became its

495

Director in 1980. Among his publications are *Piecework Bargaining* and *The Changing Contours of British Industrial Relations.*

Stephen Chiu is Lecturer in Sociology at the Chinese University of Hong Kong. He has a Ph.D. from Princeton and has co-authored a number of papers on industrial change and various aspects of labor relations in Hong Kong.

Braham Dabscheck is an Associate Professor in the School of Industrial Relations and Organizational Behavior at the University of New South Wales. He has published several books and numerous articles on various aspects of Australian industrial relations. He is also editor of the *Journal of Industrial Relations.*

Anne Daly is a Research Fellow in the Aboriginal and Economic Policy Research Unit at the Australian National University. She has undertaken research and published widely on labor market issues in Australia.

Edward Davis is Professor and Director of the Labour–Management Studies Foundation at the Graduate School of Management, Macquarie University, Sydney, Australia. He holds a Master of Arts from the University of Cambridge, England; a Master of Economics from Monash University; and a Ph.D. from LaTrobe University in Australia. His research has covered such areas as democracy and government in trade unions, technological change, and workers' participation in management. He is co-editor, with Russell Lansbury, of *Technology, Work and Industrial Relations* (1984), *Democracy and Control in the Workplace* (1986), and *Managing Together? Consultation and Participation in the Workplace* (forthcoming).

Carlo Dell'Aringa is Professor of Economics and Director of the Institute for Labor and Industrial Economics at the Catholic University of Milan. He has published widely in the field of labor and industrial relations. Recently, he has been conducting research into wage differentials and collective bargaining.

Lee Dyer is Professor of Human Research Studies and Director of the Center for Advanced Human Resource Studies at the Industrial and Labor Relations School, Cornell University. He holds BBA, MBA, and Ph.D. degrees from the University of Wisconsin–Madison. His teaching and research interests cover human resource strategy and planning and the role of the human resource function. He has published numerous articles in academic journals and has undertaken research and consulting assignments in a number of corporations throughout the world. His recent books include

Human Resource Management: Evolving Roles and Responsibilities (1988), *Personnel/Human Resource Management* (1989), and *World Class Workplaces: Toward the Twenty-first Century* (forthcoming).

Hanna Fisher works for the Histadrut: the Federation of Labor in Israel. She has undertaken research on trade unions and has published joint papers with Gideon Ben-Israel.

Ludwik Florek is a Professor at the University of Warsaw Law School and Director of the Institute of Legal and Administrative Sciences. He is the author of eight books and many articles and studies on Polish, international, and European law and social security. He has been a lecturer at many European and American universities. He is also Secretary of the Polish branch of the International Society of Labor Law and Social Security, and a Senior Legal Adviser for foreign companies in Poland.

Amira Galin received a BA in Sociology and Political Science from the Hebrew University, Jerusalem; and an MSc and DSc in Management Science and Industrial Relations from the Technion (Israel Institute of Technology). She is Professor of Management in the Faculty of Management, Tel Aviv University, where she teaches industrial relations and human resource management. In recent years she has been the coordinator of the Study Group on Flexible Work Patterns for the International Industrial Relations Research Association and editor of the *Work Flexibility Review.*

Robert Gregory is a graduate of the University of Melbourne and the London School of Economics and Political Science. He is currently Professor of Economics and Head of the Division of Economics and Politics in the Research School of Social Sciences at the Australian National University. He is a member of the board of the Reserve Bank of Australia and the Australian Institute of Family Studies. He has been Principle Consultant in a series of Aged Care Reviews for the Department of Community Services and Health. He is currently a member of the Committee on Employment Opportunities, which is preparing a Discussion Paper as a precursor for the Australian Government's Full Employment White Paper.

Olle Hammarström received an MBA from Gothenburg School of Economics and Business Administration in 1967. He was a consultant in personnel administration before joining the Sociology Department of Gothenburg University. He worked as a researcher and change agent during the first generation of industrial democracy experiments in Sweden, from 1969 to 1974. He has worked with the Ministry of Labor in Sweden and Australia.

He joined the Swedish Work Life Center as a Research Director in 1978. Beginning in 1981 he was Research Director and then Assistant Secretary with the Swedish Union of Clerical and Technical Employees in Industry. He has published several books and articles in the area of industrial democracy and industrial relations.

Lajos Héthy graduated from the University of Budapest with degrees in both Economics and Sociology. He has been the Director of the Institute of Labor Research, Budapest, since 1980. He is an Honorary Professor in the Faculty of Economics at Janus Pannonius University in Hungary. He was Deputy Secretary of State for International Programs in the Hungarian Ministry of Labor from 1990 to 1991, and has been president of the Hungarian Industrial Relations Association since 1991. He has published widely in the area of labor relations.

Thomas A. Kochan is the George M. Bunker Professor of Management and a Leaders for Manufacturing Professor at MIT's Sloan School of Management. He came to MIT in 1980 as a Professor of Industrial Relations. From 1988 to 1991 he served as Head of the Behavioral and Policy Sciences Area in the Sloan School. He also served as a member of the MIT Commission on Industrial Productivity. From 1973 to 1980 he was on the faculty of the School of Industrial and Labor Relations at Cornell University. Recent books include *The Transformation of American Industrial Relations* (with H. Katz and R. McKersie) and *Transforming Organizations* (with M. Useem).

Russell D. Lansbury is Professor of Industrial Relations at the University of Sydney. He holds degrees in Psychology and Political Science from the University of Melbourne, and a Ph.D. from the London School of Economics. He has extensive experience as a consultant to organizations in both the private and public sectors, as well as the trade union movement in Australia and overseas. He has worked for British Airways in London and has been the recipient of a Senior Fulbright Fellowship at Harvard University and MIT. His publications cover a wide range of subjects, including technological change, new forms of work organization, and employee participation in management; and his recent books include *International and Comparative Industrial Relations* (with G. J. Bamber) and *Workplace Industrial Relations: Australian Case Studies* (with D. Macdonald).

David A. Levin is Senior Lecturer and Head, Department of Sociology, University of Hong Kong. He has a master's degree in Labor and Industrial Relations from the University of Illinois. His publications include *Labour Movement in a Changing Society: The Experience of Hong Kong* (co-edited with Y. C. Jao, S. H. Ng, and E. Sinn) and "Dependent Capitalism, a Colonial State, and Marginal Unions: The Case of Hong Kong" (co-authored with Stephen Chiu) in *Organised Labor in the Asia-Pacific Region.*

Manuela Samek Lodovici is a Senior Researcher at the Instituto per la Ricerca Sociale of Milan. She also teaches labor economics at the Catholic University of Milan. Her recent publications include "Industrial Relations and Economic Performance" (with Carlo Dell'Aringa) in *Participation in Policy Making.*

John Mathews is Director, Industrial Relations Research Center; and Senior Lecturer, School of Industrial Relations and Organizational Behavior, University of New South Wales. He directs the research program in Case Studies in Organizational Innovation. He was a senior executive in the Victorian government, first with the Department of Labor and then with the Ministry of Education. He has published widely in the fields of organizational innovation and workplace reform, and is the author of *Tools of Change, Health and Safety at Work,* and his latest book, *Age of Democracy.*

John R. Niland is Vice-Chancellor of the University of New South Wales. He has held the Chair in Industrial Relations since 1974, and has served periods as Head of the School of Economics, Head of the School of Industrial Relations, Director of the Industrial Relations Research Centre, and Dean of the Faculty of Commerce and Economics. His academic qualifications include a Bachelor of Commerce and Master of Commerce from the University of New South Wales, and a Ph.D. from the Institute of Labor and Industrial Relations at the University of Illinois. He has held academic positions at Cornell University the University of Illinois, and the Australian National University.

Eng Fong Pang teaches at the Faculty of Business Administration in the National University of Singapore. He was formerly Director, Economic Research Center, National University of Singapore. He has also taught at the University of Michigan and Columbia University. His recent books include *Foreign Investment and Industrialisation in Malaysia, Singapore, Taiwan and Thailand* (with Linda Lim) and *Labour Flows and Regionalisation in Pacific Asia.*

Se-Il Park is Professor of Law and Economics at Seoul National University. He was previously a Senior Fellow at the Korea Development Institute. He holds a law degree from Seoul National University as well as a master's and a Ph.D. from Cornell University.

John Purcell is University Lecturer in Management Studies and Fellow in Industrial Relations at Templeton College, Oxford University. He is currently conducting research on strategic choice in the management of employee relations in multidivisional companies, focusing on the links with corporate strategy and business policy. His publications include *Good Industrial Relations: Theory and Practice* and *Beyond the Workplace and Human Resource Management in the Multi-Divisional Company* (with Bruce Ahlstrand).

Marino Regini is Professor in the Department of Social Policy at the University of Trento in Italy. He was a visiting scholar at the Center for European Studies at Harvard University in 1978-1979, and a Visiting Professor at Johns Hopkins University and at the European University Institute. He teaches courses in economic sociology, comparative industrial relations, and political economy. He is the author of *Uncertain Boundaries: The Social and Political Construction of the Economy* and *State, Market and Social Regulation: New Perspectives in Italy* (with Peter Lange).

John Storey is Senior Lecturer in Human Resource Management in the Loughborough University Business School and Director of the Human Resource and Change Management Research Unit. He was formerly a Principal Research Fellow in the Industrial Relations Research Unit at the University of Warwick. His most recent works include *New Perspectives on Human Resource Management, Managing Human Resources and Industrial Relations* (with Keith Sisson), and *New Wave Manufacturing Strategies*. He is review editor for the *Human Resource Management Journal*.

Kazuo Sugeno is Professor of Law at the University of Tokyo, where he also received his law degree. He has been a visiting scholar at both the Yale Law School and the University of Michigan Law School, and he was a Visiting Professor at the Harvard Law School.

Clive Thompson is the Director and Associate Professor of the Labor Law Unit at the University of Cape Town. He has practiced extensively as a trade union lawyer, arbitrator, and mediator in South Africa. He is co-editor of the *Industrial Law Review* and co-author of *South African Labour Law*.

Chrissie Verevis is Executive Officer to Professor John Niland in his capacity as Vice-Chancellor of the University of New South Wales. She holds this position as a secondment from her substantive position of Lecturer in Industrial Relations at the University. She has worked in industrial relations in various capacities, including as a research officer for a blue-collar trade union, as a researcher and advocate for the government, and as an industrial relations academic. Her interests lie chiefly in industrial law.

Jelle Visser is Professor at the Institute for Sociology at the University of Amsterdam in the Netherlands. He has published extensively on trade unions in an international context.

Janet Walsh is a Lecturer in Economics at the University of Leeds. She was formerly a Research Officer at the Department of Applied Economics, and a Fellow of Girton College, Cambridge University. She has published in the areas of structural change and multinationals in the British textile and clothing industry, and pay bargaining and economic performance. Her current research is on the European pay strategies of British-based multinationals, and the dynamics and changing forms of internal labor markets in Britain and Australia.

Kirsten S. Wever is a political economist and is currently Assistant Professor of Human Resource Management at the College of Business Administration, Northeastern University. She received BA and MA degrees from the University of California at Berkeley, and a Ph.D. from the Political Science Department and the Sloan School of Management at MIT. She is the author of *Negotiating Adjustment: Business, Labor, Government and Competitiveness in the United States and Germany,* and has published articles on German and American employment relations and labor politics in a variety of journals, including *Journal of Public Policy, Industrial Relations,* and *The Harvard Business Review.*

Isik Urla Zeytinoglu is an Associate Professor of Industrial Relations at McMaster University, and Faculty Adviser to the Women's Studies Program. She is also Co-Chair of McMaster University's Research Center for the Promotion of Women's Health. She has published articles on topics of women and paid/unpaid work, part-time workers, and international labor standards and collective bargaining legislation. Her writing has appeared in a number of books and in such journals as *Relations industrielles/Industrial Relations, Industrial and Labor Relations Review,* and *Comparative Labor Law Journal.*